EMPRESS JOSEPHINE.
Gallica Rose. *See page 36.*
Williams-Ellis

The heritage of the ROSE

David Austin

Foreword by Graham Stuart Thomas
with
original paintings by Susan Williams-Ellis

Antique Collectors' Club

ISBN 1 85149 020 5

First published 1988
Revised edition 1990, reprinted 1993

British Library Cataloguing in Publication Data
Austin, David, *1926*
The rose
1. Roses
I. Title II. Antique Collectors' Club
583'.372

Printed in England by the Antique Collectors' Club Ltd., Woodbridge, Suffolk

To my wife, Pat

ACKNOWLEDGEMENTS

I wish to express my thanks to a number of people who have helped me in the production of this book.

Susan Williams-Ellis for allowing me to use her superb paintings of roses.

Graham Stuart Thomas for reading the manuscript and making numerous helpful suggestions.

Barry Ambrose of the Royal Horticultural Society, Wisley, for much help, encouragement and practical advice, including suggestions for plants for association with roses.

Messrs. Faber & Faber, for permission to include an extract from T.S. Eliot's *Four Quartets;* the Literary Trustees of Walter de la Mare and the Society of Authors, for permission to include an extract from Walter de la Mare's *All That's Past;* the Trustees of Vita Sackville-West, for permission to include an extract from *The Garden*.

My publishers, Diana and John Steel, of the Antique Collectors' Club, who have allowed me an unusual amount of latitude and been very understanding throughout the production of this book, and Cherry Lewis, their assiduous and sympathetic Editor.

Diane Ratcliff and Doreen Pike for typing the scripts and much other help.

CONTENTS

ILLUSTRATIONS

The eleven superb watercolour paintings of roses in this book are part of a collection by Susan Williams-Ellis, better known for her Portmeirion Pottery.

The photographs are by the following photographers:

David Knight, A.B.I.P.P., A.R.P.S., A.S.I.A. (Art and Design), of the School of Art and Design, The Polytechnic, Wolverhampton. Knight

Michael Warren, A.B.I.P.P., A.M.P.A., who specialises in horticultural photography and has a large library of pictures. Warren

Vincent Page, Picture Editor of *The Sunday Times Colour Supplement,* who possesses one of the largest collections of rose pictures, and who gave extensive and valuable assistance in the editing of photographs. Page

Claire Calvert, B.A. (Hons.), née Austin, who assists the author at his nursery, specialising in hardy plants. Calvert

Graham Stuart Thomas, O.B.E., V.M.H., D.H.M., V.M.M., formerly Garden Adviser to the National Trust and author of many books on gardening. Thomas

Professor G. Fineschi, Italy, whose garden in Florence contains one of the finest collections of roses in Europe. Fineschi

Other photographs are from R.C. Balfour, Harry Smith's Horticultural Photographic Collection, Paul Edwards, garden designer, and the following nurseries/nurserymen: Cants of Colchester, James Cocker & Sons, Dickson Nurseries Ltd., Fryer's Nurseries Ltd., R. Harkness & Co. Ltd., Le Grice Roses, John Mattock Ltd., Wisbech Plant Co. Ltd. and B.J. Tysterman.

FOREWORD

Graham Stuart Thomas, O.B.E., V.M.H., D.H.M., V.M.M.

My memories of David Austin go back to the early 1950s when he used to make an annual visit to my first commercial collection of Old French Roses. He was, like me, almost bowled over by their unique beauty and gradually built up a selection from them. I think it was during our visit to the Paris rose gardens with Gordon Rowley that he first stated that one of his main aims in life was to breed roses of a shrubby nature. He had already made a start. We could all see that British, French and American breeders were intent on creating more and more hybrids set in the moulds of the Hybrid Teas and Floribundas, oblivious of the fact that only slight progress — of ever larger flowers and brighter colours — was likely to occur. They all had it firmly fixed in their minds that lovers of the rose simply desired bush roses along these stereotyped lines. (In this they were, and ever have been, encouraged by the competitive trials of the leading rose societies.) They had forgotten that the rose was originally a shrub. The Reverend Joseph Pemberton was of the same mind about the matter earlier in this century when he was producing 'Penelope', 'Felicia', 'Cornelia' and others of the Hybrid Musks. These did not become popular at the time because nobody was then looking for shrub roses, apart from the species which had always been favoured by shrub specialists.

It is now part of rose history that the resurgence in popularity of the Old Roses since the mid-1950s has resulted in dedicated groups of their admirers being formed throughout the English-speaking world, though it is improbable that anyone will try seriously to raise fresh varieties along the old lines; the old varieties reached a perfection of their own and are not likely to be surpassed. Having once broken into the store-house of beauty exhibited by the shrub roses, I am sure there is no stopping the movement. The bush Hybrid Teas and Floribundas have earned their special popularity through providing floral colour from midsummer until autumn, but during the rest of the year they are not particularly attractive. It was obvious what was needed: shrubs of grace and beauty in a variety of sizes, with good foliage, capable of producing flowers of all shapes — doubles and singles, simple or sophisticated — in a range of colours and fragrances, so that they could play their part in the general furnishing of the garden, and not merely in beds on lawn or paving. It was such thoughts as these which spurred David on to use some of his spare time as a farmer to raise his first seedlings.

I think it would be right to say that David is a nonconformist when it comes to roses. After all, why should a new rose have to conform to the stereotyped lines of modern bush roses, so freely used for bedding? When I asked one of the panel of judges of the Royal National Rose Society why so few of David's roses had received any recognition I was told they were 'too lanky'. I realised afterwards that this meant they did not conform to the standards laid down for modern bedding roses nor to the Society's version of a shrub rose, which is really nothing more than an overgrown Floribunda. We need graceful shrub roses for gardens of all sizes. But just think how these judging criteria limit our appreciation of a great shrub rose. Should it be said that the splendid 'Nevada' or 'Frühlingsgold', 'Fritz Nobis' or 'Golden Wings' are too lanky? We should welcome more roses of such superlative value, but there is also a great need for shrub roses of similar grace, beauty, individual charm and scent for smaller gardens; roses of, say, three to five feet in height and width, which will bloom from summer until autumn. This is what David has set himself to produce.

Breeding from garden roses is very unpredictable. The plants are of such mixed origin, with so many generations behind them, that to cross a pink rose with a white, for instance, may result in a whole range of colours including red, purple and yellow. We must remember when contemplating the welter of dazzling colours of modern roses, that these vivid tones all stem from hybridizing the Old Roses with three species only from among the 150 existing around the Northern Hemisphere. First the pale yellow of *Rosa gigantea* and the crimson of *R. chinensis,* followed by the strong yellows and flames of *R. foetida.* Crosses with these three put into reverse the continuation of the whites, soft pinks, mauves, purples and maroons of the Old French Roses. As if these giant strides were not enough for over a hundred years of breeding, a strident new colour — pelargonidin, a vermilion of neon-brilliance — suddenly cropped up without initiation by man sometime shortly after 1929.

It has been my privilege for some years to visit David's rose fields and see the results of his labours. Though his stud book records the many thousands of crosses made each year, owing to the unpredictability of breeding in a non-stereotyped group of plants it seems to me that almost anything may happen, but to his experienced eye the results are more recognisable. The result is that from the initial sowing of the precious grains (any one of which may just as well develop into a plant of superlative beauty as into one which may prove to be an utter dud) selection must be made from the first flowering onwards. This happens in the first year with repeat-flowering roses. Any likely candidates are propagated and after three or four years and several acres of plants, perhaps ten of a kind may be the reward. Further assessment of the growth, foliage, flower and scent will be made two or three times a week, at different times of the day, for three or four months. And in the meantime successive years' crosses will be made and sown, all to be watched likewise. Assessing and reassessing each variety is difficult. Wandering down the rows of a morning may bring quite different opinions from following the same paths later in the day. It is only by ruthless selection and the destruction of over ninety per cent that a handful of good plants may be re-propagated, perhaps a hundred of each. If these in bulk pass muster after three or more years, a few of them may be named and may prove a success, such as 'Mary Rose' and my own namesake. It is interesting to recall that the latter was the only rich soft yellow amongst hundreds of seedlings. But on looking back one can see that it has ever been a rare colour, cropping up first in the old Noisettes, such as 'Alister Stella Gray', and then again in 'Lady Hillingdon' and the Hybrid Musk 'Buff Beauty', with pale echoes in 'Barbara Richards' and 'Golden Dawn'.

We are very fortunate that David has had the initiative and vision, persistence and faith, to have given us the selection — from his thousands of crosses — which are named and described in Chapter 6 under his chosen title of English Roses. It is high time that his roses should receive proper evaluation, and who better than by the raiser, who, as he rightly claims, should know more than any one else about the failings of each seedling as well as its assets.

This book is a survey of the garden roses of today. Only an author and rosarian of considerable standing could have written such an impartial evaluation of so many disparate classes of roses. They embrace not only the species but the groups which have been selected by rose growers for over 150 years, each representing some particular style of perfection in the raiser's eyes. There is no doubt that David is well on the way to giving us a new class, the small graceful shrub of repeat-flowering habit which will fit into our complex gardens of today. He has fortunately been able to bring to his work the eye not only of a commercial nurseryman but also that of a lover of gardens and the imagination that goes with both.

It must be encouraging to him to know that his productions are already being listed by rose nurseries in ten different countries.

I am sure that the opinions expressed in this book will help us all to reassess the manifold beauties of the Rose.

Chapter 1
THE ROSE

Throughout the history of western civilisation, from the earliest times to the present day, the rose has been the flower closest to the heart of man. In Greek mythology Aphrodite, goddess of love, was regarded as the creator of the rose, which was supposed to have arisen from a mixture of her tears and the blood of her wounded lover Adonis. In Roman legend it was said to have sprung from the blood of Venus. Again and again we find it appearing in ancient history as a symbol of love and beauty, and sometimes of licentiousness and excess.

With the rise of Christianity the rose was at first looked upon with disapproval due to its pagan past, but this attitude soon changed, and we find the rose becoming intertwined with the Christian faith: for example, the rosary and the idea of the five petals of the rose representing the five wounds of Christ. Indeed, it was the church which was in a large degree responsible for carrying the rose across Europe to many lands.

Although we in the West, and in Britain in particular, like to think of the rose as being very much our own, this is in fact by no means entirely true. Roses appear at one time or another in association with Brahma, Buddha, Mahomet, Vishnu and Confucius, and the origins of the roses we enjoy today lie in a large degree in the lands of the Middle and Far East. This is perhaps best summed up in the following extract from Vita Sackville-West's long poem *The Garden:*

> June of the iris and the rose,
> The rose not English as we fondly think,
> Anacreon and Bion sang the rose;
> And Rhodes the isle whose very name means rose
> Struck roses on her coins;
> Pliny made lists and Roman libertines
> Made wreaths to wear among the flutes and wines;
> The young Crusaders found the Syrian rose
> Springing from Saracenic quoins,
> And China opened her shut gate
> To let her roses through, and Persian shrines
> Of poetry and painting gave the rose.

The earliest known representation of a rose was found in Crete, dated somewhere between 1700 and 2000 B.C. Since that time it has appeared in painting and sculpture, on pottery and fabrics, and as a decoration of all kinds, in all ages and in many lands.

It is, however, in poetry and literature that this affection is most vividly proclaimed, both for the beauty of the rose itself and as a symbol of all that is best and most beautiful in human nature. As early as the fifth century B.C. what is probably the first poem to the rose was written by the poet Anacreon:

I sing of Spring, flower crowned
I sing the praises of the Rose
Friend aid me in my song.
The rose is the perfume of the Gods, the joy of men,
It adorns the Graces at the blossoming of Love,
It is the favoured flower of Venus,
It is the chief care of the Nymphs,
It is the joy of the Muses,
In spite of its many thorns
We gather it with delight.

The Bible mentions the rose on frequent occasions, as for example in *Isaiah,* Chapter 35:

> The wilderness and the solitary place shall be glad for them; and the desert shall rejoice and blossom as the rose.

Nearer to our own time, Shakespeare mentions the rose more than sixty times, using it (as indeed do most poets) more as a symbol than in praise of the flower itself:

I have seen roses damask'd, red and white
But no such roses see I in her cheeks.

And yet, by heaven, I think my love as rare
As any she belied with false compare.

The great herbalist, Gerard, writing in 1596 in the beautiful language of the time, says of the rose:

> The plant of Roses, though it be a shrub full of prickles, yet it has been more fit and convenient to have placed it with the most glorious flowers of the worlde, than to insert the same here among base and thornie shrubs: for the Rose doth deserve the chiefest and most principall place among all flowers whatsoever, being not only esteemed for his beautie, vertues, and his flagrant [sic] and odiferous smell; but also because it is the honour and ornament of our English Scepter, as by the conjunction apeereth in the uniting of these two most royall houses of Lancaster and York.

John Keats, in the nineteenth century, wrote:

But when, O wells, thy roses came to me
My sense with their deliciousness was spell'd.
Soft voices had they, that with tender plea
Whispered of peace and truth and friendliness unquelled.

In our own time we have Walter de la Mare's much-quoted lines from his poem *All That's Past:*

Very old are the woods;
And the buds that break
Out of the brier's boughs,
When March winds wake,
So old with their beauty are —
Oh, no man knows
Through what wild centuries
Roves back the rose.

In more sombre mood, from T.S. Eliot's *Little Gidding,* are the lines:

Ash on an old man's sleeve
Is all the ash the burnt roses leave.
Dust in the air suspended
Marks the place where a story ended.

It would not be difficult to compile a sizeable book of such poems and quotations.

In painting, too, the rose has been very much in evidence, particularly from the Renaissance onwards, although it seems to be less so today, due, perhaps, to the less sympathetic nature of the various modern schools and also perhaps to the less sympathetic nature of the modern rose. In painting, the rose is more often used as an embellishment rather than as a main subject, but time and again it is chosen by the artist for this purpose. Any rose lover who visits a gallery in this country or abroad cannot have failed to notice this, and may even have found it hard to resist studying these roses and perhaps trying to name them.

At times we find the rose painted for its own sake, particularly in the paintings of the Dutch school of the late sixteenth and seventeenth century. Jan Brueghel, Jan Davidsz de Heem, Rachel Ruysch, Jan van Huysum and Daniel Seghers all painted flowers, and among their works are to be found many paintings of roses. In the nineteenth century Fantin-Latour stands out as a painter of roses; Renoir, too, painted roses.

If we consider the rose as decoration, it soon becomes clear that it stands supreme above all other flowers. Indeed it is difficult to walk into any house in the West without finding some representation of a rose. This, I think, illustrates better than anything else the very special place the rose holds in our lives. Only recently I was talking to the chief designer from one of our largest firms of pottery manufacturers, who told me that the rose is by far the most popular decoration for china and pottery, the demand for rose designs exceeding those of all other flowers put together.

The history of the rose has been written and rewritten on numerous occasions and makes intriguing reading. I do not intend to go over this ground again, except in so far as it helps us to understand and appreciate our subject. Nor is it necessary to go too deeply into the long history of roses to realise how important they have always been. Since those far-off days when we first hear of the rose many flowers have come to the fore as garden plants, but none has come anywhere near to supplanting it.

Today roses are to be found in almost every garden in the country in which there are any flowers at all. They are also to be found in almost every country in the world, sometimes struggling in the most unsuitable of climates. What is the fascination of this flower? How is it that the rose has always been the best loved of all flowers? It seems to have the ability to evoke by its beauty (and, to some degree, through the long accumulation of its history) many of the emotions, principles, desires and joys fundamental to the spirit of man, and to do this as no other flower can. For this reason, it is worthy of closer attention than we would afford other flowers; for the rose is more than other flowers — it is part of the very fabric of our lives; it has about it a humanity that we do not find in any other flower. It is only necessary to consider the few brief notes I have made so far to realise how true this is.

In the flower of a rose there are many flowers. It is seldom quite the same on any two days. From the opening bud to the fall of the flower, at every turn of its petals as they unfold, it is always presenting us with a different picture. Its colouring, too, is the same: perhaps deep and rich at the centre, maybe softer towards the outer edges, but the balance will always be changing, sometimes paling with time, or taking on a new hue, or occasionally intensifying. The flower varies according to where it is grown, from garden to garden, from one soil to another. It varies according to weather conditions; it will be quite different on a sunny day than on one which is cool and overhung. It will take on one appearance in early summer and quite another in the autumn. Here perhaps is one reason why we do not easily tire of it.

Between one variety and another, from one class to another, and from species to species, the rose has many forms: from the simple wild flower of our hedgerows, through the Old Roses, to the sophisticated Hybrid Tea of modern gardens. The flower may, for example, be in the form of a rosette as in the old Alba Rose 'Queen of Denmark'; it may be a rounded cup as in the Bourbon Rose 'Reine Victoria'. There are the heavy voluptuous blooms of *Rosa centifolia,* the wide open semi-double flowers of the Damask 'Celsiana' with its long stamens. Again the beauty of the flower may lie in the tiny pompon blooms of a Polyantha Rose, or the perfect scrolled buds of a Hybrid Tea Rose like 'Madame Butterfly'.

Then there is fragrance, which has been described as the very soul of a rose, and here we find no less diversity. The sense of smell is a hard one to tie down; it is the least developed of all our senses, yet it has great power to move us. Various people at various times have found the scent of many different flowers in roses and I doubt if there is a wider range to be found in any other flower. Not only are there the rich, heady fragrances of the Old Roses, as in the Centifolias and Damasks, which have been handed down over the ages to many roses of the present day, but there is also the sharp, fruity scent of many Rambling Roses, the scent of Musk Roses, the Tea Roses, and the myrrh-like fragrance of many of the English

Roses. And more than these too, for the scent of violet, clove, peony, lilac, apple, raspberry and others have been detected in various roses. The great majority of roses are fragrant, usually strongly so, but in some it is a slight fragrance, in a few it is barely detectable, but it is almost never entirely absent.

There is more to the rose than its flowers and their fragrance; growth too is important, as is the foliage and the manner in which the flower is poised upon that growth. The rose is a brier and this sometimes leads to an untidiness of growth. However, this does not seem to matter, for the very untidiness somehow adds to its charms. Indeed the brier growth contributes to its durability in that it gives the rose the ability to renew itself with constant new stems from its base. Roses may vary in height from the tiniest of Miniatures of as little as 3 or 4ins., to the most massive of Climbers which may reach 30 to 40ft. They can be bushes, as with a Modern Rose which is pruned almost to the ground each year, or they can be shrubs of 4 to 6ft. in height, as with the Old Roses; sometimes the Species may be 10ft. or more in height and as much across. They may climb a wall or ramble over trees or other shrubs, they may even creep along the ground. The flowers may be held singly or produced in great sprays of a hundred or more. It is this manner and diversity of growth that contributes much to the many attractions of the rose.

Man has taken a wild flower and over many centuries, at first by the selection of chance seedlings and later by design, moulded it to his wishes. The rose is a flower that belongs in the main to those parts of the garden that are close to the house, and those parts most closely controlled by the gardener. Here it is always with us as we pass; one of those small but not insignificant parts of our life that makes it worth the living.

With all this, the rose is the most practical of plants, often flowering intermittently from early summer to the coming of the first frosts. Once planted it will live for many years, and while it will certainly reward careful cultivation, many of its varieties will survive quite happily with little or no attention. Even those with no particular feeling for flowers can plant it in the knowledge that it is not going to give very much trouble. It is a flower for all people, from the great garden to the smallest suburban plot. What other flower can combine so many qualities? It is small wonder that the rose is known as the 'Queen of Flowers'.

THIS BOOK

It is my purpose in this book to take the reader from the earliest known roses, all the way through their history to those of the present day. As each class or group takes its place I shall try to give some idea of its particular charms, beauties and virtues, as well as something of its weaknesses. I shall say something of its history and development and add to this a few notes on the cultural requirements peculiar to each kind. I shall then describe what I regard as the best and most beautiful varieties in each group.

At the very start I am faced with a problem: what to include and what to leave out. *Modern Roses,* the rather deceptive title of what is in fact the 'stud book' of roses, contains over thirty thousand different varieties. Many of these have long since been lost, although many remain, and to describe all of them in detail would obviously be impossible and counter-productive. We hear much about the preservation of our heritage these days, and the rose has little to fear in this respect. Few plants can be so well preserved, and this is very good. But the fact is that many of the varieties listed in *Modern Roses* are of small garden value and it is necessary to make a selection. This is what I try to do. With a few exceptions (which are included to complete the story), the roses mentioned, both old and new, are here because I think they are worth their place in the gardens of today. I can see little virtue in extending my list beyond this point.

Even so, those who are new to the subject may find my list somewhat bewildering and might even be happier if it had been shorter. I do in fact include some eight hundred different kinds, but it is important to remember that roses are grown in nearly all gardens. Nothing can be more dispiriting than to walk along a road and see only 'Queen Elizabeth', 'Peace', 'Super Star' and a few others time and time again. What we need above all is variety if the rose is not to become a bore. This need be no problem, for no flower has received so much attention from breeders, few are so well provided for by nature, and no other flower can offer such diversity. I have tried, therefore, to give a balanced selection which covers the rose in all its forms, and gives due attention to each.

As a rose nurseryman, I am continually surprised at the knowledge displayed by many of my customers, not a few of whom are very keen gardeners. It is, however, true to say that most garden owners are not aware of the great range of roses available to them: the Old Roses, with their fragrance and unsophisticated charm; the more recent Shrub Roses which offer such great garden value; the Wild Roses with their natural grace; the brightly coloured Hybrid Teas and Floribundas; the many beautiful and diverse Climbing and Rambling Roses; to say nothing of the various developments that are taking place today. It is the chief aim of this book to make this great wealth of beauty known to a wider public.

A great divide exists among present day rose lovers; it lies between those who prefer roses of the 'old' type and those who prefer the 'modern' type. Or, to put it another way, those who favour Shrub Roses and those who favour Bush Roses. It will become clear that my preference lies with the former, but this does not mean that I am entirely blind to the virtues and possibilities of the latter. Many books have been written on roses in recent years, some might say too many. Some of these have been concerned with the Old Roses and others with the Modern Roses, seldom do they cover both. It is my intention to discuss the whole and give a balanced view. It forms a fascinating story. Some of the roses that I shall

BLAIRI NO. 2.
Bourbon Climber. See pages 277 and 286.
Williams-Ellis

ROSA MUNDI.
Gallica Rose. *See page 46.*
Williams-Ellis

THE REEVE.
English Rose. See pages 207 and 215.
Williams-Ellis

PRÉSIDENT DE SÈZE.
Gallica Rose. *See page 46.*
Williams-Ellis

COMTE DE CHAMBORD.
Portland Rose. *See page 83.*
Williams-Ellis

LUCETTA.
English Rose. See pages 187 and 194.
Williams-Ellis

PERDITA.
English Rose. *See pages 195 and 202.*
Williams-Ellis

EMANUEL.
English Rose. *See pages 190 and 220.*
Williams-Ellis

Wise Portia.
English Rose. See pages 209 and 215.
Williams-Ellis

SEVEN SISTERS' ROSE.
Multiflora Rambler. *See page 319.*
Williams-Ellis

be discussing are very old, many belong to the nineteenth century, still more will belong to the twentieth century, but from whatever era they originated, they are included not for any quaint fascination with the past, nor for any desire to be 'up to date', but for their virtues as garden plants.

There has been a movement in recent books towards listing garden roses in some sort of botanical order. No such classification is really possible and the attempt strikes me as being bogus. Garden roses, over the course of their history, have become so much intertwined, one species with another and one class with another, through breeding and selection, that such a method can only cause confusion. It is for this reason I have chosen a historical grouping. The garden rose is man made, and it is better to hold to those classifications which he has found convenient over the years. This method, I think, also gives roses an added interest.

For those who may be new to roses and who wish to make a selection, I would ask them not to be dismayed by the sheer number and complexity of varieties. Each chapter of this book from 2-11 contains a certain group of roses and is, in its way, complete in itself. Within a chapter there are various subsections, but for all practical purposes they each contain roses that are much of a kind. If we study each group as a whole, the picture becomes much clearer and selection easier.

Only the enthusiast will read this book from beginning to end, but I suggest that all readers study not only this chapter but also Chapters 12 and 13, as well as the introductions to each chapter and to the various classes of roses contained therein. The reader will in this way discover not only the interesting story of the rose but, more importantly, he or she will also get a good idea of the wide range of roses available, and can then choose to study in more detail the descriptions of the individual varieties. In this way I hope the book may be a useful source of reference.

THE RETURN OF THE OLD ROSES

Before I embark on the long journey around the family of the rose, it is necessary to give due credit to those who have been responsible for a comparatively recent development. As the reader turns the pages of this book he or she will see that there was a steadily increasing development and diversification of roses up to the end of the nineteenth century and a little way into our own century. From this point on what we now frequently call Modern Roses — the Hybrid Teas and Floribundas — took over and swept all else on one side. It was rather like destroying a beautiful and ancient city and replacing it with something inferior.

While this was going on there was already a movement taking place to preserve the old. It is interesting to note that George Paul, writing in the Royal Horticultural Society's Journal in 1896, speaks in this manner: 'Wanted: a refuge for the old roses where they may be found again when tastes change'. He was, in fact, showing remarkable insight, for within little more than a quarter of a century such outstanding gardeners as Edward Bunyard, G.N. Smith, George Beckwith, Maud Messel, Constance Spry, Ruby Fleischmann, Murray Hornibrook, A.T. Johnson, Bobbie James, Anastasia Law, Vita Sackville-West and others, were already gathering together collections of Old Roses.

It is, however, to Graham Thomas that we owe the greatest debt. It was he who put together all these collections into one great collection — and indeed added many more, as Nursery Manager first at Hillings & Co. of Woking and later at Sunningdale Nurseries. His collection of different varieties numbered well into four figures, and from these nurseries the old varieties spread into many gardens in the United Kingdom and eventually into nurseries around the world, so that we now have a movement which is continually gathering momentum.

Graham Thomas did more than just preserve these roses, he changed the way we looked at them through his three volumes entitled *The Old Shrub Roses, Shrub Roses of Today* and *Climbing Roses Old and New.* In these books he observes the rose so acutely and describes them so well, that it would be difficult to improve on him. Indeed, almost all subsequent writers on this subject have felt the need to state their debt to him, and for me perhaps more so than for others as he has been my friend and adviser over the last thirty-five years. I do not, in this book, attempt to attribute information to him where it may be due for fear of repetition.

Others, however should not be forgotten: Nancy Steen in New Zealand, Pat Wiley of 'Roses of Yesterday and Today' in California, Peter Beales, who has gathered together one of the largest commercial collections of roses, Trevor Griffiths in New Zealand, who has another exceptionally large commercial collection, and many others too numerous to name or unknown to me.

A name that will be cropping up from time to time is that of Dr. C.C. Hurst. Working at Cambridge, he was one of the pioneers of the science of genetics in the period between 1900 and 1914, studying many plants and animals, including man. When he returned to his work after the First World War, he turned his attention more particularly to the rose, and much of what we now know about the origins of the various groups of garden roses must be attributed to his work. Students of the rose should consider themselves fortunate to have had such an authority working with their chosen flower.

Chapter 2

OLD ROSES I

In this chapter I include all those classes which were established prior to the introduction of the repeat-flowering China Rose at the end of the 18th century, and which had such a revolutionary effect on the development of the rose and eventually led to the Hybrid Teas and Floribundas of the present day. That is to say the Gallicas, the Damasks, the Albas, the Centifolias and the Moss Roses. As most readers will be aware these are not small upright bushes, as are Modern Hybrid Teas, but genuine shrubs like any other shrub in the garden. Their growth will reach somewhere in the region of 4 to 6ft. according to variety, although there are among them many smaller shrubs that fit nicely into a small garden.

The formation of their flowers is quite different to that which we have become accustomed to today. In the Modern Rose the ideal lies in the bud with its high-pointed centre, and this is indeed often beautiful, but the disadvantage is that the mature flower tends to be muddled and almost completely lacking in form. Old Roses are quite different; their buds, though often charming, are likely to open as small cups, with little petals developing within, but it is as the flower gradually expands into the full bloom that its true beauty is revealed. At this later stage it can take on many forms: it may remain cupped, it may become flat with many petals, or it may reflex at the edges to form an almost domed flower. Between these shapes there are many gradations. The flower may also, of course, be semi-double, exposing an airy bunch of stamens at the centre. Thus we have a bloom that is beautiful at all stages, from the opening of the bud to the eventual fall of the petals. It is this variety of form that makes these roses so worth while. Fine as the Hybrid Tea may be, the Old Roses offer so much more scope, and for this reason we have, at our nursery, thought it worth while to proceed further with the breeding of roses of the old type. I shall be discussing these in Chapters 6 and 7.

It has to be admitted that Old Roses are rather limited in their colour range. We have white through pink all the way to a maroon-crimson, mauve and purple — all colours often of exceptional purity and softness of tone. Susan Williams-Ellis (who has spent many weeks at our nursery painting roses for her Portmeirion Pottery) speaking in terms of fabrics has suggested that these are like vegetable dyes in comparison with the harsher 'chemical' colours of Modern Roses. I think this puts it rather well. There are, unfortunately, only one or two yellows and not many whites, although 'Madame Hardy' and 'Madame Legras de St. Germain' can produce some of the most perfect blooms. Pink is the true colour of the rose, and in the Old Roses it often has a clarity seldom found elsewhere. The colour crimson is seldom pure in these early roses, but it does have the great virtue of turning to wonderful shades of purple, violet and mauve.

The Old Roses of this section do have one disadvantage, if in fact it can be truly described as a disadvantage; they flower only once in a season, whereas their successors are repeat flowering. It should, however, be borne in mind that we expect no more of any other shrub. We do not, for example, expect repeat flowering of the lilac or the rhododendron. If your garden is reasonably large, you may not wish to have all your roses in flower throughout the summer, even though you will probably like to have at least some in bloom later in the season. You may prefer that they should take their place in due season, like any other flower. It should also be remembered that a rose which flowers but once tends to give a better show for that limited period, during which it is able to devote all its energy to one glorious burst of flowers. It will also usually form a more shapely shrub for, unlike bush roses, shrub roses produce long growth from the base of the plant. This does not flower in the first season but subsequently sends out flowering branches. It is this strong growth that forms the basic structure of a well-shaped shrub which is not only more pleasing to the eye, but which also displays its flowers in a more natural and satisfactory manner. In addition to this the plant is likely to be much more robust because it has not had to expend its energy on the continual production of flowers.

Almost all these roses are over one hundred years old, and a few may well be over a thousand years old. There must have been many more of their brethren who have fallen by the wayside. Those that remain really are great survivors. It is, therefore, not surprising that they are extremely tough and hardy. It is our experience that they are also more disease resistant that most roses, mildew being their worst fault, though this is not difficult to control. They are easy to grow and will do well with minimal care, although a little extra attention can yield rich rewards (see Chapter 13).

The rose has received far more attention from the plant breeder than any other flower, so it may seem strange so many gardeners should turn back to the beginning and start growing varieties from the distant past. There is little doubt this has something to do with the attractions of the antique, and I see no reason to decry this. There is, however, much more to the Old Roses than this, for they possess a very special charm that is not always to be found in roses of more recent date.

It is my personal opinion that we are today much too obsessed with the past, and often too little concerned with the creations of our own time. If we consider the devotion that we put into the preservation of old buildings and how little concern we show for new ones, it sometimes seems a little unhealthy. Having said this, there is a certain satisfaction to be gained from the sheer permanence of these roses; we have had time to get to know them and to love them, something that cannot be said for Modern Roses that come and go with bewildering speed. In spite of this, it cannot be stressed too strongly that these are not mere curiosities but first-class shrubs in their own right, and their gentle colours and more natural growth melt perfectly into the garden scheme. Finally, but by no means least, it is hardly necessary to say that their fragrance excels that of the majority of those which have come after them. Considered as a group they are, to me, still the most beautiful of all roses.

The naming of Old Roses is always a source of controversy and many Old Rose enthusiasts like to show their knowledge on the subject. These roses suffered a long period of neglect before re-emerging in our time, and inevitably many names were lost. Although a great deal of research has gone into finding the correct names this has not always been possible. A description found in an old book or catalogue may have been adequate for the gardeners of that time, but it is frequently insufficient for us to give a name to a particular rose. It has often been necessary simply to do the best that we can, and, in fact, this does not matter very much, for as we all know, a rose by any other name will smell as sweet. The important thing is to agree on a name so that we all know what we are talking about.

GALLICA ROSES

Rosa gallica is a native of central and southern Europe. It forms an upright shrub of 3ft. in height which suckers freely, with slender stems and many small thorns. It bears deep pink flowers of 2 to 3ins. across, followed by round, red hips. Our garden Gallicas have been developed over the centuries from this species.

Although so much of the history of Old Roses is shrouded in mystery it is safe to assume that the Gallicas are the oldest of garden roses and have been involved, to a greater or lesser extent, in the development of all the four other classes of Old Roses. Their influence is present, at least in some small degree, in nearly all our garden roses down to the present. Long before they received their name, their predecessors were grown by both the Greeks and Romans and almost certainly by others before them. Although they are the oldest of the truly Old Roses they also became the most highly developed. In 1629 the great English botanist and gardener John Parkinson listed twelve varieties. A little later the Dutch began raising seedlings to produce new varieties. It was not long before this activity spread to France, where breeding was carried out on a large scale and they became known as Gallicas. Soon after 1800 there were said to be over one thousand varieties. Most of these have long since been lost, but we still have more of them than any other group of the truly 'old' roses, and these still include some of the most beautiful roses that can be grown today.

Not surprisingly, all this work led to highly developed flowers in a variety of colours. These tend to be in the stronger shades: deep pinks and near crimsons, as well as rich mixtures of purple, violet and mauve. There are a number of good striped varieties as well as others that are attractively mottled, marbled or flecked, and there are also a few soft pinks, though these are probably hybrids of other classes. No other Old Rose produces such subtle and fascinating mixtures of colour. They are nearly all very fragrant.

The Gallica Rose or, as it is sometimes called, the 'Rose of Provins', is not difficult to recognise. It usually forms a small shrub, generally not more than 4ft. in height, with strong rather upright growth and numerous small, bristly thorns. The leaves are oval, pointed at the tip, of rather rough texture and often dark green in colour. The flowers are usually held either singly or in threes, and the buds are typically of spherical shape.

These roses are excellent garden subjects, with low, easily managed growth that is ideal for the smaller garden. They will, if required, grow in poor, even gravelly soil, and demand a minimum of attention. If grown on their own roots they will sucker freely and quickly spread across a border. Although they are often effective when grown in this manner they can become a problem, and for this reason it is usually better to plant budded stock and not to plant too deeply.

ALAIN BLANCHARD. This variety has almost single flowers of deep purple-crimson, with contrasting golden stamens, the colour later turning to a purple which is attractively dotted and mottled with pink. Its growth is thorny, about 4ft. in height, with pale green foliage. Fragrant. Probably a Gallica/Centifolia cross. Bred by Vibert (France), introduced 1839.

ANAÏS SÉGALAS. This rose has perfectly shaped flowers which open flat and are well filled with petals, showing a green eye at the centre. The colour is a rich mauve-crimson, turning with age to a pale lilac-pink. It forms a low-growing, branching and free-flowering bush with light green foliage. Strong fragrance. Height 3ft. Vibert (France), introduced 1837.

ASSEMBLAGE DES BEAUTÉS ('Rouge Éblouissante'). Very double flowers of a vivid cherry-red, unusual amongst Gallicas; later becoming tinged with mauve, the petals reflexing almost to a ball, with a button eye at the centre. Very fragrant. Height 4ft. Introduced 1823.

BELLE DE CRÉCY. One of the finest, most free-flowering and reliable of Gallica Roses. On opening the flowers are a cerise-pink mixed with mauve, later turning to soft parma-violet and ultimately to lavender-grey; a wonderful succession of tints. They are shapely in form, the petals opening wide and reflexing to expose a button centre. A very rich fragrance. This variety will grow to about 4ft. in height and about 3ft. across. Bred prior to 1848. See page 42.

BELLE ISIS. A charming little rose of short growth that is ideal for the small garden. The flowers are not large but are full petalled, opening flat, neatly formed and of a delicate flesh-pink colour. It has tough, sturdy growth, with many prickles and small light green leaves. Its origins are something of a mystery as it is unusual to find so delicate a pink among the Gallicas, but it is probable that one of its parents was a Centifolia. It has the unusual fragrance of myrrh, and this would seem to indicate there is also Ayrshire 'Splendens' in its make up, for this scent was unique to those roses. Height 3ft. Bred by Parmentier (Belgium), introduced 1845.

BURGUNDY ROSE ('Parviflora', 'Pompon de Burgogne'). A charming miniature Gallica which forms a dense, very short jointed shrub, with very small dark green pointed leaves and tiny claret-coloured pompon flowers made up of numerous small petals. It is as though a large shrub had shrunk in all its parts, resulting in something quite unlike any other rose. The growth is about 3ft. in height. It can become rather too narrowly upright, but careful clipping will enable it to maintain its shape. In existence before 1664.

CAMAIEUX. One of the most pleasing of the striped roses. Its flowers are only loosely double but of shapely formation. They are white and heavily striped and splashed with a crimson that soon turns to purple, later becoming pale lilac and remaining attractive at all stages. There is a sweet and spicy fragrance. It forms a small shrub of about 3ft. in height. Introduced 1830.

CARDINAL DE RICHELIEU. One of the darkest of all roses. The flowers are mauvish-pink in the bud, becoming mauve, and ending in the richest pure purple. They are quite small and as they develop the petals reflex back almost forming a ball. This is an excellent garden shrub, developing into an arching mound of growth with dark green leaves and few thorns. It requires good cultivation and fairly severe pruning if it is to attain its full potential, otherwise the flowers may be rather insignificant (see Chapter 13). It is advisable to thin out the shrub by the annual removal of some of its older growth. The height is 5ft. by 4ft. across. Fragrant. It is said to have been bred by Laffay of France in 1840, but may have been bred in Holland by Van Sian and originally named 'Rose Van Sian'. See page 39.

CHARLES DE MILLS. The largest flowered and most spectacular of the Old Roses. Each bloom has numerous evenly-placed petals which open so flat that they give the impression of having been sliced off with a sharp knife. The colour is rich purple-crimson gradually turning to pure purple. It is an erect grower but forms a rather floppy shrub of 4ft. in height and may require some support. Unfortunately there is no more than a slight fragrance. Breeder and date of introduction not known. See page 39.

CRAMOISI PICOTÉ. A pretty and unusual little rose with small, full, almost pompon flowers which are crimson in the bud, opening to a deep pink with crimson at the edges. The growth is short and compact with small dark green leaves. Little fragrance. Height 3ft. Bred by Vibert (France), introduced 1834.

D'AGUESSEAU. This rose has the brightest red colouring to be found among the Gallicas. For this reason we find it is in great demand — perhaps greater demand than its qualities warrant. Its colour is a bright cerise-scarlet although this soon fades to cerise-pink. The flowers are full petalled and fragrant, the growth strong with ample foliage. Height 5ft. Bred by Vibert (France), introduced 1837.

DUC DE GUICHE. A magnificent Gallica with large flowers of a rich wine-crimson shaded with purple. They have many petals and are beautifully formed, opening at first to a cup and gradually reflexing. It is one of the finest of its class, but in a dry season the colour can become dull and altogether less pleasing, particularly in light soils. Height about 4ft. Fragrant. Bred by Prévost, introduced 1829. See page 64.

DUCHESSE D'ANGOULÊME. This little charmer is probably not wholly Gallica. The delicacy of its transparent blush-pink globular flowers, which hang so gracefully from its arching growth, strongly suggests some other influence — *Rosa centifolia* has been suggested, but it is difficult to be sure. It has few thorns, light green foliage and a spreading growth to about 3ft. in height and as much across. It was, at one time, also known as the 'Wax Rose'. Bred by Vibert (France), prior to 1827. See page 38.

DUCHESSE DE BUCCLEUGH. A variety with unusually large flowers that open flat and quartered with a button eye. Their colour is an intense magenta-pink which does not appeal to everyone. The growth is very strong and upright, to 6ft. in height, with fine luxurious foliage. One of the latest of the Gallicas to flower. Bred by Robert (France), introduced 1846.

DUCHESSE DE MONTEBELLO. A rather loose-growing shrub bearing sprays of soft pink full-petalled flowers of open-cupped formation. These have a delicate charm and blend nicely with its grey-green foliage. It is unlikely that it is a true Gallica. I have used it for breeding purposes crossing it with repeat-flowering English Roses and, much to my surprise, obtained a proportion of repeat-flowering seedlings. This would suggest that it was itself the result of a cross with a repeat-flowering rose. Such mysteries contribute much to the interest of Old Roses. A beautiful rose with a sweet fragrance. Height 4ft. Bred by Laffay (France), introduced prior to 1829. See page 65.

DU MAÎTRE D'ÉCOLE. A variety producing some of the largest flowers found among Gallicas. They are full petalled and open flat and quartered, later reflexing to reveal a button centre. Their colour is a deep pink, gradually turning to lilac-pink and taking on mauve and coppery shading as the flowers age. The growth is lax, about 3 or 4ft. in height, arching under the weight of its heavy, fragrant blooms. Meillez (France), 1840.

EMPRESS JOSEPHINE. The origins of this rose are not known. If it did exist in the time of Empress Josephine, it certainly did not bear her name, which it acquired quite recently. It is, however, an entirely appropriate name, as it is one of the most beautiful Old Roses and Josephine perhaps did more than anyone else to establish and encourage interest in roses throughout Europe, gathering together at Malmaison the largest

TOUR DE MALAKOFF, *Centifolia Rose. A graceful shrub and one of the most beautiful of the purple shades.* *See page 72.* Knight

SURPASSE TOUT, *a typical, strongly coloured Gallica Rose. See page 46.* Page
DUCHESSE D'ANGOULÊME', *a Gallica Rose of unusually delicate colouring. See page 36* Page

CARDINAL DE RICHELIEU, *one of the darkest of all Gallica Roses. See page 35.*
CHARLES DE MILLS, *the largest of the Gallica Roses. See page 35.*

Warren Knight

A Border At *David Austin's rose garden illustrating the natural growth of Shrub Roses. 'Nyveldt's White', 'Cardinal de Richelieu', 'Sea Foam',* Rosa *'Complicata', 'D'Aguesseau', 'Maiden's Blush' and 'Fred Loads'.*
Warren

A BORDER AT *David Austin's rose garden. 'Chapeau de Napoléon', 'Wilhelm', 'Katharina Zeimet', 'Gloire de Guilan', 'Ipsilante',* Rosa *'Dupontii', 'Tuscany', 'Smarty', and* Rosa virginiana.

Warren

BELLE DE CRÉCY, *one of the most attractive of the Gallica Roses.* *See page 34.* Knight

TUSCANY SUPERB. *Gallica Rose. An excellent garden shrub.* *See page 47.* Calvert

MARIE LOUISE, *Damask Rose. One of the most sumptuous of the Old Roses.* *See page 49.* Warren

collection of roses ever established up to her time. This variety is far removed from the typical Gallica and is classed as *Rosa × francofurtana.* It is probably a hybrid of *R. cinnamomea.* The flowers are semi-double with wavy petals of an unusual papery appearance. Their colour is a rich tyrian rose veined with a deeper shade. Unlike the majority of Old Roses, the flowers are followed by a fine crop of large turbinate hips. 'Empress Josephine' forms a low, shapely, rather flat growing bush some 3ft. in height, with very coarse textured grey-green foliage and few thorns. Excellent in every way, the only possible complaint being that it has no more than a faint fragrance. It has one close relative, 'Agatha', which is of the same class, but which is an altogether taller and coarser rose with, rather surprisingly, an intense fragrance. See frontispiece.

GEORGES VIBERT. Rather small flowers which open flat, with narrow quilled petals of blush pink striped with light crimson. The growth is narrow and upright, about 5ft. in height, with many thorns and unusually small leaves. Bred by Robert (France), 1853.

GLOIRE DE FRANCE. A small shrub with somewhat spreading growth of 3ft. in height and rather more across. It bears beautifully shaped full lilac-pink flowers with reflexing petals which hold their colour at the centre while paling with age towards the edges. Bred prior to 1819.

HYPPOLYTE. A tall, vigorous shrub of 5ft. in height, with few thorns and small dark green leaves. The flowers, too, are small, flat at first, later reflexing into a ball-like formation. The colour is mauve-violet.

NESTOR. Lilac-pink flowers, deepening towards the centre, opening cupped, later becoming flat and quartered and gradually taking on mauve and grey tints. It has almost thornless growth of 4ft. in height. Introduced about 1846.

OFFICINALIS (the 'Apothecaries' Rose'). This historic rose is said to be the 'Red Rose of Lancaster', the emblem chosen by the House of Lancaster at the time of the Wars of the Roses, and there is little doubt it is the oldest cultivated form of the Gallica Rose that we have. It seems to have first appeared in Europe in the town of Provins, south east of Paris, where it was used in the making of perfume. It was said to have been brought there by Thibault Le Chansonnier on his return from the Crusades. Thibault IV, King of Navarre, wrote the poem *Le Roman de la Rose* in about 1260, and in it he refers to this rose as the rose from the 'Land of the Saracens'. Whatever the truth may be, this is a rose of great antiquity. For centuries it was grown for its medicinal qualities, and for this reason it is known as the 'Apothecaries' Rose'. Today we appreciate it for its excellent garden qualities, for it certainly deserves a place among the very finest of garden shrubs of any kind. It forms low branching growth, carries its semi-double light crimson fragrant flowers (with golden stamens) nicely poised above ample dark green foliage, blooms very freely, and provides a most satisfactory effect in the border. If grown on its own roots it will quickly spread by suckering and might well be used on banks and in other areas where ground cover is required. Budded on a stock it will grow to about 4ft. in height and about the same across. The colour varies widely according to climate and season and is much paler under hot conditions. In autumn it produces small round hips which are not without ornamental value.

POMPON PANACHÉE. A pretty little miniature-flowered rose with neatly-formed blooms that have deep pink stripes on a cream ground. They are held in ones and twos on wiry upright stems with small leaves. Erect growth of 3 or 4ft. in height.

PRÉSIDENT DE SÈZE ('Jenny Duval'). A perfect bloom of this rose can be more beautiful than any other to be found among the Gallicas. Its attractive lilac buds open to magnificent large full-petalled flowers that display a bewildering array of tints. Graham Thomas mentions cerise, magenta, purple, violet, lilac-grey, soft brown and lilac-white, and all these colours are to be found, depending on the stage of development of the flower and the prevailing weather conditions. Perhaps it is simpler to say the overall colour effect is lilac, violet and silvery-grey. It forms a sturdy shrub with ample foliage, and will grow to about 4ft. in height. For some years now a rose named 'Jenny Duval' has been distributed by nurserymen, including ourselves. It is now generally agreed that this is the same as 'Président de Sèze'. To those who have known this rose under both names, it may seem strange that we have taken so long to arrive at this conclusion. My only defence is that this rose is so various and ever-changing in its colour that the confusion between the two was understandable. I have had more than one not inexperienced rose enthusiast come to me with what they thought was yet another entirely different sport, and this too has turned out to be the same variety. The truth is that 'Président de Sèze' differs so widely according to the conditions under which it is grown that it seldom looks the same on any two occasions. There is a pleasing fragrance. Nothing is known of its origin, but Graham Thomas obtained it from Babbink & Atkins of New Jersey and distributed it in Britain. See page 22.

ROSA MUNDI (*Rosa gallica versicolor*). This is a striped sport of 'Officinalis', having all the virtues of that excellent rose, to which it is similar in every respect except colour. This is palest blush-pink, clearly striped and splashed with light crimson which provides an attractively fresh appearance. Occasionally a flower will revert to the colour of its parent. It has the same strong bushy growth, and flowers in the same happy profusion as 'Officinalis', providing a wonderful massed effect. Both roses make fine low hedges — indeed it would be hard to find better roses for this purpose. The date of this rose is not known, but it certainly goes back to the sixteenth century and earlier. Like its parent it will make a 4 by 4ft. shrub. See page 20.

SURPASSE TOUT. Large full, tightly-packed flowers of light rose-crimson, turning with age to cerise-pink. The petals reflex and there is a button eye at the centre. The growth is strong and bushy, the height about 4ft. Strong fragrance. In existence before 1832. See page 38.

TRICOLORE DE FLANDRE. Large, fairly full white flowers heavily striped with shades of lilac, purple and crimson. The growth is short, about 3ft. in height, but vigorous with plentiful smooth foliage. Fragrant. Bred by Van Houtte (Belgium), 1846.

TUSCANY. A rose which can be compared with 'Officinalis' and 'Rosa Mundi', both in its habit of growth and for its excellence as a garden shrub. It has fairly large semi-double flowers of the darkest maroon-crimson; these open wide, with bright golden stamens lighting up the centre. It forms a sturdy bush of 4ft. and, on its own roots, will spread freely if permitted. The foliage is dark green. We do not know the age of this beautiful variety, but it probably goes back a very long way. There is only a slight fragrance. It was once known as the 'Old Velvet Rose' — the herbalist Gerard, writing in 1597, mentions a 'Velvet Rose', and it is likely that this is the same variety.

TUSCANY SUPERB. A larger version of 'Tuscany', with taller more vigorous growth to about 4ft. in height, larger, more rounded leaves and larger flowers with more numerous petals. It is in fact 'more' everything, while remaining at the same time very similar in its general character and colouring; the stamens are partially obscured, as these tend to be hidden by the extra petals. Its origins are not known, but it was recorded by Paul in 1848. It must have been either a sport or a seedling from 'Tuscany' — probably the latter. See page 43.

DAMASK ROSES

The Damask Rose, like the Gallica, dates back to ancient times. It is said to have been widely grown by the Persians and brought to Europe by the Crusaders. S.F. Hamble gives the credit for this to a Robert de Brie whom, he says, brought it to his castle in Champagne at some time between 1254 and 1276, whence it was distributed throughout France and later brought to this country.

According to Dr. Hurst, the Damask Rose originated from a natural hybrid of the Gallica Rose and a wild species known as *Rosa phoenicea.* The latter rose is a sprawling shrub or climber of no particular garden merit, bearing corymbs of small white flowers. We thus have two widely differing parents, and it is therefore not surprising that this family is itself somewhat diverse in its nature. In general Damask Roses are taller than Gallicas, perhaps 5ft. in height, more lax in growth, with more and larger thorns. The leaves are elongated and pointed, of a greyish-green colour and downy on the underside. Where there are hips these will usually be long and thin. The flowers are nearly always a lovely clear pink and have not inherited any of the purplish-red shades of their Gallica parent. They are often held in nicely poised sprays. The Damasks are usually strongly fragrant, the very name being synonymous with this quality. They bring elegance to the rose, both in leaf and general habit of growth.

Closely related to these roses is the Autumn Damask. This is a rose of great antiquity. It is not, perhaps, of the highest value for the garden, but is of great interest to the student of roses in that it was the only rose to have the ability to repeat flower prior to the introduction of the China Rose late in the eighteenth century. It is of equal interest for its very long history. Dr. Hurst tells us that it is first noted in the Greek island of Samos towards the end of the tenth century B.C., where it was used in the cult of Aphrodite. It was later introduced to mainland Greece and then to Rome where it continued to play a part in ceremonies connected with Venus. In the first century B.C. Virgil in *The Georgics* mentions the rose which flowers twice a year, and this was no doubt the Autumn Damask. This is a rather prickly shrub, with the leaves running right up to and clustering around the flowers. It has an unsophisticated charm and the typical Damask fragrance. It eventually led to the Portland Roses, through which it played an important part in the development of repeat-flowering roses about which I write in the next chapter.

CELSIANA. A typical Damask Rose, with fine, graceful grey-green foliage. The flowers are large, opening wide, semi-double, and of a soft pink colour that later fades to blush, with a central boss of golden stamens. They are held in delicately poised sprays, and the petals have the appearance of crumpled silk. There is a strong fragrance. Height approximately 5ft. I place this rose high on any list of Old Roses. Known to have been in existence before 1750. See page 56.

GLOIRE DE GUILAN. In 1949 this rose was collected by Nancy Lindsay from Iran, where it is used for the making of attar of roses. It forms a loose sprawling shrub with apple-green leaves. The flowers are cupped at first, later becoming flat and quartered. Their colour is a pink of unusual clarity and purity, and they are very fragrant. I have found it to be particularly resistant to disease. Height 4ft. See page 57.

HEBE'S LIP (*Rubrotincta*). A modest rose but not without its attractions. It has cupped semi-double flowers, with red-tipped petals that give it its name. The growth is short and thorny with fresh green foliage. Height 4ft. It is probably of hybrid origin, perhaps Damask × *Rosa eglanteria*. See page 58.

ISPAHAN ('Pompon des Princes'). A very fine shrub which begins to flower early and continues over a long period. The flowers are large and very full, opening flat, and of a rich warm pink that does not fade. A good cut flower, lasting well in water. It has a glorious fragrance. Height 5ft. In cultivation before 1832. See page 58.

KAZANLIK (*Rosa damascena trigintipetala*). One of the roses grown at Kazanlik in Bulgaria for the production of attar of roses. The blooms are pink and of no great merit, but it does form a graceful and typical Damask shrub, and has, as might be expected, a rich fragrance. Height 5 or 6ft. Probably of great antiquity.

LA VILLE DE BRUXELLES. Exceptionally large full-petalled blooms of a clear rich pink. When fully open the petals reflex at the edges, leaving a slightly domed centre filled with small petals. A truly luxurious flower of fine quality. The foliage is large and plentiful, pale green in colour and of typical Damask shapeliness. Its growth is upright but often weighed down by the heavy blooms, particularly in moist weather. Rich fragrance. Height 4ft. Vibert (France), 1849.

LEDA. Milk-white flowers with the slightest suggestion of pink. As they open they develop a picot effect, the rim of the petals becoming stained with crimson, so giving rise to its other name the 'Painted Damask'. The blooms are full petalled, reflexing to reveal a button centre. Although not perhaps quite so exciting as the description implies, it is a pretty rose with good foliage. Slight fragrance. Height 3ft. Prior to 1827.

MADAME HARDY. One of the classic Old Roses — only a few others can approach it for the sheer perfection of its flowers. They are not very large, of pretty cupped formation at first, later becoming flat and finally reflexing. There is the slightest hint of blush in the early stages, but later they become a pure glistening white, while at the centre a small green eye adds to the attraction. They are held in nicely poised clusters, and are fragrant with just a hint of lemon. It will grow to about 5ft. and is reasonably strong, although it will repay more generous treatment with manure and fertiliser. The foliage is pale green. We cannot be sure of its origin, though it is obviously not pure Damask, the leaves and growth showing signs of Centifolia influence. Bred in 1832 by Hardy (who had charge of the Empress Josephine's famous rose collection at Malmaison) and named after his wife. See page 59.

MADAME ZOETMANS. A charming rose not often seen but gaining in popularity. Its flowers are of medium size, fully double, of cupped formation at first, opening to reveal a button eye. Their colour is white, tinted with blush at the centre, and they are borne on graceful growth on a nice bushy plant with fresh green foliage. Height 4ft. Bred by Marest (France), 1830.

MARIE LOUISE. A lax-growing shrub vying with 'La Ville de Bruxelles' for the splendour of its flowers. These are unusually large and full, of deep pink with the petals reflexing, and very fragrant. The sheer weight and quantity of the flowers often weighs down the branches to the ground. The height is about 4ft. with plentiful large foliage. Here we have a rose that might well be encouraged to flop over a low retaining wall. Raised at Malmaison, 1813. See page 44.

OEILLET PARFAIT. A compact, twiggy shrub of 3 to 4ft., with small pale green leaves. The flowers open flat with numerous petals of warm pink colouring, later reflexing almost to a ball. There is also a striped Gallica of the same name.

OMAR KHAYYAM. This rose is perhaps of more historic interest than garden value. It is the rose that grows on the poet Edward Fitzgerald's grave at Boulge, Suffolk, and which was itself first raised from seed from a rose on Omar Khayyam's grave at Nashipur in Persia. The flowers are soft pink, fragrant, of medium size, and quartered, with a button eye. The foliage is grey-green and downy. Height 3ft. About 1893.

PETITE LISETTE. A miniature-flowered Damask carrying small bunches of perfect little flowers, each well filled with clear pink petals. It has small, neat, downy grey-green foliage, and forms an excellent well-rounded shrub of 3 to 4ft. in height. Bred and introduced by Vibert (France), 1817.

QUATRE SAISONS (*Rosa damascena bifera,* the 'Rose of the Four Seasons'). This is the repeat flowering Autumn Damask I mentioned in the introduction to this section. The flowers are clear pink, loosely double, with long sepals and a powerful fragrance. It has rather spreading growth and greyish-green foliage. An ancient and most historic rose. Height 5ft.

SAINT NICHOLAS. A recent addition to this very old class, which occurred as a chance seedling, in 1950, in the garden of The Hon. Robert James, at Richmond, Yorkshire. The flowers are semi-double, opening flat, and of a rich pink colour with yellow stamens. It forms a short prickly bush of 5ft. in height, with good, dark green foliage. See page 58.

YORK AND LANCASTER (*Rosa damascena versicolor*). A tall shrub, with clear downy grey-green foliage, which carries its flowers with elegance in dainty open sprays. These are unusual in that they may be pink or almost white, or a mixture of both, the white being flecked with pink and vice versa, all these variations being found on one shrub at the same time. The individual flowers are informal and semi-double, usually exposing their stamens. It is not a dramatic shrub, but it does have a certain airy elegance. The story that the two factions in the Wars of the Roses each took a bloom from a bush of this rose — a red and a white — is probably not true. The roses of the two houses were in fact more likely to have been *R. gallica officinalis* and *'R. alba semi-plena,* although there is no firm historical evidence for this. It is important to obtain bushes from correct stock, as the flowers can easily revert to pink. Fragrant. Height 5ft. Known to be in existence before 1550.

ALBA ROSES

The Alba Roses form another very old group. In existence in classical times and probably brought to Britain by the Romans, they were widely grown in the Middle Ages, no doubt mainly for medicinal purposes, and appear in many paintings of that period. The other classes of ancient roses have a great deal in common and a casual observer might see them as all of one type, but this is not the case with the Albas which are quite distinct. It is generally agreed that they are the result of natural hybridization between the Damask Rose and *Rosa canina,* the Dog Rose of our hedgerows, or at least a species closely allied to it. A cursory inspection of the growth of the Dog Rose will show its close affinity to Alba Roses. As with other Old Roses many of its varieties appear to be the result of further hybridization with roses of other classes.

The Albas form a small but important group which includes some of the best and most beautiful of the Old Roses. Their growth is larger than that of the other old classes, often 6ft. or more in height, and it is no doubt for this reason that they were formerly known as Tree Roses. The flowers, as the name suggests, are rather limited in their colour range, being restricted to white, blush and pink, but they have a delicacy and refinement that is hard to match elsewhere. Their foliage is frequently grey-green in colour, and this tones well with their soft tints and provides an excellent contrast with other roses and plants. They nearly all have a pleasing and characteristic fragrance.

The delicate appearance of the flowers is in sharp contrast to the undoubted toughness of the plant which will grow under difficult conditions. Albas are, in fact, among the most easily grown of all roses, and even in partial shade will do better than most others, although no roses really like such conditions. Whenever we are asked at our nursery for roses that will grow in partial shade, it is always to these we first turn. They are ideal for the border or as individual specimens, or for planting in the more wild areas of the garden. They will also form a particularly fine hedge, different varieties of similar stature mingling together most satisfactorily. The taller varieties may be trained as climbers and they are quite happy when grown on a north wall.

ALBA MAXIMA ('Great Double White', the 'Cheshire Rose', the 'Jacobite Rose'). An ancient rose known to have existed in classical times, it has been grown in cottage gardens in this country for many centuries, where it lives on almost indefinitely, continually renewing its growth. It is not uncommon to see this variety growing, apparently wild, in hedgerows, such plants marking the place where a cottage once stood but which has now long since gone and only the rose remains. There can be no better testimony to its durability. Surely this must be one of the longest lived of all roses? It forms a tall if rather top-heavy shrub of 6ft., and although the individual flowers are not particularly distinguished they are most effective in the mass. Fully double, they are blush-pink at first but soon turn to creamy-white. Strong fragrance. See page 58.

ALBA SEMI-PLENA. Said to have been the 'White Rose of York', this is a luxuriant shrub with fine grey-green foliage and elegant shapely growth. The flowers are large, almost single, symmetrical in outline and milky-white in colour, with a large boss of stamens. They are followed in the autumn by typical Dog Rose hips. This is one of two roses cultivated at Kazanlik, Bulgaria, for the production of attar of roses. In every way a first class garden shrub. Very fragrant. Height 6ft. See page 63.

AMELIA. Here we have a smaller shrub than is usual among Albas. It bears large strongly fragrant pure pink semi-double flowers with pronounced golden stamens. Its height is about 4ft. Bred by Vibert (France), 1823.

BELLE AMOUR. A strong shrub, 6ft. in height, bearing clusters of semi-double slightly cupped flowers of a soft salmon-pink — a shade almost unique among Old Roses. These have a myrrh fragrance which suggests this rose may have some Ayrshire 'Splendens' in its make up. It was originally discovered growing on the wall of a convent at Elboeuf, Normandy.

CELESTIAL ('Céleste'). A modest rose, much treasured for the charm and delicacy of its exquisitely scrolled buds and semi-double flowers of lovely soft pink colouring. These are not large and have yellow stamens. The blooms are beautiful against the grey-green of the typically Alba foliage, and have a sweet fragrance. However the growth is anything but delicate, forming a robust shrub which, in our experience, should not be pruned too severely, otherwise it tends to make growth at the expense of flowers. It forms a shrub of 5ft. in height by 4ft. across. It is said to have been bred in Holland towards the end of the eighteenth century.

FÉLICITÉ PARMENTIER. At its best this is a most beautiful rose, with perfect quartered flowers very tightly packed with petals of clear fresh pink; these later reflex and fade to cream at the edges. The growth is quite short, about 4ft. in height, but bushy, with many thorns and pale green leaves. It is an excellent rose, but in dry seasons on sandy soil the flowers sometimes fail to open properly; with good management this should not be a problem. Known to have been in cultivation in 1834. See page 63.

MADAME LEGRAS DE ST. GERMAIN. A rose of exceptional beauty. Starting as a prettily cupped bud, it opens to form a perfectly shaped slightly domed flower with many petals. The colour is a glowing white with just a tinge of yellow, and this gives us a hint as to its origins — there has to have been a Noisette somewhere in its breeding. It would be hard to think of a more perfect marriage than Alba and Noisette, although in this case it has led to one weakness: the flowers can be damaged by wet weather. Otherwise it is sheer perfection. The growth is tall and lax, forming a graceful shrub of 6ft. in height, with few thorns and pale green leaves. Fragrant. It can equally well be grown as a Climber. Introduced prior to 1848. See page 54.

MADAME PLANTIER. This is an Alba/Noisette hybrid and, in fact, is sometimes classified as a Noisette. It forms a sprawling mound of graceful growth covered with large clusters of rather small pompon-like blooms against pale green foliage. The colour is creamy-white, lightly tinged with yellow at first, later turning to pure white, and there is a pointed green eye at the centre of each flower. Its sweet and powerful fragrance fills the air. It is equally effective when trained as a Climber, and I have vivid memories of a visit to Sissinghurst Castle and being shown this rose climbing up the trunks of fruit trees where they made a wonderful sight like billowing dresses. The height is 6ft. spreading to 6ft. across. Bred and introduced by Plantier (France), 1835. See page 54.

QUEEN OF DENMARK, *Alba Rose. This is one of the most beautiful of the Old Roses.* *See page 69.*
Knight

MADAME PLANTIER, *Alba Rose. An excellent free-flowering shrub or Climber. See page 52.* Page
MADAME LEGRAS DE ST. GERMAIN, *Alba Rose. One of the most perfect of the Old Roses. See page 52.* Calvert

CHAPEAU DE NAPOLÉON, *Centifolia Rose. Similar to 'Centifolia', but with moss-like growth.* *See page 70.* Calvert

CENTIFOLIA, *the 'Old Cabbage Rose', fading slightly.* *See page 70.* Calvert

CELSIANA, *Damask Rose. Wide open flowers on an excellent shrub.* *See page 48.* Calvert

GLOIRE DE GUILAN, *Damask Rose. Beautiful flowers of a very clear pink — here a little faded. See page 48.*
Calvert

ISPAHAN, *Damask Rose. See page 48.* Page
ALBA MAXIMA, *Alba Rose. See page 51.* Calvert

ST. NICHOLAS, *Damask Rose. See page 50.* Calvert
HEBE'S LIP, *Damask Rose. See page 48.* Warren

MADAME HARDY, *Damask Rose. One of the most perfect flowered of all Old Roses.* *See page 49.* Knight

MAIDEN'S BLUSH, *Alba Rose.* *See page 69.* Page

FANTIN-LATOUR, *Centifolia Rose.* *See page 71.* Warren

PAUL RICAULT, *Centifolia Rose. Like the other roses on this page it has high quality blooms.* *See page 72.* Page

A BORDER AT *David Austin's gardens, illustrating the natural growth of Old Roses. 'Ispahan', Damask Rose; 'Nozomi'; 'F.J. Grootendorst', Rugosa Rose; 'Cardinal de Richelieu', Gallica Rose.* Warren

OLD ROSES AND *Climbers at David Austin Roses. 'Surpasse Tout', Gallica Rose; 'Georges Vibert'; 'Pink Perpétue'; 'Tuscany Superb', Gallica Rose; 'Paul's Himalayan Musk', Climbing Rose.* Warren

DE MEAUX, *Centifolia Rose. This makes one of the most perfect Standard Roses, but flowers only once in the season. See page 71.* Knight

PETITE DE HOLLANDE, *Centifolia Rose. Another pretty miniature-flowered variety. See page 72.* Calvert

ROSA ALBA SEMI-PLENA, *an excellent shrub for partial shade and difficult positions. See page 51.* Knight
FÉLICITÉ PARMENTIER, *Alba Rose. Beautifully-formed flowers of delicate colouring. See page 52.* Calvert

DUC DE GUICHE, *a Gallica Rose with magnificent heavy blooms. See page 36.* Warren

DUCHESSE DE MONTEBELLO, *an unusual blush-pink Gallica Rose.* *See page 36.* Warren

NUITS DE YOUNG, *the darkest of all the Moss Roses. See page 75.* Warren
COMTESSE DE MURINAIS, *a tall-growing Moss Rose with flowers of delicate beauty. See page 74.* Calvert

WILLIAM LOBB, *a good, reliable, tall Moss Rose for the back of the border.* *See page 76.* Calvert
JEANNE DE MONTFORT, *a Moss Rose with plenty of brown moss on the buds.* *See page 75.* Page

MARÉCHAL DAVOUST. *Moss Rose. A particularly good garden shrub. See page 75.* Page

MOUSSELINE. *another good Moss Rose. See page 75.* Warren

JAMES MITCHELL. *Moss Rose. See page 75.* Page

HENRI MARTIN. *Moss Rose. A good rose, but not very much moss. See page 74.* Knight

SHAILER'S WHITE MOSS. *probably the best white Moss Rose. See page 76.* Knight

LOUIS GIMARD. *Moss Rose. See page 75.* Warren

MAIDEN'S BLUSH (known in France as 'Cuisse de Nymphe' and at other times and in various countries as 'La Royale', 'La Seduisante', 'Virginale', 'Incarnata'). This forms a graceful arching shrub of 5ft. in height with typical grey-green Alba foliage. The flowers are loosely double, of soft blush-pink, the petals reflexing slightly with age and paling towards the edges. They have a delicate fragrance. An old and much loved rose and certainly in existence before the beginning of the sixteenth century. See page 59.

MAIDEN'S BLUSH (small). This has smaller flowers than the above rose and grows to only 4ft. in height. I do not know whether it was a sport or a seedling from 'Maiden's Blush', but it is similar in every respect except size. Raised at Kew in 1797.

POMPON BLANC PARFAIT. An unusual rose and difficult to compare with any other. It has little round buds which open to small, flat, tightly-packed pompon flowers on short thin stems. The flowers are pale lilac-pink in colour and of very neat formation. They appear late in the season and are then produced a few at a time in long succession. The growth tends to be slow to develop, with small grey-green leaves and twiggy, rather stiff, almost reluctant growth, of perhaps 4ft in height. Slight fragrance. Introduced 1876.

QUEEN OF DENMARK ('Koenigin von Danemarck'). Few old roses can equal this for the perfection of its individual blooms. These are prettily cupped in the bud and later develop into a full perfectly quartered, slightly reflexing flower with a button eye at the centre. The colour is a warm rose-pink. Strong fragrance. The growth is comparatively short, perhaps 4 or 5ft. in height, with typical grey-green foliage. Like all Albas it is easily grown, but superb blooms can be obtained with good cultivation. Raised in 1816 by John Booth, who recorded it as a seedling from 'Maiden's Blush', and introduced it in 1826. See page 53.

CENTIFOLIA ROSES

The Centifolias were for a long time thought to be the most ancient of all roses, but subsequent research has proved this to be far from the truth. They are mere children by comparison with the three classes discussed so far. It seems that they evolved over a period extending from early in the seventeenth century to the beginning of the eighteenth century, that they were largely the result of the work of Dutch breeders, and that during the period mentioned some two hundred varieties were known to have been introduced. It is not easy to say exactly how they arose, but Dr. Hurst's work shows that *Rosa gallica, R. phoenicea, R. moschata* and *R. canina* all come into their make up. This would seem to indicate that a Damask/Alba cross might have occurred at some time, although it was probably rather more complex than that. It is likely that a series of crosses took place over a long period, resulting in what came to be regarded as a distinct breed. Centifolias were great favourites with our forefathers who seem to have prized them above all others, and evidence of this is provided by the Dutch and Flemish flower painters who used them in their work more frequently than any other roses.

The typical Centifolia has lax, open, rather lanky growth with a mixture of large and small thorns; the leaves are large, rounded and broadly toothed; the flowers tend to be heavy and globular with numerous petals. In spite of all this Centifolias are seldom clumsy and their luxuriant blooms nod gracefully on their stems. Their colours are, in the main, warm clear shades of pink, which do not normally fade in the sun. There are also a number of varieties of hybrid origin which tend towards crimson and pleasing shades of purple and mauve, as well as one or two whites. They are rightly famous for their rich fragrance.

The Centifolias have a strong tendency to produce sports, and this has resulted in a number of unusual forms. Foremost amongst these are the Moss Roses, but there are also quaint and unusual varieties such as 'Chapeau de Napoléon', 'Bullata' and a number of charming miniatures.

It is sometimes worth while giving some of the more lax-growing varieties a little support to stop them bending too near the ground. Pruning can be rather more severe than with other Old Roses, and should be just enough to keep the bush in order, without losing the grace of their arching growth.

BLANCHEFLEUR. Heavy, full-petalled, creamy-white flowers with a tinge of blush at the centre and red on the tips of the petals. It forms a vigorous 5ft. bush with many thorns and apple-green foliage, and shows signs of hybrid origin. Perhaps a little coarse in appearance for my taste, but it is the only white Centifolia we have. Fragrant. Raised by Vibert (France), 1835.

BULLATA (the 'Lettuce-leaved Rose'). This is probably a sport of 'Centifolia' to which it is similar, with the same cupped flowers and rich fragrance. The difference lies in the leaves, which are excessively enlarged and deeply crinkled, like the leaves of a lettuce. It is perhaps due to the effort of producing such foliage that the flowers tend to be rather inferior to 'Centifolia' and do not always open well. The height is 4ft. An interesting curiosity that seems to have originated in 1801.

CENTIFOLIA (the 'Rose of a Hundred Leaves', 'Rose des Peintres', the 'Provence Rose'). The type from which this group derives its name. Even those who know little or nothing about Old Roses will usually have heard of it by its name of 'Old Cabbage Rose'. To the old herbalists it was the 'Queen of Roses', and indeed it is the most beautiful of the Centifolia Roses with its heavy nodding blooms of warm glowing pink and rich Old Rose fragrance. It has strong, nicely arching growth of about 5ft. The flowers are at their best in warm, dry weather. Prior to 1600. See page 55.

CHAPEAU DE NAPOLÉON (*Rosa centifolia* 'Cristata', 'Crested Moss'). This rose is very similar to 'Centifolia', described above. It is distinguished by the fact that the calyx is greatly enlarged in much the same way as a Moss Rose, giving the bud the appearance of a three-cornered cockade hat. Closer observation will reveal that this is not the same as the 'moss' of a Moss Rose, but what Bunyard describes as 'an exaggerated development of the sepals'. However we describe it, the result is very attractive. Although the open flower is not quite so deep as 'Centifolia', it is otherwise indistinguishable, with the same clear pink colouring. It is said that it was originally found in 1820, growing in the crevice of an old wall at Fribourg in Switzerland. This suggests, rather surprisingly, that it was a seedling, not a sport. There is a rich fragrance. Height about 5ft. Introduced by Vibert (France) as 'Crested Moss', 1826. See page 55.

COTTAGE MAID. A rose which has had many names in its time: 'Belle des Jardins', 'La Rubanée', 'Village Maid', 'Panachée à Fleurs Doubles', 'La Belle Villageoise', 'Dometil Beccard' and 'Dominic Boccardo'. It is perhaps more properly known as 'Variegata', but we have chosen 'Cottage Maid' as being rather more picturesque. The flowers are quite large and globular in shape with numerous petals, the colour creamy-white, delicately striped with pale pink. It is a vigorous bushy shrub of 5ft. in height, with dark green foliage and many thorns. Rich fragrance. Introduced by Vibert (France), 1845.

DE MEAUX. A miniature Centifolia which has to be compared with other miniatures of this class — 'Petite de Hollande' and 'Spong'. Each of these is charming in its own way, like the little roses we might expect to see decorating tea cups. They are ideal for very small gardens. In spite of some reports to the contrary I suspect that they are all sports of larger Centifolias. 'De Meaux' forms a bushy, twiggy shrub of 3½ft. in height, with tiny flowers of only a little more than 1in. across, and small light green foliage to match. The flowers open as little miniature cups and develop into small pompon flowers of typical Old Rose pink. It is in every way a charming little shrub. Said to have originated with a man named Sweet in 1789. See page 62.

FANTIN-LATOUR. We do not know the date or origin of this variety, but it is clearly not of pure Centifolia descent. The leaves and growth show signs of China Rose influence. The flowers, however, have much of the character of a Centifolia, being of a nicely cupped shape, the outer petals reflexing as the flower ages to reveal a button centre. The colour is a blush-pink which deepens towards the centre and there is a delicate and pleasing fragrance. It forms an excellent shrub with good broad growth of 5ft. in height. Named, most appropriately, after the great French artist Henri Fantin-Latour, whose finest paintings were nearly all of flowers and whose favourite flower was the rose. In every way a fine shrub. See page 59.

IPSILANTE. A most beautiful rose, producing some of the finest blooms in this group. They are large, of a lustrous warm pink colouring, cupped at first, opening flat and quartered. The growth is shapely with fine foliage, and in my garden it is more disease resistant than any other Old Rose. Rich fragrance. Height 4ft. Introduced 1821.

JUNO. Like 'Fantin-Latour', this rose has more modern affinities and is probably connected with the Bourbons. It bears fragrant globular flowers of soft blush pink, later opening flat to reveal a button eye. The growth is rather lax and about 4ft. in height. In cultivation before 1832.

PAUL RICAULT. A 5ft. shrub of medium vigour. The flowers are deep pink, very full petalled and rather globular, the outer petals later recurving. It has a strong fragrance and is free flowering, the blooms hanging gracefully upon the stem. Raised by Portemer (France), 1845. See page 59.

PETITE DE HOLLANDE ('Petite Junon de Hollande', 'Pompon des Dames', 'Normandica'). This is another pretty miniature, with charming little Centifolia flowers of pure rose-pink. It forms a nice bushy little shrub of 4ft. with small leaves and tiny flowers all to scale. Although all are delightful, it is perhaps the best of the miniature-flowered Centifolias, and there is very little to choose between it and 'De Meaux'. Fragrant. First raised in Holland about 1800. See page 62.

ROBERT LE DIABLE. A lax shrub with dark green leaves and thorny stems. The flowers are purple, shaded with slate-grey and splashed with carmine, providing a most pleasing mixture of colour, particularly in hot weather. Of neat rosette shape, the blooms are not large, the petals reflexing towards the edges. Both foliage and flowers show signs of Gallica influence. Late flowering. Height 4ft.

SPONG. A miniature Centifolia of bushy, branching growth, about 4ft. in height, with typical Centifolia leaves. Its flowers are rich pink, paling a little towards the edges. It is rather less formal than 'De Meaux' and 'Petite de Hollande', and has the bad habit of holding its petals long after the flower has died, which is rather unsightly. This is a pretty little rose, but the least effective of the miniatures. Raised by Spong (England), introduced 1805.

THE BISHOP. A very double flower of rosette formation and unique colouring: cerise-magenta with pale lilac on the reverse of the petals, later becoming slate-grey and parma-violet. In certain lights the blooms appear to be almost blue. Gallica influence is very much in evidence. Fragrant. It has rather erect growth of 4ft. in height.

TOUR DE MALAKOFF. A most beautiful rose which will appeal to those who like the purple shades. The flowers are large, opening wide and slightly cupped and only loosely double, but it is the colouring which is their chief glory — a purplish-crimson tinted with magenta becoming violet and with a few stamens usually to be seen at the centre. It is magnificent at all stages. The growth is excellent, perhaps 6ft. in height, arching broadly to form a rather sprawling shrub. Given suitable support it might well be used as a climber. Raised by Soupert & Notting (Luxemburg), 1856. See page 37.

UNIQUE BLANCHE ('White Provence Unique'). Creamy-white flowers which are nicely cupped at first, later opening rather untidily with a button eye. At their best they can be most beautiful, the petals having a lovely silky texture. It has strong (if rather untidy) growth and there is a good fragrance. Height 4ft. Discovered at Needham, Suffolk, 1775.

WHITE DE MEAUX. This is a white sport from 'De Meaux', to which it is similar in every way except that the flowers are white tinged with pink. This may sound attractive, but unfortunately the pink is such that it gives the flowers a rather dirty appearance. It is, nonetheless, worthy of its place.

MOSS ROSES

The Moss Roses are Centifolias which have developed moss-like growth on their sepals and, in some varieties, a little way down the flower stem. This peculiarity is the result of a sport, or fault, in the plant. Small glandular growth is always present to some extent on the sepals of the flower, and in the case of Moss Roses this has become greatly exaggerated. The result is that the bud is covered in this mossy material, giving a most charming effect. We do not know exactly when this curious phenomenon occurred, but Dr. Hurst quotes various French sources which state that a rose of this nature existed in France at Carcassonne in 1696, where it had been for half a century, having been first brought there by one Freard Ducastrel. The earliest mention of it in England was in 1724, when it was listed in the catalogue of Robert Furber of Kensington. Mossing has probably occurred from time to time before and since; indeed it has been recorded subsequently on at least three other occasions. It has also occurred on an Autumn Damask, giving us the 'Perpetual White Moss'.

The majority of Moss Roses were bred over a short period of time, from approximately 1850 to 1870. Arriving, as they did, comparatively late on the rose scene, they show considerable signs of hybridity; in some varieties there are definite signs of China Rose ancestry. Here we have the first hint of the Modern Rose creeping in on the Old. The result is sometimes a loss of that charm which we so value in Old Roses, the first loss of innocence. Nonetheless, most Moss Roses have a beauty which is different from that of other roses. A Moss Rose bud just opening does have a certain charm that is all its own — in George Bunyard's words, 'a cosiness'; for, as he says, 'cosiness lay at the very centre of Victorian taste'. Indeed, I doubt that any other age would have taken them up quite so enthusiastically. They are often a little more stiff and upright than Centifolias, and there is more variation in quality. It is at this stage in the development of the rose that we have to become a little more selective in our choice of varieties.

Most Moss Roses have inherited the strong fragrance of their Centifolia ancestors and pruning should be as recommended for the Centifolias.

BLANCHE MOREAU. Very double, paper-white flowers, starting as a cup and later becoming flat, with contrasting brown moss. This rose is said to be a cross between 'Comtesse de Murinais' and 'Quatre Saisons Blanc', and it does occasionally flower in the autumn. It is perhaps a little lacking in refinement. The growth is rather slender and tall, up to 6ft. Raised by Moreau-Robert (France), 1880.

CAPITAINE BASROGER. Rather shapeless flowers of cerise-purple, and fairly coarse and ungainly growth which is tall and narrow, about 6ft. Little moss. Raised by Moreau-Robert (France), 1890.

CAPITAINE JOHN INGRAM. Full recurving flowers of dusky maroon-purple later becoming purple and showing a button eye. The buds are only sparsely covered with red moss. It forms a vigorous bushy shrub with dark foliage and many thorns. Fragrant. Height 5ft. Bred by Laffay (France), 1854.

COMTESSE DE MURINAIS. Pretty blush-pink buds enfolded in hard green moss, opening to superb quartered blooms with a button eye and fading to white. The growth is vigorous, tall, and erect, its many thorns and light green foliage suggesting a Damask ancestry. Height 6ft. Fragrant. A most beautiful rose. Bred by Vibert (France), 1843. See page 66.

DUCHESSE DE VERNEUIL. A charming rose of delicate refinement, with flowers of a clear fresh-pink colouring, the petals being slightly paler on the reverse side. It has well mossed buds, good foliage and forms a shapely shrub of 4ft. in height. Bred by Portemer (France), introduced 1856.

GENERAL KLEBER. Pretty buds wrapped in fresh green moss opening to form wide flat flowers with silky petals of soft clear pink and a button eye at the centre. It has good bushy growth, about 4 by 4ft., with light green foliage. One of the most beautiful of the Moss Roses. Fragrant. Bred by Robert (France), introduced 1856.

GLOIRE DES MOUSSEUX ('Madame Alboni'). This variety has the largest flowers of the Moss Roses, and indeed some of the largest flowers of all Old Roses. Its full-petalled blooms open wide and flat, reflex at the edges and have a strong fragrance. Their colour is a soft pink which pales with age. There is ample pale green moss on unusually long sepals. A beautiful flower, that may occasionally be damaged by rain. It forms a strong, rather erect, but not unshapely shrub of 5ft. with thick stems and large, light green leaves. Bred by Laffay (France), 1852.

HENRI MARTIN ('Red Moss'). Long crimson buds with contrasting but rather sparse green moss. The open flower is not very full but of attractive, neatly rounded form, and of an unusually pure crimson for a Moss Rose, later becoming purple-crimson. The flowers, which are held daintily on thin, wiry stems on a vigorous shrub of up to 6ft. in height, are followed by red hips. Fragrant. Bred by Laffay (France), 1863. See page 68.

JAMES MITCHELL. A vigorous shrub with small magenta flowers that fade to lilac-pink. The buds are dainty and wrapped in dark moss. It is usually the first Moss Rose to flower. Height 5ft. Raised by Verdier (France), 1861. See page 68.

JAPONICA ('Moussu du Japon'). This rose not only has mossy buds but also moss spreading heavily well down the stem, and even on to the leaves. The blooms are magenta-pink and not very impressive; the foliage has purple and copper tints when young. Really only valuable as a curiosity. Height 3ft.

JEANNE DE MONTFORT. A tall and vigorous Moss Rose of 6 or 7ft. in height. Its flowers are clear pink, not very full, have exposed yellow stamens, and are sweetly scented. The buds have plenty of brown moss on long sepals. Bred by Robert (France), 1851. See page 67.

LITTLE GEM. A miniature variety which has small, flat, pompon flowers of a uniform light crimson, but with very little moss. It forms a low bush, no more than 2ft. in height, with small leaves. Raised by Paul (England), 1880.

LOUIS GIMARD. Large cup-shaped flowers, tightly packed with petals of light crimson. It has deep green foliage and the buds are enclosed in dark moss. Height 5ft. Raised by Pernet Père (France), 1877. See page 68.

MADAME DE LA ROCHE-LAMBERT. Attractive crimson buds with dark moss and long sepals, opening to form flat, shapely, full-petalled flowers of crimson-purple. It makes a good bushy shrub of 4ft. in height and occasionally repeat flowers. Bred by Robert (France), 1851.

MARÉCHAL DAVOUST. One of the most satisfactory Moss Roses, when we consider it as a garden shrub. It flowers freely and has graceful, shapely, rather arching growth, creating a most pleasing overall effect. The buds are attractive, with green-brown moss, and open to form shapely flowers of light crimson tinted with purple and mauve, the petals reflexing to show a button centre and a green eye. Height about 4½ft. Fragrant. Raised by Robert (France), 1853. See page 68.

MOUSSELINE. This rose is often found under the name 'Alfred de Dalmas'. No other Moss repeat flowers quite so well, except perhaps 'Salet', which is a much less attractive rose. The buds of 'Mousseline' are pretty and have green-brown moss, although this is not very plentiful. The open flowers are medium sized, cupped, of a soft flesh-pink and delicately scented. The growth is bushy, about 4ft. in height, with pale green, peculiarly spoon-shaped leaves. It appears to be related to the Autumn Damask, probably 'Quatre Saisons Blanc'. A charming little rose. Height 3ft. Raised by Portemer (France), introduced 1855. See page 68.

NUITS DE YOUNG ('Old Black'). The darkest of all the Moss Roses, having small flowers of rich velvety maroon-purple lit by contrasting yellow stamens, with thin buds wrapped in very dark moss. Its growth is slender and wiry and it has small, dark leaves of an almost purple shade. Careful thinning at pruning time and some feeding will be worth while. Height 5ft. Bred by Laffay (France), 1845. See page 66.

OLD PINK MOSS. It seems certain that this well-known rose was a sport from *Rosa centifolia.* It is a little smaller and less deep in the flower, probably due to the burden of producing moss. Otherwise it has the same warm, rich pink colouring and strong fragrance, as well as the elegance and poise and other good characteristics of its parent. This is probably the original Moss Rose from which the others are descended. Although many varieties have followed it, none have excelled it, either for the beauty of its flowers or its value as a garden shrub. Height 4ft. It probably dates back to 1700.

RÉNÉ D'ANJOU. Pretty buds with brown-green moss opening to beautiful soft pink flowers with a delicious perfume. The foliage is tinted with bronze and it forms a bushy shrub of 4ft. in height. A charming rose. Bred by Robert (France), 1853.

SALET. A repeat-flowering Moss Rose with blooms of a good clear pink, and red moss. Unfortunately it is rather coarse both in flower and growth, although it is the most perpetual in this class. Height 4ft. Bred by Lacharme (France), 1854.

SHAILER'S WHITE MOSS (*Rosa centifolia muscosa alba,* 'Clifton Rose', also often known as 'White Bath'). This is a sport from 'Old Pink Moss', and is similar except for its colour. As one might expect, it is a most attractive rose, with cupped white flowers tinted with blush at the centre when they first open. It is certainly the best white Moss Rose, and indeed one of the most beautiful of the small band of white Old Roses. It forms an excellent shrub of 4ft. in height. Fragrant. Discovered by Shailer, 1788. See page 68.

SOUPERT ET NOTTING. A neat little rose, which is rather different to other Mosses. The flowers are quite small, deep lilac-pink, neatly rounded and flat with closely packed petals, and have an attractive formality. The growth is short and bushy, to about 3ft. in height, and it repeat flowers well in the late summer. Although the moss is not very conspicuous, this is a charming rose. Bred by Pernet Père (France), 1874.

WILLIAM LOBB ('Old Velvet Rose'). A tall and vigorous shrub of rather straggly growth, 6 to 8ft. in height, with thorny stems and leaden-green foliage. The flowers are of the most beautiful colouring: a dark crimson-purple turning to lavender and eventually almost to grey, the reverse of the petals being light magenta. They are held in large, open sprays, have plentiful green moss and a strong fragrance. This is an ideal rose for the back of the border, where it will look over the top of other smaller shrubs without showing its rather ungainly growth. It may even, as Graham Thomas suggests, be allowed to scramble into other shrubs, often combining with them to make pleasing colour effects. Raised by Laffay (France), 1855. See page 67.

Chapter 3

OLD ROSES II

Towards the end of the eighteenth century something happened which was to change our garden roses for ever. As European travellers and traders began to throw just a little chink of light on the ancient mysteries of China, it was inevitable that plants of that massive land should be brought back to Europe. China is probably the finest source of plant material in the world, and is certainly the home of some of the most beautiful wild roses, having to its credit somewhere in the region of one hundred different species. Before Europeans had seen these in the wild, certain garden hybrids were brought to Britain. These were to be known as the China Roses. Although not particularly striking in appearance, they did have one very important characteristic: the ability to flower not just in early summer but throughout the growing season. They were, as we say, repeat flowering, perpetual flowering, remontant, or recurrent, according to which term you choose. It is interesting and rather surprising that China, in spite of her wealth of wild roses and the fact that she has a very long and honourable tradition of gardens and flowers, never rated the rose very highly. The Chinese were essentially gardeners and their interests centred around peonies, chrysanthemums and other flowers, but only to a small degree the rose, although we do from time to time find it depicted on old pottery and in pictures.

The repeat-flowering characteristic of the China Roses was not entirely new — as we have already seen the Autumn Damask Rose had the same ability which it owed to *Rosa moschata,* itself recurrent flowering from late summer onwards. The ability to flower repeatedly is a phenomenon which does not usually occur in nature and is the result of a sport or mutation in the mechanism of the plant. With one or two exceptions wild roses first of all send up tall non-flowering shoots, and it is only in the next season that the shorter flowering shoots appear on these. In the case of the China Rose something went wrong — or perhaps I should say, for us, went right. A plant appeared which lost its ability to form its main non-flowering stems and produced only flowering stems, with the result that we had a bush on which every stem produced a flower. Having flowered, the rose would normally busy itself with the production of strong stems ready to bear next season's flowers and fruit, but in this case the plant continued to flower without thought for the future. This important fact was, no doubt, noted by some observant and long-forgotten Chinaman, who subsequently propagated the plant. Whoever he was, he made a most important contribution to our garden roses — greater perhaps than anyone has done since, for this discovery doubled or even trebled the period over which we can enjoy roses.

The China Rose originally arrived in this country in four different varieties. These became known as 'Slater's Crimson China', introduced 1792; 'Parsons' Pink China', 1793; 'Hume's Blush China', 1809; and 'Parks' Yellow Tea Scented China', 1824. The origin of these roses is difficult to trace. 'Parks' Yellow' can only have been the result of a cross between *R. gigantea* — which bears the largest flowers of all rose species — and a China Rose.

It may be thought that the arrival of these roses would have caused a great flurry of interest among plant breeders, but this was not, in fact, the case. For one thing, the existing native roses were far more showy by comparison. Before long, however, hybrids with the European roses (those in Chapter 2) did appear, but the gene that provided the repeat-flowering characteristic was what is known as recessive, with the result that the first hybrids were only once flowering. It was only when these hybrids were again crossed with the China Roses that perpetual-flowering varieties began to appear and the revolution began. From then on things moved apace and the rose has never looked quite the same again.

This revolution was not confined to the repeat-flowering characteristic alone. The China Rose, with its connection with *R. gigantea,* was an entirely different rose. Whereas the European roses tended to have rough-textured leaves and many thorns, the China Roses had smooth leaves and few thorns. Moreover, their whole character was different. This provided great opportunities but, as is so often the case with such opportunities. also certain dangers. These we shall be discussing later.

'Slater's Crimson China' brought the richer and purer reds we now find in many roses. Previously the crimsons invariably turned to purple and mauves, though often with very pleasing effect. 'Parks' Yellow' gave us the larger, thicker, more waxy petals of *R. gigantea.* It also provided the Tea Rose scent and tints of yellow, though not yet a rich yellow.

As China blood became mingled with that of the Gallicas and Damasks a great variety of new roses appeared, most of them with the ability to flower repeatedly, if not always well at least to some extent.

In this chapter we cover the various classes which, while showing signs of having a strong China influence, still bear flowers with much of the character of the truly Old Rose, and can generally be described as shrubs rather than bushes. These include the Portland Roses, the Bourbons, the Hybrid Perpetuals and the Tea Roses, as well as the China Roses themselves, although there is some doubt as to the inclusion of China blood in the Portlands — at least in the early varieties. All these groups tend to have foliage nearer the China Roses than the European roses; they are, in fact, beginning to look more like the Modern Roses, but the flowers still retain the full, open Old Rose formation.

This second part of the Old Rose history is rather in the nature of an unfinished story. The flower formation and shrub-like growth of the Old

Roses were soon to be superseded by the pointed buds and low bush growth of the Hybrid Teas before breeders had brought Old Roses to their full potential. It was unfortunate that the development of the two types was not allowed to continue side by side, but it was not to be. Nonetheless, we have here some roses of real value which it would be a great shame to lose. Happily, as things stand at the moment, there is very little likelihood of this happening.

As regards cultivation, it must be borne in mind that these roses are repeat flowering and therefore require more careful attention due to their greater productivity. Soil conditions should be better and manuring more generous; spraying becomes more necessary. The older once-flowering roses can often be planted and more or less forgotten; this is not possible with repeat-flowering roses if we want to obtain worthwhile results.

Now that we are dealing with repeat-flowering shrubs, pruning takes on a greater significance. It is usual to recommend that pruning be done in March, but there is a lot to be said for pruning in December. This has the advantage that the young shooting buds will not be cut away and thus force the plant to start again. The result of December pruning is that flowers appear earlier in the year, leaving the rose plenty of time to produce its second crop, and this before the soil may have dried out. Early pruning can be particularly important in more northerly areas where the seasons are shorter. These roses, being of a shrubby nature, are frequently slow in flowering again. Strong main shoots should be pruned by about one third of their length, while short side shoots should be pruned to two or three eyes. At the same time it will be necessary to remove old and dying growth completely, while always trying to create a nice shapely shrub.

CHINA ROSES

China Roses differ in character to most other garden roses; even to those unnumbered masses that are their heirs. They are altogether lighter in growth. This is perhaps because they are diploid, whereas the majority of garden roses are tetraploid; that is to say their cells contain two sets of chromosomes, whereas it is more usual to have four sets, resulting in larger cells and therefore heavier growth. China Roses have airy, twiggy growth, and rather sparse foliage, with pointed leaves, like a lighter version of a Hybrid Tea. Both growth and leaves are often tinted with red when young. The flowers are not showy, nor are they particularly shapely, but they do have a certain unassuming charm. They have an exceptional ability to repeat their flowering, and are seldom without blooms throughout the summer. Their colours are unusual in that they intensify with age, rather than pale, as is the case with European roses.

Till recently the origins of the China Rose remained a mystery. We know of the four original varieties described in the introduction to this chapter, but the wild form eluded us. Although I cannot at this stage be certain, it would appear that this rose has now been found by Mr. Mikinori Ogisu of Tokyo, in the Chinese Province of Sichuan. A photograph of this rose appeared in the Royal National Rose Society's Journal, *The Rose,* in September 1986, together with an article by Graham Thomas. Mr. Ogisu describes it as growing into trees to a height of up to 10ft., and bearing flowers of 2 to 2½ins. wide, which vary in colour from pink to crimson — the colour being darker in regions of higher altitude. Previously, this rose had been seen by Dr. Augustine Henry in 1884, who described it in *The Gardener's Chronicle* in 1902, where it was illustrated with a drawing. The species is known as *R. chinensis* var. 'Spontanea'. It will be of enormous interest for all students of the rose to see this species when it eventually comes to this country.

The China Roses of our gardens vary considerably according to the conditions under which they are grown. In an open position in this country they will not usually reach much more than 2 or 3ft. in height, although in more favourable areas they will grow much taller. In countries with warmer climates they will make quite large shrubs of 6ft. and more. As to position, it is best to select a more sheltered corner of the garden, perhaps with the protection of a south facing wall which is shielded from the wind. Here they will grow much nearer their full potential. Having said all this, China Roses are not really tender and can be relied on to withstand all but the very hardest winters in the British Isles.

Their light growth and dainty flowers make them particularly suitable for mixing with other plants, especially where something heavier and more robust might be out of place. China Roses require fertile soil, or at least soil that has been well manured, but unlike other roses mentioned in this chapter they dislike hard pruning, and this should usually be done only to maintain the shape of the shrub and to remove dead and ageing growth.

COMTESSE DU CAYLA. A dainty little shrub of 3ft. in height with almost single flowers of varying shades of coppery-pink, eventually becoming salmon-pink with yellow tints at the base of the petal. The foliage is purplish-bronze when young. Tea Rose scent. Raised by P. Guillot (France), 1902.

CRAMOISI SUPÉRIEUR. Small, cupped, fragrant flowers of a clear unfading crimson, produced in small clusters. The growth is short and twiggy, about 3ft. in height in a warm situation. There is also a good climbing form, 'Cramoisi Supérieur Grimpante'. Bred and introduced by Coquereau, 1832.

FABVIER ('Madame Fabvier', 'Colonel Fabvier'). A small low-growing plant of about 1ft. in height, rather similar in habit to a Polyantha Rose. The flowers are small and bright scarlet with a white streak in their petals. It is constantly in bloom and the petals fall before they fade, giving an effect of continuing brilliance. Laffay (France), 1832.

HERMOSA. This shows all the signs of being a Hybrid China Rose hybrid. We do not know what the other parent was, but certainly it is an excellent little rose. 'Hermosa' has something of the appearance of a Bourbon Rose, but it is smaller in all its parts and more delicate in appearance. The growth is branching and more sturdy than most China Roses, bearing small lilac-pink flowers of a pretty cupped formation. They are borne with admirable continuity throughout the summer. Slight fragrance. Bred and introduced by Marcheseau (France), 1840. See page 88.

LE VÉSUVE ('Lemesle'). Dainty scrolled buds of Tea Rose appearance, soft creamy-pink in colour, gradually deepening with age and finally taking on tints of carmine. The flowers have a Tea Rose fragrance and are produced continually on a branching twiggy bush which will, given a warm sheltered position, achieve 5ft. in height, although 3ft. would be more usual under average conditions. Introduced by Laffay (France), 1825. See page 90.

MADAME LAURETTE MESSIMY. Long slender buds with only a few petals which open quickly. They are salmon-pink at first, shaded copper at the base of the petal, the open flower soon fading. It is the result of a cross between 'Rival de Paestum' and the Tea Rose 'Madame Falcot', and is, in fact, of rather Tea Rose appearance. It will grow to 4ft. in height in a warm position. Bred by Guillot Fils (France), 1887.

MUTABILIS ('Tipo Ideale'). Often incorrectly known as *Rosa turkestanica,* this variety rivals the 'Old Blush China' for its excellence as a garden shrub. Its pointed copper-flame buds open to single copper-yellow flowers of butterfly daintiness, soon turning to pink and finally almost crimson. Given a warm sheltered position near a wall it will form an 8ft. shrub which will probably flower as constantly as any other rose. In more exposed positions it is often quite small and frail in appearance. It would be interesting to know of its origins, but unfortunately this information has been lost. See page 85.

OLD BLUSH CHINA ('Parsons' Pink China'). This is a very good garden shrub, with twiggy but quite robust growth and dainty flowers in small clusters. These are produced continually throughout the summer, starting early and finishing late, and for this reason it was formerly known as the 'Monthly Rose'. The flowers are not large and of a loose informality. They are pale pink in colour, deepening with age. The bush usually grows to about 4ft. in height but may be considerably taller in favourable conditions. I have seen it growing as a 10ft. shrub near to a wall in the warm climate of Pembrokeshire. It has a pleasing fragrance which has been described as being similar to that of a Sweet Pea. Introduced to England 1789. See page 105.

RIVAL DE PAESTUM. Long, pointed buds, tinted blush, opening to semi-double ivory-white flowers elegantly poised on a shrub some 4ft. in height. Sometimes classified as a Tea Rose. Raised by G. Paul, 1863.

SOPHIE'S PERPETUAL. A beautiful rose found in an old garden, named by Humphrey Brooke and reintroduced in 1960. The flowers are quite small, of shapely cupped formation and held in small sprays. Their colour is a deep pink. Strong growth with few thorns and dark green foliage. It will grow into a 6ft. shrub and may be used as a Climber. Of obvious hybrid origin.

VIRIDIFLORA (the 'Green Rose'). In this rose the petals are entirely missing and have been replaced by numerous green sepals giving the effect of a green rose. It is, no doubt, a sport from the 'Old Blush China' to which it is very similar in growth. It is of little value as a garden plant, except as a curiosity, although it may have its uses for inclusion in flower arrangements. Introduced 1855.

PORTLAND ROSES

The Portland Roses were the first family in which the China Rose played a part by passing on its ability to repeat flower. They had only a short period of popularity, for they were soon to be overtaken, first by the Bourbons, and not long after by the Hybrid Perpetuals, but in 1848 there were eighty-four varieties growing at Kew. Today only a handful remain, but they form, nonetheless, a not unimportant class, both for their beauty and as one of the parents of the Hybrid Perpetuals.

The origins of the Portland Roses are shrouded in mystery and writers tend to step lightly over the subject, but we do know that around the year 1800 the Duchess of Portland obtained from Italy a rose known as *Rosa paestana* or 'Scarlet Four Seasons' Rose', and that it was from this rose that the group developed. The Portland Rose was repeat flowering, and was thought to have been the result of a cross between a Gallica Rose and the repeat-flowering Autumn Damask. This is unlikely, although it could easily have been a seedling from such a rose. Hurst seems to have had little to say on the subject, although he does note that Redouté's print of 1817 has the appearance of a China-Damask-French hybrid. I would thus assume Hurst had not seen the growing plant. One would expect that there is some China Rose influence there (probably 'Slater's Crimson China'), although there is not much evidence of this in the plant. If this is so, it may well have inherited the recurrent-flowering characteristic from two different sources. The Portland Rose was sent from England to France where André Dupont, gardener to the Empress Josephine, named it 'Duchess of Portland', and it was not very long before the French had raised numerous varieties.

Portland Roses are not difficult to recognise. They usually show a strong Damask influence, but they are shorter in growth, perhaps 4ft. in height. The flowers tend to have very little stem so that the leaves are packed closely around the flowers, forming what Graham Thomas describes as a rosette or shoulder of leaves.

Although they cannot be said to be graceful in growth, being rather upright, Portland Roses are well suited to smaller gardens as they form small, compact shrubs. Their virtue lies in the fact that, though repeat flowering, they still retain much of the character of the truly Old Roses and have a strong Damask fragrance. Their ability to repeat is by no means unfailing and varies according to variety, but most of them can be relied on to provide flowers later in the year, many of them producing particularly beautiful Old Rose blooms.

ARTHUR DE SANSAL. A compact, upright shrub with ample foliage, the attractive buds opening to form flat, neatly-shaped very double dark crimson-purple flowers, paler on the reverse side of the petals. There is usually a button eye at the centre of the flower. Richly fragrant. Height 3ft. Raised by Cartier (France), 1855. See page 87.

BLANC DE VIBERT. This variety bears prettily-cupped, many-petalled white flowers with a strong fragrance. It forms an upright bush with ample pale green Damask Rose foliage. Height 3ft. Raised by Vibert (France), introduced 1847.

COMTE DE CHAMBORD. Very full quartered flowers of rich clear pink with a powerful Damask Rose fragrance. The growth is strong and rather upright, about 4ft. in height, with ample foliage, the leaves coming all the way up to the flower in true Portland style. Here we have a rose that retains the true Old Rose character, while at the same time repeat flowering well. One of the best and most beautiful of this class. Raised by Moreau-Robert (France), introduced 1860. See page 23.

DELAMBRE. A compact bush, bearing full-petalled deep pink flowers against ample dark green foliage. Height 3ft. Bred by Moreau-Robert (France), 1863.

JACQUES CARTIER. Very similar to 'Comte de Chambord', but its shapely full-petalled flowers have, if anything, a little more refinement, although it is not such a good repeat flowerer. It has the same clear pink colouring, fading a little with age, and a button eye at the centre. The growth is compact and erect with light green Damask Rose foliage. Rich fragrance. Height 3½ft. This and 'Comte de Chambord' are two beautiful Old Roses. Raised by Moreau-Robert (France), introduced 1868. See page 92.

MARBRÉE. Deep purple-pink flowers mottled with a paler pink and opening flat. The growth is strong and tall for a Portland, with plentiful dark green foliage. Slight fragrance. Height 4ft. Raised by Robert et Moreau (France), 1858.

PERGOLÈSE. Medium-sized, fully double fragrant flowers of a purple-crimson which fades to mauve as they age. They are produced in small clusters on a bushy upright shrub with ample dark green foliage. Height 3ft. Raised by Robert et Moreau (France), introduced 1860.

ROSE DE RESCHT. A shapely, bushy shrub that has quite small neatly-formed very double flowers with closely-packed petals. The purplish-crimson blooms are nicely placed on short stems against ample rough-textured deep green foliage. There are signs of Gallica Rose influence both in flower and leaf, but the fact that it produces a second crop of flowers suggests its place is in this class. Fragrant. Height 3ft. Brought to England by Miss Nancy Lindsay from Iran or France. See page 87.

ROSE DU ROI ('Lee's Crimson Perpetual'). An interesting little rose which has had a great influence on our Modern Roses, being the channel through which we obtained the clear red colouring, first of all in the Hybrid Perpetuals, and from them in the Hybrid Teas of the present day. It is a short rather spreading bush and not particularly robust. The flowers are loosely double, crimson mottled with purple. Strong fragrance. It repeats well and is, all in all, a worthwhile rose in its own right. Raised by Lelieur (France), introduced by Souchet, 1815.

ROSE DU ROI À FLEURS POURPRÉS ('Roi des Pourpres', 'Mogador'). Said to be a sport from 'Rose du Roi', its appearance casts some doubt on this. It is a pretty little rose with loosely formed purple flowers. Of spreading growth, it may achieve about 3ft. under suitable conditions. Introduced 1819.

THE PORTLAND ROSE (the 'Scarlet Four Seasons' Rose'). This forms an excellent bushy and rather spreading shrub of 3ft. in height with ample foliage. The flowers are semi-double opening wide and of light crimson colouring with conspicuous yellow stamens. A good garden shrub both in summer and autumn. Strong Damask fragrance. See pages 91 and 105.

BOURBON ROSES

The origins of the Bourbon Rose make a fascinating story and illustrate very well how the various movements in the developments of the early roses always happened by chance. Such happenings sometimes occur in what seem to be the most unlikely places. These roses take their name from l'Île de Bourbon, a small island near Mauritius in the Indian Ocean, now known as Réunion. It is said that farmers of this island were in the habit of planting both the Autumn Damask and the 'Old Blush China' together as hedges. With so many of these roses growing in close proximity there was always a chance that a hybrid would arise, and this, in fact, is what happened. The Parisian botanist Bréon found a rose growing in the garden of a man named A.M. Perchern. This rose was intermediate between the Autumn Damask and the 'Old Blush China' and had been grown in the island for some years under the name 'Rose Edward'. Bréon sent seed of this rose to his friend Jacques, gardener to King Louis-Philippe, and from this seed a rose called 'Rosier de l'Île de Bourbon' was raised. It was distributed in France in 1823 and two years later in England. Not much is known about the early development of these

MUTABILIS, *a China Rose assorting well with delphiniums and herbaceous geraniums. See page 81.* Knight

LOUISE ODIER, *Bourbon Rose. A Victorian favourite and one of the most reliably recurrent-flowering of the Old Roses.* *See page 94.* Knight

MADAME PIERRE OGER, *Bourbon Rose. Another Victorian favourite.* *See page 95.* Knight

ROSE DE RESCHT, *Portland Rose.* *See page 84.* Warren

ARTHUR DE SANSAL. *See page 83.* *Both this and 'Rose de Rescht' are unusually dark Portland Roses, both showing the influence of the Gallica Rose.* Knight

HERMOSA, *a hardy, reliable, repeat-flowering China Rose, seen here with lavender, an excellent companion.* *See page 81.*
Warren

MADAME ISAAC PEREIRE, *Bourbon Rose. A sumptuous beauty, particularly good in autumn.* *See page 95.*
Calvert

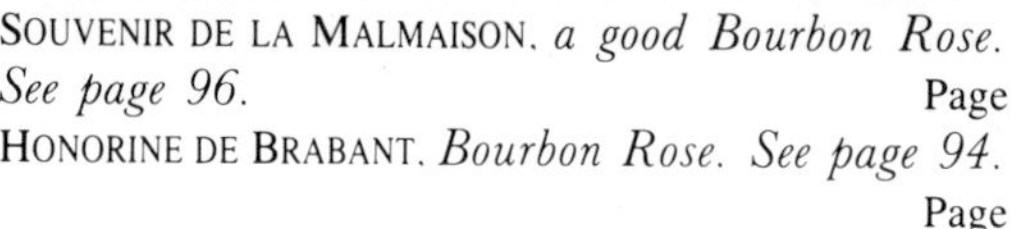

SOUVENIR DE LA MALMAISON, *a good Bourbon Rose. See page 96.* Page

HONORINE DE BRABANT. *Bourbon Rose. See page 94.* Page

REINE VICTORIA. *Bourbon Rose. See page 95.* Knight

LE VÉSUVE, *a China Rose with Tea-like buds. See page 81.* Page

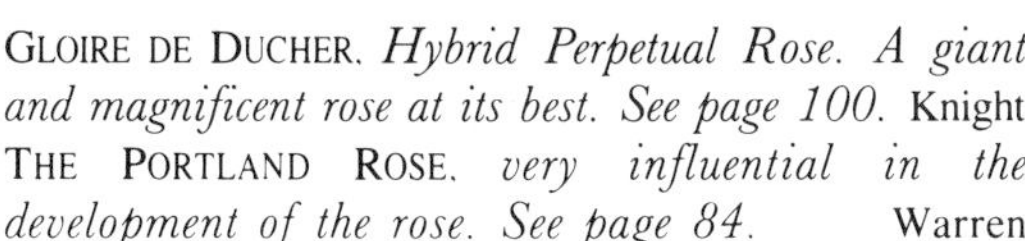

GLOIRE DE DUCHER. *Hybrid Perpetual Rose. A giant and magnificent rose at its best. See page 100.* Knight

THE PORTLAND ROSE. *very influential in the development of the rose. See page 84.* Warren

PAUL NEYRON. *a giant flowered Hybrid Perpetual Rose. See page 109.* Knight

BARON GIROD DE L'AIN. *Hybrid Perpetual Rose with attractive picoté edging. See page 98.* Calvert

JACQUES CARTIER, *one of the most charming of the Portland Roses.* *See page 83.* Knight
COMMANDANT BEAUREPAIRE, *a striped and flecked Bourbon Rose.* *See page 94.* Warren

roses, for breeding was then still confined to the chance collection of seed, but we can be sure that several other roses played a part in their development.

The Bourbons represent the first real step towards the Modern Roses. Their flowers still retain the character of the Old Roses with their strong fragrance, and they still have shrubby growth, but their leaves and stems begin to look more like those of the Hybrid Tea, and they are nearly all repeat flowering. Thus we have something of the best of both worlds. They are usually of robust growth and some highly desirable roses are to be found among them.

With Bourbons pruning becomes more important, particularly if we are to take advantage of their ability to flower a second time. Side shoots should be pruned back to three eyes, and strong main shoots reduced by one third. As the years go by, ageing and dead growth should also be removed. A liberal mulching with farmyard manure or compost, and an application of a rose fertilizer in March and again after the first crop of flowers will greatly improve the results. The removal of flowers immediately after they die is also important.

ADAM MESSERICH. A late arrival on the scene. One of its parents was a Hybrid Tea, and this shows up in the rather modern appearance of its growth and foliage — it might be argued that it is not a Bourbon at all. However, this need not worry us as it is a good shrub which may also be grown as a Climber or pillar rose. It is very vigorous, sending up long slightly arching almost thornless growth from the base of the plant. The flowers are large, semi-double, slightly cupped in shape and of a deep warm pink. The fragrance is strong, with a somewhat fruity, some say raspberry, flavour. It flowers freely in early summer but there are only occasional blooms later. Height 5ft. Bred by P. Lambert (Germany), introduced 1920.

BLAIRI NO.2. See Chapter 9.

BOULE DE NEIGE. A slender upright shrub of perhaps 5ft. in height, its neat dark green foliage betraying its partly Tea Rose ancestry. The flowers are held in small clusters, and its small, round, crimson-tinted buds open to the most perfectly formed creamy-white blooms of posy freshness, the petals gradually turning back on themselves almost forming a ball. Add to this a strong fragrance and we have one of the most charming white Old Roses. Bourbon 'Blanche Lafitte' × the Tea Rose 'Sappho'. Bred by Lacharme (France), 1867. See page 103.

BOURBON QUEEN ('Queen of the Bourbons', 'Reine des Îles Bourbon'). A rose frequently found surviving in old gardens after many years. It may be grown either as a tall rather open shrub of up to 6ft. in height, or as a Climber; on a wall it can achieve 10 to 12ft. The flowers are cupped and rather loosely formed with exposed stamens and crinkled petals. In colour they are medium pink veined with deeper pink paling towards the edges. Strong fragrance. Raised by Mauget (France), introduced 1834.

COMMANDANT BEAUREPAIRE ('Panachée d'Angers'). The three Bourbon Roses with striped flowers — 'Commandant Beaurepaire', 'Honorine de Brabant' and 'Variegata di Bologna' — are all rather similar. This one is notable for the lovely mixture of colours in its flowers: carmine pink flecked and striped with mauve, purple, scarlet and pale pink, and this so variously that they might be described in a dozen different ways. These colours are at their best in cool weather, as they tend to be rather muddy in very hot sun. The flowers are shallowly cupped in shape, strongly fragrant and produced very freely. This rose forms a dense leafy bush of strong growth that requires some thinning at pruning time to maintain the quality of its flowers. The height is 5ft. and as much across. It flowers only in early summer. Raised by Moreau-Robert (France), 1874. See page 92.

COUPE D'HÉBÉ. Cupped flowers of pale pink opening full and slightly quartered. The growth is tall, narrow and rather too upright, with light green foliage. It may be grown as a Climber. Bred from a Bourbon hybrid × a China hybrid. Laffay (France), 1840.

HONORINE DE BRABANT. A rose similar to 'Commandant Beaurepaire' but paler in colour — light pink splashed with shades of crimson and purple. It has the advantage over 'Commandant Beaurepaire' in that it repeat flowers quite well, the later flowers often being of better quality in the less intense sunlight of late summer. They are of shallow cupped-shape, opening quartered, with a strong fragrance. The growth is robust and bushy, to about 6ft., with ample foliage. It may also be grown as a Climber. See page 90.

KRONPRINZESSIN VIKTORIA. This is a sport from 'Souvenir de la Malmaison', see below, and is similar to that rose except that the flowers are creamy-white shaded with pale lemon-yellow. They can easily become discoloured in wet weather, and I have found it to be even less strong than its parent. Unless it is possible to give it exceptional care, it would probably be better not to grow this variety. It originated in 1887 and was introduced by Späth of Berlin.

LOUISE ODIER. A rose out of very much the same mould as 'Reine Victoria', having all its virtues but with more robust and bushy growth. The flowers are beautifully formed, cupped at first, opening flatter and neatly rounded, with each petal precisely in place. Their colour is a lovely warm pink and they have a rich fragrance. Like 'Reine Victoria' it repeats well throughout the summer, and for me it is the most desirable of the recurrent-flowering Old Roses. Height 5ft. I have used this rose for breeding and the results suggest that it has some Noisette in its make up. Raised by Margottin (France), introduced 1851. See page 86.

MADAME ERNST CALVAT. A sport from 'Madame Isaac Pereire' described below. It is similar in every respect, except for the colour which is a medium pink. In my opinion the flowers are a little less happy in this colour than in the deeper shades of its parents, often appearing rather coarse, but as with so many roses we get the occasional perfect flower, particularly in autumn, that makes it all worth while. It has the same strong growth and rich fragrance as 'Madame Isaac Pereire'. Height 6ft. Discovered by Vve. Schwartz (France), 1888.

MADAME ISAAC PEREIRE. A vigorous shrub some 7ft. in height with large, thick, deep green foliage. It bears huge flowers, perhaps 5ins. across. These are cupped at first and quartered on opening, the petals being rolled back at the edges. The colour is a very deep pink shaded with magenta, giving a rich effect, and there is an extremely powerful fragrance. It flowers well in the autumn when it often produces some of its best blooms. A sumptuous beauty, especially when well grown. The parentage is not recorded. Bred by Garçon (France), 1881. See page 89.

MADAME LAURIOL DE BARNY. A most beautiful rose carrying silky richly-fragrant quartered blooms of silvery-pink colouring. They are held in weighty, slightly drooping sprays on a vigorous 6ft. shrub, which may also be trained as a Climber. It has a good crop of flowers in early summer but there are rarely any blooms later. Raised by Trouillard (France), 1868. See page 107.

MADAME PIERRE OGER. A sport from 'Reine Victoria', see below, to which it is similar in every respect except for the colour of the flowers. This is a pale creamy-blush, giving the flowers a refinement exceeding even that of its parent, the beautiful chaliced blooms taking on the appearance of the most delicate porcelain. In very hot weather the colour tends to deepen and harden on the sunny side of the blooms, and in the rain the petals became speckled. The growth is narrow and upright, about 5ft. in height. Fragrant. Discovered by A. Oger (France), 1878. See page 86.

MRS. PAUL. Probably a seedling from 'Madame Isaac Pereire', with which it shares many characteristics. It has large blush-white flowers with a strong perfume. The growth is robust though rather floppy and may require a little support. Plentiful large leaves. Height 5ft. Bred by George Paul (England), introduced by Paul & Sons 1891.

PRINCE CHARLES. Dark purple-crimson flowers turning almost lilac as they age. They are large, flat when open and have petals of a veined and crimpled appearance. The growth is strong, about 5ft. in height, with large leaves and few thorns. It has little fragrance and is not recurrent. One of the few dark coloured roses in this class. A sport or seedling of 'Bourbon Queen', introduced 1842.

REINE VICTORIA. In this rose and its sport, 'Madame Pierre Oger', see above, we have two of the most beautiful and best loved roses of this period. They both form slender shrubs of about 5ft. in height, with the blooms elegantly poised above the foliage, indicating a close relationship with China Roses. The flowers are medium sized, chalice shaped rather than cupped, the petals incurving towards the centre to provide a charming enclosed effect and holding their form to the end. The colour is lilac-pink on the outside and paler within. This variety has few rivals among the Old Roses in its ability to flower repeatedly throughout the summer. Unfortunately, as so often happens, along with this goes a greater tendency to blackspot, but no more than we expect in most Modern Roses. Fragrant. Height 4ft. Bred by J. Schwartz (France), introduced 1872. See page 90.

SOUVENIR DE LA MALMAISON. This rose was named in memory of the Empress Josephine's famous garden at Malmaison and is one of the most popular of the Bourbon Roses. It is available both as a bush and a Climber, but we are only concerned here with the bush which is a short rather spreading shrub of about 3ft. in height. The flowers are a delicate blush-pink which pales a little with age. They are cup-shaped at first, later becoming flat and distinctly quartered to form a large and beautiful flower about 5ins. across, with a fragrance similar to that of a Tea Rose. Raised in 1843 by J. Beluze of France, from a cross between the Bourbon Rose 'Madame Desprez' and a Tea Rose, it has, as we might expect, foliage of rather modern appearance, although the flowers are of truly Old Rose persuasion. It is a reliable repeat flowerer. The growth is rather too short for the flowers, and it is, perhaps, better in its climbing form, of which a description is to be found in Chapter 9. See page 90.

SOUVENIR DE ST. ANNE'S. An almost single sport of 'Souvenir de la Malmaison', found in Lady Ardilaun's garden at St. Anne's, near Dublin. It has not grown very large at our nursery, but I am informed by Graham Thomas, who was responsible for its introduction, that it is capable of forming a fine shrub of 7ft. in height. I suspect it would repay extra generous treatment. The large flowers are a delicate blush-pink colouring and have a nice clean-cut appearance. Rather surprisingly, unlike 'Souvenir de la Malmaison', it has a strong fragrance. Graham Thomas tells me that this stems from *Rosa moschata* in its parentage, in which the fragrance comes from the stamens rather than the petals. Of course, this rose does have stamens, whereas its parent does not. Introduced 1950.

VARIEGATA DI BOLOGNA. The last of our trio of striped Bourbon Roses, and of more recent origin, having been bred in Italy by A. Bonfiglioli as late as 1909. The flowers are white, clearly striped with dark crimson-purple, giving them a purity and freshness that is very appealing particularly in cool weather. They are fully double, cupped in shape, globular at first and quartered when open, and have a strong perfume. This rose has ample foliage and forms a dense shrub of 5 or 6ft., or will climb to 10ft. A distinct and beautiful rose but susceptible to blackspot. See page 102.

ZÉPHIRINE DROUHIN. See Chapter 9.

HYBRID PERPETUAL ROSES

We now reach the final stage of development of the rose before arriving at the Hybrid Teas which are, of course, the predominant roses of the present day. It will have been noticed that none of the classes described so far can be said to be in any way pure or clearly defined in so far as their origins are concerned, although they may be quite distinct in their general character and appearance. When we come to the Hybrid Perpetuals this is more than ever true. The Hybrid Perpetuals can best be described as an idea rather than as roses of any definite origins. They are, in fact, an amalgamation of various roses with certain objectives in view — for it is at this stage that large-scale breeding comes into its own — with breeders raising numerous seedlings in the hope of arriving at an ideal. Paul tells us that the French breeder Laffay raised up to 200,000 seedlings annually — more than many large-scale breeders grow today.

It cannot be said that breeding on such a scale led to an all round improvement; indeed there is, to me, a decline in the beauty of the rose since Hybrid Perpetuals first appeared. It is true that, as their name suggests, the Hybrid Perpetuals are repeat flowering, but they are rather clumsy and their growth too tall, narrow and upright, making them unsuitable for use as shrubs in the garden. The nature of their development was in no small degree due to the advent of the rose show which was, during the latter half of the nineteenth century, at the height of its popularity. Roses were exhibited in boxes in which six or more blooms would be placed at equal distances in order to show each of them individually. So keen was the competition that it resulted in a tendency to breed for exhibition only, and the flower as a bud became the exhibitor's ideal. Unfortunately this led to the notion of a rose perfect in bud formation only, while the open bloom, so much appreciated by Old Rose enthusiasts today, was given little regard. At the same time, and equally unfortunately, the breeders' attention was centred on the flower alone; habit of growth was ignored. Such roses were no doubt very fine when seen on the show bench, but as garden plants they left much to be desired.

There are, however, some beautiful Hybrid Perpetuals still surviving, particularly those of earlier date, and many of them well worth a place in the garden. It is these I have included in my list. One or two of them may be a little ungainly, but they are beautiful as cut flowers and do have at least three virtues: they are nearly all very fragrant, they are recurrent flowering, and many of them have the Old Rose flower formation. In this class we also find varieties of a rich pure crimson colouring, something not found in many other roses before this time.

Hybrid Perpetuals are gross feeders and will repay generous treatment. Some, if left to their own devices, become too tall, and it is best to prune them down by about half their height in order to maintain reasonable proportions and ensure quality and continuity of bloom.

ARRILLAGA. A very late arrival with interesting parentage (*Rosa centifolia* × 'Mrs. John Laing') × 'Frau Karl Druschki', and therefore by no means a pure Hybrid Perpetual, if indeed there is such a thing. It forms a tall shrub, often growing to over 6ft. in height. The flowers are in the Old Rose tradition, soft pink in colour, with a light fragrance. The first flowering is very prolific, but there is only an occasional bloom later in the summer. Bred by Schoener (U.S.A.), introduced 1929.

BARONESS ROTHSCHILD. Large shallowly cupped flowers, frequently of the most perfect formation, the petals later recurving. They are of a soft pink colour, deepening towards the centre. The growth is erect, to 4ft. in height, and thorny, with greyish-green foliage coming close up to the flower in the manner of a Portland Rose to which it is probably closely related. It is free flowering and repeats quite well. This variety produces some of the most beautiful flowers in this section — it is unfortunate that it has little fragrance. A sport of 'Souvenir de la Reine d'Angleterre'. Discovered by Pernet Père (France), 1868. See page 104.

BARON GIROD DE L'AIN. A 'Eugène Fürst' sport, discovered by Reverchon of France in 1897. Unlike many Hybrid Perpetuals it forms a broad shapely shrub which grows strongly without being too upright. It has fine large foliage. The flowers, like those of its parent, are a dark heavy crimson, but with the added and unusual attraction that the petals are neatly edged with a thin line of white. They are large and of shapely cupped formation, and their colour holds well, showing off the dual effect to perfection. It repeats quite well under good conditions and has a rich fragrance. Height 4ft. See page 91.

BARONNE PRÉVOST. Large flowers in the Old Rose tradition, opening flat and quartered with a small button eye. The colour is pale rose-pink. Its growth is strong and very upright, about 4ft. in height. Fragrant. Bred by M. Desprez (France), 1842. See page 108.

DUKE OF EDINBURGH. One of the best of the bright red Hybrid Perpetuals, forming a strong erect bush of about 3ft. in height. The flowers are full, of open incurved formation and fragrant, repeating quite well in the autumn. A hybrid of 'Général Jacqueminot'. Bred by George Paul (England), 1868.

EMPEREUR DU MAROC. This variety is chiefly notable for the richness of its dark velvety maroon-crimson colouring. The flowers are not very large, opening flat, quartered, and well filled with petals which later reflex. Strong fragrance. Unfortunately the growth is rather weak, often resulting in poor flowers, and it requires a high standard of cultivation to produce worthwhile results. Its foliage is similar to that of a Hybrid Tea and is rather sparse. Only slightly recurrent. Height 3ft. A seedling from 'Géant des Batailles'. Bred by Bertrand-Guinoisseau (France), 1858.

EUGÈNE FÜRST. Large globular flowers of rich velvety crimson-purple, paler on the reverse side of the petals. These are borne on a broad well-formed shrub of about 4ft. in height with large foliage. There is a good fragrance. Its breeding is 'Baron de Bonstetten' × an unnamed variety. Bred by Soupert & Notting (Luxemburg), 1875.

FERDINAND PICHARD. A striped rose that can be compared to the striped Bourbon varieties such as 'Commandant Beaurepaire'. Its flowers are pink, striped and splashed with crimson, the pink gradually fading almost to white while the crimson intensifies. They are of medium size, cupped in shape, not very full and fragrant. This rose forms a bushy shrub by the standards of a Hybrid Perpetual and flowers intermittently in late summer after the first crop. One of the best striped roses, as good as its Bourbon rivals, and perhaps the best one for the smaller garden. Height 5ft. It was raised by R. Tanne of France as recently as 1921, and may well be a sport, but from which rose we do not know. See page 101.

FISHER HOLMES. Pointed buds of scarlet and crimson, in the manner of a Hybrid Tea, the colour soon fading. It flowers both in summer and autumn and forms a healthy bush of about 4ft. in height. Fragrant. Thought to be a seedling of 'Maurice Bernardin'. Bred by Verdier (France), 1865. See page 108.

FRAU KARL DRUSCHKI ('Snow Queen', 'Reine des Neiges', 'White American Beauty'). This rose belongs theoretically to the Hybrid Teas, being a cross between the Hybrid Perpetual 'Merveille de Lyon' and the Hybrid Tea 'Madame Caroline Testout', but the growth is so tall, up to 6ft. in height, that it would be misleading to place it anywhere else but here. The flowers, however, which are white with just a hint of lemon, are very close to those of a Hybrid Tea, and even today it is difficult to find a white Hybrid Tea flower that is better than this. It should be pruned as described in the introduction to this section, and will then form a tall, narrow, but slightly arching shrub, ideal for the back of the border. A group of two or three plants will knit together into a more shapely whole and give a more satisfactory effect. The foliage is light green. This is a tough old campaigner, although it may require spraying against mildew. Little or no fragrance. Raised by Lambert (Germany), 1901.

GÉNÉRAL JACQUEMINOT ('General Jack', 'Jack Rose'). An important variety in the development of the Modern Rose and perhaps of more interest for this than for any particular qualitites of its own. In fact, most of the red roses of the present day relate back to this variety. It has rich crimson full-petalled flowers, opening rather untidily. The fragrance is particularly strong, and it was perhaps because of this rose and other similar Hybrid Perpetuals that the idea grew up that a red rose should have a strong rich fragrance — something that is sadly no longer always true today. Height 4ft. A hybrid between 'Gloire des Rosomanes' and 'Géant des Batailles'. Bred by Roussel (France), 1853.

GEORG ARENDS ('Fortune Besson'). The breeding of this rose was 'Frau Karl Druschki' × 'La France' and it should, therefore, technically be placed with the Hybrid Teas. In practice it conforms to neither of these classes, forming as it does a fine shapely, slightly arching shrub of 5ft. in height with plentiful foliage. The flowers, on the other hand, are of distinctly Hybrid Tea persuasion, with large high-centred buds, the petals rolling back at the edges in the most attractive manner. Its colour is a clear rose-pink and it has a delicious fragrance. It is interesting to note that even a Hybrid Tea flower can be displayed to greater advantage on taller more shrubby growth. Raised by W. Hinner (Germany), 1910.

GLOIRE DE DUCHER. No other Hybrid Perpetual can match this variety for the splendour and richness of its flowers. They form very large informal cups of a deep purple-crimson shaded with maroon and are very fragrant. The blooms are particularly fine in the cool of the autumn. The growth is strong and rather sprawly, up to 7ft. in height, with large dark green leaves, and it might well be grown on a pillar or some other form of support. Its only drawback is a susceptibility to mildew. The breeding is not known. Bred by Ducher (France), introduced 1865. See page 91.

HENRY NEVARD. The most recent variety on my list, this rose was bred by Cant's of Colchester as late as 1924 and may have some Hybrid Tea in its make up. Its large deep crimson flowers are of cupped formation, with a powerful fragrance. They are held on long stems and repeat well. It has the tall upright habit of growth of a Hybrid Perpetual, perhaps 5ft. in height. The leaves are large, leathery and deep green.

HUGH DICKSON. Introduced in 1905, this was one of the most popular roses of its day, but in spite of this it does not have very much to recommend it — perhaps an indication of a decline in taste at the time — at least in so far as the rose was concerned. The flowers are large, scarlet-crimson, of a globular formation and produced on long shoots. They tend to lack character, being unshapely and rather coarse. The growth is very tall and ungainly, 7ft., and it is perhaps more effective as a Climber when it will easily achieve 10ft. In its heyday it was frequently grown by pegging the long growth to the soil, so that it became effectively a climbing rose trailing along the ground. In this way numerous flower shoots are sent up along the stems, thus rendering it more suitable for bedding and providing an attractive 'Edwardian' effect. It flowers freely and recurrently and has a strong fragrance. The result of a cross between 'Lord Bacon' and 'Gruss an Teplitz', it was bred by H. Dickson.

JOHN HOPPER. Large fragrant lilac-pink flowers, deepening towards the centre. Vigorous, upright growth of 4ft. 'Jules Margottin' × 'Madame Vidot'. Bred by Ward (U.K.), 1862.

MABEL MORRISON. A white sport of 'Baroness Rothschild', see above, with the same Portland Rose characteristics and fine, shapely, shallowly-cupped blooms. In autumn these will sometimes take on delicate blush tints. Very little scent. Discovered by Broughton (U.K.), introduced 1878.

MRS. JOHN LAING. Bred by Henry Bennett, this may be regarded as his finest production. The flowers are large, deeply cupped, fully double and of a silvery-pink colouring. The growth is vigorous and upright, up to 4ft.

FERDINAND PICHARD, *a striped Hybrid Perpetual Rose. The best of the repeat-flowering striped roses for the small garden.* *See page 99.* Calvert

VARIEGATA DE BOLOGNA, *a Bourbon Rose of fresh beauty, unfortunately summer flowering only.* *See page 96.* Knight

BOULE DE NEIGE, *Bourbon Rose. One of the most perfect white roses.* *See page 93.* Calvert

CATHERINE MERMET, *Tea Rose. Representative of one of the two main classes of the late Victorian period. See page 112.* Page

BARONESS ROTHSCHILD, *one of the most beautiful Hybrid Perpetuals, and representative of the other main class of late Victorian roses. See page 98.* Knight

OLD BLUSH CHINA. *See page 81.* Calvert

THE PORTLAND ROSE. *See page 84. Both this and 'Old Blush China' are very influential varieties in the development of the rose. Both are still first-class garden plants.* Page

REINE DES VIOLETTES, *Hybrid Perpetual Rose. The best of the repeat-flowering purple Old Roses.* *See page 109.*
Warren

MADAME LAURIOL DE BARNY. *Bourbon Rose. An elegant free-flowering shrub or Climber blooming mainly in the autumn.* *See page 95.* Knight

SOUVENIR DU DOCTEUR JAMAIN. *Hybrid Perpetual Rose. See page 110.* Calvert

BARONNE PRÉVOST. *Hybrid Perpetual Rose. See page 98.* Calvert

FISHER HOLMES. *Hybrid Perpetual Rose. See page 99.* Warren

MRS. JOHN LAING. *Hybrid Perpetual Rose. See page 100.* Page

in height, with greyish-green foliage. 'Mrs. John Laing' is a good reliable rose, truly recurrent flowering and strongly scented. Introduced in 1887, and one of the most popular roses of its time, it was said that Bennett received $45,000 for the distribution rights in America, an unheard of sum in those days. It was a seedling from 'François Michelon'. See opposite.

PAUL NEYRON. In the past this rose was regarded as having the largest flowers of all roses, and I suspect this may not be far from true today. It is in every way a large shrub, with large leaves and strong upright growth. Unfortunately with size comes clumsiness, as is so often the case, but if the flowers are cut and mixed with an arrangement of other flowers they can be very effective. Their colour is deep rose-pink flushed with lilac; they are cupped in shape and have a light fragrance. A cross between 'Victor Verdier' and 'Anna de Diesbach'. Bred and introduced by A. Levet (France), 1869. See page 91.

PRIDE OF WALTHAM. Large, open, thick-petalled blooms that might appear coarse were it not for its delicate pink colouring. It forms a strong plant that repeats well, but there is a possibility of mildew. Light fragrance. Height 4ft. A sport from 'Comtesse d'Oxford'. Discovered at the nursery of W. Paul & Son (U.K.), 1881.

PRINCE CAMILLE DE ROHAN ('La Rosière'). This variety has long held the reputation of being the darkest of all roses, and for this reason it continues to be in demand. I often fear that our customers may sometimes be disappointed, as it is of very weak growth, except when well grown under favourable conditions. It will form a bushy plant of 3ft., bearing medium-sized very double flowers of the richest velvety crimson-maroon. These are carried on weak stems but have a powerful fragrance. Raised by R. Verdier (France), 1861.

REINE DES VIOLETTES ('Queen of the Violets'). A unique and charming rose with flowers closer to the Gallica Rose than to a typical Hybrid Perpetual. These are of full-petalled rosette formation, opening flat and quartered, with a button eye at the centre. Their colour is a deep velvet purple, turning with time to soft parma-violet. The growth is upright, about 4 or 5ft. in height, with grey-green foliage and hardly any thorns. It is reliably repeat flowering which, combined with the Old Rose form of flower, makes it particularly valuable. This rose requires good cultivation if it is to give of its best. A seedling from 'Pius IX'. Bred by Millet-Malet (France), introduced 1860. See page 106.

ROGER LAMBELIN. A sport from 'Prince Camille de Rohan', see above, with all the failings of that rose, having very weak growth and poor flowers in all but the best of conditions. In appearance, too, it is similar to 'Prince Camille de Rohan', except for the fact that its deep crimson petals are prettily edged with white. Like its parent it can be beautiful if well grown, but for most gardens it might be better to grow 'Baron Girod de l'Ain' which is much stronger. Very fragrant. Height 3ft. Discovered by Schwartz (France), distributed 1890.

SOUVENIR DU DOCTEUR JAMAIN. Not a typical Hybrid Perpetual, this rose is notable for its deep rich dark crimson colouring and its equally deep and rich perfume. The flowers are of medium size, shallow, showing just a hint of their yellow stamens. It is repeat flowering but, like so many crimson roses, does not make ideal growth, being rather lean and lanky, and about 5 or 6ft. in height. However, since there are few shrub roses with flowers of such colouring it is worth its place in the garden. It has for some years also been on sale under the name of 'Souvenir d'Alphonse Lavallée', though it is impossible to see any difference between the two roses. Introduced by Lacharme (France), 1865. See page 108.

TRIOMPHE DE L'EXPOSITION. Full-petalled cherry-red flowers, opening almost flat and quartered, with a button eye. The growth is strong and bushy with recurrent blooms. Height 5ft. Bred and introduced by Margottin (France), 1855.

ULRICH BRUNNER. A tall, robust and durable shrub of narrow, ungainly and upright habit, about 6ft. in height. The flowers are cupped in form and of a rather crude pale crimson colour. Fine blooms are sometimes produced and it is a useful rose for cutting. Strong fragrance, recurrent flowering. It creates a spectacular display at Sissinghurst Castle, where its long shoots are pegged down. Bred by Levet (France), 1881.

VICK'S CAPRICE. Very large full-cupped flowers, their colouring of deep pink lightly striped with paler pink and white providing a delicate effect. It is very fragrant, recurrent flowering, with ample foliage that comes all the way up to the flower. Height 4ft. A sport from the pure pink 'Archiduchesse Élisabeth d'Autriche' (to which it frequently reverts) found in the garden of a Mr. Vick of Rochester, New York, introduced 1891.

TEA ROSES

The Tea Roses were the result of crossing two of the original China Roses, 'Hume's Blush China' and 'Parks' Yellow Tea Scented China', with various Bourbon and Noisette Roses. The first Tea Rose was introduced in 1835 and most appropriately named 'Adam', having been bred by an English nurseryman of that name. The class was originally known as Tea Scented China Roses, but this was soon abbreviated to Tea Roses. How they came to be known by this name is a mystery; there is, in fact, a range of fragrances to be found amongst them, but none of them, to my nose at least, have much in common with that of tea, although Graham Thomas insists that the scent of a typical Tea Rose is exactly like that of a freshly opened packet of China tea. However this may be, we still refer to certain roses as having a Tea Rose scent, and the name has now acquired a meaning of its own.

The Tea Rose was destined to become one of the parents of the Hybrid Tea, and could perhaps be best described as a rather slender version of that class while at the same time exhibiting a fairly close affinity to the twiggy, branching growth of the China Rose. Like the Chinas they are diploids. The popular, rather romanticised impression of a Tea Rose is of a long, slender and refined bud of the most delicate colouring, but this is only partly true; in fact they come in various forms and sometimes in quite harsh colours.

These roses cannot be recommended for general garden use, indeed I am not entirely sure that they should even be included in this book were it not for the fact that they complete the historical picture. I have grown a number of them in my garden but have never found them satisfactory in our climate. If they survive the winter they are frequently cut back by frost, and although some of them are hardier than others, they often have the appearance of rather run down Hybrid Teas. When grown in the warmer parts of the British Isles, such as Cornwall or Devon, it might be quite a different matter, and I have seen them growing as fine large shrubs in Mediterranean countries. If space can be found for them in a cold greenhouse you may expect some very beautiful roses and the connoisseur may feel this worth while; after all, is it not true that many alpine plant enthusiasts go to equal lengths to grow their own particular treasures? Another less extreme method is to plant them against a warm and sheltered wall and treat them as short Climbers.

However, it would be very worth while planting them in countries with warm and frost-free climates — most of the survivors in this class have, in fact, come from such countries. The Climbing Teas are usually much hardier and can be recommended for the average garden. Whether this is due to different breeding or to the fact that they are usually grown on walls, I cannot say — perhaps it is a bit of both. These are described in Chapter 9.

Tea Roses prefer a well-drained, fertile soil and, as the reader will have gathered, should be planted in a warm and sheltered position. Like their parents the China Roses, they object to too much pruning. This should consist only of the thinning out of old growth, the removal of dead wood, and general maintenance of the shape of the bush. Height will vary enormously according to climate. They seldom achieve more than 3ft. in the United Kingdom, but I have no doubt that in more southerly countries they could form much larger bushes.

Included here is a short list of Tea Roses that are still obtainable. As I have not grown many of them under garden conditions I have not had sufficient experience of some of the varieties to say which are the best. I have included mainly those with flowers in softer shades as I think these are more appealing.

ANNA OLIVER. Flesh-pink pointed blooms with the reverse side of the petals deep pink. Quite vigorous and bushy for a Tea Rose. Fragrant. Bred by Ducher (France), 1872.

ARCHIDUC JOSEPH. One of the most hardy of the Tea Roses, forming a strong bush or Climber, with plentiful dark green foliage. The flowers are of a purplish-pink, opening flat with many petals, gradually turning to blush at the centre. A seedling from 'Madame Lombard'. Bred by Nabonnand (France), 1872.

CATHERINE MERMET. This beautiful Tea Rose was once widely grown for the cut-flower trade. When well grown it has exquisitely formed buds which are blush-pink at the centre and tinted with lilac-pink at the edges. Only suitable for the greenhouse in the U.K. Bred by Guillot Fils (France), 1869. See page 104.

DR. GRILL. Pointed rose-pink buds shaded with copper, opening flat and full petalled. Branching growth. Fragrant. 'Ophirie' × 'Souvenir de Victor Hugo'. Bonnaire (France), 1886.

DUCHESSE DE BRABANT. Large full-petalled cupped blooms varying from soft rosy-pink to bright rose-pink. This variety is hardier than many of the others and has strong branching growth with good foliage. Very fragrant. Bernède (France), 1857.

HOMÈRE. Nicely cupped soft pink flowers with red tints at the edges, paling almost to white at the centre. An early variety that is hardier than most. It has bushy, twiggy growth with dark green foliage. Bred by Robert et Moreau (France), 1858.

LADY HILLINGDON. The only bush Tea Rose that can be said to be in anything like general circulation, and virtually as hardy as a Hybrid Tea. The recorded parentage is 'Papa Gontier' × 'Madame Hoste', both of which are Tea Roses, but this is doubtful due to the fact that the chromosome count indicates a cross with a Hybrid Tea. This illustrates very well that we should not place too much credence on early breeding records. 'Lady Hillingdon' has large petals, forming long slender buds of a lovely deep apricot-yellow which eventually open to rather shapeless flowers with a strong Tea Rose fragrance. It has fine contrasting dark green foliage which is coppery-mahogany when young. There is a particularly good climbing sport, better by far than the bush, and it is wiser to grow it in this form wherever space is available; see Chapter 9. Bred by Lowe & Shawyer (U.K.), 1910.

LADY PLYMOUTH. Large well-formed pointed buds of ivory-cream faintly flushed with pink. Bushy growth, with rather sparse dark green foliage. Slightly scented. A. Dickson (U.K.), 1914.

MADAME BRAVY ('Adele Pradel', 'Madame de Sertat'). Large creamy-white flowers shaded buff, with a strong Tea Rose fragrance. Guillot Père (France), 1846.

MADAME DE TARTAS. Large, full blush-pink flowers of cupped formation. Fairly vigorous with spreading growth and good frost resistance. A very important rose in the development of the Hybrid Teas, but there is some doubt as to whether the rose now in circulation is the correct one. Fragrant. Bernède (France), 1859.

MAMAN COCHET. Large globular blooms of pale pink, deepening towards the centre with lemon-yellow shades at the base. The growth is quite vigorous with dark green foliage. Once a famous exhibition rose. 'Marie van Houtte' × 'Madame Lombard'. Bred by Cochet (France), 1893.

MARIE VAN HOUTTE. Large pointed buds of cream tinged carmine-pink, with buff at the base of the petals. Fragrant. Sprawling habit. 'Madame de Tartas' × 'Madame Falcot'. Ducher (France), 1871.

PAPA GONTIER. Long, pointed, deep pink buds, with the reverse side of the petals carmine-red, opening semi-double. Bushy growth. Nabonnand (France), 1883.

PERLE DES JARDINS. Pointed buds developing into fragrant full-petalled flowers of a straw-yellow colour. These fail to open well in damp weather. The growth is slender but reasonably hardy. Fragrant. 'Madame Falcot' × a seedling. Levet (France), 1874.

ROSETTE DELIZY. Pointed buds of apricot and yellow, the reverse of the petals being tinted with carmine. 'Général Gallieni' × 'Comtesse Bardi'. Nabonnand (France), 1922.

SAFRANO. Pretty pointed buds of saffron-yellow and apricot, opening to semi-double flowers paling with age. Bred by Beauregard (France), 1839.

THE BRIDE. A white sport of 'Catherine Mermet', see above, and similar in every way except colour. Only for the greenhouse. Discovered by May (U.S.A.), 1885.

TRIOMPHE DU LUXEMBOURG. Full-petalled flowers borne in clusters. Salmon-pink becoming salmon-buff. Hardy (France), 1839.

WILLIAM R. SMITH ('Charles Dingee', 'Blush Maman Cochet', 'President William Smith', 'Jeanette Heller'). Shapely pointed buds; pale-pink at the centre, with the outer petals creamy-blush tinted with yellow at the base. Bred by Bagg (U.S.A.), introduced 1908.

Chapter 4

HYBRID TEA ROSES AND FLORIBUNDA ROSES

HYBRID TEA ROSES

The Hybrid Teas are far too well known to require any introduction here. They are to be seen in almost every garden in the land and are grown, to a greater or lesser extent, in almost every country in the world.

Although we refer to them as Modern Roses to differentiate them from the Old Roses, the Hybrid Teas have now been with us for a long time, and as early as the middle of the last century the stage was set for their arrival on the scene. There were, as we have already seen, two main classes of roses in the latter half of the nineteenth century — Hybrid Perpetuals and Tea Roses. It was the cross fertilization of these two breeds that gave us what we now call Hybrid Teas. This was in many ways a happy combination of talents. The Hybrid Perpetuals provided the hardiness, vigour, size of flower, fragrance and stronger shades of colour; while the Tea Roses brought recurrent flowering qualities together with those characteristics that they had themselves drawn from *Rosa gigantea* — the large, thick, sheeny petals which provide us with the long pointed buds that are so popular today. The Tea Roses also brought something of their own fragrance.

For a long time it was supposed that 'La France' was the first Hybrid Tea and that with its arrival a new class was born, but this was not, in fact, true. The first reliably documented rose that could be classified as a Hybrid Tea was 'Victor Verdier'. Bred by Lacharme of Lyons and introduced in 1859, it was a cross between the Hybrid Perpetual 'Jules Margottin' and the Tea Rose 'Safrano'. It is by no means impossible that there were other unrecorded crosses before this, but it was only when Guillot crossed a Hybrid Perpetual named 'Madame Victor Verdier' (not to be confused with 'Victor Verdier') with the Tea Rose 'Madame Bravy', to produce 'La France' in 1867, that people began to realise a new class of roses had arrived. Even then it was a long time before the Hybrid Teas were officially recognised in countries other than France, where they were classified under the heading *R. odorata indica*.

In Britain it was Henry Bennett who first bred Hybrid Teas. He was a farmer and cattle breeder of Stapleford, Wiltshire, and later of Shepperton, Middlesex, who turned his attention to the rose, and I must admit to a certain fellow feeling for this man, as I myself started life as a farmer. Bennett quickly saw the possibilities of the Hybrid Teas and in a very short time bred a number of important varieties — no doubt he used his experience with livestock to good effect. He was the first to use the term Hybrid Tea or, as he put it, Pedigree Hybrids of the Tea Rose. It was Bennett and a French breeder called Jean Sisley who first applied systematic cross breeding to roses. Before this, rose breeding had been a much more haphazard affair, but Bennett and Sisley made deliberate crosses with certain objectives in view and may thus be said to be the first modern rose breeders. Unfortunately Bennett's career in this field only lasted from 1879 until his death in 1890. Even so, he is usually regarded as the father of the Hybrid Tea Rose.

The Hybrid Tea was quite different from all the roses that had preceded it. In the first place it is a bush rose, whereas previous roses had usually been true shrubs. It was designed for planting in rose beds, being about 3 to 3½ft. in height and of upright growth. With such growth, together with hard pruning, there came a remarkable ability to flower repeatedly throughout the summer — something that is hard to equal in roses of taller, more shrubby growth. No comparable garden flower can come close to it in this respect, and it is to this, more than anything else, that it owes its great popularity.

The second important difference is the formation of its flower. Interest in the Hybrid Perpetuals, which were bred primarily for the show bench, had for some time tended towards the bud-shaped flower and some, but not all, Tea Roses had flowers with pointed buds. In the Hybrid Teas the process was complete, and we have the bud-shaped flower only. The whole nature of the flower had been completely changed — a happening that must be almost unique in horticulture. Its arrival heralded what was, to all intents and purposes, a new flower. So popular was this flower, that all other types were pushed almost into oblivion.

We have had Hybrid Tea Roses now for over 120 years, although they did not fully come into their own until the turn of the century. Many thousands of varieties have been introduced in that time — far more than any other type of rose. Most of them have gone the way of all flesh and disappeared from the scene, for obviously they could not all survive and most are not worth preserving. The question is, what should we do with those earlier varieties that are still with us? Would it not be better to let them go? For the average garden, I would say 'yes'. But for those with a rather deeper interest in roses there is much to be said for retaining at least the best from the past. Certainly my experience as a commercial rose grower suggests the demand is there.

In the first place, they are always of interest to the collector and those who like the antique with all its associations. More importantly, there are a number of old Hybrid Teas that earn a place in the garden on pure merit — for the beauty of their flowers and their value as garden plants. The majority of the earlier Hybrid Teas, however, do not come up to the standard of present day varieties for sheer performance. What they do have is a character of flower that is different from later introductions. Some of the first Hybrid Teas had flowers that were closer to the Old Rose formation, but it was not long before these were superseded by roses with the bud formation of the present day. Even then they were different to present day Hybrid Teas, being less heavy in all their parts and usually with lighter, more pastel shades of colour. They were, in short, often close to the Tea Rose. As the rose proceeds on its way through history it is always evolving: new species and strains are brought into its breeding, and every time this happens the rose changes. The roses of the last twenty years are different from those of the 1920s and 1930s. It is for this reason that we should retain and grow them.

On the other side of the scales, it is important to remember that these earlier varieties do not always have the vigour of their descendants. Whether they have lost it, or never had it, is a moot point. Certainly deterioration does take place. Why this should be is a matter of some speculation — it would be easy to write a chapter on this subject alone. It may be the result of a virus entering the stock, or it may be due to some form of genetic breakdown. What is rather odd is that the truly Old Roses, like the Gallicas or Albas, which may be hundreds of years old, do not seem to suffer in this way.

The selection of Hybrid Tea Roses described here represents only a small fraction of those that still survive. I cannot be sure that they are necessarily the best. They are simply those that appeal to me. I have tried to include such varieties that seem to have something to offer which is not to be found in Modern Hybrid Teas. I have also included a few single-flowered varieties, of which there were a number in the early days. They have their own particular charm and are sufficiently different from other singles to be worthy of inclusion.

Three further important developments in these roses should also be mentioned. The first was due to the work of the French breeder, Joseph Pernet-Ducher. He spent many years in the latter part of the nineteenth century in an effort to bring the uniquely brilliant yellow of *R. foetida* into the flowers of the Hybrid Tea Roses. His first successful variety was 'Soleil d'Or', a seedling from a rose that was itself the result of a cross between the Hybrid Perpetual 'Antoine Ducher' and *R. foetida* 'Persiana'. 'Soleil d'Or' was one of those roses that was due to make a shift in the general character of the rose. Through it came not only the first of the truly intense yellows, but a whole range of associated shades. The successors to 'Soleil d'Or' were first known as Pernetiana Roses, but gradually they were absorbed into the family of Hybrid Teas. Some of the colours produced have not been very desirable, but this development has increased the colour range of all types of roses that came after 'Soleil d'Or' and will no doubt continue to do so indefinitely.

A second development was the appearance of the colour vermilion in Hybrid Teas. This was a unique happening among roses. It was due to the occurrence in the plant of a chemical called pelargonidin, instead of the normal cyanidin. These are two of the chemicals that control the

A SUPERB *formal layout of Hybrid Tea and Floribunda Roses at the Royal National Rose Society's Gardens at St. Albans, U.K.* Thomas

OPHELIA. *Hybrid Tea Rose. See page 129.* Warren
PICTURE. *Hybrid Tea Rose. See page 130.* Warren
THE DOCTOR. *Hybrid Tea Rose. See page 130.* Warren
LA FRANCE. *Hybrid Tea Rose. See page 128.* Warren

These four older Hybrid Tea Roses still have garden value.

WHITE WINGS. *Hybrid Tea Rose. See page 130.* Warren

DAINTY BESS. *Hybrid Tea Rose. See page 126.* Calvert

MRS. OAKLEY FISHER. *Hybrid Tea Rose. See page 129.* Knight

ESCAPADE. *a good Floribunda. See page 154.* Harkness

'White Wings', 'Mrs. Oakley Fisher' and 'Dainty Bess' are three good single-flowered Hybrid Tea Roses produced in the early days.

MICHÈLE MEILLAND, *a Hybrid Tea Rose which, along with the others here, is of soft colouring. See page 136.* Smith

PASCALI, *Hybrid Tea Rose. See page 137.* Smith

JULIA'S ROSE. *A Hybrid Tea Rose of unusual parchment-like colouring. See page 135.* Cants

ELIZABETH HARKNESS, *Hybrid Tea Rose. See page 133.* Harkness

PRISTINE, *Hybrid Tea Rose. See page 139.* Smith
JUST JOEY, *a Hybrid Tea Rose which, like the other roses on this page, has long elegant buds. See page 135.* Cants

PAUL SHIRVILLE, *Hybrid Tea Rose. See page 137.* Harkness
SUTTER'S GOLD, *Hybrid Tea Rose. See page 149.* Smith

PRIMA BALLERINA, *Hybrid Tea Rose. See page 139.* Smith

BLUE MOON. *The most reliable of the lilac Hybrid Tea Roses. See page 132.* Smith

PINK FAVORITE. *Hybrid Tea Rose. See page 138.* Smith

SILVER JUBILEE, *one of the strongest and best of recent Hybrid Tea Rose introductions. See page 140.* Cocker

DUTCH GOLD. *Hybrid Tea Rose. A reliable variety. See page 133.* Wisbech
CHAMPION. *Hybrid Tea Rose. See page 132.* Fryer

TROIKA. *Hybrid Tea Rose. See page 149.* Mattock
GRANDPA DICKSON. *Hybrid Tea Rose. Both this and 'Champion' have giant flowers. See page 134.* Dickson

PEAUDOUCE. *The pale primrose yellow colouring illustrates a new tendency towards softer colours among recent Hybrid Tea Roses.* *See page 138.* Dickson

colour of the flowers.

The first Hybrid Tea to carry pelargonidin in its make up was the popular 'Super Star'. It had occurred earlier among Floribundas in a little known rose called 'Independence' in the year 1951. Before this it had appeared in two Polyantha Pompon Roses, 'Golden Salmon' and 'Gloria Mundi', both of which were sports from 'Superb'. It is extremely rare to find a chemical change of this kind and we know of no similar case in roses. The new colour, like the yellow of *R. foetida,* has had a profound effect on the character of modern roses. It has resulted in many new shades and mixtures of colour. Pure vermilion is a beautiful colour, but perhaps a little foreign to the rose, and roses of this shade should be planted with restraint. Used with care it can have value in the garden scheme.

With the arrival of the Floribundas, which we shall be discussing in the latter half of this chapter, another important shift was to take place. The Floribundas have many sterling qualities. They are, on the whole, tough, hardy and very free flowering. For this reason, breeders have mixed their genes with those of the Hybrid Teas, and this has led to an improvement in their hardiness and ability to flower freely. Unfortunately, with these improvements there has frequently been some loss of beauty in the flowers, for the Floribundas lack the character we find in the Hybrid Teas.

The present day Hybrid Teas, then, are much stronger in growth and are altogether better and more reliable performers than those of earlier days. They have better disease resistance and flower more continuously and freely than earlier varieties. Moreover their colour range has been continually extended. Unfortunately, these new colours have too often tended towards the gaudy, while the tone of colour is frequently too harsh. Such colours tend to swamp the more gentle shades and even clash with each other. Although a certain amount of nonsense is sometimes talked about the arrangement of colour in the garden, when it comes to the Modern Roses it is necessary to be very careful indeed and avoid the temptation to use the more brilliant shades too freely. A greater choice of colour makes more demands on our skill, but fortunately good colours are to be found and, if we select with care, pleasing effects can be achieved. Indeed I have recently detected a tendency towards better colours and more refined flowers. The more brilliant shades should, in my opinion, be used sparingly to highlight the others, rather than fill the garden with a continual blaze of colour which, in the end, can only become tiresome.

To achieve their full potential the Hybrid Teas require generous treatment. A mulch of farmyard manure or compost will work wonders and should be combined with the application of a balanced fertilizer in spring, and again after the first flush of flowers; if this too is organic-based, so much the better. Spraying against mildew and blackspot is desirable. Good proprietary brands of spray are available at all garden centres.

Pruning is, of course, quite different from that of Shrub Roses. In the first year, when the rose has just been planted, it is best to prune back severely to 4 to 6ins. from the soil. This will help to form the basis of a good bush. In subsequent years, prune away all weak, ageing and dead wood, and then cut back the remaining growth to perhaps 10 to 12ins. Stronger growers can be left longer. On the whole, hard pruning produces fewer but finer flowers; lighter pruning a greater quantity of flowers.

SOME OLDER HYBRID TEA ROSES

ANGÈLE PERNET. Large loosely-formed flowers of pale orange-red shaded with chrome-yellow. Shiny, bronzy-green foliage. Fragrant. Height 2ft. 'Bénédicte Seguin' × a Hybrid Tea. Bred by Pernet-Ducher (France), 1924.

ANTOINE RIVOIRE. Cupped flowers of rosy-blush colouring shaded cream, with yellow at the base of the bloom. Fragrant. A hybrid between the Tea Rose 'Dr. Grill' and the famous early Hybrid Tea 'Lady Mary Fitzwilliam'. Pernet-Ducher (France), 1895.

AUGUSTINE GUINOISSEAU ('White La France'). This is thought to be a sport from 'La France' to which it is very similar, the difference being that the flowers are white, tinted with flesh-pink. Like its parent it has globular Old Rose flower formation. Introduced by Guinoisseau (France), 1889.

BARBARA RICHARDS. Buff-yellow, the reverse of the petals being flushed with pink. Free flowering and sweetly scented. Inclined to hang its head. A. Dickson (U.K.), 1930.

BETTY UPRICHARD. Long, elegant buds opening to semi-double flowers of salmon-pink with carmine reverse. Vigorous and free-flowering, with light green foliage. Very fragrant. A. Dickson (U.K.), 1922.

COMTESSE VANDAL. A perfect bloom, with high pointed buds and delicate colouring. Salmon-pink at first, veined with gold, becoming buff-pink with yellow-flame on the outside. Slight scent. Some mildew. ('Ophelia' × 'Mrs. Aaron Ward') x 'Souvenir de Claudius Pernet'. M. Leenders (Holland), 1932.

CRIMSON GLORY. The leading crimson rose of the period immediately preceding the Second World War. The colour is deep and velvety, later becoming a pleasing purple, particularly in hot weather. It opens to a rather cupped flower with a rich fragrance. It is not very vigorous and has a spreading habit of growth. Particularly fine in its climbing form which has ample vigour. A 'Cathrine Kordes' seedling × 'W.E. Chaplin'. W. Kordes (Germany), 1935.

DAINTY BESS. A single rose and one of the finest of its class. It has large rose-pink flowers with a deeper pink on the outside and contrasting red-brown stamens. The petals are slightly fringed or cut at the edges. Light refreshing fragrance. 'Ophelia' × 'K. of K'. W.E.B. Archer (U.K.), 1925. See page 119.

DAME EDITH HELEN. Large, shapely, slightly globular, very double flowers of pure glowing pink, with a rich fragrance. Bred by A. Dickson (U.K.), 1926.

DIAMOND JUBILEE. This rose, although introduced in 1947, has much in common with the earlier Hybrid Teas, for it was the result of a cross between the famous old Tea-Noisette rose 'Maréchal Niel' and 'Feu Pernet-Ducher'. The flowers are very fine, of a lovely corn-yellow colouring, with petals of great substance and perfect formation. It has the Tea Rose fragrance of its Tea-Noisette parent. The growth is strong and hardy, but unfortunately the flowers rot in damp weather. Bred by Boerner (U.S.A.), 1947.

ELLEN WILLMOTT. A single flowered rose rather similar to 'Dainty Bess' from which it was a seedling, the result of a cross with 'Lady Hillingdon'. It has creamy flowers which are tinged with pink at the edges, with golden anthers and red filaments. The petals are attractively waved. Dark purple-tinted foliage. It does not perform quite so well as 'Dainty Bess'. Bred by Archer (U.K.), 1936.

EMMA WRIGHT. A charming little button-hole rose. It has small, perfectly formed nearly single orange-salmon buds on a dwarf plant. Glossy green foliage. McGredy (U.K.), 1918.

GEORGE DICKSON. Very large though not very full flowers of deep scarlet-crimson. The stems are rather weak, so that it tends to hang its head. Growth, strong and tall. Fragrant. A. Dickson (U.K.), 1912.

GOLDEN OPHELIA. Not a sport from 'Ophelia', as the name would suggest, but a seedling from that rose. It has perfectly formed creamy-yellow buds which deepen to yellow at the centre. B.R. Cant (U.K.), 1918.

GUSTAV GRÜNERWALD. An early Hybrid Tea with large, cupped, deep pink flowers. The growth is vigorous and reliable, with glossy, deep green foliage. It is a cross between the Tea Rose 'Safrano' and 'Madame Caroline Testout'. Bred by Lambert (Germany), 1903.

HOME SWEET HOME. Perhaps the most remarkable thing about this rose is the fact that it was ever introduced in the first place. The flowers are not large, being globular in shape and opening to a cup like an Old Rose — something quite out of line with the accepted standards of its time. It is of a particularly clear and rich rose-pink, with no trace of any other colour. The petals are short, thick and velvety and there is a rich fragrance. A small but healthy bush. Bred by Wood & Ingram (U.K.), introduced 1941.

IRISH BRIGHTNESS. Single flowers of cerise-crimson with a pleasing fragrance. Date and breeding not known. Bred by A. Dickson (U.K.).

IRISH ELEGANCE. This is one of a number of single roses from A. Dickson of Northern Ireland, most of which bear the prefix 'Irish'. It has long, slim buds opening to quite substantial deep pink flowers shaded with gold. Bronze-green foliage. Slightly fragrant. Introduced 1905.

IRISH FIREFLAME. Single orange and gold flowers veined with crimson, and with attractive light fawn-coloured anthers. Fragrant. A. Dickson (U.K.), 1914.

ISOBEL. Slightly cupped single flowers of delicate rose-pink flushed with yellow at the centre. Vigorous growth. Slight fragrance. McGredy (U.K.), 1916.

JOSEPHINE BRUCE. Although this rose has its weaknesses it is still planted quite widely. The reason is to be found in the purity of its deep rich crimson colouring — a purity which has been largely lost in the crimson roses of today. It has fair vigour, the growth being broad rather than upright with the branches coming out at an angle. This makes it an ideal rose for a standard. Rich fragrance. Somewhat susceptible to mildew. 'Crimson Glory' × 'Madge Whipp'. Bred by Bees (U.K.), 1949.

K. OF K. Named after Kitchener of Khartoum. Bright crimson-scarlet flowers opening semi-double with about ten petals. A strong bush that blooms with exceptional continuity, providing a brilliant effect. A. Dickson (U.K.), 1917.

LADY ALICE STANLEY. Large open flowers with many petals of silvery-pink, deeper pink reverse. Free, branching growth and leathery green foliage. Fragrant. McGredy (U.K.), 1909.

LADY BARNBY. Shapely, highly-scented buds of clear glowing pink shaded with red. Bushy growth. Fragrant. Bred by A. Dickson (U.K.), 1930.

LADY BELPER. Large, rather globular flowers opening to a cup shape. Bronze-orange shaded with light orange. Fragrant. Dark, glossy foliage. 'Mevrouw G.A. van Rossem' × a seedling. Bred by Verschuren (Holland), 1948.

LADY FORTEVIOT. Large high-centred buds varying from golden-yellow to deep apricot. Glossy bronzy-green foliage. Fragrant. B.R. Cant (U.K.), 1928.

LADY SYLVIA. A sport from 'Madame Butterfly'. Discovered by Stevens (U.K.), 1926. See 'Ophelia' below.

LA FRANCE. This famous rose is one of the earliest Hybrid Teas. Its origins are not known for certain but Guillot, who bred it in 1867, was of the opinion that it was probably a hybrid of the Tea Rose 'Madame Falcot'. It is still a worthwhile rose, although it is said to have lost some of its vigour. The blooms are full petalled and of globular Old Rose formation, remaining so until the petals fall. The colour is a silvery-pink with a rose-pink reverse. The flowers are richly fragrant. A climbing sport is also available. See page 118.

MADAME ABEL CHATENAY. Another historic Hybrid Tea and, to me, still one of the most beautiful, retaining much of the charm of a Tea Rose at its best. Raised by Pernet-Ducher and introduced in 1895, it is the result of a cross between the Tea Rose 'Dr. Grill' and the Hybrid Tea 'Victor Verdier'. The flowers are of a charming scrolled bud formation, pale pink in colour, deepening towards the centre, the reverse side of the petals being a deeper pink. An exquisite rose that seems to retain its vigour. Delicious fragrance. There is a climbing sport but, rather unusually amongst early Hybrid Teas, this is not particularly vigorous.

MADAME BUTTERFLY. Discovered by Hill (U.S.A.), 1918. See 'Ophelia' below.

MRS. OAKLEY FISHER. One of the most beautiful of the single-flowered Hybrid Tea Roses, with neatly outlined deep orange-yellow flowers. These are delicately poised in small clusters on a branching bush of reasonable vigour. The foliage is bronzy-green and there is a light, pleasing fragrance. B.R. Cant (U.K.), 1921. See page 119.

MRS. SAM MCGREDY. A popular rose of the 1930s and 1940s. Its modern but pleasing colouring is coppery-orange flushed with scarlet that tones in nicely with its glossy, coppery-red foliage. The flowers are not large and have shapely, high centred, clean-cut buds that last well. The growth is branching and of moderate vigour. This rose is perhaps better grown in its more vigorous climbing form. Fragrant. ('Donald Macdonald' × 'Golden Emblem') × (seedling × 'The Queen Alexandra Rose'). McGredy (U.K.), 1929.

OPHELIA, (including 'Madame Butterfly', 'Lady Sylvia' and 'Westfield Star'). It is convenient to discuss these four varieties together, as the last three are all colour sports of the first. More than others, these roses set the ideal for perfect Hybrid Tea buds. These are not large but are of exquisitely scrolled formation; indeed, for perfection of Hybrid Tea form, they have few rivals even today. They differ only in the colour of the flowers: 'Ophelia' is blush pink, 'Madame Butterfly' is a slightly deeper shade and 'Lady Sylvia' is blush suffused with apricot. In all three the colour deepens a little towards the centre to give the most delicate effect. 'Westfield Star' is creamy-white. Although they do not form large bushes — they are rather slender and grow to about 2½ft. in height — all are reliable growers. The foliage is neat and of a greyish-green colour. All four have a delicious fragrance and are first-class as cut flowers. With the exception of 'Westfield Star' each has excellent climbing sports and, as is so often the case with old Hybrid Teas, this may be the best way to grow them. See Chapter 9.

The origin of 'Ophelia' is a mystery. It was introduced by Arthur Paul of Waltham Cross in 1912. Paul was unable to say where it came from, though thought it arrived with a consignment of 'Antoine Rivoire' he had bought from Pernet-Ducher in 1909. It was probably a seedling that had been included by mistake. The French firm should, therefore, share the credit, even though it must have failed to realise the true worth of the variety. It attracted little attention at the time but, eventually, both it and its sports became some of the most popular roses ever introduced and they are still in demand. It is interesting to note that 'Ophelia' was responsible for no less than thirty-six sports in all; this must be some kind of record. See page 118.

PICTURE. A dainty and much loved button-hole rose, with small perfectly formed buds of a clear velvety rose-pink with reflexing petals. These are produced on a short, free flowering bush. Height 2½ft. Slight fragrance. McGredy (U.K.), 1932. See page 118.

POLLY. Long, elegantly formed buds of cream with gold at the base, paling with age. Fragrant. 'Ophelia' × 'Madame Colette Martinet'. Beckwith (U.K.), 1927.

SHOT SILK. Once much prized for its colour effect: cerise-pink shot with orange, shading to lemon deep in the centre. Glossy green foliage. Fragrant. A. Dickson (U.K.), 1924.

SOLEIL D'OR. This is one of the most important varieties in the history of garden roses, and I have already given a few details on its origins in the introduction to this class. The rose itself has considerable beauty, being in the Old Rose style, cupped, opening rather flat and of an attractive orange-yellow shade with a hint of red. The growth is upright and has some of the appearance of the 'Persian Yellow'. Unfortunately, it is so subject to blackspot that it is doubtful whether it should be grown. If it is, it will require continual spraying. Bred by Pernet-Ducher (France), introduced 1900.

SOUVENIR DE MADAME BOULLET. Long, pointed buds of deep yellow. Spreading habit of growth. 'Sunburst' × unnamed variety. Bred by Pernet-Ducher (France), introduced 1921.

SOUVENIR DU PRÉSIDENT CARNOT. Exquisite buds of delicate flesh-pink shading to shell-pink at the centre. Fragrant. Unnamed seedling × 'Lady Mary Fitzwilliam'. Pernet-Ducher (France), 1894.

THE DOCTOR. This rose has exceptionally long narrow petals resulting in long, pointed buds of unusual character and large satiny-pink blooms. Rather short growth for such a large flower. It has a particularly strong and unusual fragrance. 'Mrs. J.D. Eisele' × 'Los Angeles'. Bred by F.H. Howard (U.S.A.), 1936. See page 118.

VESUVIUS. A large single rose with long pointed buds opening to velvety-crimson flowers. McGredy (U.K.), 1923.

VIOLINISTA COSTA. A typically modern flower, opening carmine-red and becoming strawberry-pink shaded with orange. This is a reliable rose by any standards, with vigorous, branching growth and glossy green foliage. It retains its place among Modern Roses for its ability to produce an unfailing mass of bloom. 'Sensation' × 'Shot Silk'. Camprubi, 1936.

WESTFIELD STAR. A sport from 'Ophelia', with perfectly formed creamy-white flowers. Still one of the better white Hybrid Teas. Discovered by Morse (U.K.), 1922. See 'Ophelia' above.

WHITE WINGS. One of the most beautiful of the single Hybrid Teas. Long buds opening to large pure white flowers with conspicuous chocolate-coloured anthers. Dark green foliage. A healthy bush, but it may require a little time to establish itself. Height 4ft. A cross between 'Dainty Bess' and an unnamed seedling. Bred by Krebs (U.S.A.), introduced 1947. See page 119.

MODERN HYBRID TEA ROSES

ADOLF HORSTMANN. Very large full flowers of a yellow that tends a little towards bronze. The growth is tall, robust and healthy. Little scent. Height 3½ft. 'Königin der Rosen' × 'Dr. A.J. Verhage'. R. Kordes (Germany), 1971.

ALEC'S RED. One of the most reliable red roses. It is vigorous, free flowering and repeats well. The flowers are large and tend towards a globular shape. Their colour is cherry-red but with a rather purplish tinge, making them perhaps a little dull. It has a powerful fragrance for which it was awarded the Edland Medal of the Royal National Rose Society. The growth is upright, with healthy, medium green, slightly glossy foliage. Height 3ft. 'Fragrant Cloud' × 'Dame de Coeur'. Cocker (U.K.), 1970.

ALEXANDER ('Alexandra'). Similar to its parent 'Super Star', but of an even brighter shade of vermilion, and taller and stronger, being about 4ft. in height. It must have one of the most brilliant and luminous colours to be found in roses. Slight fragrance. 'Super Star' × ('Anne Elizabeth' × 'Allgold'). Harkness (U.K.), 1972.

ALPINE SUNSET. Exceptionally large, very full flowers of cream, flushed peach-pink on the inside of the petals. Glossy foliage. Very fragrant. Healthy, vigorous, upright growth. 'Grandpa Dickson' × 'Dr. A.J. Verhage'. Bred by Roberts (U.K.), introduced 1973.

APRICOT SILK. This is not the most robust of roses, being more subject to blackspot than some, but it is one of the most beautiful of its colour. It has elegant buds in an attractive shade of apricot and the petals have a silky texture. Glossy, bronze-tinted foliage. Height 4ft. A seedling from 'Souvenir de Jacques Verschuren' × unnamed variety. Bred by Gregory (U.K.), 1965.

BEAUTÉ. Particularly fine, long slender buds of apricot-yellow, opening to a rather loosely formed flower. The growth is bushy, not very strong, but free flowering. There is only a slight fragrance. Glossy, dark green foliage. Height 2½ft. 'Madame Joseph Perraud' × unnamed seedling. Bred by Mallerin (France), 1953.

BETTINA. Nicely shaped orange-coloured flowers, the petals being attractively veined with copper and shading to gold at the base. This is an attractive rose but of only moderate vigour. It may require protection from blackspot. Little scent. Glossy, bronze-tinted foliage. Height

2½ft. The breeding is 'Peace' × '(Madame Joseph Perraud' × 'Demain'). Bred by Meilland (France), 1953.

BLACK BEAUTY. Popular for its exceptionally deep garnet-red colouring which, unlike most dark roses, seems to survive well in the sun. It is free flowering and bushy, but only slightly fragrant. Height 3ft. ('Gloire de Rome' × 'Impeccable') × 'Papa Meilland'. Delbard (France), 1973.

BLESSINGS. A reliable, prolific and continuous flowering variety of soft pink colouring. The blooms are not large, rather loosely formed, with only a slight scent. It is an ideal bedding rose, with strong, upright, branching growth. Healthy, medium green foliage. Height 3ft. The result of a cross between 'Queen Elizabeth' and an unnamed seedling. Bred and introduced by Gregory (U.K.), 1967.

BLUE MOON. The Old Roses, particularly the Gallicas, have provided us with flowers in beautiful shades of purple, lilac and mauve. The Hybrid Tea has never been able to do this. 'Blue Moon' is, of course, not blue, its flowers being of a silvery-lilac or perhaps lilac-pink shade. This colour cannot be said to be pleasing for it is altogether too dead and metallic. Nonetheless, it is certainly the best Hybrid Tea of this colour group. It has medium sized flowers of shapely, high centred form with a strong lemony fragrance. Its growth and disease resistance are satisfactory. Foliage medium green and glossy. Height 3ft. It is said that one of its parents was 'Sterling Silver', but we do not know the other. Bred by Tantau (Germany), 1964. See page 122.

BLUE PARFUM. Another rose that, like 'Blue Moon', is far from being blue. Blush-mauve would be nearer to the correct shade. The flowers are large and very fragrant with ovoid shaped buds. The foliage is dark green and glossy. Height 3ft. Bred by Tantau (Germany), 1978.

BONSOIR. Large, full, shapely peach-pink flowers with deeper shading. The growth is quite vigorous and upright, with large, glossy, deep green leaves. Moderate fragrance. The blooms can be damaged by rain. Height 3ft. Bred by A. Dickson (U.K.), 1968.

BUCCANEER. This rose is now dropping out of catalogues, but we retain it for its long, narrow, slightly arching, almost shrub-like growth, which makes it suitable for positions farther back in the border. The flowers are medium sized, of a bright, clear and unfading yellow, pointed at first and opening to an urn shape. Height 4ft. Good, healthy, medium green, matt foliage. Fragrant. Breeding 'Golden Rapture' × ('Max Krause' × 'Captain Thomas'). Bred by Swim (U.S.A.), 1952.

CHAMPION. As the name suggests, this variety has exceptionally large flowers, their colour being cream and gold heavily flushed with pink. They are borne on a strong and healthy bush. It may be it could be used to a good effect by the flower arranger, where one or two really big blooms are required. Strong fragrance. Height 2½ft. 'Grandpa Dickson' × 'Whisky Mac'. Bred by Fryer (U.K.), introduced 1976. See page 123.

CHESHIRE LIFE. Large, well formed flowers of vermilion-orange. Strong, bushy growth of medium height, with ample, dark, leathery foliage. One of the best of its colour, but with little fragrance. A good bedding rose. Height 2½ft. 'Prima Ballerina' × 'Princess Michiko'. Fryer (U.K.), 1972. See page 142.

CHICAGO PEACE. A colour sport from 'Peace', see below, to which it is similar in every way except for the fact that the flowers are phlox-pink shading to canary-yellow at the base. Otherwise it has all the virtues of its parent. Large, glossy foliage. Healthy, vigorous growth. Slight fragrance. Height 3½ to 5ft. Discovered by Johnston (U.S.A.), 1962.

CHRYSLER IMPERIAL. Large, well formed flowers of velvety-scarlet with a paler reverse, but with little scent. The growth is tall, about 4ft. in height, with medium green foliage. Some mildew. 'Charlotte Armstrong' × 'Mirandy'. Bred by Dr. W.E. Lammerts (U.S.A.).

DIORAMA. Large, apricot-yellow flowers that become flushed with pink as they open. The growth is vigorous and branching, making it a good bedding rose. It flowers particularly well in the autumn. Height 3ft. Fragrant. 'Peace' × 'Beauté'. Bred by de Ruiter (Holland), 1965.

DORIS TYSTERMAN. Shapely, medium-sized flowers of coppery-orange, freely produced on a vigorous, bushy, upright plant with glossy bronze-tinted foliage. A good bedding rose. Little fragrance. Height 3ft. 'Peer Gynt' × unnamed seedling. Wisbech Plant Co. (U.K.), 1975. See page 141.

DUTCH GOLD. Large, unfading golden-yellow flowers with a strong fragrance. The growth is vigorous and upright, with good healthy medium green foliage. Height about 3ft. 'Peer Gynt' × 'Whisky Mac'. Wisbech Plant Co. (U.K.), 1978. See page 123.

ELIZABETH HARKNESS. For me one of the most beautiful of the more recent Hybrid Teas. It has large flowers of shapely spiral formation, and its colour is ivory-white delicately touched with pink and amber. It can be affected by damp weather but, at its best, it produces buds of pristine perfection. The growth is upright, bushy, of medium height and strength, with medium green foliage. Light fragrance. It is particularly fine when grown under glass. Height 2½ft. The breeding rather surprisingly is 'Red Dandy' × 'Piccadilly'. Raised by Harkness (U.K.), introduced 1969. See page 120.

ERNEST H. MORSE. A vigorous and healthy red Hybrid Tea that has been widely grown over the past twenty years. The colour is quite bright at first but soon becomes rather dull. A frequent problem with red roses is that the really rich deep crimsons seem to lack vigour, while the vigorous ones tend to lack intensity of colour. This is, however, a very reliable variety, and an excellent bedding rose that repeats well and has a strong fragrance. Large, dark green foliage. Height 3ft. Kordes (Germany), 1965.

EVENING STAR. Large flowers of pure white which seem to resist the damp better than most white roses. Good fragrance. The growth is vigorous and upright, with healthy, dark green foliage. 'White Masterpiece' × 'Saratoga'. Bred by Warriner (U.S.A.), 1974.

FANTAN. Not a typical Hybrid Tea, nor is it very widely grown but I include it for its cupped flowers and unusual burnt-orange colouring. It is of moderate vigour. Slight fragrance. Height 2½ft. ('Pigalle' × 'Prélude'), self fertilized. Meilland (France), 1959.

FRAGRANT CLOUD ('Duftwolke'). Large flowers, coral-scarlet at first, taking on smoky overtones as they develop, and becoming a purplish-red as they fade, particularly in hot weather. The growth is strong and bushy, about 3½ft. in height, with plenty of large leaves. Free flowering and continuous. It lives up to its name with its strong fragrance. Occasional mildew. Unnamed seedling × 'Prima Ballerina'. Tantau (Germany), 1963.

GAIL BORDEN. Large flowers tending towards a globular shape, the colour being rose-pink on the inside of the petals and pale gold on the reverse. Ample large, leathery foliage. This is a reliable rose — prolific in flower and vigorous in growth. Height 3ft. Slight fragrance. 'Mevrouw H.A. Verschuren' × 'Viktoria Adelheid'. Bred by Kordes (Germany), 1956.

GRACE DE MONACO. This rose is now rarely listed in catalogues, but we continue to grow it for its large, warm, rose-pink blooms. These are full and rather globular in shape, and have a very strong fragrance. The growth is tall and angular. 'Peace' × 'Michèle Meilland'. Meilland (France), 1956.

GRANDPA DICKSON ('Irish Gold'). Large and perfectly formed flowers of pale yellow colouring, though the growth is rather short and the foliage too sparse for their size. However, it is a good bedding rose and repeats very well. It requires good soil and cultivation if it is to give of its best. Slight fragrance. Height 3ft. ('Perfecta' × 'Governador Braga da Cruz') × 'Piccadilly'. Dickson (U.K.), 1966. See page 123.

GREAT NEWS. Large blooms of rich plum-purple, the petals being silver on the reverse side — a pleasing colour effect, and one that is entirely new to the Hybrid Tea. The growth is of medium strength, but it flowers freely and has a strong perfume. Height 2½ft. Breeding 'Rose Gaujard' × 'City of Hereford'. Le Grice (U.K.), 1973.

HARRY WHEATCROFT. This rose was named after one of the great characters of the rose world who, up to the time of his death, was as well known to the public as a pop star. He also brought some of the best foreign Hybrid Teas and Floribundas to this country. It is a good choice to bear his name as it is unlikely to be superseded for a very long time. A sport from 'Piccadilly', see below, it has most of the qualities of that rose. The difference is that the outside of the petals is yellow, while the inside is red striped with yellow. Such colour effects are uncommon among Old Roses, but very rare indeed among Hybrid Teas. Slight fragrance. Height 2½ft. Introduced by Harry Wheatcroft & Sons (U.K.), 1972.

HONEY FAVORITE. A sport of 'Pink Favorite', see below, with all the excellent practical qualities of that rose, but with flowers of pale saffron yellow lightly suffused with pink. It is surprising that although 'Pink Favorite' has always been widely grown, this rose is seldom seen, in spite of the fact that reliable yellow roses are more difficult to come by. Height 2½ to 3ft. Excellent disease resistance. Discovered by Von Abrams (U.S.A.), 1962.

JOHN WATERER. Large, well formed flowers of a deep, rich, unfading crimson. Here, as so often happens, we have a red Hybrid Tea with little fragrance. This apart, it is one of the best of its colour. Its growth is strong and upright with dark green, disease-resistant foliage. Height 2½ft. 'King of Hearts' × 'Hanne'. McGredy (U.K.), 1970.

JULIA'S ROSE. A rose of unique colouring. This is usually described as a mixture of copper and parchment, but I find it hard to give an exact impression; perhaps it is more parchment than copper. Its nicely shaped buds open to rounded flowers. The growth is not very strong. Slight scent. Height 2½ to 3ft. Named for Miss Julia Clements. 'Blue Moon' × 'Dr. A.J. Verhage'. Raised by Wisbech Plant Co. (U.K.), 1976. See page 120.

JUST JOEY. Elegant pointed buds of a coppery-fawn colour, with attractively waved petals which pale a little towards the edges, the flowers remaining pleasing to the end. The growth is spreading and of medium strength, with dark green matt foliage. Quite healthy. Height 2½ft. Fragrant. 'Fragrant Cloud' × 'Dr. A.J. Verhage'. Raised by Cants (U.K.), 1972. See page 121.

KING'S RANSOM. For a long time this variety was the most popular deep yellow Hybrid Tea. There may be better varieties coming along, but it is still a good rose and is easily obtainable. It has well formed, high-centred flowers of medium size, whose colour does not fade and which are freely produced. Light fragrance. The foliage is dark green, glossy and abundant. It is not really happy on light or poor soil, where it requires careful cultivation. Height 3ft. 'Golden Masterpiece' × 'Lydia'. Bred by Morey (U.S.A.), 1961.

KRONENBOURG ('Flaming Peace'). A sport from 'Peace' which occurred at McGredy's Nurseries, then in Northern Ireland. 'Peace' is yellow, but in this variety the colour has become a rich crimson on the inside of the petals, the outside remaining the same yellow as its parent. The overall effect is predominantly a rich crimson which quickly turns to purple, varying considerably according to weather conditions: in cool weather it can be magnificently rich; in hot weather it becomes a not unpleasing dusky purple. It is interesting to note how a change of colour can alter the whole character of a rose — the heavy blooms of this rose being perhaps better suited to the crimson colouring. In all other respects it is similar to its redoubtable parent. Height 4ft. 1965. See page 142.

LAKELAND. Very large full-petalled, shapely blooms of soft shell-pink, with a slight fragrance. It is fairly vigorous, with branching growth and medium green foliage. Healthy. Height 2½ft. 'Fragrant Cloud' × 'Queen Elizabeth'. Bred by Fryer (U.K.), 1976.

L'OREAL TROPHY. An orange-salmon coloured sport from 'Alexander', with all the health and strength of that variety — useful attributes in roses of this colour, which are not notable for these virtues. Height 4ft. When used for cut-flower arrangements, it is suggested this rose and its parent 'Alexander' are best cut when quite young and before the outer petals separate. Discovered by Harkness (U.K.), 1980.

MADAME LOUIS LAPERRIÈRE. I would place this variety very high on any list of deep red Hybrid Teas. It is particularly good as a bedding rose; its growth is short and bushy, sending up numerous base shoots; it flowers very freely and continuously — well into autumn. The individual blooms are quite short in the petal which means that the buds are rather globular, though still attractive. The flowers are of medium size and have a rich fragrance. Medium green foliage. Good disease resistance. Height 2½ft. 'Crimson Glory' × unnamed seedling. Laperrière (France), 1951.

MAESTRO. For some time Sam McGredy has been producing what he has called 'hand-painted' roses. These are bicoloured, with one colour splashed upon another, and are usually Floribundas. This is the first of his Hybrid Teas of this kind. The background is crimson which is delicately flecked and edged with white, giving very much the same effect we find in Old Roses. It has good bushy growth of about 2½ft. in height. Introduced in 1981.

MESSAGE ('White Knight'). A beautiful rose, with shapely flowers of pure white, the buds being tinted with green at first. Unfortunately it is not a strong grower and is subject to mildew. Slightly fragrant. Height 2½ft. Its breeding is ('Virgo' × 'Peace') × 'Virgo'. Meilland (France), 1956.

MICHÈLE MEILLAND. Although this rose is now seldom found in catalogues, I regard it as one of the most pleasing of modern Hybrid Teas. It has quite small flowers with exquisitely shaped buds of soft pink, flushed with salmon and amber as they open, deepening towards the centre. They are borne on a branching bush of about 2½ft. in height, with light green matt foliage and hardly any thorns. Slightly fragrant. Good disease resistance. Cross between 'Joanna Hill' and 'Peace'. Bred by F. Meilland (France), 1945. See page 120.

MISCHIEF. Medium-sized flowers of pointed formation, their colour being pink tinted with coral. This is a vigorous medium-sized, compact bush with ample light green foliage. Ideal for bedding. Slight fragrance. Height 2½ft. 'Peace' × 'Spartan'. McGredy (U.K.), 1961.

MISTER LINCOLN. A deep velvety crimson rose of strong fragrance, the result of a cross between 'Chrysler Imperial' and 'Charles Mallerin'. Its growth leaves something to be desired, being rather straggly with poor foliage, but its fragrance and colour make it very worth while. The buds are nicely formed, opening to rather cup shaped flowers exposing their golden stamens. Height 3½ft. Swim & Weeks (U.S.A.), 1964.

MOJAVE. A beautiful and unusual rose, with very tightly scrolled buds. The flowers are not large, orange-pink in colour, attractively veined with orange-red. It forms an upright bush of medium vigour, with medium green glossy foliage. Slight scent. Height 3ft. 'Charlotte Armstrong' × 'Signora'. Bred by W.C. Swim (U.S.A.), 1954.

MULLARD JUBILEE. Very large, full, deep pink blooms on a vigorous bushy plant of medium height. Dark green foliage. Fragrant. Height 2½ft. 'Paddy McGredy' × 'Prima Ballerina'. McGredy (U.K.), 1970.

NATIONAL TRUST. It is interesting to compare this rose with 'Mister Lincoln' or 'Papa Meilland'. It has all the virtues required of a Hybrid Tea: stiff, upright growth, ample dark green disease-resistant foliage and good repeat flowering. The flowers are of the required spiral formation and of a bright unfading crimson, but lack fragrance, and there is something almost mechanical in the general appearance of this variety, both in flower and growth. The secret lies perhaps in its parentage, which is 'Evelyn Fison' × 'King of Hearts'. It is thus a cross between a Floribunda and a Hybrid Tea, and that cannot but affect the whole character of the rose. What we gain in productivity and efficiency, we can lose in character. This rose illustrates very well the remarks I made in the introduction to this class. Height 2½ft. McGredy (U.K.), 1970.

PAPA MEILLAND. Here we have one of the most perfect crimson Hybrid Tea Roses: the colour is rich and of remarkable purity, the flowers well formed, and there is a delicious perfume. Up to this point it is everything a red rose should be. Unfortunately there is a snag — it has very poor growth. We have to make the choice between a perfect flower and reliable constitution. If you decide to grow this variety, it is essential you treat it generously. Very fragrant. Height 2½ft. 'Chrysler Imperial' × 'Charles Mallerin'. A. Meilland (France), 1963. See page 142.

PASCALI. This variety has for some time been regarded as being the best white Hybrid Tea. It is a cross between 'Queen Elizabeth' and 'White Butterfly', the former having passed on some of her strong growth as well as disease resistance, and in this respect it is unusual among white roses of this class. Although 'Queen Elizabeth' does not have flowers of classic bud shape, many of its progeny do and, as this rose's other parent was a hybrid of 'Madame Butterfly', it is not altogether surprising that 'Pascali' is a beautifully formed rose. The flowers are not very large and have an appearance of delicate refinement. Although they give the impression of being pure white, there is a barely noticeable tinge of pink in their make up. It is free flowering, but has only a moderate fragrance. Height 2½ft. Bred by Lens (Belgium), introduced 1963. See page 120.

PAUL SHIRVILLE. A beautiful rose of elegant bud formation, with delicate apricot and peach-pink colouring. It has good spreading growth with plenty of foliage, making it suitable for the mixed border. It has a strong fragrance, for which it was awarded the Edland Medal. Height 3ft. A cross between the Climbing Rose 'Compassion', which probably gives it its excellent habit of growth, and 'Mischief'. Bred by Harkness (U.K.), 1983. See page 121.

PEACE ('Gloria Dei', 'Madame A. Meilland'). This is probably the most popular and widely grown rose ever bred. It is, in fact, the only rose to have had a book written about it — *For the Love of a Rose* by Antonia Ridge. Its influence on the development of the Hybrid Tea Rose has been enormous, not only as a parent, but also as a standard set for roses that came after it. To my way of thinking this influence has not always been for the best, and has led to a much coarser bloom. One thing is certain: it is a rose of exceptional vigour, being both tall and branching. In fact, it will form an excellent specimen shrub growing to about 4ft. in height, taller with light pruning. The foliage is large, healthy, glossy, of deep green colouring and seldom affected by disease. The flowers are very large and full, yellow flushed with pink, paling with age. They are produced freely both in early summer and autumn, with frequent flowers in between, and are not without beauty, being heavy and rather globular. 'Peace' was bred by Meilland in France and first budded in 1936. By the time it was ready for distribution the Second World War had started, though buds had already been sent to the United States. After the War it was distributed in the States under the very appropriate name by which we now know it and was an instant success. In France it is known as 'Madame A. Meilland'. Its rather complicated parentage is as follows: ('George Dickson' × 'Souvenir de Claudius Pernet') × ('Joanna Hill' × 'Charles P. Kilhan') × 'Margaret McGredy'. Meilland (France), 1945.

PEAUDOUCE. A beautiful and refined rose in the best Hybrid Tea tradition, with perfect bud formation, the colour being ivory-white itensifying to lemon at the centre. The growth is bushy, about 3ft. in height, with plentiful foliage of mid- to dark green. Breeding 'Nana Mouskouri' × 'Lolita'. Dicksons (Northern Ireland), introduced 1985. See page 124.

PEER GYNT. A strong growing, bushy rose of medium height. The flowers are of large size, bright yellow, lightly flushed with pink towards the edges, and of a rather globular shape, opening to form an attractive cupped bloom. The flowers are produced with unusual continuity, usually in clusters. Healthy, glossy, dark green foliage. Only slight fragrance. 'Colour Wonder' × 'Golden Giant'. Bred by Kordes (Germany), 1968.

PICCADILLY. A scarlet and yellow bicolour; scarlet on the inside of the petals and yellow on the reverse, becoming suffused with orange as the flower ages. The blooms are medium sized and fairly full, with a slight scent. The growth is strong and branching, with glossy, bronze-tinted foliage. Height 2½ft. 'McGredy's Yellow' × 'Karl Herbst'. McGredy (U.K.), 1959.

PINK FAVORITE. The result of a cross between the Hybrid Tea Rose 'Juno' and a seedling that was itself a cross between the Hybrid Perpetual 'Georg Arends' and the repeat-flowering climber 'New Dawn'. This most unusual combination has resulted in one of the strongest, most reliable and disease free of all the Hybrid Teas. Unfortunately the flowers, although large and well formed, are lacking in character, and its rose-pink colouring rather lifeless. The foliage is glossy and dark green, the growth branching. This said, there can be few Hybrid Teas better suited for use in a difficult site. Little scent. Height 2½ to 3ft. Bred by Von Abrams (U.S.A.), 1956. See page 122.

PINK PEACE. Not a sport from 'Peace' as the name seems to suggest, and it has little resemblance to that rose. It does, however, have something of the same robust and reliable constitution. The flowers are a deep rose-pink in colour, large and full and of cupped formation, with a good scent. It has healthy, bronze-tinted foliage and vigorous, upright growth of 3½ft. in height. It is interesting to note that the breeder, Meilland, has returned to the Old Hybrid Perpetual 'Mrs. John Laing' for part of its parentage, the breeding being ('Peace' × 'Monique') × ('Peace' × 'Mrs. John Laing'). Introduced 1957.

POLAR STAR. A comparatively new white rose that promises to become popular. The flowers are quite large and of perfect high-centred form but with little fragrance. The foliage is dark green and the growth vigorous, to about 3 or 3½ft. in height. Bred by Tantau (Germany), introduced 1982.

POT OF GOLD. Fragrant, well formed, small to medium-size flowers of clear yellow colouring. It is very free flowering, usually in large sprays, with strong bushy growth and plentiful glossy foliage. The height is about 2½ft. which makes it an ideal bedding rose. 'Eurorose' × 'Whisky Mac'. Raised by Dickson (U.K.), 1980.

PRECIOUS PLATINUM ('Red Star', 'Opa Potschke'). The outstanding characteristic of this rose is the sheer brilliance of its crimson colouring. The flowers are of medium size, the foliage plentiful and glossy, and its vigorous and bushy growth makes it a first class bedding rose. Fragrant. Height 3ft. 'Red Planet' × 'Franklin Engelmann'. Dickson (U.K.), 1974.

PRIMA BALLERINA ('Première Ballerine'). For a long time this was considered to be the best pink Hybrid Tea, and it is still high on the list. The blooms are of medium size, beautifully shaped in the early stages, with a strong fragrance. The growth is vigorous, upright and about 3ft. in height. It has healthy, dark, glossy foliage. Bred by Tantau (Germany) from a seedling by 'Peace', 1958. See page 122.

PRISTINE. Large shapely blooms of ivory-white, delicately flushed with pink and held upon a tall bush against contrasting large dark green leaves which set them off beautifully. It has good, robust leafy growth of 3ft. in height. Strongly fragrant. A cross between 'White Masterpiece' and 'First Prize'. Bred by Warren (U.S.A.), 1978. See page 121.

RED DEVIL ('Coeur d'Amour'). Exceptionally large blooms of rosy-scarlet, the reverse of the petals being a lighter shade. These are of a perfect high-centred formation, and are much valued by exhibitors, though unfortunately they are easily damaged by rain. Strong, bushy growth, with healthy, dark green, glossy foliage. Powerful fragrance. Height 3½ ft. 'Silver Lining' × 'Prima Ballerina'. Dickson (U.K.), 1967.

ROSE GAUJARD. A reliable and easily grown rose with strong, spreading growth and dark green, glossy foliage. The flowers are large, carmine-pink on the inside of the petals and a contrasting silvery-white on the outside. They are of globular shape, produced freely, but have little fragrance. A cross between 'Peace' and a seedling from 'Opera'. Bred by Gaujard (France), 1957.

SILVER JUBILEE. Perhaps the finest rose bred by Alec Cocker in his short but highly successful career as a rose hybridist, whose work, it is good to know, is carried on by his wife and son. 'Silver Jubilee' is one of the most robust and reliable Hybrid Teas and has exceptionally large and plentiful foliage. The flowers are not very large, but they are well formed and of a lovely salmon-pink colour, shaded with peach and coppery-pink. They have only a slight fragrance, but are produced with exceptional freedom. Very healthy. Height 3ft. Named to commemorate the Queen's Silver Jubilee, the breeding was ('Highlight' × 'Colour Wonder') × ('Parkdirector Riggers' × 'Piccadilly') × 'Mischief'. 1978. See page 122.

SILVER LINING. Large, well-formed high-centred blooms of silvery-pink with a silvery reverse. It is fairly vigorous and branching, 2½ ft. in height, with glossy, dark green foliage. Very fragrant. A cross between 'Karl Herbst' and 'Eden Rose'. Bred by A. Dickson (U.K.), 1958.

SORAYA. I include this rose for its pleasing and unusual colour. This is bright orange-red, the reverse of the petals crimson-red, resulting in a pleasing effect. The flowers, which are held on long stems, are of medium size and tend towards a cupped formation. They have only a slight fragrance. The foliage is dark green, tinted crimson at first. Growth, vigorous, upright. Height 2½ ft. ('Peace' × 'Floradora') × 'Grand'mère Jenny'. F. Meilland (France), 1955.

SUNBLEST ('Landora'). A reliable pure yellow rose ideal for bedding. The flowers are not large, hold their colour well, even in strong sunlight, and have a slight fragrance. The growth is bushy and compact. Seedling × 'King's Ransom'. Raised by Tantau (Germany), 1970.

SUNSET SONG. Medium-sized blooms of a pleasing golden-amber to copper colouring. It forms a vigorous, upright bush of 3ft. in height, with plentiful foliage. Slight fragrance. Parentage seedling × 'Sunblest'. Raised by Cocker (U.K.), 1981.

SUPER STAR ('Tropicana'). This is one of the most widely planted of all roses, largely because its colour — a bright vermilion — was new among Hybrid Tea Roses when it was first introduced in 1960. Although it has now to some extent been succeeded by certain of its numerous progeny, it is still a good rose, with medium-sized, well-shaped flowers and vigorous, branching, free-flowering, if somewhat top-heavy, growth. Roses

DORIS TYSTERMAN. *a reliable Hybrid Tea Rose with shapely flowers of attractive modern colouring.* *See page 133* Tysterman

SUPER STAR, *Hybrid Tea Rose. See page 140.* Smith

PAPA MEILLAND, *Hybrid Tea Rose. A rather weak rose, but with a wonderful colour. See page 137.* Smith

CHESHIRE LIFE, *Hybrid Tea Rose. See page 133.* Fryer

KRONENBOURG, *Hybrid Tea Rose. See page 135.* Smith

ENGLISH MISS, *a Floribunda Rose with charming buds. See page 153.* Cants

EYE PAINT, *a Floribunda Rose which is almost a shrub. See page 154.* Knight

QUEEN ELIZABETH, *a Floribunda Rose and one of the most reliable of all roses. See page 159.* Smith

PLENTIFUL, *a Floribunda Rose with old type flowers. See page 158.* Le Grice

KORRESIA, *best of the yellow Floribunda Roses. See page 156.* Mattock

GLENFIDDICH, *Floribunda Rose. See page 154.* Tysterman

ANNE HARKNESS, *a Floribunda Rose which is almost a shrub. See page 151.* Harkness

BEAUTIFUL BRITAIN, *Floribunda Rose. See page 152.* Dickson

PINK PARFAIT, *a Floribunda Rose with nice buds. See page 158.* Smith

APRICOT NECTAR, *a Floribunda Rose with flowers similar to those of a Hybrid Tea Rose. See page 151.* Warren

VICTORIANA, *a Floribunda Rose with unusual colouring. See page 159.* Le Grice

CLARISSA, *a Floribunda Rose with small buds rather like those of 'Cécile Brunner'. See page 152.* Harkness

YESTERDAY, *Dwarf Polyantha Rose. See page 167.* Page
MARIE PAVIÉ, *Dwarf Polyantha Rose. See page 166.* Knight
YVONNE RABIER, *Dwarf Polyantha Rose. See page 167. Polyanthas are excellent hardy little bushes that flower repeatedly.* Calvert

KATHARINA ZEIMET, *Dwarf Polyantha Rose. See page 165.* Page
CÉCILE BRUNNER, *Dwarf Polyantha Rose. See page 164.* Knight
PERLE D'OR, *Dwarf Polyantha Rose, and with 'Cécile Brunner' one of the most perfect of miniature-flowered roses. See page 166.* Knight

HAPPY THOUGHT, *Miniature Rose. See page 173.* Page
KIM, *Patio Rose. See page 169.* Page
TOPSI, *Patio Rose. See page 170.* Harkness
SNOW CARPET, *Miniature Rose. See page 174.* Page
STARGAZER, *Patio Rose. See page 170.* Page
PETIT FOUR, *Patio Rose. See page 170.* Page

Slightly larger than a Miniature Rose, the Patio Rose is a new type of rose similar to the Polyantha Rose, with short growth and ideal for small gardens.

GREEN DIAMOND. *Miniature Rose. See page 173.* Page
STARS 'N STRIPES. *Miniature Rose. See page 174.* Page
DRESDEN DOLL. *Miniature Rose. See page 172.* Page
STARINA. *Miniature Rose. See page 174.* Page
SHERI ANNE. *Miniature Rose. See page 174.* Page
A BORDER OF *Miniature Roses.* Balfour

Miniature Roses are usually no more than 15ins. tall and are ideal for tubs, troughs and very small areas. The garden scene, above right, gives a further idea as to how these roses may be grown.

of such brilliance should be planted only sparingly if they are not to dominate all else in the garden. Only a faint fragrance. Height 3ft. Unfortunately, 'Super Star' seems to have developed a susceptibility to mildew in recent years. (Seedling × 'Peace') × (seedling × 'Alpine Glow'). Tantau (Germany), 1960.

SUTTER'S GOLD. A beautiful Hybrid Tea with elegant slender buds of delicate appearance and without the heaviness of so many recent varieties. Its buds are of orange-red, developing into light orange-yellow flowers flushed with pink and veined with scarlet, becoming paler with age. The blooms have a strong and pleasing fragrance. The growth is robust, although of slender appearance in keeping with the flower. I have noticed that American roses are sometimes of more refined appearance than their European counterparts. The foliage is a glossy dark green and quite healthy. Height 3ft. 'Charlotte Armstrong' × 'Signora'. Bred by Swim (U.S.A.), 1950. See page 121.

TROIKA ('Royal Dane'). Medium-sized flowers of a coppery-orange shade, occasionally veined scarlet. One of the strongest, most reliable and healthy roses of its colour. Glossy, medium green foliage. Little fragrance. Height 3ft. Breeding unknown. Poulsen (Denmark), 1971. See page 123.

VIRGO. Beautiful white flowers frequently tinged with blush-pink. These can easily be damaged by rain and like 'Message', above, the growth is rather weak. It is also subject to mildew, and spraying may be necessary. Dark green, matt foliage. Slight fragrance. Height 2ft. Breeding 'Blanche Mallerin' × 'Neige Parfum'. Mallerin (France), 1947.

WENDY CUSSONS. It is difficult to describe the colour of this excellent rose, but it could be said to be a rose-red or very strong bright pink. However this may be, it is a most beautiful shade. The flowers are well formed and very fragrant. The growth is strong and bushy, about 2½ft. in height, with glossy, dark green foliage. It is the result of a cross between 'Independence' (mentioned under 'Super Star', see above) and 'Eden Rose', the first parent being perhaps responsible for its unusual colouring. Breeder Gregory (U.K.), introduced 1963.

WHISKY MAC. This is not a very strong nor a particularly good rose by conventional Hybrid Tea standards, and yet is is one of the most popular. The reason for this lies in its lovely clear amber-yellow colouring which contrasts so effectively with its dark green foliage. Very fragrant. Height 3ft. Parentage not known. Raised by Tantau (Germany), in 1967.

YELLOW PAGES. Full flowers of golden-yellow flushed pale pink. These are not of the highest quality and there is little fragrance, but it is robust, reliable and easily grown, flowering freely and continuously. Good disease-resistant light green foliage. Height 2½ft. An unfortunate name, no doubt chosen for advertising purposes. 'Arthur Bell' × 'Peer Gynt'. McGredy (U.K.), 1972.

FLORIBUNDA ROSES

The Floribundas share with Hybrid Teas the major position in modern gardens. Whereas the Hybrid Teas are notable for the size and quality of the individual flower, the purpose of the Floribundas is to provide a massed effect by the production of many flowers in large clusters. They were originally produced by crossing Hybrid Teas with Polyantha Roses. I shall be discussing the Polyanthas in the next chapter: it is sufficient here to say that they are a small class of very hardy and extremely free-flowering bedding roses, with numerous small rambler-like pompon blooms held in very large clusters. By combining the two groups it was possible to produce a class of hardy, free-flowering and colourful roses. This is exactly what the Floribundas are.

The credit for their origination goes to the firm of Poulsen in Denmark which, in the early part of this century, became interested in the development of hardy roses for the Scandinavian climate. P.T. Poulsen crossed the Polyantha 'Madame Norbert Levavasseur' with the Hybrid Tea 'Richmond' and produced a rose that he named 'Rödhätte' (or 'Red Riding Hood') with semi-double cherry-red flowers in large clusters. Distributed in 1912, this rose seemed to get lost in the turmoil of the war and little more was heard of it. After the war Poulsen's son, Svend, crossed the Polyantha 'Orléans Rose' with the Hybrid Tea 'Red Star', and the result was 'Kirsten Poulsen', a bright red rose, and 'Else Poulsen', which was pink. These were distributed in 1924. Both proved great successes.

These roses were followed by others, and it was not long before breeders were producing numerous varieties. At first the class was known as Hybrid Polyanthas but, in about 1950, this was changed to the less attractive name of Floribundas. Since then there has been a continual admixture of Hybrid Tea genes, with the result that the two classes draw closer together, so that at times it is difficult to know where to place some varieties. The flowers of the earlier Floribundas were often single or semi-double, opening flat, but more recently they have taken on the Hybrid Tea form, and indeed at one stage it seemed as though they might overtake the Hybrid Tea in popularity. However, this has not happened, for people still seem to want what they think of as a 'real rose', and at our nursery we sell about three Hybrid Teas for every two Floribundas.

I often feel it might have been better if breeders had concentrated more on the single or semi-double flowered Floribunda Roses, for such flowers provide a better and more natural massed effect. However, having said this, it cannot be denied that few other flowers of any kind have the capacity to produce so much colour over so long a period. It should also be remembered that the Floribundas are a mixed bag. Apart from the simple colour makers, there are roses for all tastes: single-flowered varieties like 'Dainty Maid'; varieties with flowers of almost Old Rose formation like 'Geranium Red', 'Rosemary Rose' and 'Plentiful'; those that have flowers of almost Tea Rose perfection such as 'Chanelle', 'English Miss' or 'Clarissa'; the near shrub-like growth of 'Iceberg', and the wild rose beauty of 'Escapade'.

Floribundas are on the whole hardier, more free flowering and have better disease resistance than the Hybrid Teas. They are therefore less demanding in their cultural requirements. Nevertheless, it is still worth while giving them the same generous treatment as Hybrid Teas, which they will repay with an even more plentiful and continuous display of colour. Pruning should be much less severe than for a Hybrid Tea, and it is only necessary to remove ageing, dead and diseased growth, as well as weak, twiggy branches, and then to cut back the remaining growth to about two-thirds of its length, taking care to leave a tidy, balanced bush.

ALLGOLD. A low growing Floribunda long valued for its unfading, clear, buttercup-yellow colouring. It has a depth and purity of colour that is still unequalled in this class. ('Korresia' is a better rose, but of a rather different shade.) The flowers are rather shapeless and the growth is not very strong, but the overall effect is dainty and pleasing. It has medium green, glossy, disease-resistant foliage. Slightly fragrant. Height 2½ft. Breeding 'Goldilocks' × 'Ellinor Le Grice'. Bred by Le Grice (U.K.), 1958.

AMBERLIGHT. This is one of a number of brownish shades bred by E.B. Le Grice. They are generally not very strong but have their uses, particularly for flower arrangers. This variety has large, semi-double flowers held on wiry stems in small clusters. Its colour is a pleasing clear amber. Fruity fragrance. Height 2ft. (Seedling × 'Lavender Pinocchio') × 'Marcel Bourgouin'. Introduced 1961.

AMBER QUEEN. Full-petalled, shapely buds of a lovely shade of amber-yellow. The colour is similar to that of 'Whisky Mac', and blends nicely with its dark green foliage. It has a low, spreading, bushy habit of growth. The fragrance is quite strong. Height 2 to 2½ft. Parentage 'Southampton' × 'Typhoon'. Harkness (U.K.), 1984.

ANNE HARKNESS. Large sprays of apricot-coloured flowers on long stems. The growth is unusually tall and robust, and it might be used as a shrub. A good cut flower. 'Bobby Dazzler' × ('Manx Queen' × 'Prima Ballerina') × ('Chanelle' × 'Piccadilly'). Harkness (U.K.), 1980. See page 144.

APRICOT NECTAR. An attractive Floribunda with flowers of almost Tea Rose form and delicacy. These are apricot-yellow in colour and have a good fragrance. The growth is tall and angular, forming a rather open bush. Medium green foliage. This is one of those Floribundas that comes very close to a Hybrid Tea, with large flowers held in small groups. Height 3ft. Seedling × 'Spartan'. Boerner (U.S.A.), 1965. See page 145.

ARTHUR BELL. A strong and reliable pale yellow Floribunda whose colour fades to a rather unattractive cream. The growth is tall, vigorous and upright, with leathery, medium green, healthy foliage. Good fragrance. Height 3ft. 'Cläre Grammerstorf' × 'Piccadilly'. Bred by McGredy (U.K.), 1965.

AUGUST SEEBAUER. An early Floribunda which is perhaps worth retaining as it is a little different from the general run of roses in this class. The flowers are deep rose-pink and have pointed buds opening to rather Old Rose flowers with quite a good fragrance. The growth is vigorous and it flowers profusely. 'Break o'Day' × 'Else Poulsen'. Bred by Kordes (Germany), 1944.

BEAUTIFUL BRITAIN. Shapely Hybrid Tea buds opening to form double flowers of a bright tomato-red colouring. It is very free flowering with medium green foliage, and has upright growth to about 2½ft. in height. Little fragrance. Breeding 'Red Planet' × 'Eurorose'. Dickson (U.K.), 1983. See page 144.

BROWNIE. Flowers of an unusual shade of tan edged with pink, with a yellow reverse. They are large, cupped, opening flat and held in small clusters. Height 2ft. 'Lavender Pinocchio' seedling × 'Grey Pearl'. Boerner (U.S.A.), 1959.

CAFÉ. Another rose with brown colouring, usually described as 'coffee-and-cream'. The growth is short and stocky and the foliage an olive green colour. Fragrant. ('Golden Glow' × *Rosa* × *kordesii*) × 'Lavender Pinocchio'. Bred by Kordes (Germany), 1956.

CHANELLE. This is one of my favourite Floribundas. It is a charming and distinctive rose with pretty Tea Rose buds of a delicate shell-pink. The growth is vigorous and branching and it can, if required, be grown as a small shrub. It has a light fragrance. Height 2½ft. Breeding 'Ma Perkins' × ('Mrs. William Sprott' × 'Fashion'). McGredy (U.K.), 1958.

CHINATOWN ('Ville de Chine'). An exceptionally tall and strong Floribunda, often classified as a shrub. It has large, double rosette-shaped yellow flowers that are sometimes edged with pink. Although it has its uses where a large display is required and will grow in poorer soils, all in all it is a rather stiff and coarse rose. Good fragrance. Height 5ft. Breeding 'Columbine' × 'Cläre Grammerstorf'. Poulsen (Denmark), 1963.

CIRCUS. Quite large, very double rosette-shaped flowers that are cupped at first and have a spicy fragrance. Their colour is light yellow, marked with pink, salmon and scarlet. A strong, bushy plant with good, leathery foliage. 'Fandango' × 'Pinocchio'. Swim, (U.S.A.), introduced 1956.

CITY OF BELFAST. A reliable bedding rose, with medium-green, glossy disease-resistant foliage. The flowers are medium size, orange-red in colour and held in large sprays. Slight fragrance. Height 2½ft. Breeding 'Evelyn Fison' × ('Circus' x 'Korona'). Bred by McGredy (U.K.), 1968.

CITY OF LEEDS. Bud-shaped flowers of rich salmon-pink held in large sprays. A reliable and easily grown variety, with bushy growth and good dark green, disease-resistant foliage. Slight fragrance. Height 3ft. 'Evelyn Fison' × ('Spartan' × 'Red Favorite'). McGredy (U.K.), 1966.

CLARISSA. This is something a little different from the usual run of

Floribundas, being a cross between the very strong growing 'Southampton' and the Miniature Rose 'Darling Flame'. The flowers are like very small Hybrid Tea Roses, similar to those of the much loved 'Cécile Brunner', although they do not quite have the delicacy of that rose. They are apricot in colour,with a slight scent, and held in many flowered clusters. The growth is upright with glossy foliage. Height 2 to 2½ft. A very welcome addition to this class. Named after Mrs. James Mason. Harkness (U.K.), 1983. See page 145.

DAINTY MAID. A beautiful single Floribunda with large flowers that are clear pink on the inside, carmine on the reverse. They are held in small and medium-sized clusters on a plant of vigorous, bushy growth with healthy, dark green, leathery foliage. This excellent rose is one of the parents of 'Constance Spry' and thus plays an important part in the foundation of our English Roses. Slight scent. Height 3ft. 'D.T. Poulsen' × seedling. Le Grice (U.K.), 1938.

DAIRY MAID. Dainty pointed yellow buds splashed with carmine, opening to form single flowers of cream colouring eventually turning to white. These are quite large and borne on a bush of medium height. Breeding ('Poulsen's Pink' × 'Ellinor Le Grice') × 'Mrs. Pierre S. du Pont'. Bred by Le Grice (U.K.), 1957.

DEAREST. A beautiful rose of open, full petalled, rather Old Rose formation. The colour is a soft rosy-salmon, and the flowers are produced freely in large trusses on a vigorous bushy plant of about 2½ft. in height. They have a good fragrance for a Floribunda. Dark, glossy foliage. Unfortunately the blooms are easily damaged by rain and there is a tendency to mildew. Seedling × 'Spartan'. Dickson (U.K.), 1960.

DUSKY MAIDEN. An early Floribunda with large almost single flowers of dark red with deeper shadings and contrasting golden stamens. To me this is still one of the most pleasing of the crimson Floribundas, and all the better for being single. It has some fragrance. Breeding ('Daily Mail Scented Rose' × 'Étoile de Hollande') × 'Else Poulsen'. Bred by E.B. Le Grice, introduced 1947.

ELIZABETH OF GLAMIS ('Irish Beauty'). This once popular rose is not much grown now as, unlike the lady in honour of whom it was named, its vigour diminished not long after introduction. This is a shame, as it is a pretty little rose with nicely shaped open flowers of soft salmon-pink. Given good soil it will grow quite adequately. It has a good scent. Height 3ft. Breeding 'Spartan' × 'Highlight'. Bred by McGredy (U.K.), 1964.

ENGLISH MISS. A charming variety producing large sprays of light pink, medium-sized flowers which start as pretty pointed buds and open to a camellia-like shape. Thus we have a good example of an ideal bloom — one that is beautiful at all stages. The growth is upright, rather short, and the foliage dark green with a purplish tinge. It has a good fragrance. Height 2½ft. Breeding 'Dearest' × 'Sweet Repose'. Bred by Cant (U.K.), 1977. See page 143.

ESCAPADE. The almost single flowers of this variety have a simple wild rose charm far removed from that of the typical Floribunda. The colour is a rose-pink with a hint of violet and the flowers are held in dainty profusion above the bush. The result of a cross between 'Pink Parfait' and the little purple Polyantha 'Baby Faurax', it is from the latter that it gains its originality, providing us with a hint as to what the breeder might do with Floribundas as a whole. It is vigorous, hardy, disease resistant and reliable. Light fragrance. Height may vary between 2½ and 4ft. Harkness (U.K.), 1967. See page 119.

EUROPEANA. A strong growing and exceptionally free flowering dark crimson Floribunda, which is a cross between 'Ruth Leuwerik' and 'Rosemary Rose'. It relates back to 'Gruss an Teplitz' through both parents, and this shows up in its growth which is unusually strong, lax and spreading. It bears huge clusters of flowers that weigh down its branches to such an extent they have been known to break. The individual flowers are quite large, full of petals and of an informal rosette shape, but of modern appearance. Bronze-tinted, glossy foliage. Unfortunately 'Gruss an Teplitz' has handed down a tendency to mildew. Slight fragrance. de Ruiter (Holland), 1963.

EVELYN FISON ('Irish Wonder'). Unfading scarlet flowers of exceptional brilliance. The growth is strong and healthy with dark green, glossy foliage. This is a very reliable Floribunda providing a mass of colour, but perhaps a little ordinary in its overall appearance. Even so, it is a particularly good bedding rose for the production of colour. It produces numerous small to medium-sized flowers on a vigorous, bushy plant. Height 2½ft. 'Moulin Rouge' × 'Korona'. McGredy (U.K.), 1962.

EYE PAINT. A rose of exceptional vigour, with branching, bushy growth that would perhaps be better regarded as a shrub. Its parentage is an unnamed seedling × 'Picasso'. It thus relates back, rather distantly, to *Rosa pimpinellifolia,* and something of this species is still evident in its growth. It bears small scarlet flowers with a white eye and reverse in large clusters. The growth is tall, dense and bushy. Unfortunately it is rather subject to blackspot. Height 4ft. McGredy (New Zealand), 1976. See page 143.

GERANIUM RED. This has something in common with an English Rose, with flowers similar to those of an Old Rose, opening flat, full-petalled and rosette shaped. I do not quite know why it is called 'Geranium Red', for the colour is, in fact, a dusky red which becomes tinged with purple as the flower ages. It is not, in my experience, excessively strong, although it is a rose of considerable beauty. Good fragrance. Height 2½ft. 'Crimson Glory' × seedling. Boerner (U.S.A.), 1947.

GLENFIDDICH. Pointed buds opening to medium-sized flowers with a slight fragrance. The growth is bushy and of medium height, with healthy, glossy, dark green foliage. It is said to perform better in Scotland: perhaps the name may have something to do with this. In the south it is at its best in the autumn. Height 2½ft. Breeding 'Arthur Bell' × ('Sabine' × 'Circus'). Cocker (U.K.), 1976. See page 144.

GOLDEN SLIPPERS. This variety has been popular in America where it was bred, but it has never received much attention here. It has a nice, airy, spreading growth and the flowers are quite small and of delicate appearance, their colour being Indian yellow flushed with vermilion, with golden-yellow at the centre. Moderate vigour. Height about 2ft. Slight fragrance. 'Goldilocks' × unnamed seedling. Von Abrams (U.S.A.), introduced 1961.

GREENSLEEVES. One of the few roses with green flowers. They are, in fact small, semi-double and pale pink, but turn to green as they age, particularly in warm sun. Occasionally beautiful, but frequently dull and uninteresting. 'Rudolph Timm' × 'Arthur Bell' × ('Pascali' × 'Elizabeth of Glamis') × ('Sabine' × 'Violette Dot'). Harkness (U.K.), 1980.

HONEYMOON ('Honigmond'). Medium-sized canary-yellow flowers of full-petalled rosette shape, but without the charm of an Old Rose. The growth is medium to tall, strong and upright, the foliage pale green and healthy. Slightly fragrant. Height 3ft. Breeding 'Cläre Grammerstorf' × 'Spek's Yellow'. Kordes (Germany), 1960.

ICEBERG ('Fée des Neiges', 'Schneewittchen'). This is probably the best rose ever to come out of the Floribunda class. The flowers are white, of medium size, double, opening wide, and held in large clusters. If we study both growth and flower, we soon notice it is no ordinary Floribunda. The growth is tall, very bushy and branching; the leaves glossy, light green and rather narrow; the stems smooth and slender. The fact is, it is not of typical Floribunda breeding, being a cross between a Hybrid Musk Rose, 'Robin Hood', and a Hybrid Tea Rose, 'Virgo'. Although 'Robin Hood' was a Polyantha on the one side, it is probable that its other parent was one of Pemberton's Hybrid Musks. This shows up in 'Iceberg' which, although it makes a first class bedding rose, is really more of a Shrub Rose. The whole plant has a Hybrid Musk appearance. Lightly pruned it will form an excellent shrub of 4ft. in height. It flowers early and late and is seldom without bloom in between. In the cool of the autumn the flowers have a distinct blush tinge, and are then particularly attractive. Undoubtedly, no Floribunda makes a better standard and grown thus it seems to flower even more abundantly, forming a large, well-shaped head of growth. It will also make a fine low hedge. Its only weakness is a tendency to blackspot as the season advances, but it seems to have the ability to outgrow this. All the same, spraying is advisable for the best results. It has a pleasing, light fragrance. Bred by Kordes (Germany), 1958.

ICED GINGER. Clusters of large Hybrid Tea-shaped flowers in an unusual blend of ivory, pink, yellow and copper. The growth is vigorous and upright, the flowers fragrant, and the foliage light green and disease resistant. It lasts well when cut. 'Anne Watkins' × unnamed variety. Height 3ft. A. Dickson (U.K.), 1971.

INTRIGUE. Neatly rounded, rather small flowers of an intense dark crimson which, unlike many dark roses, does not burn in the sun. The blooms are held in large, well spaced sprays. The growth is bushy and of medium height. 'Gruss an Bayern' × seedling. Kordes (Germany), 1979.

IVORY FASHION. This is a favourite of mine, although it is not particularly strong and somewhat subject to disease. It was bred from 'Sonata' × 'Fashion' and, like many Floribundas with 'Fashion' in their make up, the flowers tend to have an added delicacy. These are ivory-white, large and semi-double. They have some fragrance. Bred by Boerner (U.S.A.), introduced 1958.

JOCELYN. Flowers of an unusual matt mahogany tint that become a purplish-brown with age. They are very double and flat in shape, and held in clusters above shiny foliage. Le Grice (U.K.), 1970.

JOYBELLS. Unusual and attractive large rose-pink flowers shaped like those of a double camellia. The growth is strong and branching, about 2½ft. in height, with many thorns and glossy, medium green leaves. Worthy of attention by those who like something a little different. Slight fragrance. Breeding unnamed seedling × 'Fashion'. Bred by Robinson (U.K.), 1961.

KORRESIA ('Fresia', 'Friesia', 'Sunsprite'). This rose stands alone as the best yellow Floribunda. It is of a particularly pleasing shade, not quite so deep as that of 'Allgold', but equally unfading, making a good splash of colour across the garden. Its flowers are held in small clusters and are of average size, opening wide, with quite a good fragrance. The foliage is a glossy light green and has good disease resistance. It flowers well and repeatedly. Height 2½ft. 'Friedrich Wörlein' × 'Spanish Sun'. Kordes (Germany), 1974. See page 144.

LAVENDER PINOCCHIO. This is quite the most beautiful Floribunda among the lavender and mauve shades. The colour is a brownish-lavender, which may not sound very attractive but is, in fact, most pleasing. The flowers open to a full, slightly cupped formation and have a lot of character. The growth is quite vigorous and bushy. Slight fragrance. Height 2ft. 'Pinocchio' × 'Grey Pearl'. Boerner (U.S.A.), 1948.

LILAC CHARM. Single or almost single flowers of the clearest mauve colouring, with golden anthers and red filaments. This is not a very strong rose, but it is bushy and its single flowers and purity of colouring give it a dainty beauty. Dark matt foliage. Slight fragrance. Height 2ft. Le Grice (U.K.), 1962.

LILLI MARLENE. A standard variety that can always be relied upon to provide a mass of scarlet-crimson. It is, however, rather uninteresting and mechanical in the individual flower. The growth is vigorous, bushy and of medium height. ('Our Princess' × 'Rudolph Timm') × 'Ama'. Kordes (Germany), 1959.

MA PERKINS. Pale salmon-pink flowers of a deeply cupped formation unusual amongst Floribundas; a little like an old Bourbon Rose. It is strong, healthy and has rather upright growth. Light fragrance. Height 3ft. 'Red Radiance' × 'Fashion'. Bred by Boerner (U.S.A.), 1952.

MARGARET MERRIL. An excellent white rose of recent introduction. The flowers have exquisite high pointed buds, with just a tinge of blush, and eventually open wide. They have what is probably the strongest fragrance of any in this class. The growth is of medium height, about 3ft., and it has dark green foliage, with particularly good disease resistance. 'Rudolph Timm' × 'Dedication' × 'Pascali'. Harkness (U.K.), 1978.

MASQUERADE. The rose that many gardeners love to hate. This I suspect is because it was at one time very much overplanted, and although it is a great performer its flowers are lacking in character. They are semi-double, quite small, and in various shades of colour — yellow at first, turning to salmon-pink and becoming red, with all these different tints to be seen at one time. They are produced very freely in large clusters, and continually if the hips are removed. The fact is, that when seen in the mass or featured in a mixed border, this can be quite an effective rose even if there is little to be said for the individual blooms. Its growth is very vigorous and bushy. It is more attractive in autumn when the red is less in evidence. Light fragrance. Height 3ft. 'Goldilocks' × 'Holiday'. Bred by Boerner (U.S.A.), 1949.

MATANGI. Semi-double open blooms of bright orange-red, with a distinct white eye and a white reverse. A good bedding rose of vigorous growth, with healthy dark green foliage. Slight fragrance. Height 2½ft. Seedling × 'Picasso'. McCredy (New Zealand), 1974.

MOUNTBATTEN. This is very nearly a Shrub Rose and only suitable for the largest rose bed. The colour is usually described as mimosa-yellow. It has many virtues: strong, very bushy growth, excellent disease-free foliage, and it flowers abundantly and continually. The individual blooms are large, fragrant and fully double, starting as nice buds and retaining their beauty when fully open. Height 5ft. Parentage 'Peer Gynt' × ('Anne Cocker' × 'Arthur Bell') × 'Southhampton'. Harkness (U.K.), 1982.

NEWS. A cross between an Old Rose, 'Tuscany Superb', and the Floribunda 'Lilac Charm'. It thus has a similar origin to my English Roses, but whereas these lean towards the old type of flower, this rose is of typical modern character. However, it takes from its Old Rose parent a rich purple colouring which was not previously found in Floribundas or Hybrid Teas. A more exact description of the colouring is beetroot-purple. The flowers are large, semi-double, with contrasting creamy-yellow stamens. It has excellent strong, bushy growth and flowers freely over a long period. Medium green matt foliage. Slight fragrance. It is perhaps a little surprising that the parents mentioned above should have produced a repeat-flowering variety, and that this should be of typical Floribunda growth. It may well have been a second cross-back to a Floribunda. Le Grice (U.K.), 1968.

OLD MASTER. A low growing, vigorous, bushy variety with glossy, dark green foliage. The flowers are quite large, semi-double, opening wide with about eighteen petals. Their colour is a deep carmine, becoming purple with age, with a white eye at the centre. The reverse of the petals is silvery-white. The whole adds up to an Old Rose effect. Slight fragrance. Healthy. ('Maxi' × 'Evelyn Fison') × ('Orange Sweetheart' × 'Frühlingsmorgen'). McGredy (New Zealand), 1974.

ORANGE SENSATION. Fairly large clusters of medium-sized, semi-double, bright orange-vermilion flowers on a vigorous, bushy plant. It has quite a good fragrance for a Floribunda. Light green matt foliage. Height 2½ft. de Ruiter (Holland), 1961.

PADDY MCGREDY. A bushy, low growing Floribunda of little more than 2ft. in height, with deep pink flowers of almost Hybrid Tea shape and size. These are produced with exceptional freedom, covering the plant with bloom. There is usually a period when there are few flowers after the first flush, but a second good crop appears in the autumn. Slight fragrance. Breeding 'Spartan' × 'Tzigane'. Introduced by McGredy (U.K.), 1962.

PAPRIKA. An attractive Floribunda with a little more character than many of its kind. Its flowers are semi-double, of dusky brick-red colouring, with a bluish tinge towards the centre. It forms a vigorous, bushy plant of about 2½ft. in height, with good, glossy, dark green foliage. Good disease resistance. Some fragrance. 'Märchenland' × 'Red Favorite'. Tantau (Germany), 1958.

PICASSO. A vigorous, branching bush, bearing large scarlet flowers with a white ring and yellow stamens at the centre, the reverse of the petals being white. 'Marlena' × '('Evelyn Fison' × 'Frühlingsmorgen' × 'Orange Sweetheart'). McGredy (U.K.), 1971.

PINK PARFAIT. Pointed Hybrid Tea buds of pink and cream, prettily shaped and held on slender stems. The growth is strong and healthy with abundant foliage and it is possible to grow this variety as a shrub. It is very free flowering and excellent in every way, except that it has no scent. Medium green foliage. Good disease resistance. Height 2½ft. Parentage 'First Love' × 'Pinocchio'. Introduced by H.C. Swim (U.S.A.), 1960. See page 145.

PLENTIFUL. This rose is distinguished by the Old Rose formation of its flowers. These are of a bright, strong pink, with numerous petals in a full, quartered, shallow cupped shape. They are produced in large trusses and are, indeed, plentiful. The foliage is a shiny light green, but unfortunately rather subject to blackspot which can reduce the vigour of the bush. Little scent. Height 2ft. Introduced by Le Grice (U.K.), 1961. See page 143.

PRISCILLA BURTON. One of McGredy's 'hand-painted' roses, having deep carmine flowers with a white eye when open; an attractive effect. The buds also are pretty and it repeat flowers well. The foliage is dark, shiny and plentiful. Slight fragrance. McGredy (New Zealand), introduced 1978.

PURPLE SPLENDOUR. The result of a cross between 'News' and 'Overture', with brighter and purer purple colouring than 'News'. The flowers are double and carried on erect growth. The foliage is dark green. Slightly fragrant. Le Grice (U.K.), 1976.

QUEEN ELIZABETH (the 'Queen Elizabeth Rose'). Every now and again a rose appears that will sooner or later be found in almost every garden. 'Queen Elizabeth' and 'Peace' are two varieties that spring to mind when we consider the period since the Second World War. Both have the quality of extremely strong growth and near indestructibility, particularly this variety. 'Queen Elizabeth' has more in common with the Old Roses than other Floribundas. The flowers are large, clear pink and deeply cupped in shape. Although the plant is on the whole a little coarse and of rather ugly, upright habit, the individual flowers are not without their beauty, particularly when cut. The bush or shrub grows to a great height, at least 4½ft., but often when lightly pruned it may be seen growing to 6ft. or more. It is ideal for the back of a large mixed border. When allowed to develop without restraint the flowers tend to perch on top of the growth where they cannot be seen properly. There is no other Hybrid Tea or Floribunda quite so accommodating as regards growing conditions, for it will grow anywhere that a rose can reasonably be expected to grow. It has few, if any, practical weaknesses. The foliage is large, dark green and very disease resistant. It flowers freely and continually. Faint fragrance. Breeding 'Charlotte Armstrong' × 'Floradora'. Raised by Dr. W.E. Lammerts (U.S.A.), 1954. See page 143.

ROSEMARY ROSE. This variety and the pink Floribunda 'Plentiful' were two roses frequently requested by our customers before the arrival of the English Roses. The reason lies in the fact that people were looking for recurrent-flowering roses of the old type, and these two fulfil this requirement better than any of the others. The flowers of 'Rosemary Rose' are large, rosy-red, full petalled, slightly cupped at first, opening flat, with something of the Old Rose charm. They are freely produced on a vigorous, branching, bushy plant of medium height, and have quite a good fragrance. Its parentage is 'Gruss an Teplitz' × unnamed seedling and, like other roses with the first of these parents, it has inherited a tendency towards mildew. Height 2½ft. de Ruiter (Holland), 1954.

SOUTHAMPTON ('Susan Ann'). A very robust Floribunda of up to 4ft. in height, with plenty of glossy, disease-resistant foliage. The flowers are large and apricot-orange flushed with scarlet. It will make a fine show when used as a bedding rose. Slightly fragrant. ('Queen Elizabeth' × 'Allgold') × 'Yellow Cushion'. Harkness (U.K.), 1971.

SWEET REPOSE ('The Optimist'). Well formed Hybrid Tea shaped flowers of creamy-pink, remaining attractive when open; the colour becoming deeper and shaded with crimson at the edges. Strong growth, of medium to tall height, about 3ft., with plentiful bronze-tinted foliage. Slightly fragrant. 'Golden Rapture' × seedling. de Ruiter (Holland), 1956.

VICTORIANA. Large, full, rounded flowers carried in clusters on a short, sturdy bush. They are of a most unusual mixture of colours — vermilion on the inside of the petal with a soft silvery reverse. The result is an attractive effect. Sweetly scented. Le Grice (U.K.), 1977. See page 145.

VIOLET CARSON. This rose has something in common with 'Pink Parfait', with small Hybrid Tea buds of a creamy-peach colour and a silvery shade on the reverse of the petals. The growth is vigorous and branching, with bronzy-tinted foliage. It is not, perhaps, quite so beautiful as 'Pink Parfait', but does have the advantage of a mild but pleasing fragrance. Height 2½ft. Breeding 'Madame Léon Cuny' × 'Spartan'. McGredy (U.K.), 1964.

YELLOW CUSHION. Not a widely grown Floribunda, but it does have attractive yellow cup-shaped flowers, unusual amongst Floribundas. It blooms freely in small clusters and has some fragrance. The growth is low and bushy, with glossy foliage. Height 2ft. 'Fandango' × 'Pinocchio'. Bred by Armstrong (U.S.A.), 1966.

AN AFTERWORD

Readers may have gathered that I favour the open flower and more shrub-like growth of the Old Roses, but this is not to say that the Hybrid Tea, with its shapely buds and bush-like growth, does not appeal to me. A perfectly scrolled bud of a Hybrid Tea can be a thing of great beauty. If the life of the flower in this form is of necessity short, this is unfortunate; it can, however, be of such perfection that it is still very worth while. It is not so much the type of flower that I dislike, but what the breeder has made of them.

There is nothing to be lost by a rose breeder — or anyone else for that matter — stating his ideas as to the proper development of roses, and I shall therefore take this opportunity of laying out a few of my own very personal opinions regarding the future of the Hybrid Teas and Floribundas.

To breed a really beautiful Hybrid Tea is a very difficult task. The early varieties were not strong in constitution, and after the Second World War breeders set to to give them more strength. In this they have succeeded admirably. New strains and species have been brought in to provide further health and vigour. The trouble has been that too little thought has been given to the quality of flowers, or even to the attractions of the plant itself. It has been assumed that any rose must be beautiful as of right; that this side of the breeding would take care of itself. This has not proved to be the case. Too often the flower has been clumsy and the growth without grace. To me the bud flower should be essentially one of delicate elegance, but when it is heavier due attention must still be paid to the qualities of refinement. Colour, too, has been considered something to be extended regardless of suitability, but the addition of a new colour or colour mixture is not necessarily a virtue. What we need are good colours. Why, too, must the Hybrid Tea always be of rigid growth? Its ancestors, the China Roses and the Tea Roses, were not so; could they not sometimes be more lax in growth, with finer stems and more natural and shrub-like habit? After all, roses today are seldom grown in beds; most are grown in borders, so it might be better to develop something a little more natural and suitable for such positions.

There is an assumption that so long as roses are pointed in the bud and of symmetrical form this is all that is required. I suggest that this is not really enough. If we take early Hybrid Teas like 'Madame Butterfly' or 'Madame Abel Chatenay', with all their weaknesses, we cannot but be impressed by the beauty of form and general character of their flowers. Perhaps it is from such roses that we should take our inspiration. The breeding of Modern Hybrid Teas has been affected by many outside influences, not least by *Rosa multiflora*, via the Floribundas. These influences, for all their beneficial effects on the performance of the plant, have done little to enhance the beauty of the flower; indeed the effect has been very much the reverse. *R. multiflora*, in particular, has flowers of so different a character that it is difficult to blend them satisfactorily with a Hybrid Tea. The genes of a rose are not infinitely flexible.

Happily, there are signs that a change is already taking place. Breeders are now more alive to the demand for more suitable colours.

One of the most recent developments is the Patio Rose (Chapter 5), and here we often find small bushes of a very satisfactory habit of growth. Perhaps with time breeders will also pay more attention to the quality and form of the flowers.

As for the Floribundas, these I would like to see in single or semi-double form, producing flowers in great profusion, but with a natural, almost wild rose appearance. Their purpose should be to produce colour, but without crudeness.

If anything, the Hybrid Teas and their close relations the Floribundas suffer from over exposure. They are seen with such frequency that it is easy to take them for granted. Moreoever, no flowers have been so packaged, presented and promoted almost to the stage where they are regarded as something apart from other garden flowers, and hardly as flowers at all. They seem to survive only on the stimulus of a new injection of publicity. They are talked of and written about by the media, often in rather silly terms, frequently with more regard for the person or worse still the product after which they may be named, but seldom with much regard for the attraction of the rose itself. The rose nurserymen are not without blame for all this. Breeding roses is a costly business, and it is sometimes hard to resist the temptation to recoup some of the expenses by charging a fee for the name. This does not matter so long as it is a name that is going to help the rose as well as the nominee.

I cannot pass on without some comment on the trials, held in many countries throughout the world, at which new roses are tested and awards made to those considered to be of greatest worth. These trials are, no doubt, a very good idea. Hundreds of new roses are bred each year, and nurseries cannot grow them all; indeed many are not worth a place in their lists. Unfortunately these trials do have a negative aspect. They are enormously influential, and their decisions can mean life or death to new roses. They are conducted on a points system: so many for health, so many for freedom of flowering, so many for scent, and so on. The shortcoming of such a system is that these figures do not necessarily add up to a beautiful rose, and I suspect that those who judge at these trials do not have the question of beauty very much in mind. Their concern is for a bush that will grow well, be free from disease, etc. The trouble is that they think quantitively, not qualitatively: more colour, more flowers, indeed more of everything. Not only this, but they also have to be concerned with the maintenance of the status quo — they can only judge by the standards that are already accepted and these can sometimes be a hindrance rather than a spur to progress.

To be fair, judges do have an impossible task and, as these trials are planned at present, there is little else they can do. There are, I think, two ways that might help us out of this plight. The first is that nurserymen should not take trials too seriously; that they should be a little more adventurous and not take the easy route of growing just what they are told. They should think a little more of what might appeal to their customers. The second is that trials should be divided into two sections. The first should be devoted to judging the practical virtues, the second to the assessment of aesthetic appeal. Even then it would be necessary for those considering the findings to use their own judgement and assess for themselves what exactly is implied by the judges when they make their decisions.

Chapter 5
SOME SMALL ROSES

Having completed our survey of the two main classes of Modern Roses — the Hybrid Teas and Floribundas, we are left with three other modern groups. These are all either short with small flowers, or miniature with miniature flowers: Dwarf Polyantha Roses, Patio Roses and the Miniature Roses. All these are very free and continuous in bloom and ideal for the very small gardens we frequently find with today's new houses.

The Polyanthas and the Patio Roses are both strongly influenced by *Rosa multiflora* and have inherited much of the hardiness and floriferous nature of that species. The Miniature Roses are descendants of a miniature China Rose, but have felt the influence of many other roses, including species from the Synstylae* section to which Multiflora belongs.

* See Chapter 11.

DWARF POLYANTHA ROSES

For the origins of the Dwarf Polyantha Roses we have to go back to the year 1860, when the French breeder, Guillot, of Lyons, sowed seed of the climbing species *R. multiflora* which is, as we shall see, the parent of many Rambler Roses. The resulting plants turned out to have not single white flowers, as would be expected, but flowers of varying shades of pink, some double and others single or semi-double. Most of these were sterile, but one produced hips. Guillot sowed seeds from this rose and, to his surprise, some of the resulting seedlings were not Ramblers, but short, perpetual-flowering bushes. It is almost certain that his original *R. multiflora* had, by pure chance, been pollinated by a China Rose — in all probability the 'Old Blush China'. Guillot chose two of these seedlings and named one 'Paquerette', which he introduced in 1875, and the other 'Mignonette', which he introduced in 1880; both bore large sprays of very small pompon flowers like those of a Multiflora, and both were a soft rosy-pink fading to white with age. Thus it was a new class was born.

Like their *R. multiflora* parent, the Dwarf Polyanthas are extremely tough and hardy, and produce their flowers with the greatest freedom in large, tightly packed clusters. They also repeat with continuous regularity. No sooner has one branch of flowers come into bloom than another flower shoot appears just beneath it. This virtue, together with their toughness, was to have a profound effect on the development of the rose — an effect that has by no means yet run its course. Unfortunately Dwarf Polyanthas usually have little or no fragrance.

These roses cannot be said to have reached great heights of popularity and few varieties were bred. Indeed, not long ago they had all but been dropped from catalogues. Recently, however, there has been a revival of interest, and we ourselves sell them in quite large numbers. Dwarf Polyanthas are very different to other bush roses and are ideal for the edges of borders where something low growing is required, particularly if the soil is not of the best. In recent years one or two new varieties have appeared, but these are usually of taller growth, as, for example, 'Yesterday'.

Cultivation is less demanding than for any other comparable roses. Pruning consists merely of cutting off last year's flower heads and the removal of old and dead growth. They shoot continually from the base of the plant, and this can result in a mass of ageing growth which will require some thinning.

I include with this class a small group of roses that are so different as hardly to warrant inclusion here, except for the fact that one of their parents was a Polyantha. They are 'Cécile Brunner', 'Perle d'Or', 'White Cécile Brunner', 'Madame Jules Thibaud' and 'Jenny Wren', which are often included with the China Roses, where they probably have less right to be. We have to place these particularly charming roses here as they are so much out on their own and they do not really fit in anywhere else. They are like exquisite little miniature flowered Tea Roses, with perfectly formed scrolled buds.

BABY FAURAX. A short grower, no more than 12ins. in height, that might well be at home amongst the Miniature Roses. It is usually regarded as being as close to blue as it is possible to get in a rose. This I think is true, with the possible exception of 'Reine des Violettes' and 'Veilchenblau'. The colour is, in fact, reddish-violet. A very useful little rose with close sprays of tiny cupped flowers on a continuously flowering bush. Lille (France), 1924.

CAMEO. Neatly shaped clusters of dainty salmon-pink, semi-double flowers, with a slight fragrance. 1½ft. de Ruiter (Holland), 1932.

CÉCILE BRUNNER ('Madame Cécile Brunner', the 'Sweetheart Rose', 'Mignon', 'Maltese Rose'). An exquisite little rose with buds no larger than a thimble. Each of these is of perfect pointed Tea Rose formation and retains its beauty even when fully open. The colour is a pale pink which deepens towards the centre of the bud. The flowers are borne singly on thin, wiry stems, and later in the season strong base shoots appear bearing open sprays of bloom. The foliage too is small, but otherwise like that of a Tea Rose. It usually grows to a height of 3ft. and repeat flowers throughout the summer. There is a faint perfume, and the bush is free of disease. One of its parents was the famous old Tea Rose 'Madame de Tartas'. Bred by Pernet-Ducher (France), distributed 1881. See page 146.

Another rose, 'Bloomfield Abundance', is almost identical except that it is much taller. This variety does not have quite such perfect flowers, but it is worth while referring to Chapter 8 before deciding which variety to grow. There is also an excellent climbing version of 'Cécile Brunner'.

CORAL CLUSTER. Pure coral-pink flowers in large clusters. Its rich, glossy-green foliage has some tendency to mildew. Height 1½ft. R. Murrell (U.K.), 1920.

GLOIRE DU MIDI. A sport from 'Gloria Mundi', with small globular flowers of brilliant orange-scarlet which retain their colour well. This is a well formed bush with bright green foliage. Slight fragrance. Height 1½ft. de Ruiter (Holland), 1932.

JENNY WREN. A hybrid of 'Cécile Brunner', its pollen parent being the Floribunda Rose 'Fashion'. The flowers are of a creamy-apricot colour with the reverse of the petals a pale salmon-pink. They are rather too large to be compared with those of either 'Cécile Brunner' or 'Perle d'Or', and open more loosely, but are still small and prettily shaped in the bud. They are held in open sprays and have a strong fragrance. This is an attractive little rose and it is surprising more breeders have not attempted such hybrids. Height 3ft. Ratcliffe (U.K.), 1957.

KATHARINA ZEIMET. This rose and 'Marie Pavié' both have a pleasing delicacy of flower not often found in the Polyanthas, and it is interesting to note that 'Marie Pavié' was one of its parents. The flowers are small, fully double, pure white with a sheeny texture, and are held in large clusters. It has good short, bushy growth and smooth, rich green foliage. Sweet fragrance. Height 2ft. 'Etoile de Mai' × 'Marie Pavié'. P. Lambert (Germany), 1901. See page 146.

LITTLE WHITE PET. See Chapter 8.

MADAME JULES THIBAUD. A peach-coloured sport from 'Cécile Brunner', otherwise identical.

MARGO KOSTER. A pretty little plant with branches of very cupped, almost bell-like flowers in a pleasing shade of salmon-pink. They are a little larger than is usual for this group and have a slight fragrance. The growth is short and bushy, about 16ins. in height. It is used as a pot plant in some countries.

This rose is the result of a quite extraordinary series of sports, starting with the Rambler 'Tausendschon' which sported to give a short bush called 'Echo'. This gave us 'Greta Kluis', which in turn gave us 'Anneke Koster', which produced 'Dick Koster', which finally resulted in 'Margo Koster'. There is little point in describing them all, as I think 'Margo Koster' is probably the best. All Polyanthas seem to have the capacity to sport and, indeed, to revert back again to their parent, so that we often find two different colours on one bush. Koster, 1931.

MARIE-JEANNE. An attractive variety, bearing very large clusters of small blush-cream rosette-shaped flowers on a bush of some 2 or 3ft. in height. The foliage is a glossy light green. Suitably pruned it will form a nice little shrub. It is almost entirely without thorns. Turbat (France), 1913.

MARIE PAVIÉ. A bushy, twiggy plant that grows well and bears dainty clusters of fresh blush-white flowers. One of the nicest roses in this group. Height 1½ft. Alégatière (France), 1888. See page 146.

MIGNONETTE. This, as I have said, is one of the two original Polyanthas. It bears small, soft rosy-pink flowers that pale almost to white with age. They are held in large clusters on a dwarf free-flowering bush. Height 1ft. Guillot Fils (France), 1880.

NATHALIE NYPELS ('Mevrouw Nathalie Nypels'). An excellent Polyantha bearing medium-sized, semi-double rose-pink flowers on a dwarf, spreading bush. It has rather unusual parents for a rose of this class: 'Orléans Rose', a typical Polyantha × (a seedling from the China Rose 'Comtesse du Cayla' × *Rosa foetida bicolor*). It is, consequently, not of a typical Polyantha character, the flowers being a little larger and showing signs of its China parentage. Quite a strong fragrance. Height 3ft. Leenders (Holland), 1919.

NYPELS PERFECTION. Open, semi-double flowers of hydrangea-pink with deeper shadings towards the centre. They are borne in large clusters on a vigorous bush of about 2ft. in height, with plentiful light green foliage. Leenders (Holland), 1930.

PAUL CRAMPEL. This rose, together with 'Gloria Mundi' and 'Golden Salmon', was the first to have the brilliant orange-scarlet or vermilion colour we associate with such modern Hybrid Teas as 'Super Star'. As such, these three Polyanthas represented an entirely new colour in roses when they were first introduced around 1930. 'Paul Crampel' is a typical Polyantha, with tight bunches of small flowers each with a tiny white eye at the centre. The growth is vigorous and erect, and the foliage light green. It has the unfortunate habit of sporting to flowers of a rather unpleasant crimson. Height 2ft. Bred by Kersbergen (Holland), 1930.

PERLE D'OR. Almost a replica of 'Cécile Brunner', with similar perfect, miniature Tea Rose buds. The flowers are a buff-apricot shade that deepens towards the centre, becoming tinged with pink as they open, finally fading to cream. They are of rather looser formation than 'Cécile Brunner' when fully open, but are equally, if not more, beautiful. Like 'Cécile Brunner' they are held on long, wiry stems and have a sweet fragrance, though the growth is perhaps a little stronger. Height 4ft. It is probably the result of a cross between a Polyantha and the Tea Rose 'Madame Falcot'. Rambaud (France), 1883. See page 146.

THE FAIRY. See Chapter 8.

WHITE CÉCILE BRUNNER. A sport from 'Cécile Brunner', see above. Unfortunately it is not quite white but tinged with buff, giving it a rather dirty appearance.* Nonetheless, it is a worthwhile rose for those who are particularly attracted to miniature flowers. Slight fragrance. Height 3ft. Discovered by Fauque (France), 1909.

YESTERDAY. A much more recent introduction, bred by Harkness and introduced in 1974. Its parents were ('Phyllis Bide' × 'Shepherd's Delight') × 'Ballerina'. Both 'Phyllis Bide' and 'Ballerina' have connections with *Rosa multiflora,* and 'Yesterday' therefore has a right to be included here. It forms a rather taller bush than the older varieties, being 3ft. in height. The flowers are small, flat and typically Polyantha, produced in graceful sprays and of a pleasant lilac-pink colouring paling a little towards the centre. They are sweetly fragrant. It has a natural bushy, branching habit of growth that fits easily into the garden scene. See page 146.

YVONNE RABIER. Said to be a cross between *Rosa wichuraiana* and an unknown Polyantha, it is therefore surprising that this rose is so very perpetual flowering, as first crosses between once-flowering and repeat-flowering roses are almost always summer flowering only. It is a vigorous bushy rose of 3ft in height. As one would expect from two such parents, it is extremely hardy and disease resistant. The flowers, which are sweetly fragrant, are white with just a tinge of yellow and produced in abundance. It has long, slender, glossy-green foliage that shows signs of both parents. Turbat (France), 1910. See page 146.

* Graham Thomas thinks this remark is libellous. He says that it is pure white with lemon at the centre. This has not been my experience with this rose in the short time I have had it. I hope Graham Thomas is right.

PATIO ROSES

The Patio Roses do not form a clearly defined class, nor are they officially recognised as a class. It is, however, becoming increasingly necessary to place the roses I describe here in some sort of group. The name is not one I would have chosen, as it seems to have a rather artificial ring, but since no one has yet thought of a better one I shall continue to use it. It no doubt arose from the fact that these roses, being small, are rather suitable for growing in containers on patios; however, as they are also equally suitable for the garden in general, it seems an illogical name.

The Patio Roses are closely connected with the Dwarf Polyanthas and the Miniature Roses and are frequently the result of crossing these with Floribundas. It is, however, dangerous to be too dogmatic as to their origins for they are, in reality, the result of a variety of influences.

I regard Patio Roses as being one of the more satisfactory developments in present-day roses. They are usually small, bushy plants, rather like miniature Floribundas but much more compact, indeed some of them could be described as very small bushy or spreading shrubs. They have very numerous small flowers and repeat particularly well. The growth, though short, is often cushion-like or arching, and some varieties have flowers of attractive rosette shape. Others have small pompon flowers like those of a Polyantha. The foliage is often small and dark and there is little trouble with disease. If breeders will concentrate on beauty of flower, and not necessarily on a brilliant colour or a Hybrid Tea shape, I feel sure we could be hearing a lot more about these roses in the future, particularly if they can continue to develop a good bushy habit of growth. Unfortunately they tend to have little or no scent and it may be difficult to breed this into them.

Cultivation provides no problems, and pruning usually consists of little more than removing dead flower heads and a little thinning and reshaping of the bush.

ANNA FORD. An excellent spreading, bushy plant of 1½ft. in height, with shiny, polished foliage. This is covered with small mandarin-red, semi-double flowers that pale to orange-red with a touch of yellow at the centre and golden stamens. It is very free flowering, forming a mound of colour and repeating well throughout the summer. Its many small hips will have to be removed if further flowering is required. Slight fragrance. Harkness (U.K.), 1980.

BIANCO. Small creamy-white, rosette-shaped flowers, produced with great freedom in large clusters on a short, rather open and spreading bush. There is some fragrance. Height 1½ft. 'Darling Flame' × 'Jack Frost'. Cocker (U.K.), 1983.

BOYS' BRIGADE. Dwarf, bushy growth bearing single crimson flowers with a yellowish-white centre. Very free and continuous bloom. It bears many hips which should be removed before they develop. Height 1½ft. ('Darling Flame' × 'St. Alban') × ('Little Flirt' × 'Marlena'). Cocker (U.K.), 1984.

BRIGHT SMILE. Slightly larger flowers than is usual for this group, with deep yellow pointed buds, later opening wide to show their stamens, eventually fading. The growth is strong, neat and bushy with plentiful healthy, shiny, foliage; it is close to a Floribunda in general appearance. Free and continuous flowering. Slight fragrance. Height 2ft. Dickson (U.K.), 1980.

CAROLINE DAVISON. Fairly large pink flowers with a white centre. These are held in close bunches creating a Floribunda-like effect. Slight fragrance. Height 1¼ft. Harkness (U.K.), 1980.

DAINTY DINAH. A bushy, spreading plant with numerous full-petalled, neatly-rounded flowers of a strong rosy-coral colour. The height is 2ft. and as much across. A charming little rose with an excellent habit of growth. Slight fragrance. 'Anne Cocker' × 'Wee Man'. Cocker (U.K.), 1981.

ESTHER'S BABY. Bright rose-pink flowers starting as pretty buds and opening to a semi-double star-like formation. It is very free flowering with low, spreading, bushy growth of 1¼ft. in height. Small, dark green foliage. Slight fragrance. Harkness (U.K.), 1979.

FAIRY CHANGELING. Attractive rosette-shaped flowers of Polyantha-like appearance, but of rather larger than usual size and in pleasing shades of very deep pink showing off well against a leafy background of dark foliage. A most satisfactory, spreading, cushion-like plant of 1½ft. in height. Light fragrance. Harkness (U.K.), 1981.

FAIRY DAMSEL. A nice, spreading bush bearing broad sprays of small Polyantha-like, rosette-shaped deep crimson flowers. It has plentiful foliage and is seldom without bloom. A pretty little rose. Slight fragrance. Height 1½ft. Harkness (U.K.), 1981.

HAKUUN. 'Hakuun' is Danish for a cloud, and this rose produces tightly packed trusses of small buff to creamy-white flowers in such quantities that they are, indeed, like a cloud. A tough, reliable and bushy plant of 2ft. in height. Slight scent. Poulsen (Denmark), 1962.

INTERNATIONAL HERALD TRIBUNE. A particularly fine variety with attractive, rather cupped semi-double purple flowers that pale a little but remain a good colour to the end. The centre of the flower is white with an occasional streak on the petals, and there are dainty stamens. The flowers are held in large sprays and produced with excellent continuity. The growth is robust but neat and compact, with ample foliage. Slight fragrance. Height 1½-2ft. Harkness (U.K.), 1985.

JEAN MERMOZ. This charming little rose has usually been classified with the Polyanthas, but I think it can now be moved to this group. It is, in fact, a cross between *Rosa wichuraiana* and a Hybrid Tea. It bears pretty, airy sprays of tiny, very double flowers on nice spreading growth. They are of a deep china-pink shade, and have a slight fragrance. An ideal rose for the edge of a border. Height 1½ft. Bred by Chenault (France), 1937.

KIM. An upright plant, but bushy and compact. The flowers are yellow lightly suffused with pink and are larger than is usual for those in this section. A good cut flower, lasting well in water. Height 1½ft. Harkness (U.K.), 1973. See page 147.

LITTLE JEWEL. Attractive cup-shaped flowers of a bright rose-pink. Bushy, rather upright growth. Height 1½ft.

LITTLE PRINCE. Sprays of small orange-red flowers on a compact bush of upright habit. It has many hips which must be removed for the benefit of later flowers. Height 1½ft.

MARLENA. At the time of its introduction in 1964, this was a revolutionary rose. It was, in fact, the forerunner of this section. Growing to about 1½ft. in height, it is covered with small semi-double, slightly cupped, crimson-scarlet flowers in clusters, forming a mound of colour. It is seldom without bloom. Bred by Kordes (Germany).

NOZOMI. See Chapter 8.

PEEK-A-BOO. A hybrid of 'Nozomi' which is a trailing or ground-cover rose. Although 'Peek-a-Boo' has not inherited this habit, it has taken on a compact cushion-like growth which is most satisfactory. It might be described as a perfect small — or perhaps I should say miniature — shrub. The flowers are apricot becoming tinted with pink and are held in graceful sprays. Attractive small foliage. Slight fragrance. Height 1½ft. and as much across. Dickson (U.K.), 1981.

PETIT FOUR. One and a half inch semi-double, clear pink flowers with white at the centre and an occasional white stripe. Neat, cushiony growth with plentiful foliage. Slight fragrance. See page 147.

PINK POSY. It is interesting to note that this is a hybrid of 'Trier', a rose of which we shall be hearing more when we discuss the ancestry of the Hybrid Musk Roses, Chapter 8. The outcome is a charming and unusual rose, close to a Polyantha in appearance. It bears bunches of tiny, double flowers of light rose-pink. We have not heard much about fragrance in this section, for the very good reason that there is not much to talk about; however, this variety does have a sweet fragrance, no doubt due to the influence of 'Trier'. It is the type of rose of which I should like to see more in this class. Height 2ft. Cocker (U.K.), 1983.

REGENSBERG. Light pink semi-double flowers mottled and edged with white with a white centre. These are rather larger than is usual and create a good massed colour effect. Neat, free, bushy growth of 1½ft. in height. Slight fragrance. McGredy (New Zealand), 1979.

ROBIN REDBREAST. Small, almost single flowers of dark crimson, with a yellowish-white eye and yellow stamens, creating a brilliant massed effect. Spreading, bushy habit, of about 2ft. in height. Ilsink (Holland), 1984.

STARGAZER. Almost single, bright orange-red flowers with a yellow centre of star-like formation. The reverse of the petals is pale yellow, giving something of the impression of *Rosa foetida bicolor*. Low growth of about 1½ft. Slight fragrance. Harkness (U.K.), 1977. See page 147.

TOPSI. Semi-double blooms of unfading orange-red. Free flowering, slight fragrance. Somewhat subject to black spot. Height 2ft. 'Fragrant Cloud' × 'Fire Signal'. Tantau (Germany), 1971. See page 147.

WEE JOCK. A well rounded cushion-like bush that has scarlet-crimson flowers with pretty buds like miniature Hybrid Tea Roses, but opening to a rosette formation. It has bushy growth with plentiful foliage and repeats well. Height 1½ft. Cocker (U.K.), 1980.

MINIATURE ROSES

These are true miniatures, 5ins. in height in the case of 'Rouletii', but more usually from 9 to 15ins. in height, varying somewhat according to whether they are grown from cuttings or grafted on a stock — those from cuttings will be shorter. Miniature Roses are not only diminutive in height, but also in all their parts, having twiggy growth and tiny leaves and flowers. The flowers, when closely examined, can be very pretty, either in the form of little Hybrid Tea buds or as small Old Rose rosettes.

There can be little doubt that the original variety was a miniature form of a China Rose. The earliest example of this type of rose came to Britain from China at some time around the year 1800 and from here travelled to France. A number of varieties were raised which became popular in both countries, particularly as pot plants for the house. Later interest faded and they were almost entirely lost. In 1918 a Swiss Army Medical Officer named Roulet discovered plants of some of these varieties growing in pots in a Swiss village, where it was said they had been grown for a very long time; this rose became known as 'Rouletii'. The Dutch hybridist Van Vink and Pedro Dot of Spain used it as a parent, crossing it with various roses to found the modern race. After this a number of other breeders began to take a hand, and the popularity of Miniature Roses began to spread.

It is an odd fact that the Miniatures have received more attention in the land of the 'bigger and better' — the United States of America — than anywhere else. Space is usually not a problem there, while in Great Britain it frequently is. Even so, Miniature Roses have never been very popular here and their popularity in the United States must be in some degree due to the work of Ralph Moore of California. It is he who has done more than any other breeder to bring them to their present state of development. I had the great pleasure of visiting his most interesting nursery during the summer of 1985, where I had the opportunity of seeing the vast amount of work he has done and is doing in this field. He has numerous varieties on the market, but sadly many of the charming little roses he has bred have never been properly distributed. The problem seems to be the old one: the public, or perhaps more accurately the nurseryman, now demands small bud-shaped flowers like miniature Hybrid Teas. Nevertheless, at Ralph Moore's nursery I saw the most beautiful little rosette and cup-shaped flowers in good colours and in numerous varieties, including both mossed and striped roses. Moore is the only hybridist to breed Moss Roses since the time of the Old Roses.

The great problem with Miniature Roses is to know how to use them in the average garden. It would be easier if they were a little larger in growth, like the miniature Centifolias, with miniature flowers and leaves. As it is, they are useful plants for very small gardens. In larger gardens they are perhaps at their best in troughs, urns, window boxes, small raised borders and the like. Wherever they are used, it is necessary to place them where they can be seen at close quarters, otherwise their little flowers cannot be viewed with any real appreciation. There is also no reason why they should not be grown in pots and brought into the house when in full bloom, though they cannot, of course, be kept there, and must be taken outdoors at intervals so they can recover from the ordeal. One of the best ways to enjoy them is as cut flowers in posy bowls.

Miniature Roses will grow in any good garden soil, but where the soil is poor it will be necessary to improve it with a little manure. Pruning should consist of cutting back to about half the height of the plant, and removing dead and diseased wood.

ANGELA RIPPON. A compact, leafy plant, bearing full-petalled, coral-pink flowers in clusters. It is about 1½ft. in height, bushy in growth, and flowers very freely. There is some fragrance. de Ruiter (Holland), 1978.

BABY DARLING. Small orange-pink flowers with a slight fragrance. Growth dwarf and bushy. Height 8 to 12ins. 'Little Darling' × 'Magic Wand'. Moore (U.S.A.), 1964.

BABY GOLD STAR. This has rather large flowers for a Miniature Rose. Their colour is a bright yellow, but may be paler at times; the growth bushy, to about 15ins. in height. Little fragrance. 'Eduardo Toda' × 'Rouletii'. P. Dot (Spain), 1940.

BABY MASQUERADE. This is the result of a cross between 'Tom Thumb' and the Floribunda 'Masquerade', and has the appearance of a very small version of the latter rose. The flowers are double, of star-like appearance and, again like 'Masquerade', the colour changes from yellow to pink, and then to a crimson that further deepens with age. Reliable but rather coarse. Height 18ins. Tantau (Germany), 1956.

BAMBINO. A sport from 'Perla de Alcanada', see below, and similar in every way except that it has rose-pink blooms. It has the same hardy, compact growth and pretty, shapely flowers. Height 6 to 10ins. Discovered by Pedro Dot (Spain), 1953.

CINDERELLA. A cross between the pretty little Polyantha 'Cécile Brunner' and 'Tom Thumb'. It has charming 1in.-flowers of satiny-white tinged with flesh-pink which, in spite of their small size, are made up of some forty-five tiny petals. Height about 10ins. Bred by de Vink (Holland), 1953.

CORALIN ('Carolyn', 'Karolyn'). A rather larger variety for the class, up to 18ins. in height, with comparatively large flowers with about forty petals. Their colour is turkey-red with an overtone of orange. 'Mephisto' × 'Perla de Alcanada'. M. Dot (Spain), 1955.

CRICRI. A dwarf, bushy plant of 12ins. in height. The flowers are well formed and very double, their colour salmon-pink shaded with coral. ('Alain' × 'Independence') × 'Perla de Alcanada'. Meilland (France), 1958.

DARLING FLAME. One and a half inch flowers of globular shape and vermilion-red colouring. A good garden plant of above average height. ('Rimosa' × 'Josephine Wheatcroft') × 'Zambra'. Meilland (France), 1971.

DRESDEN DOLL. A most interesting rose, the result of many years work by Ralph Moore of California, who has here managed to combine the attractive mossy buds of the Moss Roses with the small growth and repeat-flowering habit of the Miniature Roses. The growth is perhaps a little large for this class, but none the worse for that. The flowers are double, opening out into a rosette formation, and of a nice soft pink colouring, occasionally showing the yellow of their anthers. The buds are quite well mossed, and this provides a most charming effect. 'Fairy Moss' × unnamed Hybrid Moss seedling. Moore (U.S.A.), 1975. See page 148.

DWARFKING ('Zwergkönig'). Fairly full, dark red flowers of average size. The growth is bushy and of medium height. 'World's Fair' × 'Tom Thumb'. Kordes (Germany), 1957.

EASTER MORNING. Fairly large full-petalled ivory-white flowers. Growth medium-tall. Slight scent. 'Golden Glow' × 'Zee'. Moore (U.S.A.), 1960.

FIRE PRINCESS. Well-formed scarlet flowers on a rather tall, upright bush, with dark green foliage. 'Baccara' × 'Eleanor'. Moore (U.S.A.), 1969.

GREEN DIAMOND. There have been very few green garden roses, and most of these are rather disappointing. This is perhaps the most satisfactory example so far. The buds are tinted with rose-pink, the flowers a soft green when open, though at times they fail to open properly. It is of medium height and bushy growth. Unnamed seedling of Polyantha type × 'Sheri Anne'. Moore (U.S.A.), 1975. See page 148.

HAPPY THOUGHT. Full flowers of pink blended with coral and yellow. Growth vigorous and bushy; profuse bloom. (*Rosa wichuraiana* × 'Floradora') × 'Sheri Anne'. Moore (U.S.A.), 1978. See page 147.

JUDY FISCHER. Pointed buds opening into full-petalled, rose-pink flowers of medium size. Good low, bushy growth with dark, bronzy foliage. 'Little Darling' × 'Magic Wand'. Moore (U.S.A.), 1968.

LAVENDER JEWEL. Quite large, full flowers in a charming combination of pink and lavender. The growth is bushy, lax and of medium height. A good garden plant. 'Little Chief' × 'Angel Face'. Moore (U.S.A.), 1978.

LAVENDER LACE. Small, pointed buds of lavender colouring. Growth bushy and of medium height. Fragrant. 'Ellen Poulsen' × 'Debbie'. Moore (U.S.A.), 1968.

LITTLE FLIRT. Orange-red flowers with an orange-yellow reverse. Light green foliage and bushy growth of 12 to 14ins. The breeding is (*Rosa wichuraiana* × 'Floradora') × ('Golden Glow' × 'Zee'). It is interesting to note that *R. wichuraiana* is a giant Rambler; 'Floradora' a strong Floribunda; 'Golden Glow' a Climber; and only 'Zee' a Miniature. Moore (U.S.A.), 1961.

MAGIC CAROUSEL. This variety has quite large flowers with pointed buds prettily edged in red. The growth is upright and of medium height, the foliage small and glossy. 'Little Darling' × 'Westmont'. Moore (U.S.A.), 1972.

MR. BLUEBIRD. A charming little rose with semi-double flowers of a lovely bluish-lavender colouring. The growth is compact and bushy. In every way an excellent variety of considerable garden value. The breeding is recorded as 'Old Blush China' × 'Old Blush China'. I understand that self-set seed was sown and this resulted in a high proportion of Miniature seedlings. These must surely have been chance hybrids with a Miniature Rose. Moore (U.S.A.), 1960.

NEW PENNY. Moderately full flowers of coral-pink becoming pink as they age. Branching habit, dark green foliage. (*Rosa wichuraiana* × 'Floradora') × unnamed seedling. Moore (U.S.A.), 1962.

PEACHY WHITE. Pointed buds opening into small semi-double flowers. Their colour is white but tinted with blush. Growth upright and bushy. 'Little Darling' × 'Red Germain'. Moore (U.S.A.), 1976.

PERLA DE ALCANADA. Small, rosy-carmine flowers with fifteen to twenty petals. Growth very dwarf and compact, 6 to 10ins. in height, with dark, glossy foliage. 'Perle des Rouges' × 'Rouletii'. P. Dot (Spain), 1944.

POUR TOI. Creamy-white, semi-double flowers tinted with yellow at the base of the petals. Very short, only 6 to 8ins. in height, but with good, bushy growth. 'Eduardo Toda' × 'Pompon de Paris'. P. Dot (Spain), 1946.

RISE 'N SHINE. Comparatively large, shapely blooms of pure yellow on a good, bushy plant of medium height. 'Little Darling' × 'Yellow Magic'. Moore (U.S.A.), 1977.

SHERI ANNE. Pointed buds, opening to a flat flower of bright orange-red. The blooms are held in sprays and have quite a strong fragrance. An excellent variety. 'Little Darling' × 'New Penny'. Moore (U.S.A.), 1973. See page 148.

SILVER TIPS. Pointed buds, opening into small 1in.-flowers with very numerous petals. The growth is vigorous and bushy, and it flowers freely. Height 12ins. (*Rosa wichuraiana* × 'Floradora) × 'Lilac Time'. Moore (U.S.A.), 1961.

SNOW CARPET. An excellent little rose of a unique habit of growth. This is a miniature creeping variety that trails along the ground, slowly building into a small mound of growth. It has tiny short-petalled, star-like and very double flowers of pure white held in sprays against small glossy leaves. It may be grown in rock gardens, although the purist might not think it correct in such a position. It will also form an attractive Miniature Standard Rose. Repeat flowering. 'New Penny' × 'Temple Bells'. McGredy (New Zealand), 1980. See page 147.

STACEY SUE. Very full, soft pink blooms with up to sixty petals. It has an excellent lax, spreading habit, making it a good garden plant. 'Ellen Poulsen' × 'Fairy Princess'. Moore (U.S.A.), 1976.

STARINA. Rather large flowers of orange-red colouring on a comparatively tall, bushy plant. ('Dany Robin' × 'Fire King') × 'Perla de Montserrat'. Meilland (France), 1965. See page 148.

STARS 'N STRIPES. Another Moore innovation. This time he has used the old striped Hybrid Perpetual 'Ferdinand Pichard' to produce a charming little striped Miniature. The flowers are semi-double with white stripes on a red ground, and have something of the appearance of a diminutive 'Rosa Mundi'. The growth is bushy and lax, forming a small shrub of 2ft. in height, and should appeal to those who like Old Roses. 1980. See page 148.

TOY CLOWN. White flowers of pretty semi-double cupped formation with carmine at the edge of the petals. The growth is bushy and of medium height, with small, leathery foliage. Slight fragrance. Height 12ins. 'Little Darling' × 'Magic Wand'. Moore (U.S.A.), 1966.

YELLOW DOLL. Large blooms, starting as pointed buds, eventually revealing many petals of pale yellow to cream colouring. Good spreading growth to about 12ins. in height, with leathery, glossy foliage. 'Golden Glow' × 'Zee'. Moore (U.S.A.), 1962.

Chapter 6
ENGLISH ROSES

I have discussed the Old Roses and I have discussed the Modern Roses, and we have seen the widening gulf that has grown between them. The English Roses bring these two lines together again. They originate from crosses made between Old Roses on the one hand — Gallicas, Damasks and others, and certain Hybrid Teas, Floribundas and Modern Climbers on the other.

These two traditions have been brought together with the objective of combining the form, character and growth of the Old Roses, with the repeat-flowering habit and wider colour range of the Modern Roses. English Roses are, in fact, repeat-flowering Old Roses and may be said to carry on where the Bourbon Roses left off.

Before going any further, I must make it clear that English Roses were bred by myself, and anything I write about them should be read with this in mind. It might also be added that the breeder should know his own varieties best, their weaknesses as well as their virtues, and if he is any good at his job he should be their severest critic. However this may be, one of the main objectives of this book is to make English Roses better known to a wider public. They are not an officially recognised class, but if the name helps us to recognise them and put them in the proper order of things, then this does not matter.

An English Rose is, or should be, a Shrub Rose. According to variety, it may be considerably larger or even smaller in growth than a Hybrid Tea. But whether large or small, the aim is that it should have natural, shrubby growth. The flowers themselves are in the various forms of the Old Roses: deep or shallow cup shapes; rosette shapes; semi-double or single, or in any of the unlimited variations between these. They nearly always have a strong fragrance, no less than that of the Old Roses, and their colours often tend towards the pastel shades, although there are deep pinks, crimsons, purples and rich yellows. The aim has been to develop in them a delicacy of appearance that is too often lacking in so many of the roses of our time; to catch something of that unique charm which we associate with Old Roses. Furthermore, English Roses nearly all repeat flower well under suitable conditions.

Their breeding began some thirty years ago, but although I had made crosses earlier than this, it was only when I hybridized the beautiful Floribunda 'Dainty Maid' (bred by E.B. Le Grice) with the charming little Gallica 'Belle Isis', to produce the now popular 'Constance Spry', that they really began to get under way. 'Constance Spry' is a large Shrub or Climbing Rose of exceptionally strong growth, bearing giant but always refined flowers of a lovely shade of glowing pink. It made a considerable stir among those who favour Old Roses, for it had all the characteristics of such roses, and this was exactly what I was looking for. 'Constance Spry' was, however, only once flowering. With this in mind I crossed 'Constance Spry' back to certain other recurrent flowering modern varieties. Among these were the Floribunda 'Ma Perkins' for its cupped, old type flowers; the Hybrid Tea 'Monique' for the purity of its pink colouring; and 'Madame Caroline Testout', a tough old Hybrid Tea with flowers of Old Rose formation.

Meanwhile, I crossed another of Le Grice's Floribundas, 'Dusky Maiden', with the deep crimson Gallica 'Tuscany' to get shades of red. This also gave me a once-flowering rose of the old type, the deep wine-crimson 'Chianti'. I again crossed this with an early Hybrid Tea called 'Château de Clos Vougeot', notable as a parent of strong crimsons which do not fade. It is also a rose of spreading habit, something which I much desired in English Roses. Unfortunately it tends to yield seedlings of rather weak growth, and it was necessary to cross its progeny with other strong-growing red varieties.

We now had two strains, a pink and a red, and these formed the basis of the breed. Since then, other roses have been brought in, always with the objective of improving the shrubby nature of the plant, while retaining and enhancing the Old Rose appearance of the flowers. Notable among these has been 'Iceberg', itself closely related to the Hybrid Musk Roses and, to my mind, one of the finest Floribundas ever bred. Its influence shows up in such varieties as 'Graham Thomas', 'Perdita' and 'Heritage'.

To gain increased vigour some Modern Climbers, such as 'Aloha' and 'Parade' have been used; both are very fragrant and vigorous and have close affinities to the Old Roses in the form of their flowers. Other roses used have been 'Louise Odier', 'Conrad Ferdinand Meyer', 'Golden Wings' and 'Chinatown' — the latter two in order to introduce yellow colouring.

As regards the cultivation of English Roses, there are a few points that should be borne in mind. It must always be remembered that these are repeat-flowering roses, like the Chinas, the Bourbons and some Modern Shrub Roses. If we wish to be sure of flowers later in the season it is necessary to give them fertile soil and to feed them well, if possible giving them some form of natural manure. It is also essential that there should be moisture if flowering is to continue throughout the summer. Without this growth must cease, and with it flowering. Mulching is helpful and, during dry spells, watering. This is true of all recurrent-flowering roses, and particularly those of a shrubby nature.

Pruning is also more important with repeat-flowering Shrub Roses, and so it is with English Roses. It may vary depending on the gardener's own requirements, but in general it is best to prune back the growth to two-thirds or one-half of its length, having first removed weak, ageing or dead branches. This may be interpreted with some freedom: longer growth will probably result in less continuous flowering; on the other hand it may provide a more attractive shrub. Due attention should be paid to the building up of well balanced growth.

I prefer to prune in January or in late autumn, although it is more usual to recommend March. The growth of roses starts very early. If we prune late we remove shoots that are already growing well. This does not matter except for the fact that we are delaying flowering because the growth will have to start all over again, and this can sometimes mean that the second or third crop of flowers arrive so late in the season that they are caught by late frosts. All repeat-flowering Shrub Roses, and particularly English Roses, require time to generate further growth and flowers. Early pruning means that the second crop will start while there is still likely to be moisture in the soil.

Alternatively, there is no reason why pruning should not be exactly the same as that employed with the Hybrid Teas or Floribundas, see pp.125 and 151. The less vigorous English varieties can be pruned to within a few inches of the ground to provide bushes, and so pruned should repeat well for it is hard pruning that makes the modern bush rose so excellent in this respect. It will also render them more suitable for beds and for very small gardens. They may not, however, show themselves to such good effect and will lose something of their natural grace.

Large growers like 'Abraham Darby', 'Charles Austin', 'Cressida', 'Gertrude Jekyll', 'Hero', 'Hilda Murrell', 'Leander', 'Lucetta', 'Mary Rose', 'Sir Walter Raleigh', and 'Windrush' may be allowed to grow into tall shrubs, and can be grown at the back of the border. In such cases very little pruning will be given, except removing old wood and trimming out weak and dead shoots. With such pruning repeat flowering would be considerably reduced.

The soft colours of the English Roses mix admirably with those of Old and Shrub Roses, providing continuity when the latter have finished flowering. English Roses also mix well with other plants in the border but, as with all recurrent-flowering roses, cannot withstand too much competition, so it is necessary to keep them at a reasonable distance from other strong-growing plants.

Most people, particularly those with smaller gardens, will plant Shrub Roses singly. This is perfectly satisfactory, but I should like to stress the advantages of planting them in close groups of two or three. In this way one plant runs into the other to provide a more bushy whole and, incidentally, probably assuring us of a more continuous flowering, for when one plant has temporarily ceased to flower the others may take over, in very much the same way as in a bed of Hybrid Teas.

English Roses come in all sizes — anything from 2 to 8 ft. in height. They are therefore suitable for all positions and gardens, both large and small. However, I wish to make a plea for the use of one or two larger kinds in even the smallest of gardens. Shrubs of some height are required to give character to small gardens and a 4ft. shrub does not take up so very much more space than a 2½ft. shrub and, proportionately speaking, will probably be more productive.

ENGLISH ROSES

ABRAHAM DARBY. This variety is unusual among English Roses in that it is the result of a cross between two Modern Roses, the Floribunda 'Yellow Cushion', and 'Aloha' a Modern Climber, although both parents bear flowers similar to those of an Old Rose. 'Abraham Darby' is very much a Shrub Rose, forming a fine plant of up to 5ft. in height with long, arching growth, and glossy foliage. The flowers, in spite of the parentage, are of truly Old Rose formation, large, deeply cupped and loosely filled with petals. The colour is soft peachy-pink on the inside of the petals and a pale yellow on the outside. The centre petals fold and turn inwards to give a mixture of yellow and pink. All these colours fade towards the edge of the flower as it ages, providing a soft and pleasing effect. There is a strong and delicious fragrance. It is hardy, disease resistant and recurrent flowering. Austin (U.K.), 1985. See page 187.

AMBRIDGE ROSE. This a good all-round garden rose. It flowers very freely and continuously, has neat, bushy growth, and could equally well be used for a border or for rose beds. The flowers are of medium size, nicely cupped at first, opening to a loose rosette formation; their colour is deep apricot at the centre, paling to the outer edges of the flower. Height 2½ft. Named at the request of the B.B.C. for their long-running 'Archers' serial. Breeding, 'Charles Austin' × 'Seedling'. Austin (U.K.), 1990.

BELLE STORY. The flowers of this rose are large, perfectly symmetrical in outline, with the petals opening wide and incurving towards the edges, with a fine boss of stamens at their centre; the whole giving the impression of a semi-double peony. They are held in small and medium-sized sprays. The colour is a delicate shade of pink, fading slightly towards the edge of the flower. It has a pleasant fragrance. A strong and healthy shrub of about 4ft. in height. Belle Story was one of the first nursing sisters to serve as an officer in the Royal Navy. Austin (U.K.), 1984. See page 186.

BIBI MAIZOON. I was very excited when I first saw this rose bloom, as it seemed to a large degree to represent an ideal English Rose. The growth is nicely arched, forming an elegant shrub, and the flowers, which are of medium size, are of perfect deeply cupped formation. They are filled with petals and are of the richest, purest pink imaginable. They are also very fragrant. Our picture, though good, does not quite portray the true cupped form of the flower. Breeding, 'The Reeve' × 'Chaucer'. Austin (U.K.), 1989. See page 183.

BREDON. Had this rose been introduced as a Floribunda it might well have made a reputation for itself on the popular market, for it has many of the qualities looked for in a Floribunda. It is a short but vigorous little bush, producing many small flowers in large sprays so that the plant is covered with bloom. The flowers, however, are much nearer the old tradition, being small, perfectly formed rosettes of about 2½ins. across and made up of numerous little petals. Their colour is a buff-yellow shade, deeper at the centre, paling towards the edge. They have a strong fruit-like Rambler Rose fragrance. It might be used as a low hedge. Height 3ft. 'Wife of Bath' × and 'Lilian Austin'. Austin (U.K.), 1984. See page 219.

BROTHER CADFAEL. Here we have a rose with exceptionally large flowers. This is not a quality we particularly look for, but there is certainly a place for such roses and they are never in any way clumsy. They are of perfect deeply cupped formation, crisp and fresh in appearance, and of soft pink colouring. The growth is strong, about 3-3½ft. in height and bushy, so that the flowers do not appear out of proportion to the shrub. It repeats well for so large a flower and has a wonderful fragrance. Such blooms make an excellent statement in a bowl of mixed roses or other flowers. Breeding, 'Charles Austin' × seedling. Austin (U.K.), 1990. See page 214.

CANTERBURY. An almost single rose, bearing large wide open blooms of a lovely warm pink with a silky glowing quality and a fine boss of yellow stamens. Although this is one of the most beautiful single roses I know, it is rather weak, and the bush not quite large enough for the flowers. In spite of this, I feel it is well worth its place in the garden. It has a nice, spreading habit of growth, about 2½ft. in height. Fragrant. Breeding Hybrid Tea 'Monique' × ('Constance Spry' × seedling). Austin (U.K.), 1969.

CARDINAL HUME. I include this among the English Roses at the suggestion of the breeders, Harkness of Hitchin, because it has many of the characteristics of an English Rose. The flowers are small and held in sprays, and are of rich crimson-purple colouring, with a strong fruity fragrance. If they lack a little in form, the excellent habit of growth more than compensates for this. In this respect it is very nearly ideal, forming a nicely rounded mound of about 2½ft. in height and 3ft. across, the flowers nestling in its dark green foliage. It blooms with exceptional continuity. Light fragrance. Harkness (U.K.), 1984.

CHARLES AUSTIN. A strong upright shrub with large shiny modern foliage and bearing exceptionally large, cupped, full-petalled flowers of an apricot-yellow colouring paling with age and becoming tinged with pink. Strong fruity fragrance. Although it does not repeat continuously, it can be relied on to provide a second crop in the autumn. It is perhaps a little coarse when put alongside our more recent productions, but can be very imposing towards the back of a border, where it will grow much taller if lightly pruned. For other positions it is better cut down to half its height

HERITAGE *bears some of the most perfect blooms of any English Rose and is also a very good shrub.* *See page 193.* Warren

CONSTANCE SPRY, *the first English Rose to be introduced, with large almost peony-sized blooms, on a large sprawling shrub. Also a good Climber. Summer flowering only. See page 210.* Warren

THE PRINCE, *English Rose. Richest crimson turning to richest purple; unique amongst present day roses. See page 207.* Knight

THE COUNTRYMAN, *English Rose. An interesting back-cross to a Portland Rose, with low arching growth and fragrant flowers of true Old Rose character. See page 206.* Seager

BIBI MAIZOON, *English Rose. Superb 'Old Rose' of purest colour. Usually more distinctly cupped than this. See page 179.* Warren

MARY ROSE, *English Rose. An excellent, reliable shrub that flowers continuously.* *See page 195.* Page

FRANCINE AUSTIN, *English Rose. A dainty Noisette hybrid, with the long, wiry stems, nicely spaced flowers and sheeny petals of its parent. A small shrub with elegant, arching growth.* *See page 191.* Knight

BELLE STORY, *an English Rose with an attractively incurved form of flower.* *See page 179.* Knight
CLAIRE ROSE, *English Rose. Large blooms of pleasing shallow cupped formation.* *See page 189.* Knight

CYMBELINE, *an English Rose which is almost grey in colour. Attractive arching growth. See page 190.* Knight

ABRAHAM DARBY, *English Rose. A shapely, medium sized shrub producing large cupped flowers with unusual freedom and continuity. See page 179.* Knight

ENGLISH GARDEN, *English Rose. Neatly formed medium to large flowers on a short bush.* *See page 191.* Knight

if it is not to become ungainly. Height 4 to 6ft. Breeding 'Aloha' × 'Chaucer'. Austin (U.K.), 1973. See page 197.

CHARLES RENNIE MACKINTOSH. Many people dislike the purple and lilac shades in modern roses, and certainly I do not find them attractive. They are often altogether too harsh and metallic. I do not feel the same about this rose. It is of a pleasing shade of lilac — a little to the lilac side of lilac-pink. The flower formation is cupped at first, opening wider. They have a somewhat frilly, feminine appearance that appeals to many people. The growth is tough and wiry, with plentiful thorns and dusky foliage. It mixes well with other colours, both in the house and in the garden. There is a strong fragrance. 3½ft. Breeding, 'Chaucer' × 'Conrad Ferdinand Meyer'. Austin (U.K.), 1988. See page 200.

CHARMIAN. Large, heavy rosette-shaped flowers of rich pink with a powerful Old Rose fragrance. These are carried on spreading rather floppy growth, similar to that of 'Lilian Austin', sometimes weighing down the branches to the ground. The height is usually about 4ft., but it will occasionally send up much taller growth. Breeding 'Lilian Austin' × unnamed seedling. Austin (U.K.), 1982. See page 220.

CHAUCER. A rose very much in the 'old' tradition. The leading flowers are quite large, deeply cupped and inclined to be of an enclosed chalice-like formation, while the side blooms will probably be more shallow, showing their stamens. Their colour is a light pink, paling towards the edges, and they have a strong myrrh fragrance. The growth is rather upright with small Gallica-like thorns and quite large, medium green foliage. Height 3½ft. The breeding of 'Chaucer' is interesting and a little surprising: 'Duchesse de Montebello' × 'Constance Spry', neither of which are repeat flowering. 'Constance Spry' has one repeat flowering parent, and it appears 'Duchesse de Montebello' must also have had one, otherwise it is unlikely these two parents would produce a recurrent-flowering seedling like 'Chaucer'. Austin (U.K.), 1970. See page 219.

CLAIRE ROSE. Large flowers of superb quality and perfect formation. They are of a delicate blush-pink at first and neatly cupped, opening by stages to a flat, many-petalled rosette which eventually recurves slightly and pales almost to white. The growth is strong and upright, with big, pale green leaves. This is one of the most beautiful of the English Roses, the only fault being that the petals tend to spottle with age if there has been rain. It would then be necessary to remove the offending blooms. Fragrant. 4 by 3ft. Named after my daughter, Claire. Austin (U.K.), 1986. See page 186.

CRESSIDA. Very large flowers of soft pink with apricot on the reverse of the petals, the two colours mingling to give a pleasing effect. The flowers are not easy to describe; they are of cupped formation with their petals arranged in an informal manner, giving them an almost artificial appearance, rather like the roses worn by Edwardian ladies, or like early Hybrid Teas that open full of petals. A vague description, but the best I can do! It does, however, illustrate the great variety of form that is possible in roses. 'Cressida' is the result of a cross between 'Conrad Ferdinand Meyer' and 'Chaucer', which may give some hint as to its appearance. It has the growth of its Rugosa parent, at least 6ft. in height, upright and perhaps a little clumsy, with many large thorns and large, rough-textured leaves. Strong myrrh scent. Austin (U.K.), 1983.

CYMBELINE. Large flowers of 4ins. or more across, opening flat and loosely filled with petals. The colouring is most unusual, a greyish almost ashen pink with tinges of brown. Although this may not please everyone, I find it beautiful and think it could be useful in garden colour schemes, the growth arching to the ground in the most elegant manner and showing its flowers to maximum effect. It is truly recurrent flowering and has a strong myrrh fragrance. Height 4ft. Austin (U.K.), 1982. See page 187.

DAPPLE DAWN. I always find it difficult to know where to place the single English Roses. The justification for putting English Roses into a group is that they have flowers of the Old Rose formation, but the singles could just as well go in with the class known, rather vaguely, as Modern Shrubs. Here we have a good example of this. 'Dapple Dawn' is a sport from 'Red Coat', see below. The flowers are large, 4 or 5ins. across, and held well apart in open sprays. They are delicate pink, veined all over with a stronger pink and have long yellow stamens. The petals are quite thin, giving them at times a gossamer-like quality, but it is the overall effect that is so pleasing. To see this variety planted in a group, with its flowers held so daintily above the foliage, can be an enchanting sight. Like 'Red Coat' it is an excellent shrub that is hardly ever without flowers. Light fragrance. Austin (U.K.), 1983. See page 218.

DOVE. A small spreading shrub of about 2½ ft. in height and 3ft. across. The flowers lean towards those of a Tea Rose, but only at the bud stage. They are of pointed formation, opening out into a nice rosette shape. Their colour is white tinged with dusky blush. It is the graceful nature of its growth together with the elegant poise of the flowers that provide its particular beauty. The foliage is dark green and of the pointed Musk Rose type. There is a fresh, apple fragrance. All in all a pretty little shrub fitting nicely into the front of the border. Breeding 'Wife of Bath' × (unnamed seedling × 'Iceberg'). Austin (U.K.), 1984. See page 203.

EMANUEL. Large, heavy, voluptuous flowers of a soft blush-pink shaded with gold at the base. They open to a rather flat bloom made up of numerous petals which are twisted and scrolled at the centre in an unusual manner, the colours mingling to create a most attractive effect. Rich fragrance. The growth is vigorous, some 4ft. in height, and it is exceptionally free flowering. The only weakness is a tendency to blackspot and it may require spraying in areas subject to this disease. This rose was named for David and Elizabeth Emanuel, the well-known dress designers. Austin (U.K.), 1985. See page 26.

ENGLISH ELEGANCE. Quite large flowers, opening wide, the outer ring of petals retaining their form, while the numerous inner petals twist and turn in all directions to give a most attractive effect. The colour is difficult to describe: the outer petals are blush, gradually becoming pink, then a rich clear salmon-pink towards the centre; at the same time the backs of the petals are shaded with gold which becomes mixed with the other colours, resulting in an ever-changing effect as they unfold. The growth is strong but graceful, 4 to 5ft. in height, with long stems bending slightly outwards and bearing well-spaced sprays of bloom. Austin (U.K.), 1986. See page 202.

ENGLISH GARDEN. Rosette shaped flowers of about 3½ins. across, with numerous small petals forming an almost perfect example of an Old Rose. The colour is buff-yellow, paling towards the edges. The growth is not very shrubby, but short and upright, about 3ft. in height, with light green leaves. When well grown there are few English Roses that can match its flowers for symmetry of form. Pleasant Tea Rose fragrance. Breeding ('Lilian Austin' × unnamed seedling) × ('Iceberg' × 'Wife of Bath'). Austin (U.K.), 1986. See page 188.

FAIR BIANCA. A small upright shrub of 3ft. in height, with something of the appearance of a Gallica Rose. The flowers are of the most exquisite Old Rose formation, and of purest white. They are in the form of a neatly sculptured, shallow cup packed with small petals. There is a button eye at the centre and, in the middle of this, the greenish dot of its stigma can be seen. It has small light green leaves and thin spiny thorns. There is a strong fragrance of myrrh. It would be no exaggeration to say that the flowers come close to 'Madame Hardy' for sheer perfection of form. The general character of both flower and bush goes right back to 'Belle Isis', which was one of the original crosses. A useful rose for the small garden. Austin (U.K.), 1982. See page 204.

FINANCIAL TIMES CENTENARY. Large, fragrant, globular blooms of the clearest, purest pink imaginable. The growth tends to be distinctly upright, which some people might regard as a disadvantage, although it can be very useful when grown behind other roses or plants. It has a pleasant fragrance. Height 3½ft. Named for the one hundredth anniversary of *The Financial Times*. Breeding, 'Seedling' × 'Seedling'. Austin (U.K.), 1988.

FISHERMAN'S FRIEND. Quite large, full-petalled flowers, cupped at first, later forming an attractive rosette — the colour varying from deep garnet-red to deep cerise-crimson as the flower ages. The growth is strong and thorny with deep green, rough textured foliage, which relates back to *Rosa rugosa*. This is an excellent tough rose which has been found to be exceptionally hardly in the Canadian climate, but has an unfortunate tendency to blackspot in England. Strong fragrance. 3½ft. 'Lilian Austin' × 'The Squire'. Austin (U.K.), 1987.

FRANCINE AUSTIN. We bred this rose by crossing the beautiful Noisette Rose 'Alister Stella Gray' with 'Ballerina', one of the most reliable of all Modern Shrub Roses. The result is a medium sized shrub of pleasing, arching growth, bearing sprays of small, pure white flowers. It could therefore reasonably be included with the Ground Cover Roses. I would, however, prefer to keep it here, as it has retained much of the refinement of the old Noisette Roses. As with the Noisettes, the flowers are held on thin, wiry stems, well apart from each other in dainty sprays. It flowers freely and continuously — its long branches often wreathed with white, providing a lovely picture. The foliage is pale green — the leaves being made up of long leaflets. Height 3 to 4ft. and as much across. It is named after my daughter-in-law. Austin (U.K.), 1988. See page 185.

GERTRUDE JEKYLL. In the breeding of the English Roses there has always been a danger that, as the generations pass, we should imperceptibly slip back towards the Hybrid Tea and Floribunda. The genes that control repeat flowering are closely linked with these roses, and when we select for the repeat-flowering characteristic in English Roses there is a tendency to bring along much of the character of the modern rose as well. If we let this happen we lose the 'old' characteristics that are the essential purpose of English Roses. It is with this in mind that I have, from time to time, back-crossed to Old Roses. This rose is a cross between the English Rose 'Wife of Bath' and the old Portland Rose 'Comte de Chambord'.

'Gertrude Jekyll' is a rich, deep, warm-pink colour, sometimes almost red in cool weather, with pretty buds not unlike those of the charming Alba 'Celestial'. These develop, almost surprisingly, into substantial well-filled rosettes with the petals spiralling from the centre, often with the most perfect precision. The flowers are quite large, although occasionally we get a giant bloom on the end of a very strong main shoot. Above all, the fragrance is particularly powerful — the true Damask fragrance of its Portland Rose parent. It is very much the Old Rose, with strong affinities to its Portland Rose parent. It has, in fact, been chosen to be grown commercially to produce the first rose perfume to be manufactured in this country for 250 years. I can think of no other rose with quite so strong a fragrance. Height 5ft. Gertrude Jekyll, as most of my readers will know, was one of the great influences in English gardening, and was the author of a beautiful book on roses, *Roses for English Gardens.* Austin (U.K.), 1986. See page 215.

GRAHAM THOMAS. This is one of the best English Roses up to the present time. It has flowers of the richest and purest deep yellow colouring, a shade which would be difficult to match in any other rose, certainly in any other Shrub Rose. In the early stages there is just a hint of apricot. This variety, a little to my surprise, came from a cross between 'Charles Austin' and a hybrid between 'Iceberg' and an English Rose. I had hoped for yellow seedlings, but did not expect a colour of such richness and purity — a colour unequalled even among Modern Roses. The flowers are of deeply-cupped formation, chaliced at first and opening wider, the petals mingling loosely within. They are of medium size, although they sometimes produce an exceptionally large bloom at the centre of a spray. They have a strong Tea Rose fragrance which I am particularly pleased to have among the English Roses. The growth is very strong, breaking freely at almost every joint as well as at the base to produce further flowers. The leaves are smooth and reminiscent of those of 'Iceberg'. If we look for faults we might say that the growth is a little too upright and narrow at the base, although it is quite bushy and, as Graham Thomas himself asks: 'Too upright for what?' It grows to 4ft. in height. Rather oddly, I have received a report from South Africa that it grows to some 10ft. in height there in the manner of a Climber, although I have no similar reports from other countries. Such variations are not uncommon when roses are grown in different parts of the world, although this example is rather extreme. Austin (U.K.), 1983. See page 216.

GRUSS AN AACHEN. I have taken the liberty of placing this beautiful Old Rose in this section. Bred by F. Geduldig of Germany in 1909, long before the English Roses were thought of, it is so close to the English Rose ideal that I can think of no better section in which to place it. It arose from a cross between 'Frau Karl Druschki' and the Polyantha Rose 'Franz Deegen', and bears little relationship to any previous class of roses, forming a bushy plant of 3ft. in height with large, cupped flowers of a pearly-pink colour fading with age to creamy-white. They are full petalled and of typical Old Rose character, with a lovely silky sheen and delicious fragrance. In addition to this it is truly repeat flowering and, as one would expect from its parentage, very tough and hardy. See page 220.

HERITAGE. This is one of the most beautiful English Roses. The flowers are of medium size and of a most perfect cupped formation. Their colour is a soft blush-pink, and the petals within the cup are each placed with exquisite perfection, giving it a shell-like beauty. The flowers are produced in small — though sometimes large — sprays and have a strong fragrance with just a hint of lemon. It has smooth stems, few thorns and pointed Hybrid Musk Rose foliage. In growth and leaf 'Heritage' has much in common with the rose 'Graham Thomas', but owes more to its 'Iceberg' ancestor. It is branching and bushy, breaking freely along the stem to produce further flowers. It forms a nice, shapely rounded shrub of 4 or 5ft. in height. The breeding was an unnamed English seedling × ('Wife of Bath' × 'Iceberg'). Austin (U.K.), 1984. See page 181.

HERO. A rather straggly shrub, its long branches shooting out in a loose and open manner. The problem is that the growth is not sufficiently full to form a shapely shrub on its own, so it is necessary to plant two or three close together to achieve a good overall effect; on the other hand, the flowers are of a pink of quite unusual warmth and purity, a colour rare among repeat-flowering Shrub Roses. The earlier blooms are in the form of large, open cups and are often very fine, but later in the season they may be of more shallow formation. The flowers are held widely spaced in small sprays and have a strong myrrh fragrance. The height is about 5ft. spreading to almost as much across. The foliage is smooth, and there are a few large thorns. Austin (U.K.), 1982. See page 220.

JAYNE AUSTIN. If the reader will refer to the description of Tamora in this chapter, he will be able to understand the derivation of this rose. Jayne Austin results from a cross between 'Graham Thomas' and 'Tamora', and may be said to represent the Noisette branch of the English Roses, as opposed to the majority which are related to the old Shrub Roses.

It is truly a beautiful rose, as our picture shows. The flowers are shallowly cupped at first, later becoming rosette shaped. In colour they are yellow, tending a little towards apricot — the outer petals being paler, and their petals have the lovely silky sheen that we find in the Noisette Roses and their descendants. The excellent growth of this rose owes much to 'Graham Thomas'; the growth being slender and upright, with the same ability to branch and repeat flower continuously. The leaves are plentiful and pale green. It has a wonderful Tea Rose fragrance. A very charming rose. Height 3½ft. Austin (U.K.), 1990. See page 213.

KATHRYN MORLEY. A dainty rose with medium sized, prettily cupped flowers of clear pink colouring. These are numerous and repeat with admirable regularity throughout the summer. The growth is bushy and there is a good fragrance. All these virtues make it a very satisfactory garden rose. The name was auctioned at The Variety Club of Great Britain in aid of The Shaftesbury Homes, raising £13,000. It was named after Mr. and Mrs. Eric Morley's daughter, who died after a long illness at the age of seventeen. Breeding, 'Mary Rose' × 'Chaucer'. Austin (U.K.), 1990.

L.D. BRAITHWAITE. 'Mary Rose' (see below) is a most satisfactory shrub. It has pleasing bushy growth and repeats particularly well. 'The Squire' has the most superb deep crimson flowers, but rather unsatisfactory growth. 'L.D. Braithwaite' combines these virtues while avoiding the weaknesses, thus providing us with perhaps the most satisfactory red rose in this group. This is most pleasing, as good red roses are notoriously difficult to obtain. It forms a low, rather spreading shrub of about 3ft. in height, is seldom without flowers, and its colour is a bright crimson which is slow to fade. The flowers are nicely, if a little loosely, formed, and fragrant. Austin (U.K.), 1988. See page 200.

LILIAN AUSTIN. This rose lacks something of the Old Rose character which we look for in English Roses. It is, however, a first class small garden shrub of an excellent, spreading, bushy habit and one which looks very much in place with other plants in the border. The flowers are semi-double, at times almost double, but showing their stamens, while their petals are slightly waved. The colour is a strong salmon-pink, shading to yellow at the centre. 'Lilian Austin' is hardy, disease resistant, and reliably repeat flowering and it has a good fragrance. Breeding, 'Aloha' and 'The Yeoman'. Austin (U.K.), 1973. See page 198.

LUCETTA. Very large, flat, semi-double, saucer-like flowers of a soft blush-pink, becoming paler with age, with a large boss of stamens. This is a particularly good shrub; healthy and strong growing, to about 5ft. in height and as much across, with long arching branches. The great blooms are nicely poised and contrast well with its ample, dark green foliage. It is seldom without flowers and is in every way tough and reliable. Fragrant. Parentage not known. Austin (U.K.), 1983. See page 24.

MARY ROSE. This rose was introduced at the Chelsea Flower Show in 1983 and, together with 'Graham Thomas' received a lot of attention from the media, which did much to make the English Roses known to a wider public. It is not at first sight a startling rose, but has a modest charm. The flowers are quite large, informally cupped, and loosely filled with petals, their colour a strong rose-pink that may be paler in the autumn. They are only slightly fragrant. 'Mary Rose' forms a very good shrub of about 4ft. in height with foliage close to that of an Old Rose. It is quite thorny. The great virtue of this rose lies in its bushy, branching habit of growth. It combines this with a truly Old Rose character. This is a difficult combination to achieve and this rose is, I am pleased to say, passing all these qualities on to its progeny. When mass planted the pink of the flowers blends most effectively with the green of its leaves. It is very tough and can be pruned hard or allowed to grow into a larger shrub. The result of a cross between 'Wife of Bath' and 'The Miller'. Named on behalf of The Mary Rose Trust, to mark the recovery of Henry VIII's famous flagship from the Solent after more than four hundred years. Austin (U.K.), 1983. See page 184.

MARY WEBB. Of all shades of yellow to be found among roses a soft lemon is perhaps the most pleasing and suitable. This rose has flowers of just such a colour; they are large and cupped with loosely arranged petals. The growth is strong and bushy, with ample large, pale green foliage. Perhaps it might be said that the flowers are a little indefinite in form and character. There is a very strong fragrance. It is named after the novelist and poet who lived not far from our nurseries. Austin (U.K.), 1984.

OLD LILAC. Quite a different rose to 'Charles Rennie Mackintosh', though of similar lilac colouring. The flowers are large, flat and rosette shaped, and have an exceptionally strong fragrance. The growth is bushy and upright, about 2½ft. in height. Breeding, seedling × 'Hero'. Austin (U.K.), 1990.

OTHELLO. A rather extraordinary variety. The blooms are very large — larger than most others in this group, deeply cupped in shape and very full with numerous petals. As it varies so much the exact colour is difficult to describe: most often it is a deep crimson that quickly turns to crimson-purple, at other times it will take on lighter shades in all but the outer petals. Often there is a most attractive combination of tints. These flowers are of a rough-hewn appearance, but this seems to add to rather than detract from their beauty. They have the deep, powerful fragrance that seems so right for this type of flower. The growth is very strong, upright but bushy, 4ft. or more in height, with numerous strong thorns and dark green foliage. It repeats very well for such a large flower. There is some tendency to mildew, although not so much as to cause great concern. The parents were 'Lilian Austin' and 'The Squire'. Austin (U.K.), 1986.

PEACH BLOSSOM. Here we have a rose of supreme delicacy and refinement. Although the blooms are quite large, they are produced very freely and nicely poised on airy growth. They are of sheeny pink colouring, and their massed effect does, to me at least, have a blossom-like quality. A good shrubby rose of 4ft. in height. It is the result of a cross between 'The Prioress' and 'Mary Rose'. Austin (U.K.), 1990. See page 201.

PERDITA. A good small shrub, with bushy, slightly arching growth to about 3½ ft. constantly shooting from the base and providing continuity of bloom. The flowers are fully double, of medium size, delicate apricot-blush in colour and of shallowly-dished, rather cupped formation. It has ample, dark green disease-free foliage and red-brown stems, the growth generally leaning towards that of the Modern Rose. The fragrance is strong, not unlike that of a Tea Rose, and it was awarded the Royal National Rose Society's Henry Edland Medal for fragrance in 1984. Its parents were 'The Friar' × (unnamed seedling × 'Iceberg'). Austin (U.K.), 1983. See pages 25 and 202.

POTTER AND MOORE. This is a descendant of 'Wife of Bath', one of the most successful of our earlier varieties, and it may be regarded as an improvement on that rose. It has the same toughness and freedom of flowering, but the individual blooms are finer and more full. The colour is a similar shade of soft pink. Its disadvantage is a tendency for the flowers to be spoiled by damp weather. A typical Old Rose flower with a pleasant fragrance. Height 3ft. Breeding, 'Wife of Bath' × seedling. Austin (U.K.), 1988.

PRETTY JESSICA. A very small bush, no more than 2½ ft. in height, of upright growth, and ideal for anyone who has only a small garden yet would like to have a rose of truly Old Rose character. The flowers are shallow, cup shaped and very full, and have a delicious Old Rose fragrance, while their colour is that rich, warm, glowing pink which we associate with the Centifolias. The foliage is somewhat sparse. A charming little rose that flowers repeatedly, it was a hybrid between 'Wife of Bath' and an unnamed seedling. Austin (U.K.), 1983. See page 218.

PROSPERO. This variety is capable of bearing blooms of the very highest Old Rose perfection. They are medium size and their colour is deepest rich crimson eventually turning to pleasing shades of purple and mauve. Their form is faultless, opening flat or slightly domed with numerous small petals. There is also a strong Old Rose fragrance. Here, unfortunately, the virtues end, for 'Prospero' is of a rather weak constitution and only when grown on good land with generous treatment will it achieve the standard described above. A rose for the enthusiast. Height 2ft. Breeding, 'The Knight' × 'Château de Clos Vougeot'. Austin (U.K.), 1982. See page 219.

QUEEN NEFERTITI. Medium sized blooms of rosette formation and soft yellow colouring, with just a hint of apricot. The growth is short, bushy and tough, branching very freely to produce exceptionally continuous flowering. Fragrant. Height 3ft. Breeding, 'Lilian Austin' × 'Tamora'. Austin (U.K.), 1988.

CHARLES AUSTIN, *English Rose. Very large flowers and strong, rather upright growth.* *See page 180.* Knight

WINDRUSH, *English Rose. Similar to 'Golden Wings' to which it is related, though stronger and more free flowering.* *See page 208.* Knight

LILIAN AUSTIN. *This is less of an Old Rose than most English Roses, but it is an ideal shrub for the border.* *See page 194.* Knight

A GARDEN OF *English Roses at David Austin Rose Nurseries. 'Perdita' is at the front; the yellow rose is 'Graham Thomas'.* Warren

L.D. BRAITHWAITE, *English Rose. An excellent small shrub with bright, unfading crimson flowers. It blooms continuously. See page 194.*
Knight

CHARLES RENNIE MACKINTOSH, *English Rose. A pleasing shade of lilac (more lilac than this picture). Free wiry growth. See page 189.*
Knight

WINCHESTER CATHEDRAL. *English Rose. A very desirable white sport from Mary Rose and equally good in every way.* *See page 208.* Knight

PEACH BLOSSOM. *English Rose. Masses of flowers, giving a delicate blossom-like effect.* *See page 195.* Knight

ENGLISH ELEGANCE, *an English Rose with intriguing colours, elegant growth and large flowers. See page 190.* Calvert

PERDITA, *English Rose. One of the best all round varieties. See page 196.* Page

WIFE OF BATH, *English Rose. A tough, short, reliable bush with medium-sized Old Rose blooms. See page 208.* Calvert

DOVE, *an English Rose with Tea Rose buds opening to rosette blooms; elegant spreading growth. See page 190.* Knight

SIR WALTER RALEIGH, *English Rose. Giant flowers, like those of a tree peony. See opposite.* Calvert
CHIANTI, *English Rose. The crimson counterpart of 'Constance Spry' with smaller flowers but better growth. See page 210.* Calvert

FAIR BIANCA, *an English Rose producing most perfect medium-sized flowers on a short bush. See page 191.* Warren
SWEET JULIET, *English Rose. Beautiful, free flowering and reliable. See page 206.* Warren

RED COAT. The parent of 'Dapple Dawn' described above: its red flowers seem to be of slightly greater substance, otherwise it is similar. The colour appears rather harsh when the flowers are viewed individually; this is a nice fresh scarlet-crimson at first, but later it hardens to a duller shade. It is, however, when seen in the mass, however, that 'Red Coat' is most impressive — the whole effect is as though a multitude of butterflies had descended upon the bushes, and this is particularly noticeable in the nursery fields. I have often wished I could persuade municipal planters to use this rose, for I can think of few varieties more suitable for massed effect. In studying 'Red Coat' and 'Dapple Dawn' at regular intervals throughout the summer, we have found them to be hardly ever without bloom, and with the exception of 'Ballerina' I know of no other roses so consistent in this respect. 'Red Coat' may be pruned as a bush when it will grow to about 4ft. in height, or as a shrub, which will achieve 5 or 6ft. There is little scent. 'Parade' × an English Rose. Austin (U.K.), 1973.

SAINT CECILIA. A small, low-growing shrub of excellent bushy habit. The flowers are medium size, of a nice deep cupped shape and pale buff-apricot colouring. It is the manner in which these are held on the bush which gives St. Cecilia its particular attraction. They are nicely poised on long, slightly arching stems, with each flower placed sufficiently apart from its neighbour. All these qualities go together to provide us with a small but elegant shrub.

The flowers appear in extended succession, and it is not long before new shoots appear to enable them to continue well in the autumn. The leaves and thorns are small, tending towards an Old Rose in appearance. There is a strong demand for small shrubs of this type, and this charming little rose has proved popular, particularly with those who have small gardens. Myrrh fragrance. A seedling from 'Wife of Bath', it has inherited much of the reliability of that rose. Austin ((U.K.), 1987. See page 218.

SHARIFA ASMA. I know of few roses that can compare with this for the sheer delicacy and charm of the individual bloom. They are of full rosette shape, with delicate but weather-resistant petals of soft blush-pink colouring. The growth is not over strong but quite adequate, forming a small bush of fairly upright growth. It has a strong fragrance. Height 3½ft. Breeding, 'Mary Rose' × 'Admired Miranda'. Austin (U.K.), 1989.

SIR CLOUGH. This variety was the result of a cross between 'Chaucer' and the Rugosa 'Conrad Ferdinand Meyer', but leans much more towards the Rugosa parent, indeed it could easily be included in that class. 'Sir Clough' forms a large shrub of perhaps 6ft. in height, with many thorns and dark, rough-textured leaves. The flowers are semi-double, of an unusual and beautiful shade of cerise-pink, rather informal in shape with contrasting stamens and a delicious fragrance. The growth is tough and hardy. This rose was named after Sir Clough Williams-Ellis, the architect, best known as the designer of Portmeirion in North Wales. Austin (U.K.), 1983.

SIR WALTER RALEIGH. A large and generous rose, the result of a cross between 'Lilian Austin' and 'Chaucer'. The flowers are rather like those of a tree peony, at least 5ins. across, not quite fully double, opening wide and slightly cupped, usually showing their stamens. They are a lovely warm pink and have a strong Old Rose fragrance. The growth is tall and strong, about 5ft. high by 4ft. across, the foliage large, with everything in proportion to the flowers. This is perhaps the nearest we have to a repeat-flowering 'Constance Spry', although the flowers are less full. Named to mark the four hundredth anniversary of the founding of the first English speaking colony in America. Austin (U.K.), 1985. See page 204.

SWAN. A strong shrub of similar growth to 'Charles Austin', having the same large, rather modern foliage and tall, upright growth. The flowers at their best are magnificent, being large, white with a slight tinge of buff, rosette shaped and perfectly formed. Their only weakness is a tendency to become spotted in wet weather — a frequent problem with white roses. 'Swan' repeats satisfactorily but, like 'Charles Austin', it may require cutting back to half way in order to prevent it becoming too lanky. Fragrant. Breeding, 'Charles Austin' × (unnamed seedling × 'Iceberg'). Austin (U.K.), 1987. See page 218.

SWEET JULIET. Very similar to 'Jayne Austin', which I have already described, having the same medium sized, shallow, saucer shaped flowers, but of apricot-yellow colouring. These, though beautiful, are a little less perfect, with an occasional tendency to split. It is of similar breeding, with a strong Noisette influence resulting in prolific growth. Strong Tea scent. Height 3½ft. Breeding, 'Graham Thomas' × 'Admired Miranda'. Austin (U.K.), 1989. See page 204.

SYMPHONY. At its best, this rose bears attractive rosette shaped blooms of soft yellow colouring. These have a tendency to turn pink at the edges as they age, and this robs them of some of their beauty. It is, however, a reliable little shrub — very free and continuous flowering — which may also be used as a bedding rose. Fragrant. 3½ft. 'The Knight' × Floribunda 'Yellow Cushion' Austin (U.K.), 1986.

TAMORA. A cross beteween 'Chaucer' and 'Conrad Ferdinand Meyer' which has resulted in a short bush, bearing cupped flowers of apricot colouring, with silky textured petals and myrrh fragrance. It appears to have drawn all its character from 'Chaucer' and 'Souvenir de la Malmaison', which was one parent of 'Conrad Ferdinand Meyer', leaving no trace of the Rugosa side of the latter rose. It is a nice little rose but has now been largely superseded by 'Jayne Austin' and 'Sweet Juliet'. 3ft. Austin (U.K.), 1983.

THE COUNTRYMAN. Like Gertrude Jekyll this is a cross between an English Rose and a Portland Rose,and it may be helpful to refer back to my remarks on 'Gertrude Jekyll'. Here we have a cross between 'Lilian Austin' and 'Comte de Chambord'. It is shorter than 'Gertrude Jekyll', perhaps 3ft. in height, the growth bending over and taking on the excellent arching habit of 'Lilian Austin'. The flowers are quite large, loosely double rosettes, deep pink in colour, with an exceptional Old Rose fragrance. For me, they have something of the spirit of the peonies we see in Chinese and Japanese paintings, both in character and the way in which they grow on the plant, although they are, in reality, much smaller. The leaves have something of the character of a Portland, quite large with well spaced leaflets. It is important to remove the dead flowers to encourage quick new growth, and we can then expect two good periods of flower, although there will only be occasional blooms in between. Austin (U.K.), 1987. See page 183.

THE NUN. Not all roses should be introduced with a peal of bells or in the hope that they will one day rate among the most popular of roses. Some may be of more modest ambition. This is such a rose. It is a seedling from 'The Prioress', with flowers of similar open-cupped formation, and almost pure white. This form is pushed a little further with 'The Nun', the stamens being visible within, almost like a tulip, which I think is a very desirable shape of flower. The difficulty is that the petals do not always remain rigid — one or two of them may fall inwards to cover the stamens, and this can happen with 'The Nun'. At its best, this is a beautiful rose, its flowers held well apart in open sprays, giving an effect of dainty purity. There is a slight scent. Austin (U.K.), 1987.

THE PRINCE. The outstanding feature of this rose is its almost unqiue colouring — a deep rich crimson which quickly turns to a remarkable ad equally rich royal purple, a shade of purple found in one or two early Gallicas, but not to be found in any later rose, and almost impossible to catch in a photograph. 'The Prince' is the result of a cross between 'Lilian Austin' and 'The Squire' and no doubt gains its excellent neatly spreading habit of growth from the former and its colour from the latter. The foliage leans towards the Modern Rose, and it has an exceptionally Old Rose fragrance. Height 2-2½ft. Austin (U.K.), 1990. See page 182.

THE REEVE. This rose has flowers of deeply cupped formation, the petals tending to incurve, sometimes forming an almost completely enclosed globe. The colour is a very dark pink and there is a powerful Old Rose fragrance. The growth is wide, unusually lax and arching, about 2½ft. in height, the leaves dark green and the stems covered with thorns. The whole effect is one of dusky darkness. 'The Reeve' is perhaps best when planted in groups of two, three, or more, which will then form a sprawling mass. It would, no doubt, provide a pleasing picture if trained over a low retaining wall. Unlike any other rose I know. A cross between 'Lilian Austin' and 'Chaucer'. Austin (U.K.), 1979. See pages 21 and 220.

THE SQUIRE. I know of no deep crimson rose that produces such superb blooms as 'The Squire'. Unfortunately it is a sparse grower and very subject to disease. Those who grow it should bear these facts in mind. The flowers are very large, deep, full cups, very fragrant and of the richest, darkest crimson imaginable. Rough textured, dark green foliage. Height 3ft. Breeding, 'The Knight' × 'Chateau de Clos Vougeot'. Austin (U.K.), 1977.

WARWICK CASTLE. 'Lilian Austin' is a particularly good garden shrub, but the flowers are of a modern type, though not necessarily any the worse for this. It is of bushy, spreading growth and repeat flowers well. 'Warwick Castle' is a cross between 'Lilian Austin' and 'The Reeve'. The result is a rose with many of the qualities of 'Lilian Austin', but with full-petalled Old Rose flowers. They are of flat formation, 3½ ins. across, with many small petals, and have a strong rose-pink colouring. It will grow into a good small shrub of some 3ft. in height, with slender, arching stems spreading wide to form mound-like growth, while continually pushing up new shoots from the base to give continuity of flowering. Very fragrant, though with a tendency to blackspot in some seasons. This rose was named to commemorate the opening of the beautiful Victorian rose garden at Warwick Castle (a replica of the original designed by Robert Marnock in 1868) which is well worth a visit. Austin (U.K.), 1986.

WENLOCK. This has proved to be a good and reliable red rose of shrubby growth, about 4ft. in height. The colour might be described as a medium crimson, which turns to cerise with age. The flowers are large shallow cups loosely filled with petals. They are produced with the greatest freedom and have a strong fragrance. 'L.D. Braithwaite' is of better colour and more pleasing growth. 'Wenlock' was bred from a cross between 'The Knight' and 'Glastonbury'. Austin (U.K.), 1984.

WIFE OF BATH. A charming little rose, forming a bushy, twiggy shrub 3ft. in height. The flowers are of medium size, starting as pretty little tightly-petalled cups of warm pink, and gradually opening into more loosely-petalled open cups which are clear pink at the centre while paling a little towards the edges. So delicate an appearance belies its toughness, for this is one of the most reliable of the shorter growing English Roses. It has a strong fragrance of myrrh and repeats very well. The breeding is Hybrid Tea 'Madame Caroline Testout' × (Floribunda 'Ma Perkins' × 'Constance Spry'). 'Madame Caroline Testout' was an early Hybrid Tea notable for its reliability, and something of this characteristic seems to have passed down to this variety. Austin (U.K.), 1969. See page 203.

WILLIAM SHAKESPEARE. This is a cross between 'The Squire' and 'Mary Rose'. At its best, it produces superb deep crimson blooms of neat full-petalled rosette formation. The growth is exceptionally strong and hardy but, like 'Fisherman's Friend', it has developed a tendency to blackspot, which is a great shame since it was a very hopeful line of development. Rich Old Rose fragrance. Height 4ft. Austin (U.K.), 1987.

WINCHESTER CATHEDRAL. This is a sport from 'Mary Rose', to which it is similar in every way except that the flowers are white, with perhaps just the faintest tinge of buff at the centre later in the season. I think it is even more beautiful in white. See 'Mary Rose' above for further details. Named in aid of The Winchester Cathedral Trust. Austin (U.K.), 1988. See page 201.

WINDRUSH. Here we have a rose of quite a different character. A second generation descendant from 'Golden Wings', it is an English rose seeding × ('Canterbury' × 'Golden Wings'). The object of the cross was to produce a single flowered rose with some of the delicacy of a wild rose.

It cannot quite be said that 'Windrush' is like a wild rose, but it does have large, almost single flowers of 5ins. across. They are pale lemon in colour with a handsome boss of light yellow stamens, and are produced with great freedom on a robust shrub. The foliage is plentiful and pale green. The fragrance is similar to that of the Scottish Brier. Height 4ft. A first class garden shrub. Austin (U.K.), 1984. See page 197.

WISE PORTIA. A small bush with fairly large flowers of cupped formation. Their colour is a mixture of purple and mauve, sometimes of outstanding richness, at other times less so, varying according to the season, but always pleasing. The flowers are usually shapely and of true Old Rose character. Not particularly strong in growth, but it frequently produces blooms of exceptional beauty and has a delicious Old Rose fragrance. Height 2½ft. Bred from 'The Knight' × 'Glastonbury'. Austin (U.K.), 1982. See page 27.

YELLOW BUTTON. A low growing shrub 2½ft. tall, with spreading, arching growth of at least as much across. The flowers are medium sized, of reflexing rosette formation, quartered, with a button-eye. The colour varies between light and deeper shades of yellow and there is often a distinct splash of yolk-yellow towards the centre. It has a strong, fruit-like fragrance. The foliage is pale green and of glossy texture. Breeding 'Wife of Bath' × 'Chinatown'. Austin (U.K.), 1975. See page 220.

YELLOW CHARLES AUSTIN. This is, as the name suggests, a sport from 'Charles Austin' (see above). It is exactly the same, except that its flowers are pale yellow.

There are a number of other English Roses I do not include here, either because they have proved to be not up to standard, or because they have been superseded by a better variety. These include 'Admired Miranda', a very beautiful blush-pink variety with rather poor Hybrid Tea growth; 'Ellen', a quite good, large deep apricot-flowered rose; 'Glastonbury', a beautiful rich crimson rose at its best, but not sufficiently reliable; 'Immortal Juno', a large, globular-flowered rose of soft pink colouring which can be magnificent but easily becomes spoiled by the damp; 'Jaquenetta', a first class rose, but too much of a Floribunda, with apricot-blush, semi-double flowers in large bunches; 'Moonbeam', very similar to 'Jaquenetta', but with white flowers; 'The Friar', which has Hybrid Tea-like blooms opening to a rosette shape, but not sufficiently strong in growth; 'The Knight', deep crimson, subject to blackspot; 'The Miller', a reliable pink of inferior quality to more recent varieties; 'The Prioress', blush-pink; 'The Yeoman', perhaps the best of those listed here, which has flowers of a glistening soft pink and apricot colour, but is insufficiently reliable; and 'Troilus', with large flowers of honey-buff colouring — perhaps better for a warm climate.

SUMMER-FLOWERING ENGLISH ROSES

In the course of breeding the English Roses it was inevitable that a number of good once-flowering varieties should occur. These are in the nature of a by-product, but I often wonder if it would not be worthwhile to breed them intentionally. I have spoken of the virtues of roses that only flower in midsummer in Chapter 2. We have introduced six such English Rose varieties at our nursery, each of which compares well with the Old Roses. I hope to do more in this direction in the future.

CHIANTI. A tall, broad, well formed shrub of 6ft. in height and the same across, this rose is the result of a cross between the beautiful old crimson Gallica 'Tuscany', and the early Floribunda 'Dusky Maiden'. The flowers are large and of fully double rosette shape, their colour a dark crimson, becoming purplish-maroon as the flower ages, and there is a deep, rich Old Rose fragrance. It forms a robust, shapely shrub and flowers freely, and although it has to some extent been overshadowed by the better known 'Constance Spry', many people think it is rather better as a garden shrub. It was the basis from which most of the red English Roses were developed. Bred by Austin (U.K.), introduced jointly by Sunningdale Nurseries and David Austin Roses, 1967. See page 204.

CONSTANCE SPRY. The result of a cross between the charming soft pink Gallica Rose 'Belle Isis' and the Floribunda 'Dainty Maid', this rose was an ancestor of the majority of the English Roses. It has truly magnificent flowers, in fact larger than any Old Rose I know, and yet they are never coarse or clumsy and are always in proportion to the shrub. Their colour is a lovely soft pink, and they are of full, deep Old Rose formation, the outer petals gradually reflexing. The growth is very strong, and it will, if left to its own devices, form a giant, sprawling shrub with large leaves and many thorns. It will require a good deal of space for development, growing to 7ft. in height, with an equal spread and, under good conditions, even more. It is, in fact, somewhat ungainly, and perhaps better grown as a Climber or over a fence; on a wall it will easily achieve 15ft. or more. However it is grown it will provide a magnificent sight, covering itself with giant blooms.

The flowers have a strong fragrance which has been described by Graham Thomas as being similar to that of myrrh, although some people have questioned this. Fragrance is hard to classify, but Graham Thomas did go to the trouble of obtaining myrrh in order to make the comparison, and he assures me his description is correct. Before the introduction of the English Roses, myrrh was a rare perfume among roses and its origin is interesting. I turn to the same source for my information: in Graham Thomas's opinion, the myrrh fragrance originates in the Ayrshire 'Splendens', and it would appear 'Belle Isis' must have had this latter rose somewhere in its ancestry. It may seem an odd combination but, from my experience in crossing very diverse roses, I would say it is entirely possible. Be all this as it may, the particular fragrance has persisted to a remarkable degree through the generations of 'Constance Spry's' progeny. Bred by Austin

(U.K.), introduced jointly by Sunningdale Nurseries and Roses & Shrubs Limited of Albrighton, 1961. See pages 182 and 278.

DR. JACKSON. Earlier in this chapter I described the variety 'Red Coat'. 'Dr. Jackson' is a seedling from that rose and is in many ways an improvement on it, the flowers being of superior quality. These are single, of purest bright crimson and of a neatly rounded formation. The growth is more satisfactory than with 'Red Coat', being slightly arched and of more elegant appearance. It will produce a huge crop of blooms, in large, nicely formed sprays. I can think of few roses that would be more suitable for a position in the border where a distinct splash of crimson is required. It was named in memory of our much-loved local Doctor. Austin (U.K.), 1987. See page 219.

HILDA MURRELL. A strong, thorny shrub of 4 or 5ft. in height with large, rough-textured foliage. The flowers are large, with numerous petals, opening flat and of symmetrical formation. The colour is a remarkable deep glowing pink in the early stage, later becoming a little darker and losing some of its brightness. It is strikingly beautiful, of true Old Rose character and has a strong Old Rose fragrance. We named this rose after Miss Hilda Murrell not long before her tragic death in 1984. Miss Murrell was one of the pioneers of the reintroduction of the Old Roses after the Second World War. Austin (U.K.), 1984.

LEANDER. A seedling from 'Charles Austin', which, in fact, looks very much like a smaller flowered version of that rose. The colour of the flowers is a very similar shade of deep apricot and there is the same strong fruit-like fragrance. The flowers are, however, of more perfect form, being a full rosette shape with their petals held in perfect spiral symmetry but, like 'Charles Austin', they lack something of the softness of character we look for in an Old Rose. They are held in large open sprays on a tall shrub of 8ft. or more in height. This is the most healthy and vigorous of all the English Roses, with shiny dark green disease-resistant foliage similar to that of a Modern Rose. As is so often the case with a large shrub of this kind, it flowers only occasionally after the first magnificent display. Austin (U.K.), 1982.

SHROPSHIRE LASS. The result of a cross between the Hybrid Tea 'Madame Butterfly' and the Alba 'Madame Legras de St. Germain', this rose forms a tough shrub of some 8ft. in height, or it may be grown as a climber that will reach 15ft. on a wall. Its blush-white flowers are almost single, 4 or 5ins. across, with a large boss of stamens. Both leaves and growth show some sign of their Alba ancestry. This is a beautiful rose that deserves to be more widely grown, particularly as a climber, when its nicely poised flowers show off to maximum effect. Austin (U.K.), 1968. See page 220.

Chapter 7

ENGLISH ROSES NOW AND IN THE FUTURE

Having completed my descriptions of the English Roses and, I hope, in the process, given some idea of their overall character, perhaps I may be permitted to discuss them a little further and put forward some ideas for their future development.

There are many gardeners who prefer the more natural rosette or cupped style of the Old Roses, and feel that such flowers are capable of greater beauty, and indeed greater variation of beauty, than are the pointed bud flowers of Modern Roses. I myself very much prefer the style of Old Roses, although I feel there is room for both in our gardens.

There is, however, a frequent complaint that the Old Roses, for all their beauty, flower only once in the year — that they are not recurrent flowering. For this reason many gardeners will not grow them, preferring to confine themselves to the Modern Roses with their extended season of bloom. Although I think non-repeating roses have an important part to play in our gardens, there are obvious advantages in having Old Roses that flower throughout the summer. It is, of course, true that the roses described in Chapter 3 — the Chinas, Portlands, Bourbons and Hybrid Perpetuals, are recurrent flowering but, with the exception of the Chinas, they do not usually excel in this respect. Beautiful though some of them are it is, I think, also true to say this is a group of roses which never reached its full potential. Before this was possible they were overtaken by the Hybrid Teas which were roses of quite a different kind.

Roses have always been changing and, like almost everything else, are changing faster than ever now. It is a far cry from the Gallicas and Damasks of long ago to the Hybrid Teas and Floribundas of today. Indeed, it is doubtful if the gardeners of earlier times would have been able immediately to recognise many present day roses as being roses at all, so great has been this change. Fine though Modern Roses may be, to me, at least, more has been lost than gained. Above all, they have lost much of that essential quality of 'rosiness': the softness that is the essential nature of the Old Roses, and that unique quality which first gave them their very special place in our lives.

Meanwhile there *have* been gains, not only in the remarkable ability of the Hybrid Teas and Floribundas to flower with such exceptional freedom

JAYNE AUSTIN, *English Rose. A beautiful rose, showing a Noisette influence in its delicate, sheeny-petalled flowers.* *See page 193.* Knight

BROTHER CADFAEL, *English Rose. One of the largest English Roses, but never lacking in refinement.* *See page 180.* Knight

GERTRUDE JEKYLL, *English Rose. Exceptionally fragrant flowers of true Old Rose character. Strong and reliable.* *See page 192.* Knight

GRAHAM THOMAS, *English Rose. Cupped flowers in a good shade of yellow. Strong tea fragrance.* *See page 192.*

Page

ENGLISH ROSES, *together with Polyantha types, left and right. English Roses are ideal for flower arrangements and, unlike most Old Roses, flower throughout the summer.* Knight

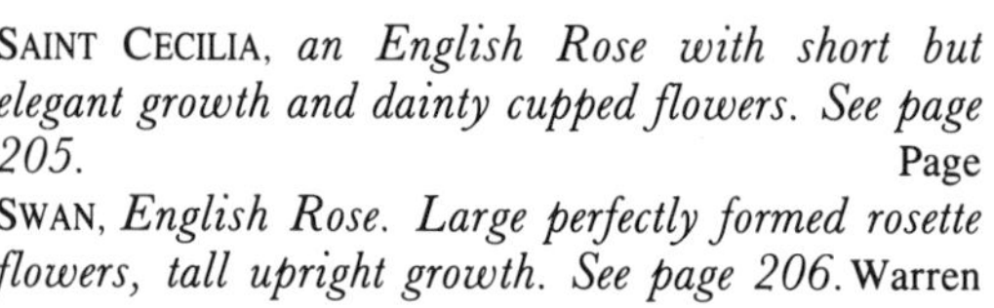

SAINT CECILIA, *an English Rose with short but elegant growth and dainty cupped flowers. See page 205.* Page

SWAN, *English Rose. Large perfectly formed rosette flowers, tall upright growth. See page 206.* Warren

PRETTY JESSICA, *English Rose. A short grower for the smaller garden. See page 196.* Warren

DAPPLE DAWN, *English Rose. This rose and its parent 'Red Coat' are two of the most continuous flowering of all shrub roses. See page 190.* Calvert

PROSPERO, *English Rose. Perfectly formed crimson rosettes. Short growth. See page 196.* Calvert
CHAUCER, *English Rose with Old rose flowers and a strong myrrh scent. See page 189.* Warren

BREDON, *English Rose. A short, tough little rose, flowering freely and repeatedly. See page 180.* Warren
DR. JACKSON, *English Rose. A good garden shrub providing a splash of dazzling colour. See page 211.* Knight

CHARMIAN, *English Rose. Medium shrub, large flowers, strong fragrance. See page 189.* Page
GRUSS AN AACHEN, *a rose of English type with charming cupped flowers. See page 193.* Page
SHROPSHIRE LASS, *English Rose. A tall summer flowering shrub or Climber. See page 211.* Knight

HERO, *English Rose. Cupped flowers of exceptional purity of colour. See page 193.* Page
YELLOW BUTTON, *English Rose. The flowers usually in deeper colours than seen here. See page 209.* Page
THE REEVE, *English Rose. Very cupped flowers and attractive arching growth. See page 207.* Calvert

and almost continually through the summer, but also in the greatly extended colour range. Formerly the colour yellow was barely known, as were all those colours allied to it — apricot, peach, buff and so on. Shades of red tended towards mauve and purple (often with the most pleasing effects), but pure crimsons and scarlets were conspicuous mainly by their absence.

The English Roses represent an attempt to go back in time, and to carry on the traditions of the Old Rose. Surely the present popularity of Old Roses suggests that the attempt is worth while? This does not mean that I recommend returning to them exactly; I do not think this would be desirable, but I should like to recapture something of their charm, while at the same time creating roses with an essential character of their own. It is, of course, possible to breed more Gallicas, Damasks, Moss Roses, etc., but to do so it would be necessary to breed from each of them alone — it is not possible to have them once we have interbred with the descendants of the China Rose for the slightest mixture of China Rose genes would change their character.

There is one point I should like to emphasise before going any further. I think that in the breeding of English Roses, or indeed any roses — or for that matter any other flower — we should approach this not just as a practical pursuit or as a science, but also as something in the nature of an art. 'Art' is a somewhat high-flown word, and ultimately perhaps a rather meaningless one, and I do not wish to sound pretentious; I only use it for the want of any better word. I think most people will see what I mean. In practice, the flower breeder does not have complete control of his craft; nature is not so accommodating. In spite of this, the breeder does have it in his power to push things in the general direction he may desire. He can at least select that which appeals to him— when he has the good fortune to find it, which is perhaps not much less than anyone can do in whatever their field of endeavour.

In the breeding of the English Roses it has always been my aim first of all to hybridize, and then to select for the overall beauty of the plant. That is to say, for the charm, character and fragrance of the flower; for the elegance and grace of growth and leaf. Only then do I consider the more practical aspects of reliability, toughness, disease resistance, and freedom and regularity of flowering, vital though these undoubtedly are. This, I believe, is the reverse of the practice of breeders in recent times. The tendency has too often been to see the rose as a machine for the production of flowers. The rose, it has been assumed, would automatically be beautiful. This unfortunately is not so. There has been a decline in the beauty of Modern Roses which has been reflected in a decline in the public's interest in them (although this decline has to some extent been offset by an increased interest in Shrub Roses). I really cannot see that the practical has much value without the aesthetic.

What then is the nature of an English Rose? What should be our aims and objectives for this group? The answer to these questions can be arranged under various headings: the form of the flower, the habit of growth, the foliage, its colour and fragrance, and the way in which all these characteristics come together to form a whole, together with such practical considerations as recurrent flowering, vigour and freedom from disease, which make it all possible.

For a hundred years now the breeder has striven for the pointed bud of the Hybrid Tea. The achievement of this ideal was made possible by the introduction of the China Roses, more particularly 'Parks' Yellow China' which had something of *Rosa gigantea* in its make up. *R. gigantea,* as we shall see in the chapter on the Species Roses, has huge, single flowers with long petals and slim pointed buds. The bud flower can be of exquisite beauty, particularly if it is not developed to the point where the bloom becomes large and clumsy. Unfortunately the open flower tends to be shapeless and lacking in quality — a jumble of petals of no particular form.

In the English Roses we return to the open flower. It may or may not have attractive buds. If it does these will probably be round, opening to tight cups filled with developing petals. The buds can be charming, but it is in the open flower that the rose is most likely to reveal its full beauty. This is how it always was in the past — no different, in fact, to the form which we find in the peony or in many other flowers. One of the great advantages of such a flower formation is the long period over which it remains attractive, from the opening of the bud to the fall of the petals. Each day, indeed almost hourly, the flower is changing from one shape to another. Although this is also true of the early stages of the flowers of a Hybrid Tea, it ceases with the collapse of the bud. Not only does the English Rose hold its shape for a long period, there is also a greater variation between the varieties. Flowers may be deeply cupped or shallowly cupped; these cups may be filled with petals or they may be open, sometimes exposing their stamens to add further to the attraction. They may be rosette shaped — indeed the very word 'rosette' derives from the rose; such flowers may open flat, or the petals may recurve. Flowers may also be single or semi-double. Nor are we restricted to these forms; there are many gradations of shape between them. To me, such roses have an appeal that is not to be found in any other flower. Why this should be is hard to say, but it is probably due to the play of the light between the petals and, indeed, through the petals, which makes possible the most delightful and ever-changing effects.

The Hybrid Teas, as I have said in the chapter on those roses, brought with them an important innovation. Unlike all the roses that preceded them they were short bushes of some 3 to 3½ ft. in height that had to be hard pruned each year. Their chief purpose was as bedding plants — the rose bed became 'the thing'. No longer was the rose to be grown with other flowers, it was to have a place all to itself. Such growth and pruning does have one great advantage; it results in more continuous flowering. The disadvantage is that these bushes can never have the grace of their more shrubby forebears. The larger the plant, the greater its capacity for graceful growth. Taller, more bushy, more spreading or arching growth cannot but carry with it the possibility of a more elegant and graceful shrub. This is our aim with the English Roses. It has to be admitted that it is a difficult task to combine shrubbiness with recurrent flowering, at least in large shrubs, but a lot of progress has been made in this direction.

Foliage is no less important than growth. This may be not only beautiful in itself, but also provides the setting for the flower and has a vital effect on the appearance of the whole plant. It may differ between varieties in size, shape, colour and texture, and varying effects can be produced, thus adding greatly to the attractiveness and interest of the shrub. The English Roses, thanks to the diversity of their parentage, offer a wide range of foliage.

The introduction of genes from *R. foetida* into the Hybrid Teas led to a great deal of development in yellow shades. New and various colour combinations became possible, but unfortunately these did not always yield the best results. Mere multiplication of colours is not necessarily desirable in itself; the important thing is that the colours should be good colours, and colours suitable to roses. In the Modern Rose colours have too frequently tended to be harsh and metallic in appearance. With the English Roses we have returned to softer, and sometimes richer, shades which seem to us to be much more in keeping with the spirit of the rose. I am not against any particular colour, but just as we would not choose any colour regardless for our homes, so we should be careful to choose suitable colours for our gardens and our roses. A colour that would be ideal for an iris would not necessarily be ideal for a rose. Moreover, many Modern Roses are in such harsh shades they do not mix well with other flowers. Worse than this, they do not mix well even with each other, and for this reason it is frequently recommended they should be planted in beds of one variety. This may be desirable at times, but it is sad that it should ever be a necessity, and in any case in most modern gardens it is not practical.

The fragrance of the English Roses is, I am pleased to say, particularly strong in the majority of varieties. This fortunately has not been too difficult to achieve. The Old Roses, from which in part English Roses spring, are, of course, noted for their fragrance, and this characteristic seems to persist down the generations, although I am always in fear of losing it. This can so easily happen — and has happened with other kinds of roses: a parent arises that is first class in every respect except fragrance, and because it is considered to be so good it is widely used for further breeding, thus reducing the fragrance of all its descendants.

The perfumes of roses are many — indeed it sometimes seems that all the fragrances of the garden are to be found in one or other rose species or variety, and many of them are to be found in the English Roses. The most unusual is that of 'Constance Spry' which, as I have said, is similar to that of myrrh, a scent that has proved very persistent in its descendants. From other sources comes the traditional Old Rose scent, the most rich and delicious of all fragrances; then there is the Tea Rose scent, the sharp scent of fresh fruit, the scent of the Scottish Brier and many shades between. I would like to think we might look forward to the time when we will breed for quality of scent as we now breed for quality of form. Scent is one of the most important aspects of a rose, but it is the one for which the breeder or nurseryman is least likely to be rewarded: it is difficult to describe, you cannot photograph it, and it is not very evident in the individual bloom at flower shows. People seldom buy a rose for its scent, although they will almost certainly be disappointed when they have it in their garden and find that it has none.

We have now discussed the five aspects of the rose: form, growth, leaf, colour and scent, but it does not quite end there; perhaps more importantly there is the manner in which all these come together, the general demeanour of the plant. There is not much that can be said about this; it is a matter of what we might call 'taste'. In the end, everything depends on the feeling an individual has for a certain rose. This really is the problem with rose trials with their point systems and awards. A rose may gain full points in all categories and yet turn out to be less than desirable.

The reader may have noticed there is one theme running through the last few pages of this chapter, and that is variety. We should not be looking for a standardised rose, or for roses that conform to a standard set of requirements. Our aim should be to create as much variation as possible between different roses. For the breeder, of course, it is often necessary to work on one theme for many generations, but within roses as a whole I should like to see developments in many different directions, whether it be in flower, growth or leaf. Variety, we are told, is the spice of life and with roses this is particularly true. They are now planted so widely and are to be found in so many gardens, that if we do not have this variety there is a grave danger people will become bored through sheer repetition and over-familiarity. This has to be guarded against, and more especially in our time when it is convenient and more profitable for commercial growers to mass produce a small number of varieties and foist them on the public — whether they like them or not.

Finally, we must consider what I have called the practical aspects of roses: their ability to grow, flower and resist disease. A rose that will not grow properly is of very little use to anyone, and it has to be admitted that some of the earlier English Roses were lacking in this respect. There were good genetic reasons for this. It is not possible to start at the beginning again, as it were, and have all the virtues at once. However, in breeding English Roses, we do have one advantage in that we do not have to strive for an artificial flower form, as is the case with the Hybrid Teas, and this does relieve us of a very considerable restriction. The drive for a particular form of flower makes it more difficult for us to develop other important qualities. With the English Roses a wide variety of species and classes of roses can be involved in their make up, without necessarily losing the desired shape of flower. The use of a wide range of roses has opened up greater possibilities. It has also afforded a degree of hybrid vigour. These factors make strong and healthy English Roses possible.

Disease resistance in English Roses is comparable to that in the Floribundas. It is an unfortunate but inescapable fact that repeat-flowering roses are more liable to disease than non-repeating. The main diseases of the rose are mildew and blackspot, both of which develop easily on young growth. The repeat-flowering rose is, by its very nature, always producing new growth in order to make more flowers. Thus we have a continual supply of soft young growth, making it easy for a disease to hop quite happily from an older leaf to a new leaf as the season progresses, multiplying as it goes. With a non-recurrent rose the pattern is quite different. These produce growth and retire for the year, leaving the leaves hard and disease resistant. With a repeat flowering Shrub Rose the problem is even greater than with Hybrid Teas. A Bush Rose is pruned very low, leaving little old growth to carry disease on into the following season. With a Shrub Rose, if it is to remain a shrub, we have to leave more growth, and thus there is a greater chance of the disease continuing. Having said this, I would not like the reader to think disease in repeat-flowering Shrub Roses is necessarily a great problem.

It is sometimes said that, other than in minor areas, there is not much scope left in roses for further development. Nothing could be further from the truth. The rose is a genus of such wealth and variety that the possibilities are almost endless. The English Roses are an example and it would be nice to think that other breeders might take them up, for only then can they come to their full potential. There is ample room for development. Should breeders do this, my only prayer is that they should devote themselves to the aesthetic qualities I have been describing, as well as to the practical. There can be little doubt that if they were to treat English Roses as so many flowers have been treated in recent times, our last state might well be worse than our first. It is not difficult to visualise giant gaudily-coloured, open roses, like huge dahlias on short bushes. Such horrors are well within the capacity of the rose and might even, for a short time, gain popularity.

It is sad to say, but it cannot be denied, that a great deal of what the plant breeder touches turns to dross. How many flowers have been taken up by the plant breeder and gained a short popularity, only to sink back into obscurity? Giant over-sized dahlias and chrysanthemums, lolloping gladioli, huge, frilly, collapsing irises, blinding geraniums and so on. Consider, too, the humble polyanthus, with its once simple charm bred from the cowslip and the primrose. How are these now? The truth is that flower breeders tend to be concerned with the more and more, while they should be concerned with the better and more beautiful. There must be a point where the search for more flowers, larger flowers, or brighter flowers becomes counter-productive and eventually ends in the downfall of the flower concerned. In time, the public always tire of such productions and true values reassert themselves. We must try to discern the essential spirit of a flower and develop it. This, of course, is no easy matter, but it provides a field that is almost endless in its extent.

Chapter 8

SHRUB ROSES OF OUR TIME

By 1920 most of the wild species roses of the world had arrived in Western Europe and, as we have seen, there had already been a huge proliferation of garden roses. It was the crossing of certain of these species and their hybrids with garden varieties that gave rise to the roses discussed in this chapter. That is to say the Rugosa Hybrids, the Hybrid Musks and the Modern Shrub Roses, as well as the more recent so-called Ground-cover Roses. The garden roses used were, in the main, Tea Roses, Hybrid Perpetuals, and more particularly the Hybrid Teas. The resulting roses are usually quite large shrubs, perhaps 5 or 6ft. in height, although they are frequently much smaller, and at times larger.

The roses in this chapter usually inherit something of the modern garden roses' ability to repeat flower, and are thus very useful garden shrubs, flowering as they do when most shrubs of other genera have finished, often continuing late into the summer. Being taller, they have a grace of growth not found in the shorter Bush Roses — it requires some length of stem to make this possible. At the same time it is difficult, if not impossible, for Shrub Roses to rival Bush Roses in continuity of bloom. It seems that the maintenance of a large shrub leaves less energy for recurrent flowering. The flowers generally do not have the bud formation of the Hybrid Tea, nor do they have the full open flower of the Old Rose, but tend to be semi-double and informal, producing a mass of colour. Having said this, it is important to stress that they are usually in no way gaudy, but provide the gentle colour effects so suitable to the rose.

Recent years have seen the appearance of certain varieties that are in effect no more than very large Floribundas. These are usually the by-products of some hybridist's Floribunda breeding programme which has turned up something too large in growth for that class. Such roses are, in my opinion, seldom very desirable.

RUGOSA ROSES

Rosa rugosa is a native of northern China, Japan and Korea. It was grown as a garden shrub in China, where it was said to have been used for pot-pourri, and Bunyard in his book *Old Garden Roses* (1936) speaks of a drawing by Chao Ch'ang who lived about A.D. 1000. It was also grown in Japan, and this explains why its descendants are sometimes known as Japanese Roses. The exact date of its arrival in Britain seems to be in some doubt, but it is thought to have been first introduced by the nurserymen Lee and Kennedy of Hammersmith in 1796. It forms a vigorous and sturdy shrub of up to 8ft. in height and as much across. It has very numerous strong thorns and rough-textured apple-green leaves. The flowers are large, 3½ to 4ins. across, of a variable purple-rose colouring, and have a light fragrance. These are followed by giant red tomato-shaped hips of 1in. or more in diameter. The stamens are creamy rather than the usual yellow, and this assorts well with the flower colour. It has two other important qualities: first, it is extremely hardy, and secondly it is almost alone among wild roses in its ability to repeat its flowering throughout the summer, so much so that later in the season the ripe hips can be seen on the branch at the same time as the last blooms. Although the colouring of the flowers may not be to everyone's taste, it is, in fact, a very fine shrub that can be relied upon to thrive in the poorest sandy soils.

With all these virtues, it is not surprising that a large number of hybrids have been raised and that these have become recognised as a class in their own right. Most of them were bred in the period immediately before and after the turn of the century when some excellent shrubs were produced combining the shrubby virtues of *R. rugosa* with the varying colours of the garden roses of the time. These hybrids are also large shrubs, and many of them have inherited the recurrent-flowering character of the species. Often they have lost some of the grace and bushiness of this parent, and some do not have its fine hips, but they form an often beautiful and very useful class. In spite of this, one cannot help feeling this group has never reached its full potential; after the first flush of interest little work has been done on them. This is perhaps largely due to the fact that the wrong parents have been used. *R. rugosa* is a diploid, while most garden roses are tetraploid and this has resulted in sterile offsprings, thus blocking further progress. However, such problems can be overcome, and a rich field of endeavour is open to future breeders. I feel sure that the Rugosas have it in them to be the best of all large garden shrub roses, so many of the required virtues are already inherent in the species.

The Rugosas are far removed from the roses of the West in their overall appearance. Indeed, they seem to have an almost Oriental character, both in flower and growth, and would look quite in place in a Chinese painting. One less fortunate result of this is that they do not always make a happy marriage when hybridized with garden roses. When the hybrid leans towards the Rugosa side of the parentage, all is well, but when it leans towards the other parent, the result can sometimes be rather clumsy. The variety 'Ruskin' is an example of this problem. In fact, these roses are rather unusual in that they seem to lean quite distinctly either towards their Rugosa parent on the one hand, or towards the garden rose on the other, seldom anywhere in between, and I shall try to make clear to which type they belong in each of the descriptions. It is necessary to take this factor into account when trying to visualise them in position in the garden.

Rugosa Hybrids are easily grown and require the minimum of attention. Pruning can be restricted to the thinning and removal of old and weak wood, also — and more importantly — to the encouragement of a shapely shrub, particularly with those varieties that tend towards a gaunt and rather upright growth.

Rugosas form excellent and impenetrable hedges or barriers, they are ideal for poor soil where other roses might find it difficult to thrive, and they are useful for seaside planting, withstanding the buffeting of the wind better than most roses. I have seen them growing quite happily on sand dunes — an ability they share only with the Scotch Roses, at least in so far as garden roses are concerned.

AGNES. This is a cross between *Rosa rugosa* and *R. foetida* 'Persiana', and the latter parent has placed a strong stamp upon it. The result is a rose that is still very much a Rugosa but with typically Old Rose flowers and many small petals of yellow tinted with amber, later fading to cream. It is, in effect, a yellow Old Rose, and this gives it a particular value to those in favour of this form. A mixture of the not altogether pleasing scent of *R. foetida* 'Persiana', and the scent of the Rugosa, has resulted in a delicate and unusual fragrance in this rose. The growth is upright, bushy and strong, perhaps 7ft. in height and 5ft. across, with rather small, pale green leaves. It is subject to rust in some gardens. Bred by B. & W. Saunders (Canada), introduced 1922. See page 260.

BELLE POITEVINE. A shapely shrub of 5ft. in height by as much across, and close to *Rosa rugosa* in its general appearance, having large semi-double, loosely-formed flowers of mallow-pink that open flat to show creamy-white stamens. They have a slight fragrance and are followed by large orange-red hips. Raised by G. Bruant (France), introduced 1894. See page 260.

BLANC DOUBLE DE COUBERT. A rose with all the appearance of a double form of *Rosa rugosa* 'Alba'. The flowers are large, pure white, sometimes tinged with blush in the bud, the petals having an almost papery appearance and opening semi-double with a strong fragrance. The growth is very similar to *R. rugosa* 'Alba', but a little less strong. The breeder, Cochet-Cochet of France, claimed that it was the result of a cross between *R. rugosa* and the beautiful Tea Rose 'Sombreuil'. It would be easy to come to the conclusion that there has been some mistake here, not an uncommon occurrence among older roses. However, *R. rugosa* is so dominant a seed parent that it frequently leaves little trace of the pollen parent, and it is quite possible the parentage is as the breeder stated. This is one of the best of the Rugosas, growing well and flowering with remarkable continuity. There are only a few hips. Height 5ft. Introduced 1892. See page 260.

CARMEN. A variety with small and, individually, quite attractive single, dark crimson flowers. Unfortunately the growth is rather upright and the flowers do not show up well, the whole effect being one of imbalance and poverty. It was a cross between *Rosa rugosa rosea* and the Hybrid Perpetual 'Princesse de Béarn'. Bred by Lambert (Germany), 1907.

CONRAD FERDINAND MEYER (more conveniently known as 'Conrad F. Meyer'). The parentage of this rose is 'Gloire de Dijon' × 'Duc de Rohan' × a form of *Rosa rugosa.* Its growth is very tall and upright, with unusually long strong stems shooting freely from the base, so that it can, if desired, be grown as a Climber. There are numerous strong thorns, and the foliage is about half-way between that of a Hybrid Tea and *R. rugosa.* This rose has always been available in nursery catalogues, even at the time when Shrub Roses were almost entirely neglected. The reason lies, perhaps, in its large Hybrid Tea-like blooms. These are of a soft silvery-pink with the petals nicely rolled at the edges. Later they open into large, cupped, informal flowers. The fragrance is, to me, one of the most delicious of any to be found among roses, and very strong. It is interesting to note that *R. rugosa* has only a light scent, but when crossed with other roses it often produces seedlings with a very strong scent. This rose is best pruned to half its height in order to form a reasonably shapely shrub, and if it is not to exhibit its flowers to the sky only. It flowers freely and produces a good second crop later in the summer. The height will depend on pruning, but left to its own devices it will easily reach 10ft. Bred by Müller (Germany), introduced 1899.

DELICATA. A rather weak shrub by Rugosa standards, growing to little more than 3ft. in height, and it would, therefore, not be a first choice except where space is limited. It is otherwise close to *Rosa rugosa* in general appearance. The flowers are semi-double and of a pleasing soft lilac-pink. Raised by Cooling (U.S.A), introduced 1898.

DR. ECKENER. One of the most massive and powerful of the Rugosas; so much so that few can find space for it, and severe pruning leads only to more growth and less flowers. It may have its uses in poor soils. The blooms are coppery-yellow, becoming pink and yellow with age, and are large and of Hybrid Tea character. Excessively thorny. A coarse rose though it has a strong fragrance. Height 10ft. The breeding is 'Golden Emblem' × a *Rosa rugosa* hybrid. Bred by Berger (Germany), introduced 1931.

FIMBRIATA ('Phoebe's Frilled Pink', 'Dianthiflora'). This pretty rose has, as its various names indicate, flowers fringed at the edges in the manner of a pink. This is probably the result of some breakdown in the genetic make up of the plant, due to the difficult step between its two widely separated parents, *Rosa rugosa* and the vigorous Noisette Rose 'Madame Alfred Carrière'. Such peculiarities do occur in many garden plants in the course of hybridization — in this case the result is a happy one. In spite of the robust nature of both parents 'Fimbriata' is not a particularly vigorous shrub, although adequately so. The growth is rather slim with quite small, light green foliage. The flowers are small, soft pink, fragrant and held in clusters. It has a delicacy that is more beautiful than we find in its more robust competitors the Grootendorst Roses. Height 4ft. Bred by Morlet (France), 1891. See page 239.

F.J. GROOTENDORST. Like 'Fimbriata' this variety has small flowers with fringed petals, but in this case the results are less pleasing. It is a cross between *Rosa rugosa* 'Rubra' and the Polyantha Pompon Rose 'Madame Norbert Levavasseur'. The flowers, which are of a rather dull crimson, lack the delicacy of 'Fimbriata' and are carried rather too tightly in their sprays. The growth is very strong, upright and bushy, and the leaves show signs of its Polyantha parentage. It has no scent. On the plus side it is strong and entirely reliable and flowers more repeatedly than any other of the Rugosas, except its own sport and the species itself. It has in fact three sports: 'Pink Grootendorst', 'Grootendorst Supreme' and 'White Grootendorst', all of which are of very similar character and detailed below. Height 5ft. Raised by de Goey (Holland), introduced 1918.

FRU DAGMAR HASTRUP ('Frau Dagmar Hartopp'). A widely planted rose and a favourite with municipal authorities, no doubt because it lends itself to mass planting, being of short, bushy growth which can be pruned fairly hard without losing bloom. It might best be described as a shorter, light pink form of *Rosa rugosa.* The flowers are beautiful and delicate in appearance, the buds long and pointed and of a rich pink, opening to a clear light pink with creamy-white stamens. They are produced repeatedly and are followed by large deep red hips. Fragrant. It is thought to be a seedling from *R. rugosa.* Height 4ft. Hastrup (Denmark), 1914. See page 238.

GROOTENDORST SUPREME. A sport from 'F.J. Grootendorst', see above, with darker, garnet-red flowers. It is said to be rather less vigorous than its parent, to which, except for colour, it is similar. Yellowish-green leaves. Slight fragrance. Height 4ft. Grootendorst (Holland), 1936.

HANSA. At first sight this variety seems to be very similar to 'Roseraie de l'Hay', but on closer observation it soon becomes clear that it is a less beautiful rose. The flowers are fully double and of deep crimson-purple. It is strong, hardy and healthy, and from a nurseryman's point of view has the advantage that it propagates much more easily than 'Roseraie de l'Hay'. Typical Rugosa type. Fragrant. Height 4ft. Introduced by Schaum & Van Tol (Holland), 1905.

LADY CURZON. The parentage of this rose is *Rosa* 'Macrantha' × *R. rugosa* 'Rubra', a very promising cross and the result does not disappoint us. It forms a tangled shrub of some 8ft. in height and the same in width. The leaves are rough textured, like those of its Rugosa parent, and there are many strong thorns. The flowers are large, single and about 4ins. across, of a light iridescent pink, paling almost to white at the centre, with petals like crumpled silk and a fine boss of golden stamens. They are fragrant but not recurrent. This variety is excellent in the border or in the more wild areas of the garden, where it will scramble quite happily for 20ft. in all directions in shrubs and trees if required, providing charming natural effects. Raised by Turner (U.K.), introduced 1901. See page 240.

MADAME GEORGES BRUANT. A cross between *Rosa rugosa* and the beautiful Tea Rose 'Sombreuil', resulting in a tall, narrow and somewhat ungainly shrub. The flowers start as shapely pointed buds of creamy-white and open to pure white flowers with three or four rows of petals and yellow stamens. They are held in small clusters which appear both in summer and autumn. Fragrant. Height 5ft. Raised by Bruant (France), introduced 1887.

MAX GRAF. A trailing rose and one of the best varieties for ground cover. The result of a cross between *Rosa rugosa* and *R. wichuraiana,* gaining its prostrate habit from the latter. It forms a thicket of growth about 2ft. deep and spreads over a wide area, its long shoots sometimes rooting themselves into the ground as they go. The flowers are of small to medium size, single, pale pink to almost white at the centre, with yellow stamens, and have the fresh, fruit-like fragrance of their Wichuraiana parent. It has plentiful, dark, glossy foliage, and flowers only in the early summer. A useful rose, not only in the border, but also for covering banks and other problem areas where dense ground cover is required. Bred by Bowditch (U.S.A.), 1919. See page 242.

MICRUGOSA. See Chapter 11.

MIGRUGOSA ALBA. See Chapter 11.

MRS. ANTHONY WATERER. Of all the Rugosas that are of obvious hybrid appearance, this is in many ways the most satisfactory. It has excellent leafy growth of 5ft. in height, spreading broadly to form a dense and shapely, domed shrub. Both flower and foliage are close to that of an Old Rose. The blooms open wide, full and slightly cupped and are of crimson colouring, with a strong fragrance. It produces an unfailingly good crop of flowers in early summer, followed by only occasional blooms later. If it was also repeat flowering this rose would be hard to beat. The parents were the Hybrid Perpetual 'Général Jaqueminot' × unnamed Rugosa hybrid. Introduced by Waterer (U.K.), 1898. See page 238.

NOVA ZEMBLA. A colour sport of 'Conrad Ferdinand Meyer', see above, the flowers being white with the very slightest tinge of pink. Equally good and similar in every way to its parent, although perhaps a little less vigorous. Discovered by Mees (U.K.), 1907.

NYVELDT'S WHITE. A beautiful single white rose, which might at first sight easily be mistaken for the excellent *Rosa rugosa* 'Alba'; closer observation reveals a rose of more refined appearance and rather more graceful growth. The leaves are smoother and their leaflets narrower and of a paler green than those of 'Alba'. The flowers are more elongated in the petal and about 4ins. across. They are fragrant, repeat well, and are followed by plentiful large, orange-red hips. A very good shrub. The parentage is stated as being (*R. rugosa* 'Rubra' × *R. cinnamomea)* × *R. nitida.* This is a little surprising, as there are no white roses in this cross, and it may be that *R. rugosa* 'Alba' was used rather than *R. rugosa* 'Rubra'. Raised by Nyveldt (Holland), introduced 1955. See page 239.

PAULII. See Chapter 11.

PAULII ROSEA. See Chapter 11.

PINK GROOTENDORST. A pink sport of 'F.J. Grootendorst', see above. Like its parent it is vigorous, though perhaps a little less so than the original, forming a strong, bushy, reliably repeat-flowering shrub. Discovered by Grootendorst (Holland), 1923. See page 239.

ROBUSTA. A recent introduction from Kordes of Germany. It bears abundant medium-sized, single, bright scarlet-red flowers continuously throughout the summer. The growth is very strong and dense, with many thorns and ample leathery, dark green foliage. There is a slight fragrance. This promises to be a useful addition to the Rugosas. The breeding was unnamed seedling × *Rosa rugosa* 'Regeliana'. Introduced 1979.

ROSA RUGOSA ALBA. An almost faultless if little sung shrub of good vigorous growth, 6ft. high by as much across, with ample foliage. It bears large 4in. pure white flowers which open from long, slender buds throughout the summer. These are followed by very large tomato-like orange-red hips that ripen together with the last of its blooms. Slight fragrance. This rose was originally a sport from *Rosa rugosa typica,* and as such would not come from true seed. However, strains have been developed that are almost pure, although the occasional purple-flowered plant will still occur. Seedling bushes of both *R. rugosa* 'Alba' and *R. rugosa typica* are ideal for massed landscape planting, particularly in public places, as both flower continuously throughout the summer, spreading and suckering freely to form a continuous thicket and, most importantly in such planting, they do not have the problem of suckering from a stock (anyone involved in landscape designing and maintenance will be well aware of the problems presented by suckers in the middle of a hundred closely planted 6ft. tall thorny shrub roses!) See page 238.

ROSA RUGOSA RUBRA (*R. rugosa* 'Atropurpurea'). A selected form from the species *R. rugosa typica.* The flowers are of a richer crimson, with the usual contrasting creamy stamens. It is a considerable improvement on the original. See page 238.

ROSA RUGOSA TYPICA (*R. rugosa rugosa).* This is a form of *R. rugosa* described in the introduction to this group. It is considered typical of the species, although it cannot be depended on to reproduce itself exactly from seed. *R. rugosa* is, in fact, a very variable species.

ROSERAIE DE L'HAY. A vigorous shrub, perhaps 8ft. in height, with fine dense spreading growth and luxurious typically Rugosa foliage. The flowers are very large and double, opening wide from attractively pointed buds, their colour a rich crimson-purple with a few creamy stamens to be seen among the petals. They are studded evenly among its leafy growth, showing themselves to perfection. It is one of the most beautiful and completely reliable shrub roses, repeating well, but with very few hips. Similar to 'Hansa', see above, but finer and of richer colouring. Said to be a double sport from *Rosa rugosa,* but this is doubtful. Bred by Cochet-Cochet (France), 1901, and named after the magnificent rose garden near Paris. See page 239.

RUSKIN. A cross between the Rugosa 'Souvenir de Pierre Leperdrieux' and 'Victor Hugo', it is the latter rose, a typical red Hybrid Perpetual, which has proved to be the dominant parent, with not altogether good results. It is true that it produces large and sumptuous rich scarlet-crimson cupped flowers of Old Rose character, but these are often misshapen and clumsy. Moreover, the growth is very tall and narrow, and by no means satisfactory. This can be improved by cutting the rose down to half its height each year, or it may be trained as a Climbing Rose. It has a rich and pleasing fragrance, but there is little or no repeat flowering. Height anything up to 8ft. Raised by Van Fleet (U.S.A.), introduced 1928.

SARAH VAN FLEET. A strong, bushy, upright shrub of 7ft. in height and 5ft. across. It is one of the most useful and reliable of the Rugosa hybrids, both for garden and municipal planting, especially at the backs of borders. The flowers are large, semi-double, opening wide and slightly cupped, china pink in colour, with yellow stamens. They are usually held in small clusters and appear both in summer and autumn. The growth and foliage is typically Rugosa, with rough-textured leaves and many thorns. Bred by Dr. Van Fleet of the U.S.A., reputedly from a cross between *Rosa rugosa* and 'My Maryland', but a chromosome count seems to place some doubt upon this. Introduced 1926. See page 260.

SCABROSA. Whether or not this is a selection from *Rosa rugosa* or a hybrid is hard to say. Certainly it has everything in common with the species, except that it is of more substance in every way. The flowers are very large, single and about 5½ins. across. Their colour is a rich violet-crimson with pale contrasting stamens. The growth is strong, spreading and bushy, with large, thick, very rugose leaves and many thorns. It has a slight fragrance and bears massive hips. Height 4 or 5ft. It was first introduced by Harkness & Co., of Hitchin, but Jack Harkness of that firm, in his book *Roses,* takes no credit for its breeding, saying it was discovered amongst a batch of a rose called 'Rose Apples', but otherwise being unable to say anything of its origin. See page 260.

SCHNEELICHT. There have been a number of successful hybrids between *Rosa rugosa* and other wild species, and this is one of them, being the result of a cross with *R. phoenicea.* It forms a broad mound of growth about 5ft. in height and 8ft. across, sending up long, arching branches that bear clusters of flowers all along their length. These start as pointed blush-tinted buds, opening to pure white single flowers of medium size with yellow stamens. It has dark green foliage close to that of *R. rugosa.* A useful Ground-cover rose. Bred by Geschwind (Hungary), introduced 1894.

SCHNEEZWERG ('Snowdwarf'). Reputedly a hybrid of *Rosa bracteata,* and from this species it may have inherited its dark, shiny foliage which bears little resemblance to a Rugosa. Its outstanding virtues are its compact, twiggy growth and shapely habit, together with its ability to flower continuously throughout the summer. The flowers are quite small, semi-double and purest white, with pale yellow stamens. They repeat well and are followed by pretty, small, orange-red hips. Height about 5ft. A good and reliable shrub, if a little unexciting. Raised by P. Lambert (Germany), introduced 1912. See page 260.

SOUVENIR DE PHILEMON COCHET. A sport from 'Blanc Double de Coubert', with very much more double flowers. These might be described as being similar to those of a double hollyhock, with large, rather papery outer petals enclosing numerous small inner petals. At their best they are very beautiful and quite unique, but unfortunately rather subject to damage in damp weather, and it would perhaps be better to avoid this rose in particularly moist areas. It forms a rather smaller shrub than its parent, but otherwise the growth is the same. 5ft. Discovered by Cochet-Cochet (France), 1899.

VANGUARD. An excessively vigorous and rather coarse shrub with large glossy foliage and large ill-formed flowers of modern appearance, orange-salmon in colour. It does not flower very freely, and if pruned continues to make more growth at the expense of flowers. Very fragrant. Breeding *Rosa wichuraiana* × *R. rugosa* 'Alba' × 'Eldorado'. Height up to 10ft. It can be used as a Climber. Stevens (U.S.A.), 1932.

WHITE GROOTENDORST. A white sport of 'Pink Grootendorst', the second in a line of sports from 'F.J. Grootendorst', see above, though the growth does not seem to be so strong as that of its forebears. In fact, there is often a decline in vigour when a sport occurs. Discovered by Eddy (U.S.A.), introduced 1962.

HYBRID MUSK ROSES

This is rather a misleading name for a group of roses that are only remotely connected with the Musk Rose via the Noisettes. It is, however, a pleasant name and conveys a more accurate feeling for the class than any other we are likely to come up with. These roses do, in fact, usually have a strong fragrance which is similar to that of the Musk Rose with its ability, in the words of Francis Bacon, to 'carry on the air'.

The Hybrid Musks are usually shrubs of 5 or 6ft. in height, although there are a few smaller varieties which are often of less value. The flowers are generally of small to medium size and held in sprays. Given adequate growing conditions they repeat flower well, sending up strong stems from the base to provide a second crop in late summer. It may be said that they are to the Shrub Roses what the Floribundas are to the Hybrid Teas, producing as they do an excellent massed effect. It is there that the analogy ends, for their growth is more graceful than that of a Bush Rose and their flowers are usually of soft colouring. Both growth and foliage are close to that of the Modern Rose, with its smooth, shiny texture.

The history of the Hybrid Musks begins in Germany in 1902, when Peter Lambert sowed what he believed to have been self-fertilized seed of a Rambler called 'Aglaia' and raised a variety that he named 'Trier'. 'Aglaia' was itself a cross between *Rosa multiflora* and the buff-coloured Noisette 'Rêve d'Or'. 'Trier', a 6ft. shrub or short Climber bearing sprays of small, nearly single white flowers tinged with cream and pink, had the great advantage that it was both repeat flowering and shrubby in growth. Lambert saw the possibilities of this variety and used it in the development of a number of roses he called 'Lambertiana'. Most of these were, in fact, of little merit, being not much more than rather large Polyantha Roses.

It was not long before the Reverend Joseph Pemberton took a hand. He lived in a village in Essex with the picturesque and appropriate name of Havering-atte-Bower, and here he raised a series of varieties we now call Hybrid Musks. These were the result of crosses between 'Trier' in particular, but also between certain Polyanthas and Noisettes, with a variety of different Hybrid Teas, Tea Roses and Noisettes. They were introduced by a nurseryman called J.A. Bentall, who also bred a few varieties himself, notably 'Buff Beauty' and 'Ballerina'.

There the story ends, for little more work has been done on the Hybrid Musks since that time. The problem seems to have been exactly the same as with the Rugosas, for in many cases the Hybrid Musks are also the result of crossing diploids with tetraploids, thus leading to varieties that are sterile and inhibiting further progress. Alternatively, it may be that no one has thought it worthwhile proceeding further. If this is so, I think it is a mistake, for it is possible to visualise many good things coming out of these roses and, as with Rugosas, the problem of sterility can be overcome.

The Hybrid Musks require good cultivation and adequate manuring if they are to reach their full potential. Well treated they will form graceful shrubs, bearing an abundance of bloom in summer and again in autumn. Being repeat flowering, pruning is important. Take out the old and weak wood as the shrub matures, and prune back the strong main shoots by one third to encourage new growth. Be careful to leave sufficient strong growth to enable the shrub to build up its structure, otherwise it may remain short.

In recent years a number of new roses have been introduced that seem to come very close to the Hybrid Musks in the nature of their growth. I am thinking mainly of the roses that I list as Ground-cover Roses, which are often not so much ground cover as sprawling shrubs. These new roses are usually without fragrance, but in growth are not dissimilar to Hybrid Musks, and the time may come when it will be convenient to place all these together in one class. Perhaps the linking factor would be that they all have some connection with the ramblers of the Synstylae family.

AUTUMN DELIGHT. As the name suggests this rose is notable for its display of flowers late in the season. These have considerable charm, being almost single and of cupped formation, yellow in the bud, creamy-yellow when open with contrasting dark stamens, and fading almost to white with age. The early blooms are held in small sprays, but later large heads are produced on shoots from the base of the plant. It grows to little more than 3ft. in height. Bred by Bentall (U.K.), introduced 1933.

BALLERINA. This is by no means a typical Hybrid Musk, being much more like a very large Polyantha, but do not let this deter you, as it is, in fact, a beautiful rose. Its small single Polyantha blooms held in many-flowered clusters are of a soft pink with a white centre. 'Ballerina' flowers with remarkable continuity, and combines this with quite exceptional toughness and reliability. It forms a tight, rounded shrub of 4ft. in height by almost as much across, while the flowers are held in close trusses, slightly reminiscent of a hydrangea. A mass planting of this rose can provide a pleasing effect, the flowers mingling attractively with its light green foliage. It is also excellent when grown as a standard. Slight fragrance. The parents are not recorded. Bred by Bentall (U.K.), introduced 1937. See page 255.

BUFF BEAUTY. One of the finest of the Hybrid Musks, bearing flowers of a lovely rich apricot-yellow and having a strong Tea Rose fragrance. They are semi-double to double, of medium size and held in small or large clusters on a well-balanced arching shrub which may be 5 or 6ft. in height and as much across. It has large, thick, dark green leaves, and its smooth stems are tinted with brown. When well grown, the whole plant has an appearance of almost tropical lushness. The breeding has not been recorded nor, so far as I know, has the breeder. Although I am well aware it is fruitless to surmise on such matters, I would hazard a guess it has 'Lady Hillingdon' as one of its parents, for its colour, growth and scent all seem to point to this. It is reliably recurrent flowering. One of the finest of the rather small number of yellow shrub roses available to us. See page 244.

CALLISTO. This is a small shrub of 4ft. in height, but quite broad and bushy. The flowers are small, rambler-like and held in tight sprays, and of a pleasing yellow shade, fading with age almost to white. Strong fragrance. A seedling from 'William Allen Richardson', it is thus probably a pure descendant from a Noisette Rose. Raised by Pemberton (U.K.), introduced 1920.

CORNELIA. A vigorous shrub bearing sprays of small, formal rosette-shaped flowers with three or four rows of petals. Their colour is apricot-pink at first, becoming creamy-pink with a distinct boss of yellow stamens at the centre. 'Cornelia' forms a fine, shapely shrub with quite small foliage. In the autumn large sprays of bloom are produced on the strong

PLEINE DE GRÂCE. *This superb Modern Shrub Rose will produce a greater mass of bloom than any other I know. It may also be used as a Rambler. See page 264.* Warren

MRS. ANTHONY WATERER, *Rugosa Rose. Rugosas are very durable and have a natural ability to repeat flower.* *See page 231.* Knight

ROSA RUGOSA ALBA. *See page 232.* Warren

FRU DAGMAR HASTRUP, *Rugosa Rose.* *See page 230.* Calvert

ROSA RUGOSA RUBRA. *Note how it is producing hips at the same time as flowers.* *See page 232.* Warren

ROSERAIE DE L'HAY, *one of the best of the Rugosa Roses. See page 232.* Knight

FIMBRIATA, *a Rugosa Rose with fringed petals like a pink. See page 229.* Knight

NYLVELDT'S WHITE *is similar to, though daintier than,* Rosa rugosa *'Alba'. See page 231.* Warren

PINK GROOTENDORST, *Rugosa Rose. Also fringed, but stronger than 'Fimbriata'. See page 232.* Calvert

LADY CURZON, *a* Rosa rugosa *hybrid with large silky-textured flowers on a sprawling shrub.* *See page 230.*
Calvert

FELICIA, *a fine example of this Hybrid Musk Rose, seen against a background of foliage.* *See page 245.*
Knight

CERISE BOUQUET, *Modern Shrub Rose. A typical spray of bloom of this large and elegant shrub.* *See page 250.* Knight

MAX GRAF, *a* Rosa rugosa *hybrid and one of the best of the Ground-cover Roses.* *See page 231.* Warren

FRÜHLINGSANFANG, *Modern Shrub Rose. Both this rose and 'Frühlingsgold' are robust shrubs that will grow in poor conditions. See page 252.* Calvert

FRÜHLINGSGOLD, *Modern Shrub Rose. See page 252.* Warren

PENELOPE, *one of the best Hybrid Musk Roses and always reliable. See page 246.* See page 246. Warren
BUFF BEAUTY, *another excellent Hybrid Musk Rose, seen here with herbaceous plants. See page 236.* Knight

new stems from the base of the plant. There is a strong fragrance that carries far. 'Cornelia' will grow to about 5ft. in height and spread to 6ft. The parents are not recorded but it appears to be closely related to 'Trier'. Bred by Pemberton (U.K.), introduced 1925. See page 256.

DANAË. A small shrub, 3 to 4ft. in height, bearing sprays of small, fragrant, deep yellow rambler-like flowers that fade to white as they age. 'Trier' × 'Gloire de Chédane-Guinoisseau'. Pemberton (U.K.), 1913.

DAYBREAK. A small shrub of about 3ft. in height with sprays of loosely formed semi-double flowers of pale yellow fading to ivory, and with dark yellow stamens. The foliage is tinted brown at first, later becoming dark green. Strong Musk Rose fragrance. 'Trier' × 'Liberty'. Pemberton (U.K.), 1918.

FELICIA. A strong and reliable shrub flowering very freely both in summer and autumn. Its parents were 'Trier' by the Hybrid Tea 'Ophelia', and the flowers, though small and held in large sprays, have something of the character of the latter rose about them. They begin as somewhat pointed apricot-pink buds, and open to rather informal blush-pink flowers with a strong aromatic fragrance. The foliage, too, leans towards the Hybrid Tea, both leaf and flower having rather more substance than is usual among the Hybrid Musks. It will form a broad, shapely, branching plant of 5ft. in height. A first class, practical shrub, that will also make a good hedge. Bred by Pemberton (U.K.), introduced 1928. See page 241.

FRANCESCA. A large, graceful shrub of 6ft. in height, with broad, arching growth. It is well clothed with foliage, the individual leaves being long and pointed. The long pointed buds of slim, Tea Rose elegance open to quite large, semi-double flowers which are nicely poised in well spaced sprays and coloured apricot-yellow fading to pale yellow. Strong Tea Rose scent. From 'Danaë' × 'Sunburst'. Raised by Pemberton (U.K.), introduced 1922.

MOONLIGHT. This is the result of a cross between 'Trier' and the early Tea Rose 'Sulphurea', although it leans heavily towards the former. The individual flowers are small, semi-double and white with yellow stamens, and are held in medium-sized sprays, followed by very large sprays late in the summer. 'Moonlight' is useful where a tall shrub is required as it will reach 8ft. or more in height, although it is more upright than broad and has been known to ascend up to 15ft. in trees. The stems are tinted mahogany, and the foliage dark green. Strong Musk Rose fragrance. Bred by Pemberton (U.K.), introduced 1913.

NUR MAHAL. One of the few red Hybrid Musks. The result of crossing the old dark crimson Hybrid Tea 'Château de Clos Vougeot' with an unspecified Hybrid Musk seedling. It is not so widely grown as many of the Hybrid Musks, which I think is unfortunate, for it is a rose of some character. The flowers are medium sized, crimson at first, opening wide and turning to mauve-crimson with contrasting yellow stamens. They have an evenness of outline that gives them a pleasing formality. The growth is wide and branching, about 4ft. in height and rather more across. Fragrant. Bred by Pemberton (U.K.), introduced 1923.

PAX. A cross between 'Trier' and 'Sunburst' resulting in a shrub rather similar to 'Francesca' which, in fact, shares 'Sunburst' as one of its parents. The growth is tall, broad and elegantly arching, with brown stems and dark green leaves. The flowers start as long pointed buds and open to large, loosely formed and semi-double white flowers with golden stamens and a pleasing fragrance. They are held in sprays of medium size which have a delicacy and natural charm the equal of any of this group. Further, often massive sprays follow late in the season. Height 6 to 8ft. Bred by Pemberton (U.K.), introduced 1918.

PENELOPE. This is usually regarded as one of the most reliable of Hybrid Musk Roses, indeed of all Modern Shrub Roses, and has for many years been widely used both in private gardens and for amenity planting. It forms an excellent full branching shrub of about 5ft. in height and a little more across. The flowers, which are of medium size and borne in large clusters, show some affinity to its mother parent, the Hybrid Tea 'Ophelia'. Coppery-salmon tinted buds open blush-pink and semi-double, soon becoming almost white, the overall effect being pale pink. They have a strong musky fragrance and are followed by pleasing coral-pink hips — a rare bonus in a repeat-flowering rose, although it may be preferable to remove the earliest of these when the petals fall to encourage further bloom. Bred by Pemberton (U.K.), introduced 1924. See page 244.

PINK PROSPERITY. Not, as the name might seem to suggest, a sport from 'Prosperity', but quite a different rose, with small tight-petalled, pompon flowers of clear pink and with a strong fragrance. It is robust and healthy and of rather upright habit. Overall, in both flower and growth, it lacks the softness and grace of other roses in this class. The breeding is not recorded — it is probably not of the usual Hybrid Musk origin and is more likely to be a Polyantha cross. Height 5ft. Bred by Bentall (U.K.), introduced 1931.

PROSPERITY. A cross between the creamy-blush Polyantha Rose 'Marie-Jeanne' and the Tea Rose 'Perle des Jardins', 'Prosperity' is, therefore, of rather different origin from most Hybrid Musks, being a hybrid of a Polyantha, and this shows up in its growth. However, the Tea Rose parent brings a softness and shrubbiness that renders this variety quite in keeping with the class. The growth is strong, bushy and rather upright, about 5ft. in height and slightly less across, with shiny, dark green foliage. The flowers are creamy-white, flushed with pink at first, later becoming ivory-white tinged with lemon at the centre. They are quite small and held in many flowered trusses. Good fragrance. Bred by Pemberton (U.K.), introduced 1919. See page 259.

THISBE. A small shrub of moderate vigour, carrying clusters of small, semi-double buff-yellow flowers soon paling to creamy-buff. It has a strong and pleasing fragrance. The breeding is the same as for

'Prosperity', see above, but this time we have a rose that is much closer in character to its Polyantha parent. Height 4ft. Bred by Pemberton (U.K.), introduced 1918.

TRIER. The foundation rose of the class described in the introduction to this section. It is not in itself a particularly outstanding variety, forming a rather upright shrub of 6 or 8ft. in height, with sprays of small, single white flowers tinted with blush and with a hint of yellow at the base. Thought to be a self-seedling from 'Aglaia'. Bred by Lambert (Germany), introduced 1904.

VANITY. A tall shrub of 8ft. in height, bearing large, almost single, light crimson flowers which are held widely spaced in open sprays. In late summer, long, strong shoots appear, often bearing huge many-flowered heads of bloom. The whole effect is one of light and airy grace. Due perhaps to its size, the branches are not plentiful and this often results in lop-sided and very open growth. For this reason it is a good idea to plant closely in groups of two or three bushes, so that they grow together to give the appearance of one fine shrub. 'Vanity' is ideal for the back of a large border, where its dainty flowers look very beautiful when seen above other plants. The foliage is dark green and rather sparse, a feature that seems only to add to its attraction by exposing its glaucous green stalks. There is a strong and pleasing fragrance. A cross between 'Château de Clos Vougeot' and unnamed seedling. Bred by Pemberton (U.K.), introduced 1920. See page 259.

WILHELM ('Skyrocket'). In 1927 Pemberton introduced a crimson Hybrid Musk called 'Robin Hood', the result of a cross with the crimson Polyantha 'Edith Cavell'. 'Robin Hood' is a rather dull variety showing a strong Polyantha influence, and in 1934 Kordes crossed it with the red Hybrid Tea 'J.C. Thornton' to produce 'Wilhelm'. The result of all this work is a rose that is rather far removed from what I would consider to be a true Hybrid Musk. It is modern in character, with rather upright growth similar to that of a large Floribunda. For all this, 'Wilhelm' provides a fine splash of colour, with a mass of small semi-double dark crimson flowers in large clusters. It repeats reliably and there are long-lasting orange-red hips in the autumn. There is only a slight fragrance. Height 5 to 6ft.

WILL SCARLET. A scarlet sport of 'Wilhelm', similar in every way except colour and providing a brilliant display. Light fragrance. Introduced by Hilling (U.K.), 1947.

MODERN SHRUB ROSES

We group under this heading a large number of Shrub Roses of widely varying origins, nearly all of them bred during the last fifty years. Perhaps the most important thing they have in common is that all but a few have some Hybrid Tea in their make up, a fact that often shows up in their appearance, both in flower and growth. They might well be said to be hybrids of the Hybrid Teas or Floribundas. The other side of their parentage may come from any one of a variety of species and classes, resulting in many widely differing shrubs.

It would be easy to draw the conclusion that these roses are a pretty ordinary lot and little more than overgrown Hybrid Teas or Floribundas. Indeed this sometimes is the case, and many of the new Shrub Roses passing through the various trial grounds fit the description perfectly. If, however, we select carefully, we can find what are undoubtedly some of the best Shrub Roses of this century. It is these that I have tried to include in my list.

Nearly all these roses are easily grown and very robust. More often than not they are recurrent flowering. They are, therefore, highly suitable for the average garden, and as this group includes some of the best known of all Shrub Roses, many of them are easily obtained at local garden centres. Most are extremely showy, producing masses of bloom. Local authorities buy them in large numbers, and no wonder, for there cannot be many shrubs of any kind that produce so much colour.

The name of Kordes occurs again and again among these roses, and it should be said that this firm has contributed more than any other to their development. Kordes was interested in breeding hardy Shrub Roses for the North European climate. Some of these may appear a little coarse, no doubt due to the pursuit of hardiness, to the exclusion of other qualities, but we have only to mention such varieties as 'Frühlingsmorgen', 'Fritz Nobis' and 'Cerise Bouquet', to realise how beautiful many of them are.

Cultivation is no problem. Good feeding and adequate pruning will yield a better performance and greater continuity of flowering, but due to the great diversity of habit of this class, it is not possible to be specific as regards pruning. Usually it is best to thin out weak wood and cut back the remaining growth by about a third, but a little imagination is called for here — where the growth is closer to the wild species greater freedom should be allowed and less pruning done.

Many of these shrubs are equally good as Climbers, perhaps for a wall, fence or pillar, and the majority of the taller kinds are suitable for growing in this manner.

ALCHEMIST. A vigorous upright shrub of 6ft. in height with plentiful, glossy foliage. The flowers, a mixture of yellow and yolk-yellow, are unusual among Modern Shrub Roses in that they are of typical Old Rose rosette shape, opening flat — in fact rather similar to those of the English

Rose 'Charles Austin', though less cupped in shape. They have a strong fragrance, but there is no second crop. 'Alchemist' can equally well be grown as a shrub or a Climber, when it might grow to 10ft. or more. This variety is the result of a cross between the Hybrid Tea 'Golden Glow' and a *Rosa eglanteria* hybrid. Bred by Kordes (Germany), introduced 1956. See page 282.

ALOHA. I have just described 'Alchemist' as being unusual among Modern Shrub Roses for its Old Rose flower formation; here we have another variety of which the same might be said.

When the once-flowering Rambler Rose 'Dr. Van Fleet' sported to produce the repeat-flowering rose 'New Dawn', the way was open to breed new and more reliably repeat-flowering Climbers. 'Aloha' is one of the results of such endeavours. However, since it is very short in growth, it is much better treated as a recurrent-flowering shrub, although it can be used as a Climber of 6ft in height. As a shrub it forms a rather floppy plant, its branches laden down with masses of heavy blooms. These are very double, deeply cupped in form and much like those of an old Bourbon Rose, while the colour is rose-pink, deeper on the outside of the flower. There is a strong fragrance. The foliage is glossy, leathery and disease resistant. If you have a low retaining wall, this rose can be planted on top and allowed to trail downwards with the most pleasing effect. 'Mercedes Gallart' × 'New Dawn'. Bred by Boerner (U.S.A.), introduced 1949.

AUTUMN FIRE ('Herbstfeuer'). An arching shrub bearing sprays of semi-double, fragrant, dark red flowers. In spite of its name, I have not found it to be particularly good in autumn, but it does have excellent, very large orange-red hips — perhaps it is to these that the name refers. Height 6ft. Kordes (Germany), 1961.

BLOOMFIELD ABUNDANCE. A miniature-flowered rose with tiny, pale pink Tea Rose buds of perfect scrolled formation. These are so like those of the rose 'Cécile Brunner', see Chapter 5, as to be almost indistinguishable at first sight. This is no doubt partly because the flowers are so small, but nevertheless the similarity is quite remarkable. The real difference is that 'Bloomfield Abundance' forms a shrub of some 6 or 8ft. in height, whereas 'Cécile Brunner' seldom grows to more than 4ft. The individual blooms can easily be recognised by one characteristic: on 'Bloomfield Abundance' the lobes of the calyx are unusually long and leafy for the size of the flower, trailing down as it opens; on 'Cécile Brunner' these are short.

'Bloomfield Abundance' is a tall, airy shrub, producing its blooms singly and in small clusters on long, wiry stems. Later in the year long shoots appear from the base of the plant in the manner of a Hybrid Musk Rose, and these produce dozens of widely separated flowers. It is a very reliable shrub, the result of a cross between a *Rosa wichuraiana* hybrid called 'Sylvia', and the Hybrid Tea Rose 'Dorothy Page-Roberts'. Bred by George C. Thomas (U.S.A.), 1920.

BONN. A strong, upright shrub of 6ft. in height and rather ungainly habit. The flowers are semi-double, orange-scarlet, becoming tinged with purple as they age. This rose is perhaps a little coarse, but repeats quite well and there are dark red hips in the autumn. Fragrant. 'Hamburg' × 'Independence'. Bred by Kordes (Germany), 1950.

CERISE BOUQUET. A unique rose that is difficult to compare with any other. It is the result of a cross between *Rosa multibracteata* and the Hybrid Tea Rose 'Crimson Glory'. The growth is tall and gracefully arching, 6 to 8ft. in height by as much across though examples of up to 12ft. are not uncommon and, when allowed to trail through other shrubs, up to 15ft. The flowers are quite small and surrounded by attractive, leafy grey-green bracts. Starting as prettily scrolled buds, they open semi-double and flat to expose their stamens and are of a pleasing cerise-crimson colour. The particular charm of this rose lies in the fact that the individual blooms are held on long, leafy, hanging stems fanning out in the most graceful manner from an already bending branch. The foliage is small, greyish-green and attractive. Although it can be a little temperamental when first planted, I can think of no faults. It has a rich, fruit-like fragrance. There is only one period of flowering, but then it is one of the most beautiful shrubs in the garden. I understand this rose will make a good Climber, and can well imagine that it would be very fine when so grown. Bred by Kordes (Germany), introduced 1958. See page 242.

CLAIR MATIN. A rose of modern appearance, bearing dainty, pale pink, semi-double flowers of medium size with a slight fragrance. It has branching, slightly arching growth of 7ft. in height and about 6ft. across. The foliage is deep green and leathery. Perhaps its greatest virtue is that it repeat flowers with remarkable reliability. 'Clair Matin' may equally well be grown as a Climbing Rose, when it will achieve a height of 12ft. 'Fashion' × ('Independence' × 'Orange Triumph') × 'Phyllis Bide'. Bred by Meilland (France), 1960.

COMPLICATA. See Chapter 11.

DENTELLE DE MALINES. Some years ago I received a number of new roses from Mr. Louis Lens of the well-known Belgian firm of rose specialists. All were bred by himself. I had them for a number of years before appreciating how good they were. They turned out to be exceptionally strong-growing shrubs, bearing masses of small rambler-like blooms in big trusses, and I selected from these three varieties which seemed to me to be the best. They were 'Dentelle de Malines', 'Pleine de Grâce' and 'Running Maid', all three of which are ideal for the larger garden or for mass planting in public places — indeed I can think of no roses that make a more impressive show. They are also beautiful and have attracted attention from visitors to the gardens at our nurseries. 'Dentelle de Malines' is a hybrid between *Rosa filipes* 'Kiftsgate' and an unspecified rose. It is particularly attractive, with the tiny, very cupped flowers of *R. filipes,* and of a lovely, soft clear pink colouring. The growth is elegantly arched and covered with shapely sprays of bloom. It is not recurrent flowering.

EDDIE'S JEWEL. A cross between the early light crimson Floribunda 'Donald Prior' and a hybrid of *Rosa moyesii,* this rose forms a shrub of 8ft. tall and 6ft. across. The growth and foliage bear some resemblance to *R. moyesii,* but the flowers, which are deep red, are semi-double. It will frequently produce some flowers in late summer. There are no hips. Bred by Eddie (Canada), 1962.

ERFURT. A well-formed shrub of branching, slightly arching growth with good foliage. The flowers, which are borne in small clusters, are of medium size, semi-double, and slightly cupped, their colour being rosy-pink with a prominent contrasting white centre and a boss of golden stamens. 'Erfurt' is not a glamorous rose, but it is reliable and repeats well. It has a light fragrance. Height 5ft. 'Eva' × 'Réveil Dijonnais'. Bred by Kordes (Germany), 1939.

FOUNTAIN. An upright shrub, 5ft. in height, bearing large blood-red typically Hybrid Tea flowers with shapely buds. They are of particularly pure colouring and have a strong fragrance. There is ample deep green disease-resistant foliage. It is nice to see a Hybrid Tea flower on a good shrub. Parentage unknown. Bred by Tantau (Germany), introduced 1970.

FRANK NAYLOR. Sprays of medium-sized, dusky-crimson semi-double flowers against complementary dusky, dark green foliage. A shrub of excellent branching habit, producing its flowers with quite exceptional continuity. This would be a good rose in every way were it not for its susceptibility to mildew, but it is worth growing in areas where this disease is not a problem. Bred by Harkness (U.K.), 1978.

FRED LOADS. A cross between two Floribundas, 'Orange Sensation' and 'Dorothy Wheatcroft', this rose will reach 6ft. in height, sending up long, strong, upright growth from the base. It is very much the giant Floribunda, but flowers freely and continually, providing a mass of semi-double flowers of orange-vermilion. The foliage is bright green, disease resistant and plentiful. Fragrant. Bred by Holmes (U.K.), 1968.

FRITZ NOBIS. A cross between the strong growing Hybrid Tea Rose 'Joanna Hill' and 'Magnifica', the latter being a direct descendant of the Penzance Sweet Brier 'Lucy Ashton'. It is remarkable how 'Fritz Nobis' has caught the strong, bushy growth of the Sweet Brier, and managed to combine this with the most charming Hybrid Tea-like flowers. The whole shrub remains in balance, growing to about 6ft. in height and the same across. The flowers start as perfect pointed buds and open to shapely semi-double flowers of a clear pink. Add to this a delicious clove scent, and we have one of the best Modern Shrub Roses. There are few roses capable of such a fine display. It is unfortunate this occurs only in early summer, but to ask more would, perhaps, be too much, and we do have the compensation of its dark red hips that last long into the winter. The foliage is large and dark green. Bred by Kordes (Germany), introduced 1940. See page 258.

FRÜHLINGSANFANG. W. Kordes introduced a number of Shrub Roses with the prefix 'Frühlings' or, in English, 'Spring', all of which are hybrids of one or other of the Pimpinellifolia group, and I list what I regard as the three best. These all flower early in the season, before most other garden roses appear. 'Frühlingsanfang' is a cross between 'Joanna Hill' and *Rosa pimpinellifolia* 'Grandiflora', and forms a large shrub, of species-like appearance, 9ft. in height by as much across. The flowers are large and single, ivory-white, opening flat, with yellow stamens, and are followed in autumn by maroon-red hips. Introduced 1950. See page 243.

FRÜHLINGSGOLD ('Spring Gold'). This is one of the most widely planted of all Shrub Roses, both in gardens and public places. The reason for this is not hard to explain, for no garden rose is more hardy, so reliable, or so easily grown, even under difficult conditions. The flowers are creamy-yellow in colour, fairly large, semi-double, with rich yellow stamens, and although they are rather untidy in form this does not matter in the mass. They have a strong fragrance that carries across the garden. There is only one period of bloom, early in the season, but what a magnificent flowering it is — the whole shrub is covered with flowers! It usually grows to about 7ft. high by as much across, although sometimes, if permitted, it will grow much larger. A hybrid of 'Joanna Hill' and *Rosa pimpinellifolia hispida.* Bred by Kordes (Germany), introduced 1937. See page 243.

FRÜHLINGSMORGEN ('Spring Morning'). The third member of this series is one of the most delicately beautiful of all single roses. The flowers are large, slightly cupped and perfectly formed. According to the strength of the sun, they can vary in colour from cherry-pink to clear rose-pink, paling a little towards the centre, and they have the most attractive, long and elegant maroon-coloured stamens. The growth is not quite so unfailingly robust as in the case of the two varieties above, but it will grow to about 5 or 6ft. in height and the same across. It cannot be said to be recurrent flowering, though there are frequently a few further blooms later in the year. The foliage is of a dark and leaden green. There is a slight fragrance. Breeding ('E.G. Hill' × 'Kathrine Kordes') × *Rosa pimpinellifolia* 'Grandiflora'. Bred by Kordes (Germany), introduced 1942. See page 258.

GOLDBUSCH. A low-growing, spreading bush with coral-tinted buds opening into semi-double or double ochre-yellow flowers with yellow stamens. These have a Tea Rose fragrance and there is a second crop later in the summer. The foliage is abundant, glossy and light green. Height 4ft. spreading to 5ft. Perhaps a little ordinary, but there are not too many Shrub Roses of this colour. Bred by Kordes (Germany), introduced 1954.

GOLDEN WINGS. It is rather surprising that good, repeat-flowering single roses are rare among Shrub Roses of garden origin, in spite of the fact that the rose is, of course, single flowered by nature. This variety does, however, have single flowers. They are large, perhaps 4 or 5ins. across, sulphur-yellow, fading slightly with age, with attractive brown stamens. They open from long, pointed buds and have a sweet fragrance. With

NEVADA, *one of the best Modern Shrub Roses, growing to 8ft. and covered in bloom.* *See page 263.* Warren

SMARTY, *a pretty modern Ground-cover Rose that repeats well. See page 268.* Warren
RUNNING MAID, *another Ground-cover Rose. It is a mass of colour when in bloom, but has one season of flowering only. See page 268.* Page

BALLERINA, *Hybrid Musk Rose. Perhaps the most reliable of all repeat-flowering Shrub Roses. See page 236.* Knight

MARGUERITE HILLING, *a Modern Shrub Rose with all the virtues of its parent 'Nevada'. See page 262.* Knight

CORNELIA, *Hybrid Musk Rose, seen here with* Rosa *'Paulii' behind.* *See page 236.* Warren

RAUBRITTER, *a Ground-cover Rose bearing sprays of unique enclosed cupped flowers. At the back a good example of 'Roseraie de l'Hay', though not in full flower.* *See page 268.* Knight

SCARLET FIRE, *Modern Shrub Rose. See page 265.* Calvert
FRÜHLINGSMORGEN, *Modern Shrub Rose. One of the most beautiful single roses. See page 252.* Calvert

FRITZ NOBIS, *a very good summer-flowering Modern Shrub Rose. See page 251.* Page
GOLDEN WINGS, *an excellent repeat-flowering Modern Shrub Rose. See page 252.* Page

VANITY, *a really beautiful tall single Hybrid Musk Rose. See page 247.* Knight

RED BLANKET, *a modern repeat-flowering Ground-cover Rose. See page 268.* Knight

DORTMUND, Rosa rugosa *hybrid. A very hardy Shrub or Climbing Rose. See page 309.* Knight

PROSPERITY, *one of the best Hybrid Musk Roses. See page 246.* Page

SARAH VAN FLEET. *See page 233.* Knight
AGNES. *See page 228.* Page
SCHNEEZWERG. *See page 234.* Page

BLANC DOUBLE DE COUBERT. *See page 228.* Calvert
BELLE POITEVINE. *See page 228.* Page
SCABROSA. *See page 233.* Page

The six Rugosa Roses illustrated here all make reliable shrubs.

these attractions goes a genuine ability to flower throughout the summer. 'Golden Wings' is a beautiful rose, with something of the charm of a wild species. If it has a fault, it is the fact that its growth is rather open, stiff and stick like, though this can be improved by careful pruning to encourage more branching growth. Its breeding is both complex and interesting: Hybrid Tea 'Soeur Thérèse' × (*Rosa pimpinellifolia* 'Grandiflora' × 'Ormiston Roy'). 'Ormiston Roy' was *R. pimpinellifolia* × *R. xanthina*. 'Golden Wings' is thus closely connected with two species of the Pimpinellifolia group. See page 258.

JAMES MASON. This is the result of hybridizing 'Scarlet Fire' and the Gallica Rose 'Tuscany Superb'. 'Scarlet Fire' is itself partly Gallica, so 'James Mason' is an interesting cross and a good example of what the breeder can do with Old Roses. The flowers are of a rich crimson colouring and have something of the formality and restraint of a Gallica. They are semi-double with two rows of petals and contrasting yellow stamens. There is abundant foliage of near Gallica appearance, which can at times obscure the flowers. Fragrant. Raised by Peter Beales (U.K.), introduced 1982.

KARL FÖRSTER. A cross between 'Frau Karl Druschki' and *Rosa pimpinellifolia* 'Grandiflora', with pointed buds opening into double pure white flowers with a slight scent. The growth is vigorous, up to 7ft. in height, with attractive greyish-green foliage showing signs of Pimpinellifolia influence. It should, I suppose, be considered together with the 'Frühlings' series, but it is rather different in character and is recurrent flowering. Bred by Kordes (Germany), introduced 1931.

KASSEL. A vigorous upright shrub of 6ft. in height, bearing semi-double cherry-red flowers in Floribunda-like clusters. It has a little more character than 'Bonn', see above, to which it is rather similar, but is still rather coarse. Slight fragrance. 'Kassel' may also be grown as a 12ft. Climber. Breeding 'Hamburg' × 'Scarlet Else'. Kordes (Germany), 1957.

LAVENDER LASSIE. Often described as a Hybrid Musk, this rose really has little in common with that group. It is more like a tall Floribunda, growing to about 4ft. in height and rather narrow. The flowers are 3ins. across and have something of the character of an Old Rose, with numerous small petals in rosette formation. The colour is a pale lavender, which is useful as there are few truly repeat-flowering Shrub Roses of this shade; it is, however, variable in this respect, sometimes being nearer to a lilac-pink shade. It is fragrant, repeats well and is free from disease. Bred by Kordes (Germany), introduced 1960.

LITTLE WHITE PET. This must be one of the best small Shrub Roses for sheer garden value. It is, in fact, a dwarf sport from the excellent old Sempervirens Rambler, 'Félicité et Perpétue'. The flowers are exactly like those of its parent, being pure white, very small, of near pompon shape, with many petals, and held in large clusters. The plant grows into a perfectly symmetrical mound of about 2ft. in height and at least 2½ft. across, and is very free flowering. Perhaps the most remarkable thing about this rose is that in spite of the fact its parent does not repeat flower it does, and does so more continuously than most others. This does seem to happen on the rare occasions that we have a dwarf sport of a Rambler. In fact, this rose is not repeat flowering in the manner of, say, a China Rose — it is more that each spray of flowers continues over an extended period by the production of further branches just beneath it. It is hardy, disease resistant and has a light but pleasing fragrance — indeed it has all the virtues! What a pity, then, that it has defied all attempts of the hybridizer to use it for breeding. It might have been discussed together with the Polyanthas, for which it can easily be mistaken, but it has a softness that we do not usually associate with those roses, and is much more of a shrub. Discovered by Henderson (U.S.A.), 1879.

MAGENTA. Like 'Lavender Lassie', see above, this rose has flowers in the Old Rose formation. They are not exactly magenta in colour, being perhaps better described as a mixture of lilac-pink and mauve. They are of medium size, full petalled, opening flat and rosette shaped, with the strong myrrh fragrance we usually associate with the English Roses. It forms a shrub of about 4ft. in height with rather straggly growth. A reliable rose, but perhaps a little coarse in appearance, it is the result of a cross between a yellow Floribunda seedling and 'Lavender Pinocchio'. Kordes (Germany), 1954.

MÄRCHENLAND. A cross between the Hybrid Tea 'Swantje' and the Hybrid Musk 'Hamburg', resulting in what is, in fact, a large Floribunda of upright growth, about 4ft. in height. Although seldom grown, I include it here for the simple charm of its large, wide semi-double flowers and clear pink colouring. These are fragrant and recurrent and are held in small and occasionally large clusters. Bred by Tantau (Germany), 1951.

MARGUERITE HILLING ('Pink Nevada'). A sport from 'Nevada', see below, to which it is entirely similar except for the colour of the flowers which is a deep pink paling a little towards the centre. It sometimes seems that this rose has been overshadowed by its famous parent, and if this were so it would be unfortunate, as I think it is better in pink than in cream, although cream is a less common colour in roses. The sport occurred in three different places over a period of years: at Sunningdale Nurseries, in Mrs. Nancy Steen's garden in New Zealand, and in the garden of a Mr. Sleet who, it seems, first discovered it. It will frequently sport back and produce a branch bearing the flowers of 'Nevada', and such branches should be cut away. Height 8ft. 'Marguerite Hilling' is always one of the major attractions in our garden. First marketed by Hilling's Nurseries (U.K.), 1959. See page 255.

MARJORIE FAIR. A hybrid between 'Ballerina' and 'Baby Faurax', this rose is similar to 'Ballerina', with closely packed Polyantha-like sprays, but its single flowers are of a deep carmine with a white eye at the centre. It forms a small bushy shrub of 3ft. by as much across, and is reliably repeat flowering, hardy and disease resistant, but not, I think, so beautiful as 'Ballerina'. Bred by Harkness (U.K.), introduced 1978.

MARTIN FROBISHER. I have recently received a number of Rugosa hybrids from the Agricultural Research Station, Ottawa, where they have been breeding roses to withstand the Canadian winters. These promise to be interesting, but I am not sufficiently acquainted with them to discuss them here. This is one of these hybrids which I happened to acquire some years previously. It was derived from open-pollinated seed from the Rugosa 'Schneezwerg', and we do not, therefore, know the other parent. Whatever this may have been, we have here a rose that bears little resemblance to a Rugosa. The flowers are charming: small, double, rosette shaped, of Old Rose appearance and soft pink in colour, the general effect being a little like that of an Alba Rose, while the foliage bears some resemblance to that of *Rosa pimpinellifolia,* although there are almost no thorns. The leaves are small and of a dull metallic green. It is regularly recurrent flowering. Fragrant. Height 4 or 5ft. Introduced 1968.

MÜNCHEN. The result of the same cross as 'Erfurt': 'Eva' × 'Réveil Dijonnais', and from the same raiser, Kordes, in 1940. The growth is very similar to 'Erfurt', about 5 by 5ft., strong and healthy with shiny, dark green foliage. The flowers are semi-double, medium sized and garnet-red with occasional streaks of white. They are held in clusters and repeat well. Almost no fragrance.

NEVADA. For many years one of the most popular Shrub Roses, and not without justification. It is the result of a cross between 'La Giralda', an extremely strong and large flowered Hybrid Tea Rose, and a form of *Rosa moyesii,* probably *R. moyesii* 'Fargesii'. It exhibits many of the characteristics of its *R. moyesii* parent, forming a shapely shrub of dense growth with long, arching, almost thornless branches. These are smothered all along their length with large creamy-white, semi-double flowers opening flat with yellow stamens. They are sometimes tinged with pink, particularly in warm, dry weather. Although a little untidy when taken individually, in the mass the blooms give a show that is hard to beat among flowering shrubs of any kind. There is a second crop late in the summer and occasional flowers at other times. It is completely free from mildew but can be affected by blackspot, although no more so than many other modern shrub roses.

'Nevada' and its sport 'Marguerite Hilling', see above, are almost unique in their ability to repeat flower while still retaining their graceful, near species-like growth and it is this that makes them so special. Most Shrub Roses that repeat flower do so by producing long shoots from the base of the plant after the first flush of bloom. These usually produce large heads of flowers as is the case with the Hybrid Musks. 'Nevada' also sends up such branches in order to renew its growth, but they do not provide the bulk of the later flowers — these come from small side shoots along the branch. In this way 'Nevada' is better able to retain the grace of its growth. Unfortunately there is a price to be paid. When the shrub is perhaps eight or ten years old it often begins to become ragged and lose its shapely form as well as some of its vigour, and it is for this reason it has sometimes been said the variety has deteriorated. This is not, in fact, the case; it is the individual plant that has deteriorated. Such a decline can be avoided by the regular removal of old wood to encourage the new. Blackspot may be a problem and spraying is worth while. When deterioration occurs, it may be a good idea to prune the shrub almost to the ground and start again, at the same time providing a liberal dose of manure. Height about 8ft. by as much across. Bred by Pedro Dot (Spain), introduced 1927. See page 253.

NYMPHENBURG. One of the best of Kordes' hybrids, introduced in 1954, from a cross between the Hybrid Musk 'Sangerhausen' × Floribunda 'Sunmist'. Its semi-double flowers are rather similar to those of a Floribunda, and are held in small clusters. They are pale pink at the edges, shading to yellow at the centre and have a strong fruit-like scent. The growth is very vigorous, upright but slightly arching, usually 8ft. high by 6ft. across, and it may be used as a pillar rose. For so large a shrub it repeats well. Big, glossy, dark green foliage. A tough, reliable variety.

PEARL DRIFT. An interesting rose from the breeders' point of view. For many years they have tried to obtain crosses with the beautiful Climber 'Mermaid', but these have nearly always proved sterile. The aim has been to produce more Climbers with the very good qualities found in 'Mermaid' — its refined beauty, its ability to climb and repeat flower well, and an almost complete resistance to disease. After so many years, this is the first such rose to appear on the market, although I have heard of other seedlings. 'Pearl Drift' is a cross with the Modern Climber 'New Dawn'. No doubt the breeder was looking for a Climber, but in this case it has turned out to be a shrub with nice compact sprawling growth of 3ft. in height and about 4ft. across. The flowers are large, semi-double, tinted with pink in the bud, opening white shaded with peachy-pink. These are held in clusters and are produced very freely and continuously over a long period. The foliage is a glossy light green and has good disease resistance. It will be interesting to see how it develops. Bred by Le Grice (U.K.), introduced 1983.

PLEINE DE GRÂCE. An exceptionally strong rose; I know of few other Shrub Roses that can match it in this respect. It might well be regarded as a Rambler, for it will cover a large area when so grown, at least the equivalent of the larger Ramblers. It was, however, sent to me as a shrub, and is of such excellence when so grown, that I think it should, first and foremost, be regarded as such. It will grow to 8ft. in height and 12 ft. across, probably considerably more, and forms a well-rounded mound of arching branches which are covered with huge sprays of small blooms forming a deluge of white. This magnificent display is followed by a positive mist of small orange-red hips in the autumn. If you have a wild spot with plenty of space, this is the ideal variety with which to fill it. Bred by Lens (Belgium), introduced in England 1985. See page 237.

ROUNDELAY. A 5ft. shrub of upright growth, flowering freely and producing trusses of medium-sized, full-petalled, cardinal-red flowers that open flat and have a strong fragrance. The growth is robust and healthy. 'Charlotte Armstrong' × 'Floradora'. Bred by Swim (U.S.A.), introduced 1953.

SALLY HOLMES. A bushy recurrent-flowering shrub of 5ft. in height, bearing large, creamy-white semi-double flowers with a light fragrance. These can be very beautiful, but those produced on the strong main stems tend to be packed together much too closely, forming a clumsy head of bloom. When they appear on side branches it is quite a different matter, for here we have fewer flowers which can show off their delicate refinement to perfection. It might be worth while cutting off the larger heads before they flower in order to encourage branching. The parents were 'Ivory Fashion' × 'Ballerina'. Bred by Holmes (U.K.), a successful amateur breeder, introduced 1976.

SCARLET FIRE ('Scharlachglut'). A tall, vigorous shrub of graceful, slightly arching growth, with plentiful foliage. The flowers are single and a brilliant scarlet-crimson with contrasting yellow stamens. Although these appear only in the summer, they are followed by fine, large pear-shaped, orange-scarlet hips in the autumn, lasting well into the winter. Little or no fragrance. An excellent shrub, providing a brilliant splash of colour without being in any way crude. It has Old Rose connections, the result of a cross between 'Poinsettia' × a Gallica called 'Grandiflora'. Bred by Kordes (Germany), introduced 1952. See page 258.

SCINTILLATION. A cross between *Rosa* 'Macrantha' and the Hybrid Musk 'Vanity', this rose forms a low, sprawling shrub of open growth, about 4ft. in height and perhaps 6 or 8ft. across. The flowers are medium to large, semi-double and of the palest lilac-pink, opening wide to show their stamens. They are held in large sprays. 'Scintillation' blooms only once in the summer, but then for a long period, the overall effect being one of daintiness and grace. The foliage, like that of its parent 'Vanity', is rather sparse. A group of two or three plants can provide a beautiful effect. Bred by Austin (U.K.), 1968.

THE FAIRY. This rose might properly have been included with the Polyanthas, as its flowers are of exactly their type. It is, however, a shrub rather than a bush with low arching growth spreading out in an almost fan-like manner, 2ft. in height by 3ft. across. The flowers are small, soft-pink in colour and borne in great quantities in broad, flat sprays. Flowering starts very late, but continues throughout the summer almost without a break, providing colour when many other roses have passed their peak. The foliage is tiny, almost like that of box. This rose has always been regarded as a sport from the Rambler 'Lady Godiva', but Peter Beales suggests it was, in fact, the result of a cross between the

Polyantha 'Paul Crampel' and 'Lady Godiva'. Looking at the plant, this would seem possible, although as far as I know its breeder, Bentall, did not record his crosses. Introduced 1932.

ZIGEUNERKNABE ('Gipsy Boy'). A variety that would look entirely at home among the Old Roses, and indeed is sometimes classified with the Bourbons, a position to which it has little claim. It is, in fact, a seedling from a rose called 'Russelliana', which was itself probably a seedling from *Rosa setigera.* Its other parent is not known, but might have been a Rugosa. The growth is exceptionally strong and bushy, at least 7ft. in height and almost as much across, with many strong thorns. It has rough, dark green, Rugosa-like foliage. The flowers are a little more than medium sized, cupped in shape at first, opening flat and almost double, while the colour is a dark crimson-purple with a little white at the centre. The blooms appear only in early summer and are followed by small orange-red hips. This rose is not unlike 'Chianti' in appearance, though the flowers held in small, tight sprays, are not of the same quality and lack fragrance. It is, however, one of the toughest of roses and ideal for a difficult position in the garden. Bred by Lambert (Germany), introduced 1909.

GROUND-COVER ROSES

In recent years there has been a swing towards what are known as Ground-cover Roses. That is to say roses which tend to form a mass of low growth rather than growing into a bush or shrub. A few of these roses have been with us for some time, 'Max Graf' and 'Raubritter' are obvious examples, but there are now so many varieties becoming available that they warrant a section to themselves. Ground-cover plants in general have become very popular, and a new type of rose has been bred with this market in mind.

The idea behind the use of ground-cover plants is that they save labour, and this is considered particularly important for public planting, because it is intended that these roses should form a thicket of growth which will smother all weeds. They have a rather tidy appearance in contrast to the often rather unruly growth of other Shrub Roses.

If weeds are a problem, it will be necessary to get rid of them before planting, for if they get a hold before the rose has grown it may be the weeds will control the rose, rather than the rose control the weeds! Moreover, it is very difficult to remove weeds or suckers from among prickly growth. For this reason, these roses are frequently grown on their own roots from cuttings, and this can be a distinct advantage.

Whether or not we favour ground-cover planting, we have here an interesting new group that brings another dimension to roses. Furthermore, Ground-cover Roses do not necessarily have to be used only for ground cover, for their growth is pleasing in itself and they can be used in the same way as any other Shrub Rose.

All are very hardy and easily grown, and bring with them a Rambler-like charm. Some of them are recurrent flowering, but even those that are not bloom over an extended period.

FAIRYLAND. The parentage of this rose was 'The Fairy' × 'Yesterday', a promising cross that has produced a good Ground-cover Rose. It bears sprays of small, cupped, rosy-pink, semi-double flowers on dense spreading growth. It will spread to about 5ft. while reaching little more than 2ft. in height. There is a strong fragrance, and it is repeat flowering. A hardy, reliable rose of considerable charm. Bred by Harkness (U.K.), introduced 1980.

FERDY. Clusters of small, salmon-pink flowers on vigorous cascading growth of about 3ft. in height spreading to about 6ft. It has plentiful, healthy, light green foliage, and produces a mass of bloom in early summer followed by a lesser crop in autumn. Bred by Keisei (Japan), 1985.

GROUSE. The parents of this rose were 'The Fairy' × a *Rosa wichuraiana* seedling, and it has retained something of the Wichuraiana's prostrate growth. It will spread over an area some 10ft. wide, flowering freely in July and August but not later. The flowers are pale pink and single, with a dainty wild rose charm. Fragrant. Bred by Kordes (Germany), 1984.

MAX GRAF. Almost the original Ground-cover Rose and still one of the best. It is a Rugosa hybrid, and I have described it with those roses earlier in this chapter.

NOZOMI. A climbing Miniature Rose which, perhaps more importantly, also has the useful ability to creep and make good ground cover. It was bred in Japan by Onodera, and introduced in 1968. Indeed, it has an oddly Japanese appearance and it is easy to picture it growing in a Japanese garden. It has small glossy leaves and sprays of tiny pearly-pink flowers in midsummer, and will spread to perhaps 5ft. while remaining little more than 1ft. high. Although sometimes mixed with larger ground-cover roses this is not advisable, as it will look out of place and will almost certainly be swamped. When grown as a short Weeping Standard it can be effective, and is frequently exhibited in this form at the Chelsea Flower Show. Such Standards have to be forced under glass, and this gives the flowers an attractive delicacy they do not possess when grown outdoors. A useful, not entirely satisfying rose, but one of the few that looks at home in the rock garden, and I have seen it grown over rocks by water, providing a charming effect. The breeding was Floribunda 'Fairy Princess' × Miniature 'Sweet Fairy'.

PARTRIDGE. A rose from the same cross as 'Grouse' to which it is similar except that its flowers are pure white. It has the same wide-spreading prostrate growth and single flowers. It blooms in late July and early August. Kordes (Germany), 1984.

PHEASANT. The third rose in the 'Game Bird' series, this time with double flowers of deep rose-pink borne in large clusters. It has the same vigorous prostrate growth of about 2½ ft. in height, spreading to perhaps 6 or 7ft. Some repeat flowering. Bred by Kordes (Germany), introduced 1986.

PINK BELLS. Large clusters of pretty soft pink, fully double rosette-shaped flowers of about 1½ ins. across, held against shiny, dark green foliage. The growth is arching and spreading, growing to about 2ft. in height and 4ft. across, providing a most charming effect. It flowers in late July and early August. Breeding 'Mini Poul' × 'Temple Bells'. Bred by Poulsen (Denmark), introduced 1980.

RAUBRITTER. A cross between 'Daisy Hill' and the Rambler 'Solarium', this rose forms a sprawling shrub of 3ft. in height and some 7ft. across, the growth developing into a low, spreading mound. The flowers are most charming: clear pink in colour, small, of a very definite cupped shape and held in clusters. It has the atmosphere of an Old Rose, although it is, in fact, quite different from any variety I know. The foliage is dark green like that of *Rosa* 'Macrantha'. Although it has some tendency towards mildew it should still be grown, for it is a most beautiful rose. Bred by Kordes (Germany), introduced 1936. See page 257.

RED BELLS. Very like 'Pink Bells', but with light crimson-red flowers. Summer flowering only. Bred by Poulsen (Denmark), 1980.

RED BLANKET. A repeat-flowering Ground-cover Rose that forms a mound of growth 2½ ft. high and 5ft. or more across. It bears sprays of medium-sized, semi-double flowers of rosy-red colouring. Good, glossy, dark green foliage. Bred by Ilsink (U.K.), introduced 1979. See page 259.

ROSY CUSHION. From the same breeder as the rose above, to which it is similar, with the exception of its flowers which are single and coloured pink with white at the centre. Good foliage, excellent habit of growth, repeat flowering. The breeding was 'Yesterday' × unnamed seedling. Introduced 1979.

RUNNING MAID. A low shrub of excellent dome shape and close twiggy growth bearing large, nicely spaced sprays of pretty little deep pink Rambler-like flowers. It blooms only in the summer, but is good in every way, whether used for ground cover or in the border. There are tiny orange-red hips in the autumn. Bred by Louis Lens (Belgium), introduced in the U.K. 1985. See page 254.

SMARTY. A third variety from the breeder of 'Red Blanket' and 'Rosy Cushion', and to my mind the best and most beautiful. It is a shrub of 2 or 3ft. in height, its spreading growth bearing sprays of single, soft pink flowers of Dog Rose appearance and providing a most charming effect. It is reliably repeat flowering, almost completely disease resistant, and has a light fruit-like fragrance. Bred by Ilsink (U.K.), introduced 1979. See page 254.

SNOW CARPET. A miniature creeping rose that I describe in Chapter 5, under Miniature Roses. Although a true ground creeper, it is much smaller than the roses in this class, and therefore fulfils a rather different role.

SWANY. It is interesting that this rose has *Rosa sempervirens* as one of its parents, and therefore has a connection with the beautiful Sempervirens Ramblers. The other parent was a Wichuraiana Rambler called 'Mademoiselle Marthe Carron'. The result is a charming rose bearing sprays of small, very double, cupped, pure white flowers that open flat. The growth is truly prostrate and it will spread to 6ft. or more. The foliage is a glossy, dark green. It is completely hardy.

TEMPLE BELLS. A pretty little creeping rose bearing numerous small, almost single white flowers, its small, glossy green leaves adding to the picture. Bred from *Rosa wichuraiana* × the Miniature Rose 'Blushing Jewel', it has something of the character of *R. wichuraiana.* Bred by McGredy (New Zealand), 1976.

WHITE BELLS. The fourth, and perhaps the most attractive, of the 'Bells' series, this rose bears small, white rosette-shaped flowers in sprays. As with its three namesakes, it has excellent dense bushy growth, flowering in late June and early August. Bred by Poulsen (Denmark), introduced 1980.

Chapter 9
CLIMBING ROSES

It is a remarkable fact that a genus that has been responsible for the production of so many garden shrubs — shrubs which, if considered alone, would be sufficient to make it the most important of garden flowers — should also provide us with what is, without doubt, the most important of all climbing plants, but such is the case. It is difficult to overestimate the value of Climbing Roses in the garden. They provide a feeling of abundance, particularly in more formal and architectural areas, which may be in need of softening and a sense of life. They bring height where it might otherwise be lacking and many of them flower intermittently throughout the summer. No plant can fulfil these functions better than the Climbing Rose.

All roses delight us, but perhaps a Climbing Rose, well grown and in full flower, more so than any other, and if not always in the individual flower, at least in the mass, although the individual flower is often particularly beautiful when seen looking down at us from the branch of a Climbing Rose. Perhaps it is the association of plant and architecture that gives Climbing Roses a certain advantage.

Before going further, it is necessary to explain that the Climbing Roses are divided into two main groups: the Climbers and the Ramblers. The division is an artificial one, for both are in reality climbing plants, but this division does help us deal with them more easily. A Climbing Rose usually has larger flowers such as we might find in the Old Roses or the Hybrid Teas.

The Rambler Roses usually have smaller flowers in larger clusters, and are often of more lax growth. They are also inclined to send up long, sometimes very long, stems from the base of the plant. In fact, they do just what their name suggests, ramble. The Climbers may be stiffer in growth, and although they, too, produce strong base shoots, they tend to build up gradually on past growth. Most Climbing Roses are repeat flowering; the Ramblers almost never are. This is a very arbitrary division, one type frequently overlapping with the other, but in spite of this, when we see these roses there is generally little doubt as to which group they belong.

In this chapter we are concerned with the Climbing Roses: the Noisettes with their delicate refinement, the Climbing Tea Roses, the Climbing Hybrid Teas with their flowers of many colours, the Modern Climbers with their continuous abundance, as well as other sorts of other classifications or of none, which are often of great beauty. Perhaps the best and most frequent use for these roses is on walls, including house walls where, with the additional warmth that these provide, they are often the earliest garden roses to flower, thus making them particularly precious, and giving them plenty of time to make further growth and so flower again. In addition, no climbing plant is more suitable for growing over arches, on pillars, on trellises, pergolas and so on.

Annual tying and pruning is, of course, necessary with Climbers, and this can be a little more arduous than is the case with shrubs, but really need not be too great a task. All we have to do is to take away some of the long main growth where this is too plentiful, or is becoming old and worn out. This may not be required for a few years. Having done this, cut back the side shoots which have flowered in the previous year to 2 or 3ins., at the same time pruning away weak or dead shoots.

When attaching the young branches to a wall or length of trellis it is best, whenever possible, to train them, if not horizontally at least on a slant. This encourages them to break and form new flowering shoots all along the branch, and so provide far more flowers. Otherwise the rose will always be pushing upwards, producing its blooms only at the top, where they cannot be seen and leaving the lower parts bare. There is a special problem with pillars, for with these we have less latitude. This can be overcome by winding the growth around the pillar in spiral form.

Climbers sometimes take time to get going and a little persuasion may be necessary. A liberal quantity of some form of natural manure, mixed with the soil where they are to grow, will work wonders. If such material is readily available, it may be used very freely, and you will be amply rewarded in the years to come. Roses planted against walls may well require the most attention for such areas are usually very dry, due to the fact that the soil here is protected and may receive little or no rain. The rose will not begin to move until its roots have themselves moved out into more moist ground. A hosepipe can be useful in the first year or two. Give Climbers in such positions an occasional very heavy watering, one that will soak down deep into the soil. It is vital to avoid drying out early in the life of the rose.

NOISETTE ROSES

Even before the China Rose was hybridized with various Old Roses to produce the first recurrent-flowering roses I describe in Chapter 3, it was cross fertilized with the Musk Rose to give us the first repeat-flowering Climbing Roses. This is rather surprising, for it has never been easy to breed such Climbers. Credit for this innovation goes to John Champney, a rice planter of Charleston in South Carolina in the early 1800s.

Champney produced a rose which was first named *Rosa moschata hybrida,* but later became known as 'Champney's Pink Cluster'. It is sometimes said he obtained this rose by crossing the then new 'Parsons' Pink China' with pollen from the Musk Rose, but it is more likely it was an accidental hybrid, as the deliberate cross fertilization of roses was not practised at that time.

Philippe Noisette, a nurseryman, also of Charleston, sowed seed from 'Champney's Pink Cluster' to produce a variety known as 'Blush Noisette' which, although not so tall in growth as its parents, was repeat flowering. Thus it was that the Noisettes were born. 'Blush Noisette' was later crossed with 'Parks' Yellow China', to give us yellow Noisettes. Noisettes were also freely crossed with the Tea Rose, further widening their range and improving their quality, and the Noisette Roses are, even today, some of the most beautiful and freely recurrent flowering of all Climbing Roses. These qualities they frequently combine with tall, rampant growth — something breeders still find very hard to achieve. In addition, the colour yellow was added to the repertoire of garden roses, and we are short enough of yellows among Climbing Roses even today.

The period of development of Noisettes was brief, and one cannot help feeling that here is a job not yet completed and with very considerable possibililties for further progress. Once again, as we found with the Rugosas and the Hybrid Musks, the problem is that Noisettes are diploids and this tends to make further development difficult, most roses being tetraploid.

The Noisettes as a class include some of the most beautiful of all Climbers. They have a refinement and delicacy of appearance that would be hard to equal elsewhere. The flowers are in the true Old Rose tradition, with petals of a lovely silky texture, and nearly all have a good fragrance.

The winter hardiness of some of them is unfortunately a little questionable, but this should not prevent us from growing them in anything but the coldest positions. Given the protection of a warm wall, they will be perfectly safe. Some are, in fact, quite hardy.

AIMÉE VIBERT ('Bouquet de la Mariée', 'Nivea'). This rose, which was raised by Vibert of France in 1828, is not a typical Noisette, but a cross between a Noisette, probably 'Blush Noisette', and *Rosa sempervirens,* the 'Evergreen Rose'. It has the plentiful, long, graceful, rich green foliage of *R. sempervirens,* and bears open sprays of small, pure white, double flowers with yellow stamens. These have a simple charm that is hard to compare with any other Climber. There is a slight musky fragrance. From the Noisette it gains the ability to flower again, starting early and often continuing well into the autumn. It is somewhat tender, although it will survive most winters it is likely to encounter in the U.K. Early flower shoots are sometimes cut back by frost and this will delay flowering until July. It will climb to a height of 15ft. in a warm position and may also be grown as a large, sprawling shrub. Either way it is a most beautiful rose. We have here a variety that is, in fact, a perpetual-flowering Rambler of strong growth, and it is thus something very unusual. It might have been more accurately included with the Ramblers, but it is by ancestry a Noisette. The only comparable Rambler with this quality is 'Phyllis Bide', a shorter and less beautiful rose, a fact which should give the plant breeder some food for thought.

ALISTER STELLA GRAY ('Golden Rambler'). Bred by A.H. Gray, a Tea Rose enthusiast, this rose was introduced by George Paul in 1894. It bears small yolk-yellow buds of tightly scrolled formation which open into prettily quartered flowers, later fading to a creamy-white and remaining beautiful at all stages. The flowers have a silky texture and are held in small sprays on the ends of long, thin stems. Later in the year large heads of bloom appear. They have a delicious tea scent. This rose may be grown either as a Climber and will achieve 15ft. on a warm wall, or as a large arching shrub. A most charming rose. See page 279.

BLUSH NOISETTE. The first Noisette Rose, it is hardy, very tough and a great survivor, and still to be seen in old gardens where it may have been planted long ago. The flowers are almost double, small, Rambler like and cupped, and are held in tight clusters. They are of a lilac-blush colour with exposed yellow stamens and have a strong clove fragrance. Although of modest appearance, the flowers are pretty and produced in profusion, repeating well and creating a pleasing massed effect. This variety has a tendency to remain short and bushy, in fact it will form a good shrub. It needs the encouragement of a wall to achieve height, where it can grow to 12ft. Noisette (France), before 1817. See page 283.

BOUQUET D'OR. A seedling from 'Gloire de Dijon', and thus one of the roses sometimes known as Dijon Teas. The flowers are quite large and full petalled with a slight scent, their colour a coppery-salmon with yellow at the centre. It is hardy and fairly vigorous, growing to a height of 10ft. Bred by Ducher (France), introduced 1872.

CÉLINE FORESTIER. Although not a strong rose, this is one of the most beautiful, and given a warm wall and careful treatment it will do well. The flowers are fully double, neatly rounded, opening quartered with a button eye. Their colour is a pale yellow, the petals having a silky texture. There is a rich Tea Rose fragrance. Given time it will grow to about 8 or 10ft., perhaps more in a warm climate. A charming rose of delicate refinement. Bred by Trouillard (France), introduced 1842.

CLAIRE JACQUIER ('Mademoiselle Claire Jacquier'). Here we have a truly vigorous Noisette that will grow to as much as 30ft. but, as is often the case with Climbing Roses, what it gains in vigour it loses in its ability to repeat flower. A very good early flush of bloom is followed by only occasional flowers later. The individual flowers are rather loosely formed, rich yellow at first, paling with age to pale yellow, and with a delicious fragrance. They are held against plentiful light green foliage. Hardy. Bred by Bernaix (France), introduced 1888.

CLOTH OF GOLD ('Chromatella'). A self-sown seedling from 'Lamarque' and, like its parent, rather tender. If planted against a warm wall it can do well, and is very fine when grown under glass. The flowers are double and of a soft sulphur-yellow which deepens towards the centre. Fragrant. Height 12ft. Introduced by Coquereau (France), 1843.

DESPREZ À FLEUR JAUNE ('Jaune Desprez'). An excellent Climber blooming freely and with remarkable continuity. The flowers are quite small, opening flat, with many silky petals and a button eye, their colour a warm yellow shaded with peach, becoming paler with age. They have a strong and pleasing fragrance. The growth is vigorous, reaching 20ft. on a warm wall. The result of a cross between 'Blush Noisette' and 'Parks' Yellow China'. Bred by Desprez (France), 1835. See page 279.

DUCHESSE D'AUERSTÄDT. A sport from 'Rêve d'Or', with large, cupped, full-petalled golden-yellow flowers, similar in form to those of 'Gloire de Dijon'. It has ample foliage and will grow to about 10ft. in height. Discovered by Bernaix (France), introduced 1888.

GLOIRE DE DIJON. A famous old Climbing Rose, once found in many a cottage garden, where it was often known as 'Old Glory'. There can be few roses that have given more pleasure to more people since its introduction in 1853. It is said to have been a cross between a Tea Rose, the name of which is not known, and the old Bourbon 'Souvenir de la Malmaison', and indeed its general appearance would seem to support this. It has large, globular, buff-yellow flowers that flatten and become quartered later, taking on pink tints, particularly in hot weather. They have a strong, rich fragrance. There is no doubt this is a much hardier rose than the typical Noisette, probably due to the fact that it is in part Bourbon. It is truly recurrent-flowering. The foliage is thick and heavy, more like that of a Hybrid Tea. Unfortunately, however, it appears to have lost some of its vigour in recent years, probably due to generations of propagation on a large scale. It might be worth making a search for a robust old plant of 'Gloire de Dijon' and to build up a new stock from this. It is still very widely distributed throughout the country, and it is unlikely that the whole stock would decline at once. Bred by Jacotot (France). See page 295.

LAMARQUE. Not, I am afraid, a rose for this country, except in the warmest areas, and even then it would be best to grow it on a south wall. Under glass it could, I am sure, be magnificent. The flowers are palest lemon-yellow (almost white), quartered and flat and of exquisite delicacy. It will grow to about 10ft., but I would expect much more in warmer climates. 'Blush Noisette' × 'Parks' Yellow China'. Bred by Maréchal (France), 1830.

LEY'S PERPETUAL. This rose was given to me by Mr. Wyatt, who for some time edited an excellent magazine called *The Rose,* which unfortunately ceased publication. A seedling from 'Gloire de Dijon', it has a great deal in common with that rose. The flowers are cupped, medium sized, and of a pleasing pale yellow colour, with a Tea Rose fragrance. It will grow to about 15ft. in height. A beautiful and worthwhile rose deserving more attention. I am not aware of the breeder, although I would expect it to be 'Ley', nor do I know the date of introduction.

MADAME ALFRED CARRIÈRE. If a very strong, reliable, repeat-flowering, white Climber is required, you need look no further than this variety. Even today, there is no white Climbing Rose to rival it in performance. The flowers are large, cupped and creamy-white with just a tint of pink, and have a Tea Rose fragrance. They cannot be said to be particularly shapely, and the growth is rather stiff and upright, though this stiffness can be overcome by careful training. It can be relied upon to give a magnificent display over a long period. The foliage is large and plentiful. Reliably hardy. Bred by Schwartz (France), introduced 1879.

MARÉCHAL NIEL. Until Pernet-Ducher introduced the blood of *Rosa foetida* into the Hybrid Teas at about the turn of the century, there was no rose of such a truly deep yellow, other than a few less developed varieties such as *R. hemisphaerica* and 'Persian Yellow'. 'Maréchal Niel' was, therefore, highly prized for this reason, as well as for the perfection of its large, pointed buds. In fact it was treated with near reverence. Its long, hanging, strongly fragrant flowers of pure yellow and perfect Tea Rose shape were unique at the time. The trouble was that it would not withstand our cold winters and damp summers, and for this reason the Victorians nearly always grew it under glass, indeed lean-to greenhouses were built with the main object of growing this rose. Whether it is worth going to such lengths today is rather doubtful, although there is still nothing finer than a perfect example of its waxy blooms. Unfortunately it does not always grow very well, and requires careful treatment if it is to thrive. Graham Thomas says it should be grown like a vine, with the roots in the open soil and the growth trained into the house on a framework, under the slope of the glass. Given such conditions it may be expected to grow to up to 15ft. Believed to be a seedling from 'Cloth of Gold'. Bred by Pradel (France), 1864.

RÊVE D'OR ('Golden Chain'). A seedling from 'Madame Schultz', itself a seedling from 'Lamarque', this too is only for a warm wall. The flowers are semi-double, buff-yellow with pink shadings, paling with age, and of a rather informal shape. They are produced freely, and repeat particularly well. The foliage is plentiful and glossy. Little fragrance. A first class Climber. Bred by Ducher (France), 1869.

WILLIAM ALLEN RICHARDSON. This once famous rose was a sport of 'Rêve d'Or', to which it is similar except for the distinct yolk-yellow colouring at the centre of its flowers. Unfortunately the growth is rather weak, and it is probably not worth growing except by the collector. It requires a warm wall. Height 10ft. Bred by Ducher (France), introduced 1878.

CLIMBING TEA ROSES

I have described the Tea Roses as bushes, but there are also a number that are, by nature, Climbers. These are nearly all sports from bush varieties. Although the bushes are usually too tender to warrant growing anywhere but in warm climates, a number of the Climbers are well worth a place in our gardens. This is partly because they can be grown on warm walls where they will withstand all but the hardest frosts. Also, many of the survivors of this group are at least remotely interbred with the Hybrid Teas which gives them added hardiness. Although some Climbing Teas are rather difficult to grow, two or three of them can be included among the most beautiful of Climbing Roses. 'Lady Hillingdon', 'Sombreuil' and 'Paul Lédé' are particularly fine.

As a class they tend to have silky or waxy petals, and some of them have long, pointed buds. The foliage and growth are similar to those of the Hybrid Teas, but they are perhaps a little less heavy and more refined in appearance. Most of them flower early, and continue late into the autumn if weather permits.

It is usually essential to plant them against a warm wall to avoid frost damage. As with bush Tea Roses minimum pruning is the rule, otherwise cultivation is the same as for other Climbing Roses.

DEVONIENSIS, CLIMBING. A sport from the bush variety discovered by Pavitt and introduced in 1858, the original bush having been bred by a Mr. Foster of Devonport, and introduced in 1838. 'Devoniensis' was the first Tea Rose to be bred in England, although due to the climate it is not surprising that very few were raised in the U.K. This variety is, in fact, quite hardy on a warm wall. Its flowers are creamy-white, attractively flushed with pink and apricot at the centre. At its best they are beautiful with a silky sheen and a strong Tea Rose fragrance. In the past this rose has been called the 'Magnolia Rose'. The parentage is not known.

FORTUNE'S YELLOW ('Beauty of Glazenwood', 'Gold of Ophir', 'San Rafael Rose'). This famous old rose was brought to England from China by the well-known plant collector Robert Fortune in 1845, having been discovered in the garden of a rich Mandarin at Ningpo. Its flowers are held either singly or in small clusters and are semi-double, bright coppery-yellow in colour, shaded with white. It will grow to about 4 or 5ft. in height, no doubt more in a favourable climate. It is not recurrent flowering, and is only suitable for the collector.

GENERAL SCHABLIKINE. A rose which is only barely a Climber, and which might well have been included among the bush varieties. On a wall it may be expected to achieve perhaps 6ft. When well grown it can produce rather small, perfectly scrolled flowers of a deep coppery-pink which hang elegantly from their stems. Under poor conditions it does not have such beautiful buds, as the petals remain short and open quickly into informal rosettes. It can be particularly fine when grown under glass. Bred by Nabonnand (France), introduced 1878.

BLAIRI NO. 2, *an old Bourbon Climber of great beauty and true old-fashioned formation. See pages 19 and 286.* Page

CONSTANCE SPRY, *a fine example grown as a Climber.* *See pages 182 and 210.* Page
A WALL WELL *clothed with Climbing and Rambling Roses.* Thomas
Both scenes are in the garden of Mottisfont Abbey, Hampshire (National Trust).

ALISTER STELLA GRAY, *Noisette Rose. See page 273.* Page

DESPREZ À FLEUR JAUNE, *Noisette Rose, sometimes known as 'Jaune Desprez'. See page 274.* Page

Some of the most beautiful Climbing Roses are to be found among the Noisettes.

PAUL LÉDÉ, *a continuous and free-flowering Climbing Tea Rose with buff-yellow blooms and a delicious scent. Quite hardy. See page 285. Gallica 'Duc de Guiche' can be seen in the background.* Knight

LAWRENCE JOHNSTON, *a very tall Climber. Few Climbing Roses make a better show. See page 310.* Warren

LADY WATERLOW, *Climbing Hybrid Tea Rose with beautiful mingling colours. See page 301.* Knight
ZÉPHIRINE DROUHIN, *a most reliable and continuous-flowering Bourbon Climber. Good for a north wall. See page 288.* Page

ALCHEMIST, *a Modern Shrub Rose or Climber with Old Rose flowers. See page 248.* Warren
EASLEA'S GOLDEN RAMBLER, *Climbing Hybrid Tea Rose. A strong Rambler with large flowers. See page 291.* Warren

ICEBERG, *a Floribunda Rose looking even better in its climbing form. See page 309.* Knight

ÉTOILE DE HOLLANDE. *The climbing form of this old Hybrid Tea Rose is very reliable. See page 291.* Calvert

BLUSH NOISETTE, *the first Noisette Rose, can be a short bushy Climber or strong Shrub. See page 273.* Page

FELLEMBERG, *a Climbing China Rose of bushy growth. See page 287.* Calvert

GOLDFINCH, a *Multiflora Hybrid Rambler seen here growing as a shrub.* *See page 317* Warren

LADY HILLINGDON, CLIMBING. One of the best Tea Roses still in existence. Indeed, I would place it high in any list of Climbing Roses. It is remarkably hardy for this class, so much so that it is hard to believe it is the result of a cross between the Tea Roses 'Papa Gontier' and 'Madame Hoste'. It would be easy to believe a Hybrid Tea comes into its breeding somewhere, but the records say otherwise. Nonetheless, I would still give it the protection of a wall. The flowers are made up of large petals which result in long, elegant buds of deep apricot-yellow. These hang gracefully from the branch and emit a strong and delicious tea fragrance. Although not shapely when they open, this does not matter so much with a Climbing Rose whose flowers are usually seen from a distance. 'Lady Hillingdon' has lush growth, with large dark green leaves tinted with red when young, and it continues to flower with admirable regularity. It may be expected to grow to 15ft. The bush variety was bred by the English firm of Lowe & Shawyer in 1910, making it one of the latest of the Tea Roses to be introduced. The sport was discovered by Hicks (U.K.), 1917.

MADAME JULES GRAVEREAUX. Large, very full flowers of soft flesh-pink, shaded with peach and yellow. I am not fully acquainted with this rose, but understand it will reach 12ft. on a wall. The foliage is dark and glossy, the scent only slight. It is not a pure Tea Rose, being a cross between 'Rêve d'Or' and the Hybrid Tea 'Viscountess Folkestone'. It would appear to be well worthy of preservation. Bred by Soupert & Notting (Luxemburg), 1901.

MRS. HERBERT STEVENS, CLIMBING. The result of a cross between 'Frau Karl Druschki' (which I have already described in Chapter 3 in the section on Hybrid Perpetuals as being very close to a Hybrid Tea) and the old Tea Rose 'Niphetos'. It could, therefore, more accurately be described as a Hybrid Tea, but it is so close to a Tea Rose in appearance that we have to place it here. The flowers are white with long pointed buds tinged with green towards the centre, and have a strong, typically Tea Rose fragrance. They are produced freely and repeat well. The foliage is light green. This rose will grow strongly on a wall, often reaching 18ft. Unfortunately the flowers are easily damaged by rain, more particularly if planted away from a wall, where it is otherwise usually quite hardy. The original rose was bred by McGredy (U.K.), and the climbing sport was discovered by Pernet-Ducher (France) in 1922. See page 298.

NIPHETOS, CLIMBING. Not a rose for the outdoors in Great Britain, for if it survives the frost, the flowers are likely to be spoiled by rain. These are large and hang their heads slightly, with perfect creamy buds opening to pure white. They have a light Tea Rose fragrance. It would be worth growing this rose under glass — in fact its bush parent was once widely used for this purpose. Discovered by Keynes, Williams & Co. (U.K.), 1889.

PAUL LÉDÉ. A sport discovered by Lowe in 1913 on the Bush Rose bred by Pernet-Ducher in 1902. Its hardiness perhaps belies its Tea Rose ancestry, but however this may be it is a rose of great beauty and has a delicious tea fragrance. The flowers are large, semi-double, with exposed stamens, and of a rather loose formation. They have a lovely buff-yellow colouring and are flushed with carmine at the centre. The growth is strong, to about 12ft., and it flowers well later in the year. All in all, a most pleasing and reliable Climbing Rose. See page 280.

SOMBREUIL, CLIMBING. A rose bred by Robert of France in 1850, little is known of its parentage other than that it was a seedling from a Hybrid Perpetual called 'Gigantesque'. However, the refinement of its flowers would make it almost certain the other parent was either a Tea Rose or a Noisette. It is, therefore, really a Hybrid Tea, but to place it in that section would be most misleading. In fact, it is really a variety that stands on its own. The flowers have numerous petals, and open to form flat rosettes that can only be described as the most perfect Old Roses. They are creamy-white with the slightest flush tint at the centre, have a delicious tea scent and in quality and refinement compare with the very best of the Old Roses. 'Sombreuil' is completely hardy and may be grown on a pillar or other support, though is perhaps best on a wall where it will reach 12ft. I know of no other old variety that produces better flowers in autumn. See page 295.

SOUVENIR DE MADAME LÉONIE VIENNOT. Not one of the finest Tea Roses, but worth a place in our list. The flowers are of loose Tea Rose shape, pale yellow shaded with coppery-pink. Although not very free flowering it is recurrent and hardy. The growth is strong and quite hardy, to about 12ft. in height. Fragrant. Bred by Bernaix (France), 1898.

CLIMBING CHINA AND BOURBON ROSES

The Chinas and the Bourbons have produced only a few climbing varieties, but I think they are sufficiently different to warrant gathering them into a section on their own. The Bourbons 'Blairi No. 2' and 'Souvenir de la Malmaison' have the advantage of producing truly 'old' blooms, while at the same time being good Climbers. 'Zéphirine Drouhin' and 'Kathleen Harrop' are both remarkably free and continuous flowering. Climbing 'Pompon de Paris' is a short, twiggy Climber that would be difficult to compare with any other rose. Some of the taller Bourbons listed as Shrub Roses may also be treated as Climbers, particularly 'Madame Isaac Pereire' and 'Madame Ernst Calvat'.

BLAIRI NO. 2. Were it not for the fact that this Bourbon Rose does not repeat flower and has a tendency to mildew, I would be inclined to regard it as my favourite Climber. The flowers are indeed the very personification of an Old Rose at its best. They are cupped in shape, full of petals, pale pink at the edges, and deepening towards the centre. The growth is rather lax, perhaps 12 or 15ft. in height, with the blooms borne elegantly on the branch. The young shoots are mahogany coloured, and the mature leaves rough textured and matt green. The whole plant makes a most charming picture. Raised by a Mr. Blair of Stamford Hill in 1845, it is said that the parents are *Rosa chinensis* × 'Tuscany'. There is also a 'Blairi No. 1', which is very similar, but the flowers are less fine, and I think there is little point in growing them both, although the colour of the latter is a more even pink. I have only seen 'Blairi No.1' growing at Hidcote Manor in Gloucestershire. See pages 19 and 277.

CRAMOISI SUPÉRIEUR, CLIMBING. This is a climbing form of the bush China Rose described in Chapter 3. I find it grows to a height of 7ft., although I understand it will reach very much further with the protection of a sunny wall. It produces small, cupped, crimson flowers in clusters. The growth is twiggy and bushy with small, dark green leaves. It repeat flowers quite well, but hardly so well as we would expect from a China Rose. Climbing sport discovered by Couturier (France), 1885.

FELLEMBERG ('La Belle Marseillaise'). A rose of doubtful origin, sometimes regarded as a Noisette, but perhaps better classified as a China Rose. It bears small, semi-double cupped flowers in rather close clusters, their colour being cerise-crimson with yellow stamens. This rose flowers freely and repeats well, while the growth tends to be bushy, to 8 or 10ft., indeed it will form a good broad shrub or may even be pruned for bedding. Good, dark green, disease-free foliage. A useful and reliable if somewhat dull rose. Bred by Fellemberg (Germany), introduced 1857. See page 283.

GRUSS AN AACHEN, CLIMBING. I have never seen the climbing form of this rose, although I can imagine its pearly-pink, full-cupped flowers looking particularly beautiful on a Climber, and would like to obtain stock of it. It was discovered at Sangerhausen, and distributed by Kordes (Germany), 1937. See Chapter 6.

GRUSS AN TEPLITZ ('Virginia R. Coxe'). A rose of no particular persuasion, but rather a mixture of Bourbon, China and Tea Rose, the breeding being ('Sir Joseph Paxton' × 'Fellemberg') × ('Papa Gontier' × 'Gloire des Rosomanes'). The flowers are dark crimson and have retained the quality of a China Rose, in that the colour intensifies rather than fades in hot sunshine. They are medium sized, loosely and informally double, and have a rich, spicy fragrance. The foliage is purplish at first, becoming green later. This rose is frequently grown as a rather straggly shrub of some 6ft. in height, but is perhaps more satisfactory as a Climbing Rose when it will grow to a height of 12ft. Bred by Geschwind (Hungary), introduced by P. Lambert (Germany), 1897.

KATHLEEN HARROP. A soft pink sport from 'Zéphirine Drouhin' with a deeper pink on the reverse of the petals, but otherwise entirely similar, except that it may be a little less vigorous. It has perhaps the more pleasing colour of the two. Discovered by Dickson (U.K.), 1919. See 'Zéphirine Drouhin' below.

MARTHA. Like 'Kathleen Harrop' a sport from 'Zéphirine Drouhin', having paler pink flowers with a creamy tinge at the centre. Discovered by Zeiner (France), 1912.

POMPON DE PARIS, CLIMBING ('Climbing Rouletii'). A sport of the Miniature Rose, it makes dense, twiggy growth up to 6ft. in height, providing a good display of small rose-pink, pompon flowers in June, but rather surprisingly has very little bloom later. The foliage is small, to match the flowers, and of a greyish-green. It enjoys considerable popularity, perhaps more than it deserves, although no doubt is useful for very small gardens and certain positions in larger gardens. Maximum height about 7ft.

SOUVENIR DE LA MALMAISON, CLIMBING. The climbing form of this famous old Bourbon Rose has strong growth and will achieve a spread of 12ft. It is possible that its beautiful, delicate, flesh-pink flowers will not be quite so fine as the bush variety. Nonetheless, they take on an added charm when seen on a Climber rather than on the somewhat squat growth of the bush. Unfortunately the Climber does not repeat quite so well. Climbing sport discovered by Bennett (U.K.), 1893.

ZÉPHIRINE DROUHIN. A Bourbon Rose. Although this variety was introduced as early as 1868 it is still one of the most popular and widely distributed of all Climbing Roses and is to be found in most catalogues and even on supermarket shelves. The reason is not far to seek, as no Modern Rose has been able to excel it for sheer performance and continuity of flowering. The blooms are of a bright cerise-carmine, semi-double, of no very definite form and with a wonderful fragrance. It is very free-flowering and seen in the mass the effect is quite outstanding. Its one defect is that it is subject to mildew, but this can be overcome by planting it against a north-facing wall; indeed, no other rose that I know thrives quite so well in such a position. For this reason, if for nothing else, it is a valuable acquisition. It will achieve anything up to 15ft., maybe more on a north wall. Although sometimes recommended as a shrub, I have never found it to be very satisfactory when so grown, the growth often appearing too open and straggly, but perhaps if closely planted in a large group the appearance would be quite different. It is said that it will form a good hedge. Parentage unknown. Bred by Bizot (France), 1868. See page 282.

CLIMBING HYBRID TEA ROSES

Very few Climbing Hybrid Teas have been bred, perhaps because it is not an easy thing to do, or because it was thought to be much less profitable than the breeding of bush roses. In spite of this there are, in fact, innumerable Climbing Hybrid Teas to choose from. The explanation for this apparent anomaly lies in the fact that bush Hybrid Teas have proved very prolific in the production of climbing sports, and this is what most Climbing Hybrid Teas are. They form an important contribution to our stock of Climbing Roses, not least because they extend the colour range considerably.

Anyone whose preferences among roses lie with the Old Rose, or perhaps have some prejudice against Modern Roses, should think again in the case of the Climbing Hybrid Teas, for even those bearing flowers which may look rather ordinary on a squat bush often have greater appeal when seen from the branches of their climbing form. This perhaps illustrates better than anything else the advantages a shrub rose has over a bush rose, or, likewise, a Climbing Rose over a bush. That is to say the advantages of scale — the balance between the size of the flower, and the growth of the plant.

There can be little doubt that, in general, the older Hybrid Teas make better climbing sports than those of more recent introduction. The early Hybrid Teas were rather weak in growth, but it is an odd fact that such roses often produce strong climbing forms. They also have the advantage that they often inherit a more lax and elegant growth from their parent (a sport only has one parent), so that the flowers, instead of looking up towards the sky, look down on us for our appreciation. They have a further advantage in that they are often more gentle in colour, substance and general appearance. Fortunately it is the early Hybrid Teas that have produced the most Climbers. This may be because they were the result of rather distant crosses and had not settled down genetically. The contemporary Hybrid Tea bushes are of much stronger growth, but sometimes their climbing sports make growth and foliage at the expense of bloom and, more often than not, their flowers stand up like ramrods. It may be possible to overcome this by training the branches horizontally and not too high up.

The climbing forms of early Hybrid Teas may then be said to be good Climbers growing strongly and often repeating well. In fact, if the early varieties are to be preserved, it is perhaps as Climbers that this is best done. Having said this, modern varieties do from time to time produce good sports, and it is important we do not ignore them.

ALLEN CHANDLER. A vigorous Climbing Rose bearing very large, semi-double flowers of brilliant crimson, opening to show contrasting yellow stamens. It blooms very freely early in the season and regularly thereafter. Good red Climbing Roses are rather scarce and this is one of the best of them. It will grow to about 15ft., sometimes much more, is fragrant and has ample large foliage. A cross between 'Hugh Dickson' and an unnamed seedling. Bred by Chandler (U.S.A.).

ALTISSIMO. Large, single flowers of unfading blood-red, each some 5ins. across, opening flat and neatly rounded, with a large boss of deep gold stamens. They have no scent but are produced freely, both in early summer and quite regularly later. The growth is strong, to at least 10ft., with large, deep matt-green leaves. A very good Climber, but perhaps a little artificial in appearance. Such a colour is best kept away from red brick and is better against a light green background or perhaps clambering over shrubs. It can also be grown as a large shrub if kept in check by pruning. Bred by Delbard-Chabert (France), introduced 1966.

BETTINA, CLIMBING. A rose which bears some of the most perfectly formed Hybrid Tea flowers, with tightly scrolled buds of orange shading to gold at the base and attractive heavy veining of red and bronze. Unfortunately, the flower shoots are of the stiff and upright type. The glossy foliage is dark green tinted with bronze. It should grow to 10 or 12ft. on a wall. Sport discovered by Meilland (France), 1958, who was also the original raiser.

CAPTAIN CHRISTY, CLIMBING. A sport of an early Hybrid Tea, bearing large, very full, globular flowers of a pale flesh-pink that deepens towards the centre. A lovely Old Rose, but with only a slight fragrance. The growth is strong, to a height of 10 or 12ft. It flowers in early summer and provides occasional blooms later. Discovered by Ducher (France), 1881.

CHÂTEAU DE CLOS VOUGEOT, CLIMBING. One of the darkest of dark red roses: rich, velvety crimson overlaid with garnet, unfading and pure. It is not a typical Hybrid Tea flower, having numerous rather short petals and opening wide, with a particularly strong and rich fragrance. The growth is suitably lax, holding its flowers well. I have not found it to be very strong, although the growth is quite adequate with good cultivation. It should reach 15ft. on a wall. Sport found by Morse (U.K.), 1920, from the original Hybrid Tea bred by Pernet-Ducher (France).

CHRISTINE, CLIMBING. A Climbing Hybrid Tea of considerable beauty. Its flowers are fragrant and quite small, with long elegantly scrolled buds of pure golden-yellow. A good first crop is followed by intermittent bloom later. Good, glossy foliage. Height 15ft. Discovered by Willink, from the bush variety bred by McGredy (U.K.), 1918.

COMTESSE VANDAL, CLIMBING. The climbing sport of a beautiful and shapely Hybrid Tea. Coppery-orange buds open to salmon-pink with a coppery-pink reverse. These are held on rather upright stems and have a slight fragrance. Good healthy foliage and growth, to a height of perhaps 10 to 12ft. Found by Jackson & Perkins (U.S.A.), from the bush bred by Leenders (Holland), 1932.

CRIMSON GLORY, CLIMBING. A particularly fine rose in its climbing form. The flowers start as typical Hybrid Tea buds of deepest velvety crimson, eventually becoming an attractive informal cup of a pleasing purplish shade. They are richly fragrant and tend to be evenly placed along the branch, holding themselves admirably. In summer the whole plant is studded with flowers, to be followed by occasional blooms later. Height 10 to 12ft. We have found it to be very successful on a tall pillar. Bush bred by Kordes (Germany), 1935; sport discovered by Jackson & Perkins (U.S.A.), 1946.

CUPID. Very large, single, delicate flesh-pink flowers shaded with apricot;

these may be 5ins. across with attractively waved and crinkled petals and ample stamens. Although summer flowering only, this variety has large orange-red hips in the autumn. It will grow to 15ft. or more. Graham Thomas suggests it might be allowed to trail over shrubs, and I can imagine it being very effective when so grown. Fragrant. Bred by Cant (U.K.), 1915. See page 297.

DAINTY BESS, CLIMBING. The climbing sport of an early, single Hybrid Tea. Its pink flowers, with their fringed edges, darker reverse, and red and brown stamens are, if anything, more dainty when grown as a Climber. The growth is slight and rather thin, but fits the flower well. It requires rich soil if it is to reach its height of 8ft. Discovered by van Bernaveld (U.S.A.), 1935; the original bush bred by Archer (U.K.), 1925.

EASLEA'S GOLDEN RAMBLER. Although this rose bears the name Rambler, it is, in effect, a Climber. The buds are tipped with red and open to large loosely-filled deep yellow flowers, with a strong fragrance. They are held either singly or in small clusters. The growth is heavy and robust with thick, olive-green, shiny leaves. A reliable rose that will reach 15ft. Bred by Easlea (U.K.), 1932. See page 282.

ELEGANCE. In spite of the strong mixture of *Rosa wichuraiana* in this Climber, it has much of the appearance of a Climbing Hybrid Tea. It does, as the name suggests, have truly elegant blooms, which start as long shapely buds of clear yellow, opening to very large, very full blooms of pale lemon. The foliage is a dark glossy green. There is one profuse blooming, with only occasional flowers later. A beautiful rose that will grow to a considerable height — 15 to 18ft. Its parentage is 'Glenn Dale' × ('Mary Wallace' × 'Miss Lolita Armour').

ENA HARKNESS, CLIMBING. This is a good climbing sport of the Bush Hybrid Tea, with pointed buds of bright crimson-scarlet. The bush form, popular in the 1940s and 1950s, had a weakness in that it tended to hang its head. In the climbing form this becomes a virtue, enabling us to view the bloom from below. Vigorous growth of at least 18ft.

ÉTOILE DE HOLLANDE, CLIMBING. A climbing sport of the once popular bush Hybrid Tea, and still one of the best and most reliable crimson Climbers. It has long buds of deepest crimson and the rich heavy fragrance we expect of such a rose. The buds open to a rather shapeless flower, but this is made up for in quantity, both early and late in the season. It has been said climbing 'Étoile de Hollande' does not like cold, but this has not been my experience. It will grow to 18ft. Discovered by Leenders (Holland), 1931, on the bush by Verschuren, also of Holland. See page 283.

GENERAL MACARTHUR, CLIMBING. A rose with loosely-formed flowers that vary in colour from crimson-scarlet to deep rosy-red. They are nicely poised on the branch and open flat, with a rich fragrance. It is both free-flowering and recurrent, growing strongly to about 12ft. Discovered by Dickson (U.K.), 1923, on the bush bred by Hill (U.S.A.), 1905.

GOLDEN DAWN, CLIMBING. The bush form of this variety was sometimes classified as a Tea Rose. Its breeding, 'Élégante' × 'Ethel Somerset', would make it a Hybrid Tea, but there is, in fact, something of the Tea Rose about it. It has a delicious Tea Rose perfume and rather lax stems that make it particularly suitable as a Climber. The buds are large, well formed, full and heavy, pale lemon-yellow in colour with just a tint of rose on the reverse of the petals. Occasionally the buds may split instead of opening properly. There is a smaller crop in autumn, when the flowers are often of the highest perfection. 'Golden Dawn' has large, deep green leaves and will grow to 12ft. This climbing sport was discovered by Le Grice (U.K.), 1947, and by others at various times; bush bred by Grant (Australia), 1929.

GUINÉE. The result of a cross between 'Souvenir de Claudius Denoyel' × 'Ami Quinard', the first of which has 'Château de Clos Vougeot' as one of its parents, and the exceptionally deep colouring of that rose has been passed down with equal intensity. 'Guinée' has pointed buds opening to attractive, flat, neatly formed blooms. They are so dark that in the shade they can appear almost black; indeed, they become barely visible against its dark green foliage. For this reason it is best grown against a light background. A few contrasting stamens are visible, and there is a very rich fragrance. Although perhaps just a little lacking in strength, with generous treatment it will grow well to about 15ft. The problem may be that it is not altogether hardy and would be better grown on a warm wall. Bred by Mallerin (France), introduced 1938.

HOME SWEET HOME, CLIMBING. I am not well acquainted with this early Hybrid Tea Rose as a Climber, but as a bush the flowers are so charming that I think it is worthy of inclusion here. Its flowers are held rather too erectly to be of much use high up, but if it is trained at a low level it might prove most effective. Fragrant, purest pink, cupped flowers. Height 10ft. Bush bred by Wood & Ingram (U.K.); we do not know who discovered the climbing form.

IRISH FIREFLAME, CLIMBING. The climbing form of the dainty, single Hybrid Tea. Its colour is a mixture of orange and gold, the petals being veined crimson, with a bunch of fawn-coloured anthers. Slender growth, but quite healthy and reliable. Height about 10ft. Discovered by A. Dickson (U.K.), 1916, on the bush by the same breeder.

JOSEPHINE BRUCE, CLIMBING. As a bush, this variety produces shapely flowers of a particularly rich and pure crimson. They are very fragrant. It is perhaps even better as a Climber, growing to 15ft. and flowering well, with another crop of flowers in late summer. Discovered by Bees (U.K.), 1954, on the bush form bred by the same firm.

LADY FORTEVIOT, CLIMBING. Large, high-centred blooms of golden-yellow and apricot, with a rich fragrance. The growth is strong, if a little stiff, with bronzy, glossy foliage. Spread 12ft. One good flowering, with occasional blooms later in the year. Discovered by the Howard Rose Company (U.S.A.), 1935, on the bush by B.R. Cant (U.K.).

LADY SYLVIA, CLIMBING. I discussed 'Ophelia' and its two sports, 'Lady

LADY SYLVIA, *a climbing sport of an early Hybrid Tea Rose with shapely blooms of soft colouring.* *See opposite.*

NEW DAWN, *a Modern Climber growing on a roof — a pleasing way to train a Climbing Rose.* *See page 307.* Page

MAIGOLD, *a hardy and reliable Climbing Rose, ideal for an exposed position.* *See page 310* Page

GLOIRE DE DIJON, *a hardy Noisette Rose, once seen in every cottage garden.* *See page 274.* Knight
SOMBREUIL, *Climbing Tea Rose. Another hardy rose with perfectly formed blooms.* *See page 286.* Knight
Both these roses flower well in summer and autumn.

MERMAID, *Climbing Rose. An aristocrat among roses, with large flowers from early summer until autumn.* *See page 311.* Knight

CUPID, *Climbing Hybrid Tea Rose. The large shapely blooms are summer flowering only.* *See page 290.*
Knight

MRS. HERBERT STEVENS, *a beautifully formed Climbing Tea Rose that is comparatively hardy.* *See page 285.*
Knight

MADAME GRÉGOIRE STAECHELIN, *one of the finest Climbing Hybrid Tea Roses, with large flowers and very tall.* *See page 302.*
Knight

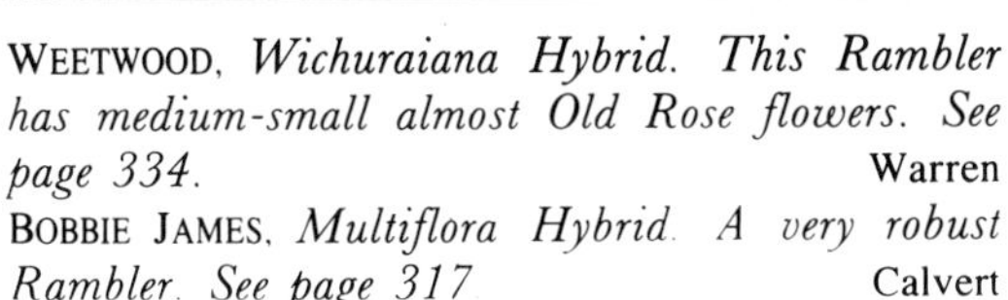

WEETWOOD, *Wichuraiana Hybrid. This Rambler has medium-small almost Old Rose flowers. See page 334.* Warren

BOBBIE JAMES, *Multiflora Hybrid. A very robust Rambler. See page 317.* Calvert

SEAGULL, *Multiflora Hybrid. A Rambler with large sprays of small flowers and wonderful fragrance. See page 319.* Warren

ROSA BANKSIAE LUTESCENS, *Banksian Rose. A single-flowered form in this beautiful group of Ramblers. See page 335.* Page

SCHOOLGIRL. *See page 308.* Calvert
GOLDEN SHOWERS. *See page 306.* Calvert
CORAL DAWN. *See page 306.* Page
SWAN LAKE. *See page 308.* Knight
PINK PERPÉTUE. *See page 307.* Knight
BREATH OF LIFE. *See page 306.* Page

Six Modern Climbers, all reliable and of fairly short growth, which will flower repeatedly.

Sylvia' and 'Madame Butterfly', under the early Hybrid Teas in Chapter 4. Climbing 'Lady Sylvia' has all the qualities of the bush form with exquisitely shaped buds of flesh-pink tinged yellow at the base. As a Climber 'Lady Sylvia' is first rate, growing to about 20ft. and repeating well. This rose, 'Ophelia' and 'Madame Butterfly' are all particularly fine in the greenhouse, where they will produce flowers of the utmost perfection. Outside, they are among the best of the Climbing Hybrid Teas, although they are a little upright in habit. Discovered by Stevens (U.K.), 1933. See page 293.

LADY WATERLOW. Large blooms opening to loosely formed, almost semi-double flowers of salmon-pink edged with carmine and with attractive veining. It produces strong growth to about 12ft., and is often recommended as a pillar rose, although it is equally suitable for a wall. Delicious tea scent. 'La France de '89' × 'Madame Marie Lavalley'. Bred by Nabonnand (France), 1903. See page 282.

LA FRANCE, CLIMBING. This early Hybrid Tea is rare as a Climber and I have not seen a mature plant in this form, though I should expect it to be attractive when so grown, particularly on a wall, where it would have some protection from the damp. It has silvery-pink cupped Old Rose flowers with a strong fragrance. Growth about 12ft. Discovered by Henderson (U.K.), 1893, on the bush by Guillot Fils (France).

MADAME ABEL CHATENAY, CLIMBING. I have already said that the bush form of this rose is one of the most exquisitely beautiful of all Hybrid Tea Roses. The Climbing form is no less desirable, although with me it has not proved too reliable. When well grown it will achieve 15ft., with attractive, not too stiff growth, and slightly nodding flowers. These are pale pink, deepening towards the centre with a darker reverse and lovely fragrance. Discovered by Page (U.K.), introduced 1917; bush form bred by Pernet-Ducher (France), 1895.

MADAME BUTTERFLY, CLIMBING. The Climbing form of the beautiful bush rose described among the early Hybrid Teas in Chapter 4, having the same perfect buds and blush-pink colouring. An excellent rose of up to 20ft., with good repeat-flowering qualities, the later blooms being finer than those in early summer. Very fragrant. Discovered by E.P. Smith (U.K.), 1926. See also 'Lady Sylvia' above.

MADAME CAROLINE TESTOUT, CLIMBING. The bush form of 'Madame Caroline Testout' was, in its day, almost as popular as 'Peace' in our time. Like 'Peace' it was extremely tough, and the climbing form is no less so. We have on our house an interesting example: photographs taken in 1919 show it as a mature Climber even then, and it is still there today, growing strongly and flowering well. This is in spite of the fact that it was cut to the ground in the winter of 1981/2 when, in Shropshire, we suffered the lowest temperatures ever recorded in England. It is interesting to note that this plant was budded on a Rugosa stock, which is usually regarded as short lived. The flowers are large and globular, of an even silvery-pink colour, not particularly full, with the petals rolled back at the edges. The growth is strong and rather stiff with the flowers held upright, though this does not seem to matter with a bloom of this form. It will achieve at least 20ft. Only a slight scent. Discovered by Chauvry (France), 1901, on the rose bred by Pernet-Ducher (France), 1890.

MADAME EDOUARD HERRIOT ('Daily Mail Rose'). A rose of unique and mixed colouring, so much so that the descriptions we read are as various as they are numerous. *Modern Roses* says: 'Coral-red, shaded yellow and light rosy-scarlet, passing to prawn-red', but in fact the overall effect is an almost terracotta shade. However we put it, it is beautiful and ever changing in appearance. The individual flowers are not outstanding, being loosely double, but they provide a sheet of bloom in early summer, and are followed by occasional blooms later on. The foliage is glossy green and there are very few thorns. It will grow to about 15ft. Fragrant. Breeding 'Madame Caroline Testout' × unnamed Hybrid Tea. Bush bred by Pernet-Ducher (France); climbing sport discovered by Ketten (Luxemburg), 1921.

MADAME GRÉGOIRE STAECHELIN. A fine Climbing Rose bred by Pedro Dot of Spain, who also gave us the Shrub Rose 'Nevada'. Known in some countries as 'Spanish Beauty', this is perhaps a more suitable name, for indeed it is one of the best of all the Climbing Roses. The flowers start as slender buds of deep pink, but soon open wide and flat to form very large semi-double blooms of fresh, glowing pink, with a deeper shade on the reverse. The stamens are visible, and there is a delicious fragrance. This Climber produces one magnificent flush of flowers in early summer, but nothing thereafter. Perhaps this would be too much to expect. It has strong growth, usually to about 15ft., but often more on a wall. The foliage is dark, glossy and luxuriant. If it has a fault, it is that the lower part of the plant becomes bare as it ages, the flowers appearing mainly on its upper branches. To avoid this it is necessary to train it horizontally so far as possible. A good rose for growing on a north wall. The result of a cross between 'Frau Karl Druschki' and 'Château de Clos Vougeot', an almost pure white and one of the darkest of dark red roses, it was introduced in 1927. See page 298.

MADAME HENRI GUILLOT, CLIMBING. It is interesting to note that the original bush form of this climbing sport is given as a cross between the Hybrid Tea 'Rochefort' and a *Rosa foetida bicolor* seedling — presumably itself a hybrid. It produces long, pointed buds which open to form flat, rounded, almost camellia-like flowers of a deep salmon-pink flushed with orange. There is a slight fragrance. The growth is vigorous, to 12ft., with glossy, green foliage. Discovered by Meilland (France), 1942, on the bush bred by Mallerin (France), 1938.

MEG. This Climbing Rose is thought to be the result of a cross between 'Paul's Lemon Pillar' and 'Madame Butterfly', and its general appearance would suggest that this is, in fact, true. It bears very large, single or semi-double flowers of pale apricot-pink, with a large boss of quite dark stamens. The flowers are fragrant and held in small clusters. This is a beautiful rose that may be grown on a pillar or wall, but is perhaps best of all when encouraged to clamber over bushes or hedges. Here its large and elegantly waved blooms display themselves with the most pleasing effect. There is only occasional repeat flowering after the first flush. Height 9ft. Bred by Dr. A.C.V. Gosset (U.K.), 1954.

MICHÈLE MEILLAND, CLIMBING. I spoke with some enthusiasm of this Modern Hybrid Tea in its bush form in Chapter 4, and it is also beautiful as a Climber, with the same perfectly formed, soft pink flowers. It will grow to 12ft. Fragrant. Discovered by Meilland (France), 1951, on the bush by the same breeder.

MRS. AARON WARD, CLIMBING. The climbing sport of an early Hybrid Tea bred by Pernet-Ducher in 1907. It produces fine, high-centred blooms of bright yellow washed with salmon, the colour varying considerably according to the season and paling with age. Strong fragrance. Growth about 12ft. Discovered by Dickson (U.K.), introduced 1922.

MRS. G.A. VAN ROSSEM, CLIMBING. A Climbing Hybrid Tea of unusual and beautiful colouring, its large flowers a mixture of dark golden-yellow and orange attractively veined with bronze. These are held on long, rather too rigid stems and have a strong fragrance. Vigorous growth to about 12ft., and deep bronzy-green foliage. Bush bred by Van Rossem (Holland); the climbing sport discovered by Gaujard (France), 1937.

MRS. SAM MCGREDY, CLIMBING. A good example of an early Hybrid Tea that is much better in its climbing form. The bush is not strong, but the Climber has no such trouble and will easily achieve 15ft. Its flowers are coppery-orange flushed with scarlet, with crisp buds, and associate well with the glossy, dark, bronzy foliage. The growth is not too rigid and the flower stems suitably lax. It repeats well. Bush bred by McGredy (U.K.); climbing sports have been discovered by various people, the first being Buisman (Holland), 1937. See Chapter 4.

OPHELIA, CLIMBING. A good Climber that will achieve anything up to 20ft., with beautifully formed blush-pink flowers repeating well and a rich fragrance. Discovered by A. Dickson (U.K.), 1920. See Chapter 4.

PAUL'S LEMON PILLAR. A cross between 'Frau Karl Druschki' and 'Maréchal Niel', two roses of classic bud formation and, as we might expect, this rose too has flowers of similar perfection. Their colour is a creamy-yellow with a tint of green at the base of the petals. They are very large, hanging slightly with their weight, the petals being neatly scrolled at the edges as the buds unfold. It will grow to a considerable height, at least 20ft. on a warm wall. However, it is surprising it should bear the name 'Pillar', for which it is not particularly well suited. There is no repeat flowering. A majestic flower with a wonderful fragrance. Bred by William Paul (U.K.), introduced 1915.

PAUL'S SCARLET CLIMBER. A once-popular Climbing Rose bearing small clusters of semi-double, scarlet-crimson flowers in late June. It is, perhaps, not so worthwhile today, as it does not repeat and the flowers are not of outstanding quality — equally good Climbers can be found amongst the 'Moderns' which do repeat. Nonetheless, it flowers freely and is hardy and reliable. Slightly fragrant. A good pillar rose; height about 10ft. The parents were probably 'Paul's Carmine Pillar' × 'Rêve d'Or'. Bred by William Paul, introduced 1916.

PICTURE, CLIMBING. This Hybrid Tea Rose is described in its bush form in Chapter 4. The climbing sport has the same charming, pink, buttonhole buds on a plant that will grow to 15ft. It flowers both in summer and autumn. Discovered by Swim (U.S.A.), introduced 1942.

REINE MARIE HENRIETTE. A cross between the Tea Rose 'Madame Berard' (which has 'Gloire de Dijon' as one parent) and the Hybrid Perpetual 'Général Jacqueminot'. Large, fully double cherry-red flowers, opening wide like those of an Old Rose. The growth is vigorous, flowering freely and recurrently. It is fragrant and will achieve 12ft. Bred by Levet (France), 1878.

RÉVEIL DIJONNAIS. The result of a cross between the Hybrid Perpetual 'Eugène Fürst' and the Hybrid Tea 'Constance', this rose is, therefore, not too distantly related to *Rosa foetida,* and this fact is evident in its appearance. It is a short growing Climber with glossy, deep green leaves. The buds are of Hybrid Tea type, opening to large, semi-double flowers of bright scarlet-crimson with a yellow centre, and yellow tints on the reverse of the petals, giving a distinct bicolour effect. It flowers in late June and, to a limited extent, later. Slightly fragrant. Growth 10ft. Somewhat subject to blackspot. Bred by Buatois (France), 1931.

RICHMOND, CLIMBING. 'Richmond' was a popular bush Hybrid Tea in the first half of this century, and this is its climbing form. It bears long, slim buds of bright scarlet turning to carmine with age and varying considerably according to the season. The open flowers are inclined to burn in the hot sun, and for this reason it is perhaps better not to plant it on a south wall. Growth 10ft. Bush bred by Hill from 'Lady Battersea' × 'Liberty', 1905; Climber discovered by A. Dickson (U.K.), 1912.

SHOT SILK, CLIMBING. A good climbing sport of the well-known early Hybrid Tea, with vigorous growth, fine, glossy green foliage and a good crop of flowers both in early and late summer. These are cerise-pink shot with orange-scarlet and shaded with yellow at the base of the petals. Fragrant. 18ft. Discovered by Knight (Australia), 1931.

SOUVENIR DE CLAUDIUS DENOYEL. The breeding of this rose is 'Château de Clos Vougeot' × 'Commander Jules Gravereaux', and it has the rare unfading crimson of the first parent, though in a brighter shade. The flowers are large, opening to a rather informal, semi-double cup shape, with a strong, rich fragrance. It is laden with bloom hanging nicely from the branches in early summer, and has a rather smaller crop later on. It may achieve at least 12ft. One of the best of our rather limited selection of crimson climbing roses. Bred by Chambard (France), introduced 1920.

SUPER STAR, CLIMBING. In spite of the excessive popularity of this rose as a bush, I do not recollect having seen the Climber growing in a garden — I myself have not grown the climbing form to maturity. I understand it is quite vigorous, reaching 8ft., and can can well imagine it might be a more pleasing rose in its climbing form given a suitable background. Its bright vermilion colouring is unique among Climbing Roses. Discovered by Blaby Rose Gardens (U.K.), 1965, and found in Europe and the U.S.A. in the same year.

SUTTER'S GOLD, CLIMBING. The climbing form of one of the most beautiful Hybrid Teas. It has the same shapely buds of orange-yellow colouring, flushed with pink and veined with red, and a delicious fragrance. Growth about 12ft. Discovered by Armstrong Nurseries (U.S.A.), 1950.

VICOMTESSE PIERRE DU FOU. It is difficult to know where to place this variety as it is the result of crossing the Noisette 'L'Idéal' with the Hybrid Tea 'Joseph Hill'. However, I think it leans towards the latter parent. The flowers are of a coppery-pink colour, deeper at first, paling a little later on. They open to a quartered formation hanging nicely from the branch. The growth is vigorous, spreading to 20ft., the foliage large and bronzy-green. Tea Rose fragrance. Bred by Sauvageot (France), introduced 1923.

MODERN CLIMBERS

If we look back over this chapter, it will be seen there has been very little in the way of the deliberate breeding of Climbing Roses. With the exception of the Noisettes, most Climbing Roses have been either sports or chance offsprings from the breeding of bush roses. It was only after the Rambler Rose 'Dr. W. Van Fleet' sported to produce 'New Dawn' in 1930, that any definite move was made towards breeding Climbing Roses, and even then nothing happened until the 1950s. 'New Dawn' had many of the characteristics of a repeat-flowering Climber having flowers of almost Hybrid Tea size and form like its parent. It was eventually crossed with various Hybrid Teas to produce a number of useful repeat-flowering Climbing Roses. Along with these, other crosses were made between bush roses and Ramblers, and sometimes between strong growing Hybrid Teas to produce further Climbers. It is a combination of all these roses that we gather together under the heading 'Modern Climbers'.

To obtain recurrent flowering in a Climbing Rose is no easy matter, and many of these roses do not grow to a great height, indeed some of them are little more than shrubs. On a pillar or more open structure they will often remain rather short, but given the benefit of a wall this will draw them up to a considerable height. Here they can achieve 10ft. or more.

There are, of course, times when a short Climber is required, as on a low wall, or fence, and here Modern Climbers come into their own. Most of them are in the modern mould, often with strong colours and with very much of the appearance of a Hybrid Tea. One thing is certain — they can be relied on to give continuity of colour over a long period.

ALOHA. I have recommended that this should be regarded as a shrub but it also makes a useful low climber. See Chapter 8.

BREATH OF LIFE. A low growing Climber of 7ft., bearing large, full, well-formed Hybrid Tea flowers of a lovely apricot colouring which turns to apricot-pink. Fragrant. Bred by Harkness (U.K.), 1982. See page 300.

CASINO. Clusters of large, globular, soft-yellow flowers, with dark, glossy, light green foliage. A cross between 'Coral Dawn' and the tall Hybrid Tea 'Buccaneer'. Height 10ft. Bred by McGredy (U.K.), 1963.

COMPASSION. Well-shaped Hybrid Tea flowers with a sweet fragrance, their colour being salmon-pink tinted with apricot-orange. The growth is rather stiff and bushy and there is plentiful dark green foliage. One of the best and most popular roses in this group, as well as being one of the most fragrant. Height 10ft. It may also be grown as a shrub. Breeding 'White Cockade' × 'Prima Ballerina'. Harkness (U.K.), 1973.

COPENHAGEN. Medium-sized flowers of good Hybrid Tea shape and dark scarlet colouring. The growth tends to be upright, to about 7ft. Quite fragrant. Breeding seedling × 'Ena Harkness'. Bred by Poulsen (Denmark), 1964.

CORAL DAWN. Quite large, full blooms of coral-pink colouring, against plentiful, healthy, dark green foliage. Fragrant. Growth 10 to 12ft. ('New Dawn' × a yellow Hybrid Tea) × an orange-red Polyantha. Bred by Boerner (U.S.A.), 1952. See page 300.

DANSE DU FEU. Bright orange-scarlet flowers of medium size, the colour deepening with age. The buds are quite short but well formed and the flowers open flat. They are produced very freely and continuously against plentiful foliage. Little scent. Growth 8ft. Breeding 'Paul's Scarlet' × unnamed Multiflora seedling. Mallerin (France), 1953.

GALWAY BAY. Large, double, Hybrid Tea flowers of salmon-pink colouring. A vigorous plant with plentiful, glossy, dark green foliage. Height 10ft. 'Heidelberg' × 'Queen Elizabeth'. McGredy (U.K.), 1966.

GOLDEN SHOWERS. A short growing Climber of many virtues. Large, open golden-yellow flowers, fading to light yellow. The individual blooms may be of no exceptional beauty, but they are produced very freely and continuously throughout the summer, providing a good splash of colour. The plant grows well and it is unusually happy on a north wall, perhaps more so than any other rose except 'Zéphirine Drouhin'. Also good as a shrub. 'Charlotte Armstrong' × 'Captain Thomas'. Lammerts (U.S.A.), 1956. See page 300.

HANDEL. Quite small semi-double flowers that are closer to a Floribunda than a Hybrid Tea in character. The colouring is unusual, being creamy-blush and edged with pink. The growth is tall, perhaps 12ft. and it repeats well. There is some tendency to blackspot. 'Columbine' × 'Heidelberg'. McGredy (U.K.), 1956.

HIGHFIELD. A sport from 'Compassion', see above, with all the virtues of that rose. Here we have light yellow flowers with occasional peachy tints. Fragrant. Harkness (U.K.), 1981.

NEW DAWN. As I said in the introduction to this section, this is a recurrent-flowering sport from the summer flowering Rambler 'Dr. W. Van Fleet', and an important influence in this group. With its conversion to repeat-flowering, the growth reduced from 20ft. in its parent to about 10ft. in this rose. It has pretty, rather pointed buds, opening to medium-sized, pearly-blush coloured flowers held in large clusters and with a sweet fragrance. The growth is vigorous with plentiful foliage. It may be pruned to form a shrub, or grown as a hedge. 'New Dawn' is one of the most disease-free of roses, and was the first rose ever to receive a patent. Discovered by Somerset Rose Nursery (U.S.A.), introduced 1930. See page 294.

NORWICH GOLD. There are three 'Norwich' varieties, all good strong-growing and very reliable Climbers. This one has clusters of full-petalled flowers of yellow shaded with orange and opening flat. Little repeat flowering. Growth 10ft. Kordes (Germany), 1962.

NORWICH PINK. Large, semi-double flowers of bright cerise-pink. Strong fragrance. Good, dark, glossy foliage. 10ft. Kordes (Germany), 1962.

NORWICH SALMON. Fully double, soft salmon-pink flowers in large clusters. Vigorous, bushy growth, with dark green, glossy foliage. Growth 10ft. Kordes (Germany), 1962.

PARADE. Here we have a rose that deserves more attention. Like 'Aloha' the growth is short, with large, deep cerise-pink flowers that are fully double and of almost 'Old Rose' persuasion. They have a strong fragrance. It is exceptionally free and continuous in flower. The growth is very vigorous and healthy, and will achieve 7 or 8ft., though it can also make a good lax growing shrub. Bred from a seedling from 'New Dawn' × 'World's Fair'. Boerner (U.S.A.), 1953.

PINK PERPÉTUE. A variety that will grow a little taller than most of the others, perhaps to 12ft. In colour it is a rather harsh pink with a carmine reverse, the flowers being medium sized, double, slightly cupped and held in trusses. The growth is vigorous and reliable and it repeats well. There is some fragrance. 'Danse du Feu' × 'New Dawn'. Gregory (U.K.), 1965. See page 300.

ROYAL GOLD. Not one of the most reliable Climbers, but with flowers of the deepest yellow colouring, a characteristic it gains from its parent 'Lydia', its other parent being the Floribunda 'Goldilocks'. The blooms are large and of good Hybrid Tea formation; the foliage is dark green and glossy. Height about 8ft. Bred by Morey (U.S.A.), 1957.

SCHOOLGIRL. This has been a popular Climber for some time, and although a beautiful rose at its best, having shapely buds in a pleasing coppery-orange shade, it is not reliable. The foliage is not good and is rather subject to blackspot, often resulting in poor growth. Fragrant. 10ft. 'Coral Dawn' × 'Belle Blonde'. McGredy (U.K.), 1964. See page 300.

SWAN LAKE. One of the most beautiful Modern Climbers, with large well-shaped, white Hybrid Tea blooms delicately flushed with pale pink at the centre. Good, dark green foliage. Slight fragrance. 8ft. 'Memoriam' × 'Heidelberg'. McGredy (U.K.), 1968. See page 300.

SYMPATHIE. Shapely, high-centred blooms of bright blood-red. Vigorous growth, with large, glossy foliage. It will achieve 10 or 12ft. A good reliable variety, flowering intermittently throughout the summer. Kordes (Germany), 1964.

WHITE COCKADE. A rose which produces some of the most beautiful and shapely flowers in this group. They are pure white and most attractive against its large, dark green leaves. Unfortunately it does not grow very quickly, nor to a great height, so would perhaps be better grown as a shrub. A good cut flower. Fragrant. 'New Dawn' × 'Circus'. Cocker (U.K.), 1969.

OTHER CLIMBING ROSES

Having covered the various classifications of Climbing Roses, we are inevitably left with a number of varieties that do not fit comfortably into any of these groups. Such roses are usually the result of crossing one or other of the garden climbers with a Climbing Species Rose.

BELLE PORTUGAISE ('Belle of Portugal'). A cross between *Rosa gigantea* and the early Climbing Hybrid Tea 'Reine Marie Henriette'. *R. gigantea* is the largest-flowered of all Climbing Species and, as we have seen, is one of the main ancestors of our modern roses. It was, therefore, obviously a good idea to back-cross some of our modern roses to this species. Unfortunately such hybrids are not hardy in this country, though this variety, and one or two others, will survive most winters in warmer areas of the U.K. if given a protected position, when it may be expected to grow to 20ft. It has long, silky, pointed buds that hang their heads in the most elegant and pleasing manner. Their colour is a pale salmon-pink and their petals beautifully scrolled, eventually opening to rather loose flowers which appear in mid-June only, but in some abundance. It has fine, long, pointed, grey-green, drooping foliage. Strong Tea Rose fragrance. Raised at the Botanic Gardens, Lisbon, 1903.

CÉCILE BRUNNER, CLIMBING. A description of the bush form of this variety is to be found in Chapter 5. This rose has miniature, blush-pink, Hybrid

Tea Rose blooms, with scrolled buds of the utmost perfection. It may, therefore, come as something of a surprise to find that its climbing form is of exceptional vigour, with fine luxuriant foliage. It can, in fact, achieve 25ft. of rampant growth. The flowers are exactly similar to those of the bush, except that they can be a shade larger, as are the leaves. Unlike the bush, however, there is little or no repeat flowering. It is a most charming and reliable Climbing Rose, and free of disease. A good variety for growing into trees. Discovered by Hosp (U.S.A.), 1894.

DORTMUND. In the early 1940s the rose 'Max Graf', a hybrid between *Rosa rugosa* and *R. wichuraiana,* produced a chance seedling which Herr Wilhelm Kordes named *R.* × *kordesii.* This turned out to be tetraploid, and may have been a chance hybrid with another rose. It was a very hardy Climber, and Kordes hybridized it with other garden roses to produce a race of hardy Climbers, most of which are repeat flowering. I include here 'Dortmund', 'Leverkusen' and 'Parkdirektor Riggers'.

'Dortmund' is a vigorous Climber, with very dark, glossy green leaves. It bears large, single, crimson flowers, with a white eye at the centre and yellow stamens, and will bloom recurrently if dead headed, otherwise there will be numerous hips. A very reliable, disease-free, hardy rose, but perhaps a little coarse. Height 8 to 10ft. Breeding seedling × *R.* × *kordesii.* Kordes (Germany), 1955. See page 259.

DREAM GIRL. A cross between the Wichuraiana Rambler 'Dr. W. Van Fleet' and a Hybrid Tea called 'Senora Gari', though it does not really fit in with the Wichuraiana Hybrids. The flowers are of a lovely soft coral-pink and of typical Old Rose rosette formation with numerous small petals. The growth and foliage is rather similar to 'Dr. W. Van Fleet', but it will achieve no more than 10ft. in height. There is a strong spicy fragrance. 'Dream Girl' flowers very late, continuing for a long time, but cannot be said to be repeat flowering. A charming rose, ideal for a pillar. Bred by Bobbink (U.S.A.), 1944.

ICEBERG, CLIMBING. Floribundas, unlike the Hybrid Teas, have not been fruitful in the production of climbing sports and I am aware of only two worthwhile varieties, this and climbing 'Masquerade'. Climbing 'Iceberg' lives up to the high expectations we would have of its parent, and even takes on a new elegance with its longer growth. Its only drawback is a tendency to revert to the bush form when first planted. When this occurs it is worth trying again with another plant. Growth 10ft. Discovered by Cant (U.K.), 1968. See page 283.

LA FOLLETTE. Like 'Belle Portugaise', this is a *Rosa gigantea* hybrid, and is in many ways similar to the former rose, with long, pointed buds and loosely-formed, open flowers. The colour is rose-pink, with coppery-salmon on the outside of the petals. A most beautiful rose, it is only for the warmest areas and sheltered walls in this country where it will grow to 20ft., although it may be massive in countries with warmer climates. Strong fragrance. One season of flowering only. Its other parent is not known. Raised by Busby, gardener to Lord Brougham, at Cannes, France.

LAWRENCE JOHNSTON (originally known as 'Hidcote Yellow'). A hybrid between the Hybrid Perpetual Rose 'Madame Eugène Verdier' and *Rosa foetida* 'Persiana', it is strange this cross should produce such a vigorous Climber which can be relied upon to reach 20ft., and often as much as 30ft. As is usually the case with *R. foetida* crosses, it is this species that dominates. The flowers are large, of loosely-cupped shape, and of a bright clear yellow that shows up well against the excellent, glossy, dark green foliage. They have a strong fragrance and are produced in one magnificent crop early in the season, with the chance of an occasional bloom later. If it has a weakness, it is a susceptibility to blackspot, a not surprising fact in a *R. foetida* hybrid, but please do not let this deter you from growing it, as it is one of our finest Climbers. Raised by Pernet-Ducher of France, in 1923, who rather surprisingly rejected it. Lawrence Johnston, of Hidcote Manor fame, rescued it when visiting the French nursery, and it was eventually made available to the public by Graham Thomas. See page 281.

LE RÊVE. A sister seedling to 'Lawrence Johnston', from 'Madame Eugène Verdier' and *Rosa foetida* 'Persiana', it was selected by Pernet-Ducher in preference to 'Lawrence Johnston', although it has, in fact, turned out to be inferior. We should not be too surprised at this, for it is difficult even to be sure of a new Shrub Rose until it has been grown in gardens for some years. With Climbers, which may take many years to reach their full potential, the task becomes even more difficult. Nonetheless, the virtues of this variety should not be totally obscured by its more illustrious sister, for 'Le Rêve' does have a certain grace that is its own. It is similar to 'Lawrence Johnston', but a little less robust, with almost single flowers of a paler yellow which are deliciously fragrant. Fine, glossy-green foliage. Growth 20ft. Introduced in 1923.

LEVERKUSEN. Perhaps the most attractive of the Kordesii hybrids, the result of a cross between *Rosa* × *kordesii* and the climbing Hybrid Tea 'Golden Glow'. It bears quite large, double rosette-shaped flowers of rather Old Rose appearance and of a creamy-yellow colouring, deepening towards the centre. There is a pleasing, fruit-like fragrance. The growth is strong and rather bushy, to a height of 10ft., and the foliage is a deep glossy green, with rather small leaflets. This rose flowers freely in summer and, to a lesser extent, later on. Kordes (Germany), 1954.

MAIGOLD. A cross between 'Poulsen's Pink' and 'Frühlingstag', which makes it three generations removed from *Rosa pimpinellifolia hispida,* and it still carries many of the qualities of that rose, particularly in that it is extremely tough and hardy and will thrive under the most difficult conditions. Indeed, it would be hard to think of any Climbing Rose of moderate height that is more suitable for such conditions. It has short, reddish buds which open to quite large, strongly-fragrant, semi-double flowers of bronzy-yellow with golden stamens. There is one very free-flowering period, early in the season, with occasional flowers later. The growth is extremely vigorous, producing strong, very thorny stems to a height of 12ft., with plentiful, glossy-green foliage. Although often recommended as a shrub, I find the growth rather too untidy for this. Little or no disease. Raised by Kordes (Germany), 1953. See page 294.

MASQUERADE, CLIMBING. The climbing sport of the Floribunda of the same name. It will grow to 18ft. and flower freely, but only in the summer. Its unusual mixture of yellow, pink and deep red has its uses in the garden scheme. Discovered by Gregory (U.K.), 1958.

MERMAID. A true classic — one of the most beautiful of all Climbing Roses, bearing large, single, soft canary-yellow flowers of 5ins. and more across, with a boss of long, sulphur-yellow stamens that remain attractive for some time after the petals have fallen. Its flowers are delicately scented and of a soft sheeny texture, the slightly waved petals giving an elegantly sculptured effect. 'Mermaid' blooms with remarkable regularity throughout the summer; in fact few Climbers can rival it in this respect. The result of a cross between *Rosa bracteata* and an unspecified yellow Tea Rose, one cannot but wonder what this Tea Rose might have been to provide such a lovely shade of yellow. The foliage is similar to that of *R. bracteata,* but larger, and almost evergreen, with a smooth, shiny surface. It is no doubt due to *R. bracteata* that 'Mermaid' is almost completely resistant to disease. Inevitably there is one snag: it is not completely hardy, but it is certainly worth growing in all but the coldest areas, and deserves the best wall you have — if this is out of the morning sun to avoid too quick a thaw after a night of frost so much the better. 'Mermaid' has, rather surprisingly, proved successful on a north-facing wall where it is protected from cold winds. It is frequently slow in the early stages, making little progress in the first two or three years, but once it starts it can grow very quickly, easily achieving 25ft. Little pruning is necessary or desirable — no more than is required to keep it within bounds. It may also be grown as a sprawling shrub, but will require a warm corner if it is not to stay short and appear impoverished. The credit for this fine rose goes to William Paul (U.K.), who introduced it in 1918, and it must be regarded as the crowning glory of that famous rose breeder. See page 296.

PARKDIREKTOR RIGGERS. A rose similar to 'Dortmund', but with large clusters of semi-double flowers of deep velvety crimson. It has similar glossy, dark green foliage. Recurrent flowering. Slight fragrance. Height 12ft. *Rosa* × *kordesii* × 'Our Princess'. Bred by Kordes (Germany), 1957.

SÉNATEUR AMIC. Another *Rosa gigantea* hybrid, along with 'Belle Portugaise' and 'La Follette'. This rose is, perhaps, a little hardier than the other two, but is still only suitable for warm walls. The flowers are borne singly or in twos and threes, and have a strong scent. They are rich pink in colour, with long buds opening to large, semi-double flowers with prominent stamens. The growth is strong, with fine foliage. It may be expected to achieve about 20ft. It is a cross with the Hybrid Tea 'General MacArthur'. Bred by Nabonnand (France), introduced 1924.

Chapter 10

RAMBLING ROSES

The typical Rambling Rose has long, lax growth and bears large sprays of often small flowers in abundance which provide a massed bower-like effect of great beauty. They flower only in the summer, although certain varieties frequently provide a few blooms later on. Many people tend to associate them with the past, and indeed their popularity was at its height in Edwardian times and soon after. They do not, however, belong to the more distant past, as most of them were introduced in the first quarter of this century. Prior to this time there was no more than a very limited selection available, bred mainly from *Rosa arvensis* (the Field Rose), *R. sempervirens* (the Evergreen Rose) and *R. moschata* (the Musk Rose). It was only with the introduction of certain species Ramblers from the Far East, notably *R. multiflora* and *R. wichuraiana,* that the majority of the varieties we now enjoy came into being. These two species were crossed with the garden roses of the day — the Tea Roses, the Hybrid Perpetuals and the Hybrid Teas, thus providing a much wider variety of colour and form of flower.

Since the Second World War the popularity of Ramblers in the average garden has given way to the more continuous flowering Modern Climbers, and there are only a few varieties to be found in the average nursery catalogue or garden centre. This could not be more unfortunate, for Rambling Roses have a place in the garden that no other rose can fill, and are capable of a beauty that is hard to equal. They have a natural grace — often exceeding that of the Climbing Roses, their branches and large sprays hanging gracefully from their support. Not only this, but they are frequently very vigorous and can grow to a great height.

The variety of different uses for Ramblers is perhaps more extensive than for any other class. While they are not always suitable for growing on walls, since they may be difficult to manage, and some of them are inclined to suffer from mildew, they are ideal for many other purposes: for trellises, arches, pergolas, pillars, tripods, the covering of small unsightly buildings and other objects as well as for growing into trees and over shrubs and hedges.

In fact the possibilities are almost endless, providing great scope for ingenuity. Rather surprisingly, some varieties can be grown successfully without support, as large shrubs, and where space can be spared they will grow into great arching mounds. There are also a number of very lax growing varieties that will creep along the ground, forming excellent ground cover. These many and varied uses will be discussed in greater detail in Chapter 12.

Ramblers are usually fragrant and, since they arise from many different species, many different fragrances can be found among them. Often this fragrance carries freely — a quality that is most desirable in any rose. Some have the fresh, sharp, fruit-like fragrance of *R. wichuraiana,* others have a Musk Rose fragrance, but it is possible to detect among Ramblers most of the fragrances of the rose, and indeed the scents of other flowers. The scent of the double white Banksian Rose (*R. banksiae banksiae*) is, for example, said to be similar to that of violets. I have not made a sufficiently close study of rose fragrances to classify them properly (the sense of smell is so personal that I do not dare to do so) , but Graham Thomas, in his book *Climbing Roses Old and New,* does go into the subject in some detail, and such knowledge adds to our pleasure in any rose.

The pruning and maintenance of Ramblers need not give us much trouble. Although there are exceptions in the case of the Multifloras, Ramblers are often best left to take their own course. Pruning is better kept to a minimum so that the plants can create their own natural effect, with no more than an occasional tidying and removal of old growth. Tying will, of course, be necessary, as will the careful and artful guidance of growth, but as time goes on new growth will often intertwine with the old and become, to some degree, self-supporting. Ramblers are in general the most disease free and trouble free of roses; the worst that we can say of them is that a few varieties suffer from mildew. This in fact does not matter so much as with other roses, since we view Ramblers from a greater distance.

AYRSHIRE HYBRIDS

Rosa arvensis is the wild trailing rose of our hedgerows that flowers a little later than the Dog Rose. The Ayrshire Hybrids are a descendant of this species, and it seems that the Sempervirens Hybrids may also have had some part in their development. Unfortunately there are no precise records, but the Ayrshire Hybrids appear to have originated in Scotland. They cannot be said to be in the front rank of Ramblers, but all of them are very hardy, and have the advantage that they will grow under the partial shade of trees better than any other climbing rose. They are useful if only for this reason and, like nearly all older roses, do have their own modest beauty. Of those that remain, the following four varieties are worth consideration.

BENNETT'S SEEDLING ('Thoresbyana'). This was raised or discovered by Bennett, gardener to Lord Manners at Thoresby, in 1840. It appears to be a double form of *Rosa arvensis* with fragrant white flowers. It is very hardy and particularly suitable for growing in partial shade. Growth 20ft.

DUNDEE RAMBLER. Small, very double, white flowers, tinted with pink at the edges. Spread 20ft. It has been suggested it is *Rosa arvensis* × a Noisette Hybrid. Raised by Martin (Scotland), about 1850.

RUGA. A hybrid of *Rosa chinensis,* it has pale pink, semi-double flowers in large, loosely-formed clusters. The growth is vigorous, often more than 20ft. Raised in Italy, prior to 1830.

SPLENDENS (the 'Myrrh-scented Rose'). One of the more worthwhile of the Ayrshire Hybrids. Its flowers are blush-white, tinted with cream and cupped at first, opening to a semi-double flower. They have a pleasing myrrh scent that was at one time almost unique amongst roses, although we do find it in the Sempervirens Hybrids, and again in the English Roses. It will grow vigorously to over 20ft. The breeding is not known, nor do we know who raised it.

SEMPERVIRENS HYBRIDS

Rosa sempervirens, the Evergreen Rose, is a native of Southern Europe and North Africa. It is a climbing or trailing species which, as its name suggests, has the ability to hold its foliage well into the winter, and has passed something of this quality on to its hybrids. Early in the nineteenth century the French breeder Jacques, gardener to the Duke d'Orléans (later King Louis-Philippe), used *R. sempervirens* to create the small but very beautiful group which we call Sempervirens Hybrids. They were almost exclusively the result of his work, and since his time little has been done with them. This is unfortunate, for few Ramblers bred since have been able to rival them for their grace of growth or for the charm of their flowers. These are small, typically Rambler, and held in graceful sprays.

Although *R. sempervirens* is not completely hardy, its hybrids seem to be almost entirely so. They have long, lax growth that is excellent for almost any purpose required of a Rambler, including growing on pillars or as weeping standards. They may also be grown as low, sprawling shrubs. Their foliage is small and neat and the flowers are usually fragrant. They flower only once in the summer.

ADÉLAIDE D'ORLÉANS. One of the most beautiful of Rambling Roses, not only for its creamy-white, semi-double flowers, but for the elegance with which they hang down, like the flowers of a Japanese cherry. Each flower is held a little apart from the next, in small dainty sprays, and the whole effect is charming. All this makes it an ideal rose for an arch or pergola. The growth can be slight by comparison with others in this robust group, but under reasonable conditions can be relied on to reach 15ft. It has a pleasant myrrh fragrance. Jacques (France), 1826. See page 327.

FÉLICITÉ ET PERPÉTUE. A very beautiful rose which must be regarded as one of the most reliable and generally useful of the Ramblers. It flowers with great abundance, the individual white blooms being small, of neat full-petalled pompon formation, and held in large, slightly hanging sprays. They have a light fragrance. The foliage is dark, small and neat, holding well into the winter. The whole plant has a look of 'rightness' and balance. It is hardy, and often to be seen in old gardens, where it may have been for a long time. This rose should not be pruned more than is necessary to keep it within bounds, as this will lead to more growth and less bloom. It flowers late in the season and is quite happy on a north wall. Growth 15ft. The name refers to two Christian martyrs who died in A.D. 203, although I am told by Professor Fineschi of Italy that these were also the names of the breeder's daughters. Bred by Jacques (France), 1827.

FLORA. A free-flowering Rambler with attractively cupped blooms opening flat and filled with petals. The colour is lilac-pink with deep pink at the centre, and there is a delicate perfume. Strong but graceful growth to about 12ft. Raised by Jacques (France), 1829.

PRINCESSE LOUISE. A very similar rose to 'Félicité et Perpétue', described above, and much of what I have said about that rose can equally well be applied to this one. It differs in the soft pink colouring of its buds which soon turns to a creamy-blush fading almost to white. The flowers are held in large clusters with typical Sempervirens elegance and are in every way delightful, while the growth is long and pliable with small, dark green foliage. Growth 12ft. Jacques (France), 1828.

SPECTABILIS. An altogether shorter rose than the other Sempervirens Hybrids, growing to about 7ft. in height. The flowers open from pretty rounded cupped buds into the most perfect delicate pink rosettes with closely packed petals, and have a sweet fragrance. It flowers late with occasional blooms in the autumn and is a charming little rose worthy of extra encouragement. This rose has also been known as 'Noisette Ayez', and there is little doubt that it is a Noisette Hybrid. Breeder unknown, introduced 1848.

MULTIFLORA HYBRIDS

The majority of the Ramblers we enjoy in our gardens today are hybrids of either *Rosa multiflora* or *R. wichuraiana.* Here we have the first of these two important groups, the Multiflora Hybrids.

R. multiflora is a native of Korea and Japan, and was introduced to Britain in 1862. It is a rather stiff-growing Climber or shrub that is both robust and hardy, and is frequently used as a root stock in continental Europe, producing large plants with few suckers. Before the introduction of the species, a garden variety known as *R. multiflora* 'Carnea' had been brought to England from Japan by Thomas Evans of The East India Company in 1804. This had clusters of small double pink flowers. In 1817 the 'Seven Sisters' Rose' arrived from Japan, and later, in 1878, another Rambler known as 'Crimson Rambler'. It was these three roses from Japan, hybridized with various other garden varieties, that gave us the basis for the Multiflora Hybrids.

It is usually not difficult to differentiate between the Multiflora Hybrids and the Wichuraiana Hybrids. The former have rather stiff growth like the original species, with many strong shoots arising from the base of the plant. Their leaves are usually of a duller, more opaque green. The Wichuraianas, on the other hand, are inclined to be more flexible in growth, with long thin stems and frequently have more polished, darker green leaves.

Multiflora Hybrids nearly always have small flowers in large, tightly packed clusters and have the advantage in that many of them flower earlier than the Wichuraianas, thus lengthening the season of bloom. *R. multiflora* has a pleasing fragrance which carries well, and this quality is often to be found in the garden varieties. Generally, the flowers of the Multiflora Hybrids have the appearance of what most people would consider to be typical Rambler Roses, whereas the flowers of the Wichuraianas tend a little more towards the Climbing Roses. They flower only once in the summer.

By the nature of their growth many varieties of this class make excellent large shrubs, as do a number of other Ramblers. Indeed it is surprising that they are not more often seen growing in this form in the wilder areas of large gardens. They are also ideal for municipal planting, roadside sites, public places, or anywhere where a large space has to be covered. I cannot think of a less expensive or more satisfactory way to do this.

It is not possible to be too dogmatic about pruning Ramblers in general, but in so far as the Multifloras are concerned we can say that much of the old growth should be removed at the base in order to encourage the remaining young growth. This is because the Multifloras tend to make so much growth from the base of the plant that they easily become choked. However, the gardener should use his discretion in this matter, paying due attention to the result that he may wish to attain and the general state of the plant. Pruning is best done immediately after flowering.

BLEU MAGENTA. The Multifloras are notable, amongst other things, for the fact that they have produced the only truly purple flowers among the Climbers and Ramblers. Later, through the Polyantha Pompon Roses, they were responsible for such purple shades as we find in the Polyantha 'Baby Faurax'. That they should have this capacity is somewhat surprising, but such are the mysteries of genetics. Other rather similar Multifloras of purplish colouring include 'Rose Marie Viaud',

'Veilchenblau' and 'Violette'. All are beautiful in their own way, valuable for the rarity of their colouring, and particularly desirable for mingling with roses of other colours, especially the pink shades. 'Bleu Magenta' is the last of the four to flower. It is of a violet-cerise shade fading to pale violet. The flowers are small, double and held in closely packed clusters. Growth of about 15ft. may be expected. There is little scent. It was brought to England by Graham Thomas from Roseraie de l'Hay. Nothing is known of its breeding.

BLUSH RAMBLER. Once one of the most popular Ramblers, this rose was bred by B.R. Cant, in 1903, from a cross between 'Crimson Rambler' and 'The Garland'. It is, therefore, one quarter Musk Rose, although in fact it is of very typical Multiflora appearance. The flowers are blush-pink, small and cupped, opening to show golden stamens. They are held in quite large, closely-packed, rather conical clusters. It flowers very freely and the growth is vigorous, with ample light green foliage. Deliciously fragrant. A good Rambler worthy of more attention. See page 332.

BOBBIE JAMES. The parents of this rose are not known, but its overall appearance indicates it has at least some connection with the Multifloras, so it seems reasonable to place it here. It is a Rambler of exceptional vigour, growing far taller than other Multiflora Hybrids. Indeed, it is one of the five or six varieties that we, as nurserymen, tend to recommend when asked for a rose to cover large areas such as an unsightly building, or to grow into a tree. It produces long, thick stems with glossy, pale green leaves. The flowers are small, semi-double, cupped in shape, pearly-white in colour, with yellow stamens, and are held in enormous clusters which, with their weight, tend to hang down from the branch. In fact each large cluster provides what I can only describe as a glistening, pearly effect. This is a very heavy rose that produces a mass of bloom, and it will require a strong structure to support it. It has an exceptional fragrance. Small oval hips. Growth to at least 25ft. Introduced by Sunningdale Nurseries (U.K.), 1961, and named in honour of the Hon. Robert James, at Richmond, Yorkshire. See page 299.

CRIMSON RAMBLER ('Turner's Crimson Rambler', the 'Engineer's Rose'). This is one of the original Ramblers brought to England from Japan in 1878. In China it was known as 'Shi Tz-mei' or 'Ten Sisters', and in Japan as 'Soukara-Ibara'. Sent to a Mr. Jenner in England from Japan, by Professor R. Smith, an engineer, Jenner named it in Smith's honour. Charles Turner, a nurseryman of Slough, purchased the entire stock of this rose and introduced it in 1893 as 'Turner's Crimson Rambler'. It soon became a popular rose, and although there are not many crimson Ramblers, we do not value it very highly today. The flowers are small, crimson, soon fading to an unattractive bluish-crimson. It is particularly subject to mildew. There is little or no scent. Height 15ft.

GOLDFINCH. A vigorous Rambler of typical Multiflora growth and character, bearing close bunches of small button-like flowers of a buff-apricot colour, fading almost to white, with yellow stamens and a strong fruit-like fragrance. There are not many yellow Multifloras and this must be regarded as one of the most satisfactory examples. It makes dense growth with many stems coming from the base and so may require quite a lot of thinning. It will also form an unusually fine, arching shrub of 7ft. in height and, eventually, considerably more across. There are almost no thorns. A hybrid between 'Hélène' and an unknown variety. Bred by George Paul (U.K.), introduced 1907. See page 284.

HIAWATHA. Small, single, crimson flowers with a white centre. The growth is vigorous, to 15ft., with light green foliage. Not perhaps one of the most beautiful Ramblers. No scent. The result of a cross between 'Crimson Rambler' and 'Paul's Carmine Pillar'. Bred by Walsh (U.S.A.), introduced 1904.

PHYLLIS BIDE. A unique rose in that it is of truly Rambler-like character, with typical small flowers in clusters, while at the same time being reliably repeat flowering. Its colour is pale yellow flushed with pink, and it has a pleasant fragrance. A dainty rose of modest beauty, which should be used in such a way as to display itself to full effect, without being lost amongst more robust neighbours. Growth about 10ft. Bred by S. Bide of Farnham, Surrey, in 1923, who gave the parentage as 'Perle d'Or' × 'Gloire de Dijon', though there is some doubt about this statement.

RAMBLING RECTOR. Rose names are not expected to amuse, but here we have an exception, evoking all sorts of images. The rose itself bears large heads of bloom which are small, semi-double, cream at first, later fading to white, with yellow stamens and a good fragrance. These are produced in great abundance on strong, unusually dense and bushy growth of 20ft. or more. Such growth makes it ideal for growing as a shrub, but it is also well suited for scrambling over trees and bushes. A magnificent sight in full bloom with numerous small hips in autumn. Origins unknown. See page 329.

ROSE MARIE VIAUD. This is the second of our purplish Ramblers, its colour being a rich violet at first, fading by degrees to a pale lilac, providing a pleasing mixture of shades. The flowers are small, of neat rosette shape, borne in large clusters, and appear late in the season. The growth is vigorous, to about 15ft. It has little or no scent. Like 'Veilchenblau', from which it is a seedling, it has some tendency to mildew, but this need not worry us too much in a Rambler. Bred by Igoult (France), introduced 1924.

RUSSELLIANA. This rose is probably a Multiflora/Rugosa cross, with predictably coarse results, but with equally predictable toughness and hardiness, giving it a certain value for demanding conditions. It has small semi-double crimson-purple flowers with the Old Rose fragrance. They are held in small clusters. The foliage is dark green, the growth robust and thorny. It flowers freely, providing a pleasing colour effect from a distance. The shrub rose 'Gipsy Boy' is a seedling from this variety. First introduced in 1840, and from time to time variously known as 'Russell's Old Cottage Rose', 'Scarlet Grevillea' and 'Old Spanish Rose'.

SEAGULL. A vigorous Rambler of some 15ft., bearing large clusters of small semi-double white flowers with the greatest freedom. Close to *Rosa multiflora* in appearance, it has a particularly strong fragrance. An excellent rose for smaller trees, producing a magnificent display of billowing white. Breeding not recorded. Raised by Pritchard, 1907. See page 299.

SEVEN SISTERS' ROSE (*Rosa multiflora* 'Platyphylla', 'Grevillei'). This rose was brought to Britain from Japan by Sir Charles Greville in 1817. Very popular in Victorian times, it is still worthy of a place in the garden. It gained its name from the varying shades of colour to be found in its flowers as they pass on to maturity — the idea being that there were seven different colours to be seen at one time. The flowers are double, quite large for a Multiflora, and held in big clusters, while the colour ranges from cerise to pale mauve, and eventually almost to white. It is free flowering and strong growing, to a height of about 18ft. Fresh, fruit-like fragrance. See page 28.

THALIA ('White Rambler'). A hybrid between *Rosa multiflora* and 'Paquerette', which was one of the two original Dwarf Polyantha Roses and itself a seedling from a Multiflora Hybrid. 'Thalia' bears large clusters of small, double, white flowers. Strong fragrance. The growth is vigorous, to about 12ft. Bred by Schmitt (France), introduced 1895.

THE GARLAND ('Wood's Garland'). An early Rambler believed to be the result of a cross between *Rosa moschata* and *R. multiflora.* The flowers are small and semi-double, with quilled petals giving the blooms an unusual daisy-like appearance, while the buds are cream tinged with blush, opening to white, with yellow stamens. The clusters are of small to medium size and are held upright on the branch. Vigorous and bushy in growth to about 15ft., with quite small, dark green leaves, it will also form a good shrub. There is a strong fragrance that carries well, and small, oval hips. Bred, or perhaps discovered, by a man called Wells, 1835.

VEILCHENBLAU ('Violet Blue'). The third of the purplish Multifloras, this is a vigorous Rambler of 12 to 15ft. and typical Multiflora character, with large, closely-packed clusters of small, cupped, purple-violet flowers. These are white at the centre with yellow stamens, and have an occasional streak of white. The colour becomes dark violet later, and finally turns to lilac-grey, presenting an attractive range of colour. Better colours are achieved in a shady position, where there may also be less likelihood of mildew, to which it is subject. There is a fresh fragrance. The foliage is light green, the growth almost thornless. A cross between 'Crimson Rambler' and 'Erinnerung an Brod'. Bred by Schmidt (Germany), 1909. See page 332.

VIOLETTE. The fourth of our purplish-coloured varieties, bearing large sprays of small, cupped, crimson-purple flowers turning to maroon-purple, with an occasional white streak and contrasting yellow stamens. Light, fruit-like fragrance. The growth is vigorous, attaining about 15ft., with few thorns and dark green foliage. Breeding unknown. Bred by Turbat (France), introduced 1921.

WICHURAIANA HYBRIDS

The Wichuraianas are the largest and most important group of Rambler Roses. The species, *R. wichuraiana,* comes from Japan, East China, Korea and Taiwan. Unlike *R. multiflora,* it is a naturally prostrate, trailing or scrambling rose, which is equally capable of being grown as a Climber, and no doubt frequently does so in its natural state. It has large clusters of quite small flowers (although bigger than those of Multiflora) of about 1½ to 2ins. across. Brought to Britain in 1891, the breeders wasted no time in making use of it in the development of new Ramblers. While *R. multiflora* is rather stiffly upright in growth — perhaps too much of a shrub to be quite what we require for a Rambler — no such complaint can be levied against *R. wichuraiana.* Its long, trailing growth, great vigour and glossy disease-free foliage have made it an ideal parent.

Whereas the Multifloras usually have small, typical Rambler flowers, the flowers of the Wichuraiana Hybrids vary considerably between varieties, having a wider range of colour and form than the Multifloras, often with flowers that are more like those of the Climbing Roses. These frequently differ from the Old Rose colouring and come closer to those of the Modern Roses, but they are never crude or garish. They are nearly always fragrant, often with the delicious fruit-like scent of fresh apples. It is interesting to note that many Wichuraiana Hybrids were hybrids of the Tea Roses, others were hybrids of China Roses, while still others were crosses with the early Hybrid Teas, which were themselves frequently close to the Tea Roses. In this Wichuraianas were fortunate, for it enabled them to perpetuate something of the delicacy of those roses. Where we have Wichuraianas crossed with Hybrid Perpetuals or with Multiflora Hybrids, we have a rose much closer in appearance to that of a Multiflora Hybrid and such varieties are often less beautiful. The Wichuraianas often grow to a greater height than the Multifloras, frequently to 20 or 25ft., and tend to be of a more branching and attractive habit of growth. All Wichuraianas have one season of flowering, although a few of them, like 'Albéric Barbier' and 'Paul Transon', frequently have a small crop of flowers in the autumn.

These hybrids can usually be left to their own devices for a long time without much pruning, making them ideal for a great many uses, such as growing into trees, over arches and pergolas, or perhaps over a wall. They also include some of the best roses for weeping standards, while others, like 'Albéric Barbier', easily take on the trailing habit of the species, making them suitable for ground cover.

When pruning Wichuraianas, we can allow a great deal of latitude, according to the position in which they are grown and the tastes of the grower. I myself prefer to see them run riot so that the growth builds up into a twiggy mass. We can afford to leave them for some years although, of course, the time will come when we have to start removing old growth.

ALBÉRIC BARBIER. A very vigorous Rambler that will easily reach 25ft. under suitable conditions. Its parents were *Rosa wichuraiana* × 'Shirley Hibberd', the latter being a yellow Tea Rose. Its pretty, yellow buds open into quite large, fully-double, quartered flowers of a creamy-white shade with a strong fruit-like fragrance. These are held in small clusters and produced with great freedom. The long, thin, flexible stems have excellent glossy, dark green foliage that will last well into the winter. I had a particularly fine specimen which grew on the wall of an old granary; gradually, without any assistance, it clambered on to the roof covering it completely and providing a most magnificent effect. Unfortunately it was killed by the exceptionally severe winter of 1981/2. In spite of this, 'Albéric Barbier' should not be regarded as tender in our climate, and hopefully we are unlikely to encounter such a winter again for a long time. This Rambler has some capacity to provide flowers later in the year, no doubt due to the influence of its Tea Rose parent. One of the best and most reliable in this class. Bred by Barbier (France), introduced 1900.

ALBERTINE. One of the most popular of Ramblers available from most garden centres and not without good reason, for it is a most reliable rose that blooms very freely. It was the result of a cross between *Rosa wichuraiana* and the Hybrid Tea 'Mrs. Arthur Robert Waddell', and its flowers, though of loose, open formation, have something of the stamp of a Hybrid Tea. Starting as salmon-red buds, they open into large, coppery-pink flowers with a rich fragrance. The growth tends to be branching and bushy, making it an excellent subject with which to cover a fence. The leaves are small, thick, deep green, and have something of the Hybrid Tea about them. It will grow to 25ft. as a Climber, and will, if desired, form a dense shrub of 5ft. in height, spreading broadly. Bred by Barbier (France), introduced 1921.

ALEXANDER GIRAULT. A useful Rambler, providing strength of colour in a class rather lacking in strong shades. The flowers are tinted red in the bud, turning to a deep coppery-carmine on opening, and have numerous slightly quilled petals. There is a green eye and yellow stamens. The growth is vigorous, to 20ft., with dark, glossy foliage and few thorns. 'Alexander Girault' will provide a magnificent and unusual massed colour effect. Parentage *Rosa wichuraiana* × the Tea Rose 'Papa Gontier'. Barbier (France), introduced 1909. See page 326.

ALIDA LOVETT. Large, double blooms of soft shell-pink, shaded yellow at the base and opening to flat flowers with a good fragrance. The growth is quite vigorous and the foliage is dark, glossy green. Height 12ft. Breeding 'Souvenir du Président Carnot' × *Rosa wichuraiana*. Van Fleet (U.S.A.), 1905.

AMERICAN PILLAR. After many years of popularity this rose has now become one of the least loved of Ramblers due, I think, to its harsh colouring and rather stiff character — both in flower and growth. Nonetheless, we still receive some demand for it. The single flowers are produced in large clusters and are bright carmine-pink with a distinct white centre. It is extremely tough and robust, but may have some mildew. There is no scent. Breeding (*Rosa wichuraiana* × *R. setigera*) × a red Hybrid Perpetual. Bred by Dr. W. Van Fleet (U.S.A.), 1902.

AUGUSTE GERVAIS. For me one of the most beautiful of the Wichuraiana Ramblers. It does not produce flowers with the abundance that we might expect of a first class Rambler, but they have a Tea Rose delicacy and are beautifully poised on elegant growth, providing the most pleasing effect. The flowers are semi-double, with large petals arranged in nicely sculptured informality, their colouring being a delicate mixture of cream-apricot and pale yellow, with copper flame-pink on the reverse. They are deliciously fragrant, and are produced over an extended period, with an occasional bloom later. Height 18ft. Good on a pillar. The breeding was *Rosa wichuraiana* × the yellow Hybrid Tea Rose 'Le Progrès'. Barbier (France), 1918.

AVIATEUR BLÉRIOT. A vigorous Rambler of rather upright growth, bearing large trusses of double apricot-yellow flowers that fade to a creamy shade later. Dark green foliage. Fragrant. Height 12ft. Breeding *Rosa wichuraiana* × 'William Allen Richardson'. Fauque (France), 1910.

BREEZE HILL. Large, very full, cupped flowers of flesh-pink tinted with apricot and held in small clusters. The growth is tall, heavy and bushy, to about 20ft. Fragrant. *Rosa wichuraiana* × Hybrid Perpetual 'Beauté de Lyon'. Bred by Van Fleet (U.S.A.), introduced 1926.

CRIMSON SHOWER. A comparatively new variety with two particularly useful qualities: it is a richer crimson than any other Rambler, and it does not begin to flower until midsummer, continuing into September. The flowers are small and rosette shaped and held in large clusters. There is little scent. 'Crimson Shower' will grow to about 12ft. in height, and has small, very glossy foliage. Its long, flexible growth makes it ideal for a weeping standard. A seedling from 'Excelsa', it was bred by the successful amateur breeder A. Norman (U.K.), introduced 1951. See page 326.

DÉBUTANTE. This excellent and charming rose bears small, cupped flowers of a fresh rose-pink colouring, the petals gradually reflexing and paling to blush-pink. They are held in quite small, dainty sprays and have a delicate and pleasing fragrance. The growth is healthy and strong, to about 15ft., with dark green foliage, the whole adding up to a most delightful picture. Rather surprisingly, there are not many soft pink Ramblers, and this is one of the most beautiful. It was the result of a cross between *Rosa wichuraiana* and the Hybrid Perpetual 'Baroness Rothschild'. It has recently provided us with an equally fine though rather different seedling called 'Weetwood'. Bred by Walsh (U.S.A.), introduced 1902.

DOROTHY PERKINS. In its day the most popular Rambler, but it has fallen from grace in more recent times. This is not surprising, as it is by no means one of the best and suffers badly from mildew. We should not be too hard on it, however, as it does have a certain appeal with its large sprays of small, double or semi-double flowers and flexible growth. The colour is a strong, almost matt pink, and unlike that of any other Rambler. It seems to require a good moist soil, and does not like to be in a baked, sunny position — certainly not against a wall where it is sure to have mildew. Fragrant. Growth about 12ft. The breeding was *Rosa wichuraiana* × Hybrid Perpetual 'Madame Gabriel Luizet'. Bred in 1901 by Jackson & Perkins (U.S.A.), who are still leading American rose specialists.

DR. W. VAN FLEET. This rose has, to a large extent, been succeeded by its own sport 'New Dawn', a repeat-flowering form that has been influential in the production of many of the Modern Climbers of the present day. The two are, in fact, identical, except that 'New Dawn' is considerably shorter in growth, due, no doubt, to the fact that more energy is taken up by the latter's long season of flowering. For this reason it is worth retaining the parent variety which will grow to at least 20ft. Its flowers are double, medium sized, with pointed buds and of a soft, even, pearly blush-pink. These are produced with great freedom, making an excellent effect in the mass. Breeding (*Rosa wichuraiana* × Tea Rose 'Safrano') × Hybrid Tea 'Souvenir du Président Carnot'. Bred by Dr. W. Van Fleet (U.S.A.), introduced 1910.

EMILY GRAY. Medium-sized clusters of semi-double buff-yellow flowers are shown off to advantage by glossy, dark green foliage, which is richly tinted with brown when young. The growth, unfortunately, is somewhat variable, and not entirely hardy, probably due to the fact that this rose is three-quarters China and Tea Rose, its breeding being 'Jersey Beauty' × 'Comtesse du Cayla'. In a warm position it will grow to 20ft., but in less favourable places it can languish at 8 or 10ft. It is, at its best, an attractive rose. Bred by Williams (U.K.), introduced 1918.

EVANGELINE. Clusters of small, single, pale pink flowers, make a dainty effect against dark green foliage. They are fragrant and appear late in the season. It is good to have a single flowered Rambler. Growth about 18ft. Breeding *Rosa wichuraiana* × 'Crimson Rambler'. Bred by Walsh (U.S.A.), introduced 1906.

EXCELSA ('Red Dorothy Perkins'). Large clusters of small, double, crimson flowers of globular formation, with white at the centre. It is vigorous, growing to 18ft., with glossy, light green leaves. Its flexible branches make it suitable for a weeping standard, or for growing in prostrate form. Somewhat inclined to mildew. Bred by Walsh (U.S.A.), introduced 1909.

FRANÇOIS JURANVILLE. An excellent, tall and vigorous Rambler of 25ft., with flowers of a rich coral-pink that deepens towards the centre, and with a touch of yellow at the base, eventually fading with age. They are of medium size, opening flat and double, with slightly quilled petals, and have a fresh, fruit-like fragrance. They are held in small clusters on graceful lax growth with purple-red stems. The foliage is glossy green, tinted with bronze at first. A useful rose for pergolas or growing into small trees, but not suitable for a wall, where it may develop mildew. A cross between *Rosa wichuraiana* and the China Rose 'Madame Laurette Messimy'. Bred by Barbier (France), introduced 1906. See page 328.

GARDENIA. Small sprays of prettily pointed buds, opening to creamy-white flowers that deepen to yellow at the centre and eventually fade almost to white. These are of medium size, very full, slightly quartered, and have a fresh apple scent. The growth is vigorous, with graceful, flexible stems and small, dark, glossy green leaves. Height 20ft. A cross between *Rosa wichuraiana* and Tea Rose 'Perle des Jardins'. Bred by Manda (U.S.A.), introduced 1899.

GERBE ROSE. Large, cupped, quartered flowers of a soft pink, with a lovely fragrance. The growth, though robust, is not typical of a Wichuraiana Hybrid, being short and rather stiff with large, glossy, dark green leaves. This is no doubt due to its Hybrid Perpetual background — it is a *Rosa wichuraiana* × 'Baroness Rothschild' cross, and it appears that the latter parent has been influential. It is, however, a good pillar rose, and has some ability to flower again after its main crop. Growth 12ft. Bred by Fauque (France), introduced 1904.

JERSEY BEAUTY. This variety is the result of crossing *Rosa wichuraiana* with the Tea Rose 'Perle des Jardins'. It has sprays of quite large single flowers of creamy-yellow colouring and deep yellow stamens. The growth is strong, to about 16ft., its magnificent dark, glossy foliage forming an excellent background for its bloom. There is a strong fragrance. Bred by Manda (U.S.A.), introduced 1899.

LADY GAY. A cross between *Rosa wichuraiana* and the Hybrid Perpetual 'Bardou Job' has resulted in a rose that is not dissimilar to 'Dorothy Perkins', though with the advantage that it is less subject to mildew. The small flowers are of a richer pink than 'Dorothy Perkins' and are held in nice sprays. The growth is vigorous, to about 15ft. Bred by Walsh (U.S.A.), 1905.

LADY GODIVA. A sport from Dorothy Perkins to which it is similar, except for the colouring of its small flowers which are blush-white, turning to almost pure white, and in this shade the effect is perhaps more distinct and pleasing. Fragrant. Growth 12ft. Discovered by G. Paul (U.K.), introduced 1908.

LA PERLE. A tall and vigorous Rambler with a spread of up to 30ft., the result of a cross between *Rosa wichuraiana* and the pale yellow Tea Rose 'Madame Hoste'. It seems that the Tea Roses, with their close relationship to *R. gigantea,* often produce tall Ramblers, and frequently combine this with flowers of exquisite delicacy. In this case they are creamy-white, deepening to yellow at the centre. They are cupped at first,

PAUL'S HIMALAYAN MUSK, *a tall and strong-growing Rambler of cherry blossom beauty.* *See page 337.*
Warren

CRIMSON SHOWER, *Wichuraiana Hybrid. Best of the crimson Ramblers. See page 322.* Fineschi
ALEXANDER GIRAULT, *Wichuraiana Hybrid. A Rambler useful for its dark colouring. See page 321.* Knight

LÉONTINE GERVAIS, *Wichuraiana Hybrid. One of the most beautiful of the large-flowered Ramblers.* *See page 333.* Warren

ADÉLAIDE D'ORLÉANS, *Sempervirens Hybrid. A Rambler with dainty, elegant hanging blooms.* *See page 314.* Warren

FRANÇOIS JURANVILLE, *Wichuraiana Hybrid. A graceful and charming Rambler of 25ft.* *See page 323.* Page

RAMBLING RECTOR, *Multiflora Hybrid. A very free-flowering Rambler with bushy growth bearing a mass of bloom with good fragrance.* *See page 318.* Warren

ROSA BANKSIAE LUTESCENS, *Banksian Rose. One of the most beautiful of Ramblers seen growing in Professor Fineschi's garden in Italy. In Britain it would require the protection of a warm wall.* *See page 335.* Fineschi

A MAGNIFICENT GROUP *of Ramblers on pillars at Roseraie de l'Hay, Paris.* Balfour

KEW RAMBLER *seen growing over a wall at Mr. and Mrs. Christopher Dumbell's garden in Worfield, Shropshire. See page 337.* Knight

BLUSH BOURSAULT, *Boursault Rose. An early flowering Rambler with attractive Old Rose flowers. See page 336.* Page

MAY QUEEN. *Wichuraiana Hybrid. A Rambler with flowers similar to an Old Rose See opposite.* Warren

VEILCHENBLAU. *Multiflora Hybrid. A mauve Rambler, here seen growing in Italy against a background of conifers. See page 319.* Fineschi

BLUSH RAMBLER. *Multiflora Hybrid. Strong growing and fragrant. See page 317.* Fineschi

PAUL TRANSON. *Wichuraiana Hybrid. A good Rambler which usually produces a small second crop in autumn. See opposite.* Knight

opening flat with quilled petals, and have a strong, fresh fragrance. The young leaves are tinted with brown, becoming a glossy green as they develop. 'La Perle' was bred by Fauque (France), introduced 1905.

LÉONTINE GERVAIS. I regard this as one of the most attractive of the Wichuraiana Ramblers. It is the result of a cross between *Rosa wichuraiana* and the dainty Tea Rose 'Souvenir de Catherine Guillot'. The flowers are a delicate mixture of pink, copper and orange; they have large, gracefully sculptured petals, and are held nicely poised on rather branching growth, providing a beautiful airy effect. Fragrant. It will grow to about 25ft., but can successfully be confined to a pillar. Bred by Barbier (France), introduced 1903. See page 327.

MARY WALLACE. A cross between *Rosa wichuraiana* and an unnamed Hybrid Tea, showing the influence of the latter parent, the flowers being large, loosely-formed, semi-double and of a warm rose-pink colouring. It has a good fragrance. The growth is strong and rather upright, spreading to about 25ft., with rather sparse foliage. Bred by Van Fleet (U.S.A.), introduced 1924.

MAY QUEEN. Graham Thomas tells us there were two Ramblers of this name, both from the U.S.A., and introduced in the same year, 1898. One was bred by Manda from *Rosa wichuraiana* × 'Champion of the World'; the other by Dr. Van Fleet, from *R. wichuraiana* × 'Madame de Graw'; the pollen parents in each case being Bourbons. It may be that neither breeder was willing to step down and change the name; it is more likely that the distributor confused two roses and sent them out under the same name. Such a confusion is by no means unheard of. The variety we have shows distinct signs of Old Rose parentage, the blooms starting as rounded shallow cups, well filled with petals, later becoming flat and eventually reflexing. They are of medium size, and, in fact, not dissimilar to those of the Bourbon 'Louise Odier'. The colour is a clear rose-pink, and there is a fresh, fruit-like fragrance. Individually the flowers are of considerable beauty, and this is equalled by the massed effect, the plant producing numerous long shoots that intertwine to form a mat of growth. It will grow to about 15ft. in height and will also form an excellent large shrub. See opposite.

MINNEHAHA. Large clusters of small, double, pink flowers, fading almost to white, on a strong Rambler. Once a very popular rose, perhaps more so than it deserved, although it will make a good weeping standard. Height 15ft. *Rosa wichuraiana* × 'Paul Neyron'. Bred by Walsh (U.S.A.), 1905.

PAUL TRANSON. Small coppery-orange buds in small sprays opening flat to form medium-sized double flowers of coppery-buff paling with age. The growth is strong and bushy with dark, glossy green foliage, the young stems and leaves being tinted with bronze. An excellent free-flowering Rambler, useful for its strong colouring. It almost invariably provides further flowers in late summer, and few Ramblers can compare with it in this respect. There is a strong, fruit-like fragrance. Growth 15ft. Breeding *Rosa wichuraiana* × the dusky red-pink Tea Rose 'L'Idéal'. Breeder Barbier (France), introduced 1900. See page 332.

RÉNÉ ANDRÉ. Gracefully hanging sprays of small, semi-double flowers of a soft apricot-yellow which later becomes flushed with pink. The growth is vigorous with long, slender, flexible stems and plentiful dark, glossy green foliage. Fresh, fruit-like scent. Occasional repeat flowering. Growth about 15ft. *Rosa wichuraiana* × 'L'Idéal'. Bred by Barbier (France), introduced 1901.

SANDERS' WHITE ('Sanders' White Rambler'). A very good white Rambler, bearing large clusters of small, semi-double flowers with golden stamens and a wonderful fragrance — more powerful than any other member of this class. The growth is vigorous, long and flexible, to 18 or 20ft., with glossy foliage. An altogether beautiful rose, it flowers with great freedom, and is useful in that it does so when most other Ramblers have nearly finished. It will also make excellent ground cover. Bred by Sanders & Sons (U.K.), introduced 1912.

THELMA. Small to medium-sized clusters of quite large semi-double flowers in a delicate mixture of coral-pink and carmine, with a hint of yellow at the centre. This variety is not always very vigorous, but it will flower freely when well grown. Height 12ft. *Rosa wichuraiana* × 'Paul's Scarlet Climber'. Bred by Easlea (U.K.), 1927.

WEETWOOD. We were asked to introduce this rose by Mrs. H.E. Bawden of Offwell, Honiton, Devon. It was a self-sown seedling found in her garden, and arose from the beautiful Rambler 'Débutante', which was itself a cross between *Rosa wichuraiana* and the Hybrid Perpetual 'Baroness Rothschild'. 'Weetwood' represents a further distillation of that cross, with slightly larger, but still small flowers, of shapely, flat, rosette formation, each one a perfect miniature Old Rose. They are a lovely soft rose-pink colour and hang from the branch in small clusters. The growth is exceptionally vigorous, and I understand that the original seedling grows to a great height in a tree. Its only weakness is a tendency towards mildew, but this need not be taken too seriously in a non-repeating Rambler. Growth possibly 20 to 25ft. See page 299.

OTHER RAMBLING ROSES

As with the Climbing Roses, there are a number of Ramblers, some of them particularly beautiful, that do not belong to any of the previous four groups. Some belong to small groups like the Banksian and the Boursault Roses; others are one-off hybrids between various species.

BALTIMORE BELLE. A hybrid between *Rosa setigera* and a Gallica Rose bred by an American nurseryman called Feast in 1843, this rose bears hanging sprays of very double cupped flowers of pale pink fading to ivory-white. They have an attractive formality which gives some hint of the Gallica parent, and are freely produced on a strong but graceful plant, with good, medium green foliage. Flowering occurs late in the season, after most other Ramblers. It will grow to 12ft.

BANKSIAN ROSES

The Banksian Roses form a small group of Ramblers that stand very much on their own. The wild species is a native of West China, growing at 5,000 ft. in Hunan, Shensi and Hupeh, and both this and its garden forms have an individuality and character that places them among the most desirable of all climbing roses. Small flowers, with a strong fragrance, are borne in hanging sprays and appear in late May or early June, long before most other Ramblers. The branches are almost thornless, the foliage pale green with long, glossy pointed leaflets of polished appearance. Unfortunately these roses are not completely hardy in this country, but they are so special that it is worth retaining your best and warmest wall for at least one of them, for their wood requires the warmth of the sun to enable it to ripen properly and resist frost. The flowers are produced on the second and third year's growth, and for this reason it is necessary to confine pruning to the removal of old wood and generally keeping the rose tidy and within bounds. In a favourable position Banksian Roses may be expected to reach the roof, or at least 25ft. Propagation is best done from cuttings or by grafting, for the Banksian Roses will not bud successfully on to the usual root stocks.

ROSA BANKSIAE BANKSIAE. This variety, frequently known as *R. banksiae* 'Alba-Plena', was brought to England by William Kerr on behalf of the Royal Society in 1807. He discovered it in a Canton garden. It was named after Lady Banks, the wife of the famous Director of Kew Gardens at that time, thus giving its name to the species. The flowers are white, small (no more than 1in. across) full petalled and form a near button-like rosette with a fragrance that is similar to that of violets, and more powerful than any other in the group.

ROSA BANKSIAE LUTEA. The most widely grown of the Banksian Roses, this is rather more free-flowering than the white form, and probably a little hardier, although it does not grow quite so strongly. The flowers are small, cupped and double, of a lovely deep yellow colour, but have only a light scent. Introduced from China by J.D. Park for the Horticultural Society of London, it first flowered in this country in 1824. One of the great classic roses. See page 330.

ROSA BANKSIAE LUTESCENS. This form has small, single canary-yellow flowers in sprays. It is believed to have been brought to England in 1870 from La Mortola, the famous garden on the Italian Riviera. It has a strong fragrance. See page 299.

ROSA BANKSIAE NORMALIS. The wild species from Western China, bearing sprays of single white flowers with a strong fragrance. Probably introduced to England in 1877.

BELVEDERE. Until recently this variety has been known as 'Princesse Marie' and placed with the Sempervirens Roses. It may well have connections with that class, but these are slender at best; indeed it is difficult to say what are its origins. Graham Thomas has suggested it should be named 'Belvedere' after the house in Ireland, whence it was procured by Lady Ross. It is a very robust Rambler of 20ft., and frequently much more under favourable conditions. It bears large trusses of small flowers that are distinctly cupped and remain so to the end. Their colour is a strong clear pink which fades a little with age, and they have a pleasant fragrance. This is a most charming Rambler, but unfortunately it has one bad fault — it tends to become shabby in the rain. It appears to require a rich soil and a cool climate. In drier areas the flowers are often a dirty white. In the richer soil at Nymans it is beautiful, growing into trees. If you can provide suitable conditions, I would certainly recommend this rose. It is also ideal as a large shrub.

BOURSAULT ROSES

These form a small group of almost thornless Ramblers which were once thought to be the result of crossing *Rosa pendulina* with *R. chinensis,* but it has since been discovered that the chromosome count excludes this possibility. We are thus left with a mystery. They have never become a major class, but they do have an Old Rose character that still appeals.

AMADIS ('Crimson Boursault'). Small semi-double, cup-shaped flowers of deep crimson-purple with an occasional white streak. These are held in both small and large clusters and produced freely on strong, rather bushy growth of about 15ft. The foliage is dark, and there are no thorns. An attractive Rambler in the mass, providing a splash of rich colouring. There is no fragrance. Bred by Laffay (France), 1829.

BLUSH BOURSAULT ('Calypso', 'Rose de l'Île', 'Florida'). Double flowers of pale blush-pink, opening flat and with a rather ragged appearance. Long, arching, thornless growth, with plentiful dark green foliage. 15ft. 1848. See page 331.

MADAME SANCY DE PARABÈRE. A unique rose, and the most beautiful of the group, with large, double, soft pink blooms of up to 5ins. across, opening flat. These are unusual in that the small inner petals are frequently, but not always, surrounded by distinctly larger outer petals, creating the attractive effect of a rosette within a single flower. They have a slight scent, and are produced early in the season. It will grow to about 15ft. and has good dark green foliage and no thorns. Its large flowers and general habit would make it more suitable for inclusion amongst the Climbers, but as it is a Boursault Rose I place it here for convenience. Bred by Bonnet (France), introduced 1874.

FRANCIS E. LESTER. One of the surest and most reliable of Rambler Roses. A seedling from the Hybrid Musk Rose 'Kathleen', this rose is thus of rather mixed origin. The flowers are single, delicate blush-pink at the edges, soon becoming almost white, and giving something of the impression of apple blossom. They are held nicely spaced in large trusses and have a particularly strong and pleasing fragrance. This rose blooms in exceptional abundance and in autumn there are plentiful small, oval, orange-red hips. The growth is strong and bushy, to about 15ft., and it will, if desired, make a first class large shrub. The foliage is elegant, a glossy dark green, with pointed, widely spaced leaflets. Bred by Francis E. Lester, founder of the Californian nursery now known as 'Roses of Yesterday and Today', introduced 1946.

KEW RAMBLER. A cross between *Rosa soulieana* and 'Hiawatha', this rose might have been included amongst the Multiflora Hybrids, but *R. soulieana* has placed a very definite stamp upon it, providing us with quite a different rose. The foliage is an attractive grey-green colour, similar to that of *R. soulieana,* the growth vigorous, bushy, and rather stiff. The flowers have a wild rose charm, being single, of soft pink colouring, with a white centre and yellow stamens. They are held in close but not over-packed trusses. The fragrance is strong and typically Multiflora, and there are small orange-red hips in autumn. It will achieve about 18ft. Raised at Kew, introduced 1912. See page 331.

LYKKEFUND. A seedling from *Rosa helenae,* thought to have 'Zéphirine Drouhin' as its pollen parent. If, in fact, this is true, it is a rather interesting cross, for I know of no other rose that has the excellent 'Zéphirine' in its make up. The two roses have this much in common — they are both entirely thornless. The flowers are of medium size, semi-double, pale creamy-yellow, deeper at the centre, and tinged with pink. They are held in medium-sized clusters and soon fade to white in the hot sun. The growth is strong and bushy, probably to 10 or 15ft., the foliage a deep glossy green, with rather small leaflets. 'Lykkefund' is suitable for growing in trees, and may also be used as a large shrub. Strong fragrance. Bred by Olsen (Denmark), introduced 1930.

MOUNTAIN SNOW. Although this rose was bred at our nursery, I am ashamed to say I have no idea of its parentage. It was one of those little mysteries that are apt to occur from time to time in rose breeding, but I feel it is worth preserving. The growth is particularly robust, with plentiful dark green foliage. The flowers, which are semi-double and of medium size, are borne in large, shapely sprays, providing a cascade of pure white. It makes a good Rambler or may be used as an elegantly arching shrub. As a Climber it may be expected to reach 12 to 15ft. and 5 by 8ft. as a shrub. Introduced 1985.

PAUL'S HIMALAYAN MUSK. This is the attractive, if somewhat fanciful, name for a very beautiful Rambler; indeed, to me, one of the most beautiful of all the Ramblers. It will grow to 30ft. over a pergola or into trees, making long, thin, flexible branches, trailing gracefully and hanging down from their support. Its small, dainty, fully-double, soft pink, rosette-like flowers are held in large open sprays, with each bloom held separately from the next on long, thin stems, giving a delicate, airy effect; the whole plant being garlanded with beauty in season. The light greyish-green foliage is long and pointed. Small, oval hips. First distributed by W. Paul (U.K.), date and parents unknown. See page 325.

PRINCESSE MARIE. Now known as 'Belvedere', see under Banksian Roses.

SILVER MOON. The breeding of this rose is thought to be (*Rosa wichuraiana* × 'Devoniensis') × *R. laevigata.* It is a particularly vigorous climber, capable of 30ft., and has abundant dark, glossy foliage, inherited from *R. laevigata.* The buds are yellow, opening to form large, single or semi-double flowers of creamy-white, with a bunch of yellow stamens. These are borne in clusters, and have a strong fruit-like fragrance. It flowers in mid-June but does not repeat. Raised by Dr. W. Van Fleet (U.S.A.), introduced 1910.

TREASURE TROVE. This aptly named, self-sown seedling, was discovered in the garden of Mr. John Treasure of Burford House, Tenbury Wells, Hereford, growing beneath a plant of *Rosa filipes* 'Kiftsgate', and was introduced in 1979. The other parent is believed to have been the Hybrid Musk Rose 'Buff Beauty', and indeed if we had been planning a yellow hybrid it would have been hard to have found a better pollen parent. 'Treasure Trove' has the vigour of 'Kiftsgate', and promises to grow to a similar size (35ft.), or at least 30ft., although it may not be quite so hardy. It flowers profusely in summer, bearing sprays of about twenty blooms which are loosely double, cupped, about 2ins. across, and have a delicious fragrance. Its colour, a warm apricot, is particularly valuable in a rose of such growth. No doubt we shall hear much more of this rose in the years to come.

UNA. The pollen parent of this rose is *Rosa canina,* the seed parent is thought to be a Tea Rose, or perhaps 'Gloire de Dijon'. The flowers are almost single, about 3ins. across, creamy-buff in the bud, opening to creamy-white, with a pleasing fragrance. They are followed by large, round hips, which have difficulty in ripening in our climate. The growth is strong, with good foliage that bears some resemblance to *R. canina.* Height 15ft. or more. Bred by George Paul (U.K.), introduced 1900.

WEDDING DAY. A seedling of *Rosa sinowilsonii,* raised by Sir Frederick Stern in 1950. The other parent is not recorded. Like *R. sinowilsonii,* 'Wedding Day' has fine, glossy foliage, although the individual leaves are smaller, but unlike *R. sinowilsonii* it is completely hardy. The growth is very strong, to at least 25ft. The flowers are single and held in large clusters which mingle with the dark foliage. They are yellow in the bud, opening to creamy-yellow, but almost immediately becoming white; the massed effect being white dotted with yellow. The petals are wedge shaped, narrow at the base, broadening to the outer edges. Its only fault is that the petals become spotted in wet weather. An ideal rose for growing in trees or to cover some unsightly object. Exceptionally fragrant.

Chapter 11

SPECIES ROSES AND THEIR NEAR HYBRIDS

Having progressed all the way from the earliest garden roses to those of the present day, and made a few suggestions as to their future, we must now return to the very first roses; the wild roses of many lands. It might quite reasonably be said that we should have begun at this point.

There are, however, certain advantages in placing them at the end of the story. We are concerned with the rose not principally from a historic point of view, intriguing though this undoubtedly is, nor from the point of view of a botanist, but as a garden plant. The Species and their hybrids are, generally speaking, quite different in character from those of horticultural origin, often occupying a different place in the garden. They are children of the wild, or, at least, close relatives of such roses, whereas the garden roses are very much the product of civilisation. The Species are all single flowered, double flowers being the result of selection by man.

Like the garden roses, the Species, too, have an interesting background, not so much from a human point of view — except perhaps for the often dauntless men who collected them — but because of the many lands and widely differing terrains which form their natural habitat. Although the cultivated rose has spread to virtually every country in the world, as a garden plant it is found wild only in the Northern Hemisphere. North America, Europe, across Russia, through China and into Japan — almost every country has its wild roses. China, in particular, is extremely rich in roses, as it is in many other plants. It is perhaps unfortunate for us, in this modern urban age, that wild roses tend to form rather large shrubs and are, therefore, not always ideal for our small gardens. Fortunately, there are many who have larger gardens, particularly those who live in the country, and for these there must always be a place for at least one or two wild roses. The Species, however, are not all large in growth; there are some that are entirely suitable for a place in the smaller garden.

The pleasure of wild roses lies not so much in their colourfulness or the showiness of their flowers, but more in their simplicity, as well as in the elegance of their growth, the daintiness of their foliage, and their often richly coloured fruit. Indeed, hardly any of the wild roses are lacking in beauty, but it is a beauty that has to be looked for. Through the long process of their evolution they have taken on many forms in order to deal with the vagaries of numerous different climates and terrains. Between one Species and another there are to be found infinitely varying patterns of growth and leaf.

We may consider growing the Species in shrub borders or mixed borders, or perhaps more particularly in the wilder outer areas of the garden; even in fields, hedges and open woodlands. The Climbing Species, which I deal with in the second half of this chapter, may be encouraged to scramble over bushes and hedges and up trees — sometimes quite large trees. In fact, the Species include some of the best roses for these purposes.

Usually the Species will not require much in the way of attention. The occasional removal of old branches to encourage the new is generally sufficient, or perhaps a little cutting back to stop them becoming excessively large or smothering their neighbours. However, pruning should not be too heavy or it may promote growth at the expense of flowers and fruit, and perhaps destroy the natural grace of the plant. For this reason it is worth studying their ultimate size with some care before making a decision on planting. Where a Species Rose has been left unpruned for many years, and perhaps been a great source of beauty during that time, there is often a tendency for it to fill up with old and dead wood, thus becoming unsightly. This is nature's pruning, but not desirable from a garden point of view. In such cases it is sometimes best to cut the shrub hard back and begin again.

The Species Hybrids are usually hybrids between Species, although sometimes they are hybrids between Species and garden varieties. All of them have the nature of wild roses with certain exceptions, such as the Scotch Roses, which I place here more for convenience than for any other reason.

The Species are not the choice of man, but a development of nature, and as such they do not come as a conveniently standardised product to fit neatly into a book. Each Species may vary considerably, according to the area from which it was originally collected. With the more varied Species, such as *Rosa moyesii,* it is important to see that your nurseryman has a good form.

There are some two hundred and fifty different Species of roses; all have their beauty, as indeed do all plants, but some are more suitable for the garden than others. As has been my policy throughout this book, I describe only those that I consider to be of true garden worth.

SPECIES SHRUB ROSES AND THEIR HYBRIDS

ROSA ALPINA. See *R. pendulina.*

ROSA ALTAICA. See *R. pimpinellifolia* 'Grandiflora'.

ROSA CALIFORNICA. A vigorous rose bearing 1½in. deep pink flowers in clusters between mid-June and early July. These are followed by a good display of hips in the autumn. Height 8ft. It is a good shrub, with pleasing dark foliage of delicate appearance, but rather overshadowed by its double form described below. A native of the U.S.A.

ROSA CALIFORNICA PLENA. Opinions differ as to the origins of this rose. Some say that it is a double form of *R. californica.* Graham Thomas, however, suggested that it may be related to *R. nutkana.* The fact that it is double suggests to me the other parent was of garden origin, for it seems rather too much of a coincidence we should find a Species Hybrid that was also double. This is a very fine shrub and a better garden plant that its parent. Its semi-double flowers are deep pink, fragrant, and borne on long, pendulous branches in cascading abundance. The foliage is small, dark and plentiful, forming dense cover. It is hardy and grows vigorously, often suckering profusely, and would, I am sure, be very useful for municipal planting. Height 8ft. Introduced by Geschwind (Hungary), 1894. See page 355.

ROSA CANINA. The Dog Rose of our hedgerows, and also to be found across Northern Europe and into Western Asia in varying forms. Although it will not require much description to people of the British Isles, for those of other countries it can be described as an open shrub of 10ft. in height, bearing 2-in. flowers either singly or in small clusters. Between different shrubs these may vary in colour from white to almost crimson, but are more often of a soft pink shade. It is unique among roses for its excessive variability, particularly in the colour of its flowers, but also in growth and leaf. In fact, if we study it in the wild, we seldom find any two plants that are the same. This is due to an unusual variability in its genetic make up, and not, as it may seem, to differences in soil conditions. The flowers have their own typical fragrance, and are followed by scarlet hips of long, oval shape. Those of us who have access to this rose will not perhaps consider planting it, although it is a beautiful shrub. Some people think it worth planting in hedgerows and wild places. I can well remember it on my parents' farm near Shrewsbury, in woodlands that had been cut some twenty years previously and where it was to be seen growing in great masses to a height of anything up to 20ft., providing an almost overwhelming profusion of bloom in season. I have come across few rose scenes to equal this since.

R. canina has been the parent of a number of hybrids, most of which are excellent shrubs, often with larger flowers, but usually keeping close to it in appearance. These include *R.* 'Complicata' and *R.* 'Macrantha' which are described separately. See page 372.

ROSA CANINA ABBOTSWOOD. A semi-double seedling of the Dog Rose showing little sign of hybridity. In spite of this I suspect it is a hybrid, as I have myself hybridized *R. canina* with other roses and obtained very similar results. This variety appeared in a hedgerow at Abbotswood in the garden of Mr. Harry Ferguson, of tractor fame, and was discovered by his gardener, Mr. Tustin, who gave it to Graham Thomas. It forms an 8ft. shrub with pink flowers of a sweet Canina fragrance followed by orange-red hips. 1954.

ROSA CANINA ANDERSONII. Probably a Canina × Gallica Hybrid with typically Dog Rose flowers but larger and of a richer, more brilliant pink, and blooming over an extended period. The leaves are long and downy on the underside. It has the bright red Canina hips. Fragrant. 6 by 8ft. First recorded by Hillier (U.K.), 1912. See page 366.

ROSA CANINA HIBERNICA. This rose has all the signs of being a Canina × Pimpinellifolia Hybrid. It forms a neat, bushy, twiggy, slightly arched shrub of medium size, with attractive pale pink flowers of about 1½ ins. across appearing late in the season. It will grow to approximately 8ft. in height, forming a dense bush, and has greyish-green foliage, midway between that of Canina and Pimpinellifolia. In autumn it bears brown-red hips. The original was discovered in 1802 by a Mr. John Templeton of Belfast who received a prize of 50 guineas from the Botanical Society of Dublin for a new indigenous plant. This was hardly an accurate description as it is, in fact, a chance hybrid. See page 367.

ROSA CANTABRIGIENSIS. See *Rosa hugonis* hybrids below.

ROSA COMPLICATA. Probably a hybrid of a Gallica Rose and *R. canina.* Indeed, it is often classified as a Gallica, although it is really very much a wild rose. It is one of the finest and most reliable of all the Shrub Roses. The flowers are large, about 5ins. across, slightly cupped at first, opening flatter, and of the purest bright pink paling to white at the centre, with a large boss of golden stamens. In mid-June the whole shrub is completely covered with a mass of over-sized Dog Rose blooms. The growth is extremely robust but quite compact, about 5ft. in height, with ample large foliage. It can be relied on to do well even under rather poor conditions — few roses are more fail-proof — and it deserves to be far more widely planted by municipal authorities. Nothing is known of its age, or origin. See page 351.

ROSA DAVIDII. A graceful, upright shrub of about 9ft. in height, bearing 2-in. mallow-pink flowers borne in large open clusters and elegantly poised along its branches. There is a pleasing fragrance, and the flowers are followed by slim, flagon-shaped hips of bright orange-red. The leaves are rough textured and of a greyish-green. It is one of the last of the Species to flower. This rose has shown a tendency to die back in my garden but soon renews itself. It grows wild in West China and South-east Tibet, and was first collected by E.H. Wilson in 1903.

ROSA DUPONTII. This beautiful rose is probably a hybrid between *R. damascena* and *R. moschata.* It may have been raised at Malmaison, and appears in Redouté as *R. damascena subalba.* The flowers are about 3ins. across and single, with occasional extra petals. Their colour is white, sometimes tinged with blush, and they are held in nice Damask-like sprays of five or more blooms. They have a clean-cut shape and a purity which adds much to their attraction, particularly when viewed against their elegant, downy-grey foliage. It is a strong and rather loose-growing shrub of perhaps 7ft. in height and rather less across. There is a sweet fragrance. Late flowering. Circa 1817. See page 351.

ROSA ECAE. A compact shrub of about 5ft. in height and almost as much across, with slender, thorny, dark brown branches and small, dark green fern-like leaves, similar to those of *R. hugonis*. The flowers are small, no more than 1in. across, deep buttercup-yellow, and set all along its branches. A good shrub, but not always easy to establish. It is best in a warm, sunny position. A native of Afghanistan, it was first collected by Dr. Aitchison in 1880. The name derives from the initials of his wife, E.C.A.

ROSA EGLANTERIA (*R. rubiginosa,* the 'Sweet Brier'). A native of Britain and Northern Europe, this rose is greatly valued for the rich and spicy fragrance of its foliage which is emitted from glands on the underside of the leaves, and is particularly in evidence on a warm, moist day, when it can fill the garden around it. An even stronger fragrance can be obtained by crushing the leaves between the fingers. Graham Thomas wisely recommends that it should be planted on the south or west side of the garden to catch the warm, moist winds. This is a strong, easily grown shrub of 8ft. in height and across, with many thorns. It will form an impenetrable barrier where this is required, and may also be used as a hedge. The flowers are clear pink, about 2ins. across, and they too are fragrant. Later there is a mass of bright red, oval-shaped hips that last well into the winter. There are a number of hybrids, all with fragrant foliage, but never of quite such power as the original.

ROSA EGLANTERIA HYBRIDS INCLUDING PENZANCE BRIERS

During the years 1894 and 1895 Lord Penzance introduced a number of Sweet Brier hybrids that he had bred himself. These were mainly crosses between *R. eglanteria* and various Hybrid Perpetuals and Bourbons. They have a certain garden value, combining as they do a variety of colours with the fragrant foliage of the wild Sweet Brier. They are nearly all extremely robust, usually about 8ft. in height, though most of them are inclined to grow into what are, to me, rather coarse shrubs of upright growth. They all have aromatic foliage, but not to the extent of the Sweet Briers. Where space can be found for only one such rose it might be best to plant *R. eglanteria* itself. It is probable that the Penzance Briers are the result of a very few crosses, with little selection.

I also include here three other hybrids — 'Janet's Pride', 'La Belle Distinguée' and 'Manning's Blush' — which come from different sources.

AMY ROBSART. Semi-double flowers of deep clear pink. Extra strong growth. Not very fragrant foliage. Good, scarlet hips. Height 9ft.

ANNE OF GEIRSTEIN. Single flowers of dark crimson with yellow stamens. Free-flowering. Many hips.

CATHERINE SEYTON. Soft pink single flowers. Orange hips. 8ft.

FLORA McIVOR. Single flowers of rose-pink, fading to blush, with a white centre. 8ft.

GREENMANTLE. Single, rosy-crimson flowers, white eye. 8ft. See page 372.

JANET'S PRIDE ('Clementine'). This was distributed by W. Paul & Sons (U.K.) in 1892, but it may well have been in existence before this date. It is a rather smaller shrub than the Species, 6ft. in height, with scented flowers that are semi-double, cherry-pink and attractively veined with pale pink, the centre being almost white. The foliage is rather more coarse and less fragrant than the Species.

JEANNIE DEANS. Semi-double, bright scarlet flowers. Foliage with above average fragrance. 7ft.

JULIA MANNERING. Single, delicate pink flowers veined with darker pink. 6ft.

LA BELLE DISTINGUÉE. An old hybrid with very double crimson flowers that make a good show of colour. It grows to about 4ft. by 3ft. across. The foliage is not very fragrant.

LADY PENZANCE. An attractive shrub, the product of a cross between *R. eglanteria* and *R. foetida bicolor.* It bears dainty single yellow flowers that are flushed with coppery-pink towards the outer edges. Unfortunately it has inherited some of *R. foetida's* susceptibility to blackspot. The foliage has only a slight fragrance, while the flowers have the scent of *R. foetida.* Height about 6ft.

LORD PENZANCE. *R. eglanteria* × 'Harison's Yellow'. Not so robust as the others, but with foliage that is quite strongly aromatic. The flowers are single, fragrant and of a soft rosy-yellow with pale yellow at the centre. Height 6ft.

LUCY ASHTON. Attractive single white flowers edged with pink. Foliage with above average fragrance. 6ft.

MAGNIFICA. A seedling from 'Lucy Ashton', and thus a second generation Penzance Brier, but it is, in fact, a much better rose than we would expect from this group. It forms a fine shrub of 6ft in height, with large, fragrant, cupped, semi-double flowers of a purplish-red. Widely used in the breeding of modern roses, it was bred by Hesse of Germany in 1916.

MANNING'S BLUSH. An old variety of a date certainly prior to 1799. It is a much smaller shrub than *R. eglanteria,* about 5ft. in height, with pretty little full-petalled flowers which are pink in the bud and pale to blush when they open. The foliage has a slight fragrance. See page 354.

MEG MERRILIES. Semi-double bright crimson flowers. The foliage has a good fragrance. Scarlet hips. 8ft.

ROSA ELEGANTULA PERSETOSA (*R. farreri* 'Persetosa'). This rose was selected by E.A. Bowles from seed of *R. elegantula,* collected by Farrer from West China in 1915. It has deeper pink flowers than is usual for the typical Species which is now very rare in cultivation. Owing to the small size of its flowers, *R. elegantula* 'Persetosa' is often known as the 'Threepenny Bit Rose', a name that may soon have little meaning to future generations of gardeners. It is a dainty little shrub, with tiny, clear salmon-pink flowers lacing its arching growth, and with small leaves and many hair-like thorns. The foliage turns to a purple shade in autumn, and there are numerous small orange-red hips which persist well into the winter. Height 5ft.

ROSA FEDTSCHENKOANA. A large and very strong growing bristly shrub of 8ft. or more in height which, if grown on its own roots, suckers very freely, spreading far and wide — so much so that it can become a problem. Perhaps its chief virtue is its pleasing grey-green foliage, but it also has the distinction of being one of five wild roses that have a natural ability to flower throughout the summer, the other four being *R. rugosa, R. beggeriana, R. foliolosa* and *R. bracteata.* The flowers are white and about 2ins. across, but although they continue over a long period I have not found them to be very plentiful. The hips are long, pear shaped and bright red with persistent hairy sepals. The flowers are fragrant, some say rather unpleasantly so. A native of the U.S.S.R. and Turkestan, it was discovered by and named after a Russian in 1868/71, arriving at Kew in 1890. See page 372.

ROSA FOETIDA (*R. foetida lutea,* 'Austrian Yellow'). This rose is often, rather misleadingly, known as the 'Austrian Brier'. It is, in fact, a native of Iran and Kurdistan, and has been with us since the late sixteenth century. *R. foetida* was a very important Species in the development of garden roses, being the main source of yellow colouring in our Modern Roses through its variety *R. foetida* 'Persiana'. This has been a mixed blessing, as *R. foetida* suffers from blackspot and has passed something of this fault on to its progeny. Indeed, it frequently and rather unfairly receives the total blame for the problem. It bears 2½-in. flowers of bright sulphur-yellow with a scent that does not appeal to everyone. The foliage is pale green and the stems brown with greyish coloured thorns. It forms a pleasing, rather sparse shrub of 5ft. in height. This Species and its varieties provide a most brilliant effect early in the season. If your garden is subject to blackspot it might be better to grow *R. pimpinellifolia* 'Lutea Maxima' which is less prone to this disease and has flowers of a similar colour, being probably a hybrid of *R. foetida.*

ROSA FOETIDA BICOLOR (*R. lutea punicea,* 'Austrian Copper'). A dramatic and intriguing sport from *R. foetida.* The upper surface of the petals has become a dazzling coppery-red, while the under-surface remains bright yellow. Otherwise it is identical to its parent. If we look at this rose, it is not hard to see how the Modern Rose arrived at its present state of often excessively bright colouring. This rose, however, is beautiful and well worth a place in the garden. It was grown in the Arab world as far back as the twelfth century. Height 5ft. See page 356.

ROSA FOETIDA PERSIANA ('Persian Yellow'). An attractive double form of *R. foetida* with flowers of similar bright sulphur-yellow colouring. It will achieve a slender 4ft. in height, although I understand that it will grow more strongly in a warmer climate. Its flowers are cupped in shape and have a rather Old Rose appearance. Introduced to England, probably from Iran, in 1838 by Sir Henry Wilcock. See page 372.

ROSA FORRESTIANA. A shrub of some 6 or 7ft. in height, and 6ft. across, bearing rosy-crimson flowers of about 1½ins. with creamy-yellow stamens. These are fragrant and borne in dense clusters, and have large, leafy bracts. The hips are flask shaped, bright orange-red and rather bristly, the green bracts persisting. An attractive shrub. A native of West China, first cultivated in 1918. See page 350.

ROSA GLAUCA (*R. rubrifolia*). A native of Central Europe usually grown for the beauty of its foliage. It is a shrub of some 7ft. in height, and nearly as much across, with smooth, almost thornless purple-red stems and glaucous coppery-mauve leaves which provide an excellent colour contrast in the border or in an arrangement of cut flowers. Its blooms are not very conspicuous, being light pink, quite small and held in rather tight bunches, but in spite of this they have a certain charm among the tinted colour of the leaves. The hips, which are small and globular, provide us with a further pleasing effect. See page 353.

ROSA GLAUCA CARMENETTA. A hybrid between *R. glauca* and *R. rugosa,* which is more robust and thorny, with larger leaves and flowers than *R. glauca.* As one would expect, it is a little coarser and lacks the elegance of *R. glauca,* but is otherwise similar with the same pink colouring. Height 7ft. by 7ft. across. Bred by the Central Experimental Farm, Ottawa (Canada), 1923.

ROSA HEMISPHAERICA (*R. sulphurea, R. glaucophylla,* the 'Sulphur Rose'). This rose has little claim to a place among the Species, but since it is difficult to know where to put it, I include it here. It bears large full-petalled, sweetly fragrant, deeply globular flowers of typical Old Rose appearance which are pale sulphur-yellow in colour. Indeed at one time it was, quite erroneously, known as the 'Yellow Provence Rose'. The growth is rather loose, up to 6ft. in height, the foliage a pale greyish-green and the blooms hang their heads from the branches: all of which sounds very attractive, and indeed it is, but unfortunately the flowers seldom open, and then only in the driest and most favourable seasons. A little rain, and they ball up and soon decay, although the plant itself is completely winter hardy. The protection of a warm sunny wall can be a help. This rose was a favourite of the old Dutch painters, and there is a particularly fine Redouté print which shows how good it can be. Unfortunately this happens only occasionally. Gordon Rowley has suggested that it is a double-flowered sport of the species *R. rapinii* which is found in Turkestan and Iran. It is known to have been in cultivation in Europe as early as 1625.

ROSA HUGONIS (the 'Golden Rose of China'). A shrub of 8ft. in height, with long, graceful branches, brown bark, many thorns and small, pale green fern-like foliage which turns a bronzy colour in autumn. It would be worthwhile for its growth and foliage alone, but in mid-May its branches are wreathed along their length with dainty, slightly cupped flowers of soft yellow colouring, each 1½ to 2ins. across. These are followed by small, round, maroon-coloured fruit. If it has a fault it is that the flowers do not always open completely, the petals tending to be crumpled. Although this is quite attractive, in some seasons it can be excessive. Possibly it may be due to our climate. *R. hugonis* is, however, the parent of some fine hybrids that are very similar and may be preferable; these are described below. They are all particularly good shrubs, with similar dainty foliage, flowering long before most other roses appear. *R. hugonis* probably grows best on its own roots. It was originally collected in West China by the missionary Hugh Scanlon (known as Pater Hugo) who, in 1899, sent seed to Kew where the original plants still thrive.

ROSA HUGONIS HYBRIDS

CANTABRIGIENSIS (*R. pteragonis* 'Cantabrigiensis'). An excellent shrub similar to *R. hugonis* but stronger in growth, easily achieving 10ft. in height. The flowers are saucer-shaped, rather larger, of a paler yellow, and more symmetrical in form than *R. hugonis*. They are produced in great profusion, providing a magnificent sight in mid-May. It has graceful growth and dainty foliage, similar to that of *R. hugonis*. There is a light fragrance. It was a self-sown seedling discovered at the University Botanic Garden, Cambridge, and was named in 1931. See page 365.

GOLDEN CHERSONESE. A comparative newcomer which is a hybrid between *Rosa ecae* and *R. xanthina spontanea* 'Canary Bird', and thus only one quarter Hugonis. It has very numerous, small, deep buttercup-yellow, sweetly-scented flowers which are held closely along its branches. A good shrub, stronger and hardier than its parents, with flowers of a particularly rich colour. It is of unusually upright growth, a fact that gives it a certain added value in the garden, even though we are grateful that most species do not share this habit. Fragrant. 6ft. Bred by E.F. Allen, 1963.

HEADLEYENSIS. A seedling of *R. hugonis,* probably hybridized with *R. piminellifolia* 'Grandiflora', and one of the best of this group. It is very vigorous, achieving 9ft. in height and considerably more across. It thus requires space if it is to develop properly. Its broad, graceful, open growth carries ample fern-like foliage. The creamy-yellow flowers are particularly fine and plentiful, and are fragrant. Raised by Sir Oscar Warburg (U.K.), 1920.

HELEN KNIGHT. This is named after the wife of the former Director of the Royal Horticultural Society's gardens at Wisley, where I understand it is a great favourite. I have only grown it for a short time, however, and have not yet got a mature shrub. It is of unusual upright growth; some might think a little too stiff and upright, but we do not require roses to be all the same, besides which there are positions in the garden where a rose of this habit can be a definite asset. It is a seedling of *R. ecae,* probably hybridized with *R. pimpinellifolia* 'Grandiflora', and will grow to 5 or 6ft. bearing deep yellow flowers with dark stamens. F.P. Knight (U.K.), 1966.

HIDCOTE GOLD. Considered to be a hybrid of *R. hugonis* and *R. sericea pteracantha,* with the fine fern-like foliage of the first rose, and large, flattened thorns showing the influence of the latter. It forms a graceful shrub with long, hanging branches which are wreathed with canary-yellow flowers in May. Height 7 by 7ft. Thought to have been raised at Hidcote in 1948 from seed collected in the wild in China by Reginald Farrer.

ROSA MACRANTHA. A fine, arching shrub, sending out long, thin growth, to a width of 10ft. and 5ft. in height. The flowers are large and borne in small clusters from mid-June to early July. Their colour is pale pink, fading almost to white, with a good boss of stamens and a pleasant fragrance. They have something of the appearance of much bigger Dog Roses. Little is known of its origin. The rather dull, rough-textured foliage and the form of its flowers seem to suggest a Gallica as one parent. *R. canina* is often suggested as the other, but cytological analysis rules this out, nor does the growth fit in with this theory. Its appearance points to the possibility of some trailing rose like *R. arvensis* in its parentage. However this may be, *R.* 'Macrantha' is a truly beautiful rose that is not only good as a shrub, but also very useful for covering banks, the stumps of old trees, or growing into other shrubs and over hedges. It has round, red hips, that persist well into autumn. See page 352.

ROSA MACRANTHA DAISY HILL. Very similar to *R.* 'Macrantha' but with semi-double flowers that are a little smaller in size. All other characteristics are very much the same, except that there is a particularly strong fragrance. 5ft. by 12ft. Raised by Smith of Newry (Northern Ireland), before 1912.

ROSA MACROPHYLLA. A very large shrub of 12ft. in height and as much across, possibly more under suitable conditions. This is one of the most magnificent of the Species, its exuberant growth and large leaves — which may be 8ins. in length and have up to eleven leaflets — forming a thick canopy. It has few thorns and dark red-brown stems. The flowers are a deep rose-pink, 3ins. across, and are held nicely poised either singly or in small clusters. In autumn it has long, bristly, bright red, flagon-shaped hips hanging elegantly from its branches. A common and widely varying shrub, found wild in an area spreading through North India, West China and the Himalayas. Introduced c.1888.

ROSA MACROPHYLLA MASTER HUGH. This rose illustrates the variability of

ROSA PAULII ROSEA, *Species Hybrid. Very large silky petalled flowers on a broadly spreading shrub.* *See page 359.*
Knight

ROSA × RICHARDII, *Species Hybrid. Also known as the 'Sacred Rose of Abyssinia', this is a good shrub with large but dainty flowers.* *See page 364.* Knight

ROSA FORRESTIANA, *Species Hybrid. An attractive shrub with flowers of almost formal appearance.* *See page 346.* Knight

ROSA DUPONTII, *Species Hybrid. An attractive shrub with shapely flowers and beautiful grey-green foliage.* *See page 342.*
Page

ROSA COMPLICATA, *Species Hybrid. One of the most reliable and free flowering of all Shrub Roses.* *See page 342.*
Page

ROSA RAMONA, *Climbing Species. A hybrid of* Rosa laevigata, *this is one of the most beautiful of single roses, but rather tender. See page 382.* Page
ROSA WILLMOTTIAE, *Species Hybrid. Dainty in growth, flower, foliage and hip. See page 375.* Page
GERANIUM, *Species Hybrid. The best form of* Rosa moyesii *for the small garden. See page 358.* Page

HULTHEMIA PERSICA, *Not a true rose, but a near relative. See page 382.* Page
ROSA FILIPES KIFTSGATE, *Climbing Species. One of the best Climbers for larger trees, its growth can be massive. See page 377.* Page
ROSA MACRANTHA, *Species Hybrid. Large flowers on an elegant spreading shrub. See page 348.* Page

ROSA SWEGINZOWII, *a giant shrub similar to* Rosa moyesii, *with the same flagon-shaped hips. See page 374.* Page

ROSA SERICEA PTERACANTHA, *Species Hybrid. Unusual four-petalled white flowers. See page 373.* Page

ROSA SERICEA PTERACANTHA, *the huge colourful thorns.* Page

ROSA XANTHINA SPONTANEA, *Species Hybrid. Commonly known as 'Canary Bird', the flowers are often a deeper yellow than here. See page 375.* Page

ROSA PIMPINELLIFOLIA, *Species Hybrid. The pretty flowers (page 356) are followed by these almost black hips.* Page

ROSA GLAUCA, *Species Hybrid. An excellent foliage plant with good hips. See page 346.* Page

MANNING'S BLUSH, *Species Hybrid. A fine example of an old Sweet Brier hybrid.* *See page 344.* Warren

ROSA CALIFORNICA PLENA, *Species Hybrid. An excellent free-flowering and entirely reliable shrub.* *See page 341.*
Knight

ROSA FOETIDA BICOLOR, *Species Hybrid. Brilliant colours with yellow on the back of the petals. See page 345.* Page

ROSA PAULII, *Species Hybrid. A large-spreading shrub with large flowers. See page 359.* Page

ROSA PIMPINELLIFOLIA, *Species Hybrid. A tough and reliable shrub which will survive poor conditions. See pages 353 and 360.* Knight

R. macrophylla. It is a form collected in Nepal in 1966 and is similar to a typical example of that rose, although it seems to be taller, more upright and more open in growth. The chief difference with 'Master Hugh', however, is its exceptionally large hips which are rather more plump than those of *R. macrophylla,* and larger than those of any other rose. They hang like miniature lanterns, or small inverted pears. Height 15ft. Mason (U.K.), 1966.

ROSA × MICRUGOSA. A hybrid of *R. rugosa* and *R. roxburghii.* The latter was formerly known as *R. microphylla* — hence this variety's name. The foliage leans towards Rugosa in character, although it is a little coarse in texture. The growth is very dense and twiggy, forming a shapely shrub with plentiful foliage. The flowers are pale pink, about 4ins. across, opening flat. Individually they are among the most beautiful of single roses, nestling amongst the leafy growth and having a lovely silky texture. They are followed by round, bristly, orange-red hips. Flowering may not be plentiful in the early stages, but as it matures it does so more freely. It will, if required, form an impenetrable barrier. Height 5 or 6ft. A self-sown seedling found at Strasburg Botanical Institute in 1905.

ROSA × MICRUGOSA ALBA. An attractive second generation seedling from the above, bearing white flowers. The growth is more upright and the leaves paler. It has the ability to repeat flower. Height 5ft. Bred by Dr. Hurst at Cambridge.

ROSA MOYESII. Certainly one of the finest of the Species Roses. A native of North-west China, it was brought to this country by E.H. Wilson and introduced in 1903, when it caused a considerable stir in horticultural circles. This is not altogether surprising, as there was nothing quite like it among wild roses. The flowers are blood-red, 2½ins. across, with overlapping petals and a neat ring of contrasting pale stamens. They have no fragrance, but are followed by magnificent, long flagon-shaped, orange-red fruit which hangs down from the branch, providing an attractive effect from late August to October — or perhaps later. The growth is open, with long, sweeping, widely spaced canes to a height of 10ft. and 8ft. across. The foliage is dark green and attractive, with up to twelve leaflets. This is a useful shrub for the mixed border, as its tall growth can be encouraged to stand above other plants without smothering them. It should be noted that in the wild *R. moyesii* is more often of deep pink colouring. The rose we grow in gardens is a selected form. As with some other Species Roses it is extremely variable. If we grow this Species from seed it will usually revert to the pink type. It is therefore important, when purchasing a plant, to be sure that you obtain a red form. I have noticed that bees prefer *R. moyesii* to any other rose in our collection; indeed, they almost ignore the rest when it is flowering. It was named after the Reverend E.J. Moyes, who was a missionary in China. See page 368.

ROSA MOYESII FORMS AND HYBRIDS

EOS. This is a hybrid, *R. moyesii* × 'Magnifica', the latter being a self-sown seedling of the Sweet Brier 'Lucy Ashton'. It bears flat, almost single flowers of coral-red along its branches, providing a brilliant effect. The growth is rather gaunt and bare at the base. Height 12ft. There is rarely any fruit. Bred by Ruys (U.S.A.), introduced 1950.

FARGESII. Similar to *R. moyesii,* but with pink flowers. The hips are rather larger. Veitch (U.K.), 1913.

FRED STREETER. A seedling from *R. moyesii,* with more bushy growth and flowers of a bright cerise-pink. It has smaller flagon-shaped hips. Discovered at Petworth in Sussex, and introduced by Jackman (U.K.), 1951.

GERANIUM. This is probably the most useful form for the average garden, as it is a smaller shrub than *R. moyesii,* with more compact growth of about 8ft. in height. The flowers are bright geranium-red, the hips rather larger, with more plentiful bright green foliage. Raised by B.O. Mulligan at Wisley (U.K.), 1938. See page 352.

HIGHDOWNENSIS. A seedling from *R. moyesii,* selected by Sir Frederick Stern at Highdown in Sussex. It is a good shrub, with tidier, less open and more bushy growth than the typical Species. The light cerise-crimson flowers with a paler centre are borne in larger clusters. It is tall and vigorous, to about 12ft. in height, and bears particularly fine orange-red hips. See page 371.

HILLIERI (*R.* × *pruhoniciana*). The outstanding feature of this rose is the dark crimson colouring of its flowers, certainly the darkest to be found in this group, and as dark as any we might find in a Hybrid Tea or Hybrid Perpetual. A mystery surrounds its breeding; some say it is a *R. moyesii* × *R. willmottiae* cross, but we would not expect this to produce such a depth of colour. The growth is more arching and graceful than *R. moyesii,* the foliage small and rather sparse, and it does not flower quite so freely, but continues over a long period. It will grow to 10ft. in height by 12ft. across. The hips are large and flagon-shaped, but not always plentiful. Light fragrance. Long thin thorns. Introduced by Hillier (U.K.), 1920.

ROSEA (sometimes attributed to *R. holodonta*). A rose related to *R. moyesii* introduced from China in 1908, with deep rose-pink flowers and good hips. The leaves are larger and there are more thorns than on the typical Species. Height 10ft.

SEALING WAX. Notable for its particularly fine scarlet hips. The flowers are of a bright pink. A seedling from *R. moyesii,* it is otherwise similar. Height 8ft. Royal Horticultural Society (U.K.), 1938.

WINTONIENSIS. A vigorous hybrid, *R. moyesii* × *R. setipoda,* but close to *R. moyesii* in general appearance. It has bushy growth and ample foliage which has a Sweet Brier fragrance. Its flowers are deep pink. Fine bristly, orange-red hips. Height 12ft. Introduced by Hillier (U.K.), 1935.

ROSA MULTIBRACTEATA. A wide and gracefully arching shrub, with prickly stems and fragrant grey-green foliage of seven to nine leaflets. The flowers are plentiful, lilac-pink, 2ins. across, with prominent bracts along their stems which provide an attractive effect. They are held singly or in small clusters. The fragrance is unusual, similar to that of *R. foetida.* One of the parents of the beautiful 'Cerise Bouquet'. Height 7ft. by 6ft. across, more in favourable conditions. Collected by E.H. Wilson from West China, introduced 1908.

ROSA NITIDA. A low growing, suckering shrub of 2ft. in height which, once established on its own roots, will spread freely, forming a thicket of excellent ground cover. It sends up slender, twiggy growth, with many thin thorns and shiny green leaves of seven to ten leaflets which in autumn develop beautiful scarlet-crimson tints. The flowers are about 2ins. across and of an unfading deep pink, but its foliage is perhaps its chief asset. Hips, small, bright red, round, and rather bristly. A native of Canada and the North-east U.S.A., first cultivated 1807.

ROSA NUTKANA. A native of western North America, growing to about 6ft. in height by 4ft. across, with ample greyish-green foliage which turns to brown in the autumn. The flowers are lilac-pink, 2 to 2½ins. in width, and are followed by a good display of globular hips which persist well into the winter. Introduced to Britain in 1876.

ROSA OMEIENSIS. See *R. sericea* below.

ROSA PAULII (*R. rugosa repens alba*). *R. rugosa* × *R. arvensis* hybrid, bred by George Paul (U.K.), and introduced at some time prior to 1903. It is an extremely vigorous, procumbent shrub of about 4ft. in height, producing long stems that can gradually spread to as much as 12ft., although it can, of course, be restricted by pruning. The flowers are pure white, about 3ins. across, the petals being wedge-shaped, narrow at the base so that they do not overlap, and providing a rather star-like effect similar to that of a clematis. They have golden stamens, the petals are inclined to be crinkled and there is a clove-like fragrance. The foliage is rough textured, similar to that of *R. rugosa* in appearance, and there are many thorns. It is very tough, growing well under adverse conditions, and ideal where a large expanse of ground cover is required. See page 356.

ROSA PAULII ROSEA. This appears to be a hybrid of *R.* 'Paulii', from which it differs quite considerably in strength of growth. Although vigorous, it is much less so than its parent. It bears large clear pink flowers with a white centre and yellow stamens. The petals have a crinkled, silky appearance, and overlap in the more usual manner. A beautiful rose with a strong fragrance. Height 3ft. by 8ft. across. See page 349.

ROSA PENDULINA (*R. alpina*). A native of the foothills of the Alpine regions of Central and Southern Europe, usually regarded as growing to about 4ft. in height, although in my experience it will easily achieve 5 or 6ft. under good garden conditions. The growth is erect and slightly arching, the stems are tinted with red and purple, and are smooth with few thorns. The foliage is finely divided, with anything from five to nine leaflets. The flowers are about 2ins. across, of a variable purplish-pink colouring with yellow stamens and are held singly or in twos and threes. They are followed by bright red pear-shaped hips of about 1in. in length, making a conspicuous show. This rose is sometimes difficult to establish, but seems to prefer light soil. An attractive shrub.

ROSA PIMPINELLIFOLIA. This rose was, until very recently, better known as *R. spinosissima,* but the botanists have now come down on the side of *R. pimpinellifolia.* It is more popularly known as the 'Scotch' or 'Burnet Rose'. A native of the British Isles, it is to be found growing in poor sandy conditions, often on seaside banks, anywhere from Cornwall to Scotland. It also grows in Europe and West Asia, and is occasionally to be seen naturalised in North America. It is one of the hardiest, toughest and most reliable of roses. Its height will vary according to conditions. In the wild, in a windswept seaside position, it may grow to no more than 6ins. In the garden it may be about 3ft. in height, but in good soil it can reach up to 6ft. It forms a thicket-like growth, sending up slender stems with many bristles and small, fern-like foliage. In May and June it produces numerous creamy-white flowers of 2 to 3ins. across close along its branches. They have a distinct, refreshing fragrance. Later, there are round maroon-black hips. When grown on its own roots it will sucker far and wide, producing dense ground cover. This may be an asset, but can sometimes be a problem, and will not occur if the union of the stock and the rose is kept above the surface of the soil when planting. It is a particularly useful rose for large scale public planting, and for this purpose it is usual to use seedlings rather than budded stock. So grown it will cover big areas at minimum cost, producing a most satisfactory effect. See pages 353 and 356.

There are a number of good forms and hybrids, and these have been used with some success in the breeding of modern garden shrubs. There is also an old race of double-flowered garden varieties (see Old Garden Varieties of the Scotch Rose below). All are similar in foliage and general appearance and are equally hardy.

ROSA PIMPINELLIFOLIA FORMS AND HYBRIDS

ROSA PIMPINELLIFOLIA DUNWICH ROSE. I know very little about the origin of this rose. It was found quite recently at Dunwich in Suffolk, and David Clark of Notcutts Nurseries, tells me that it was, at least till recently, still to be seen growing wild near the sea there. What I do know is that it is an extremely beautiful shrub — one of the finest of this group. It is typically Pimpinellifolia in flowers, foliage, thorns and hips, but differs in the habit of its growth, which is its chief virtue. It spreads broadly, fanning out into a symmetrical dome of low, arching growth. My specimen has reached 3ft. in height and about 5ft. in width in four years. How much further it will grow I cannot say. The flowers are of a creamy-yellow, about 1½ins. across, and produced in great quantities along its long, elegant branches, covering the whole shrub with a mass of bloom. I feel it must be a hybrid, but of what I cannot say. See page 366.

ROSA PIMPINELLIFOLIA GRANDIFLORA (*R. pimpinellifolia altaica, R. sibirica, R. spinosissima altaica*). Commonly known as *R. altaica*. A native of West Asia, this is very similar to *R. pimpinellifolia* but grows rather taller, to about 6ft., and has larger flowers. These are pale yellow when opening, but quickly turn to creamy-white. The hips are globular and maroon-black. It has all the hardiness of *R. pimpinellifolia*. Fragrant. An excellent hardy shrub.

ROSA PIMPINELLIFOLIA HISPIDA. A variant from North-east Asia, usually growing to about 6ft. It is not so inclined to sucker as the typical species and the stems are covered with slender brown bristles. The flowers are of considerable beauty, being a soft creamy-yellow. Known to have been in cultivation in 1781.

ROSA PIMPINELLIFOLIA LUTEA MAXIMA. Almost certainly a hybrid of *R. foetida,* from which its flowers would have obtained their strong buttercup-yellow colouring — the brightest yellow in this group. The foliage is less typically Pimpinellifolia, being more plentiful and downy on the underside. The growth is less robust and it will usually reach a height of 4ft. Hips black and globular. The fragrance shows some similarity to *R. foetida*.

ROSA PIMPINELLIFOLIA ORMISTON ROY. The result of a cross between 'Allard' (an *R. xanthina* Hybrid) and *R. pimpinellifolia* has provided a nice compact shrub, bearing neatly formed bright yellow single flowers with attractive veining. These are followed by large maroon-coloured hips. Height 4ft. Doorenbos (Holland), 1938.

ROSA PIMPINELLIFOLIA ROBBIE BURNS. So far as I am aware there have been no Pimpinellifolia Hybrids bred in this century, unless we include Kordes's excellent 'Frühlings' series, which are some way removed from the Species. This variety, which was bred at our nursery in 1985, was the result of a cross between *R. pimpinellifolia* and the English Rose 'Wife of Bath'. It is of strongly Scotch Rose appearance. The flowers are small, neat and rather cupped, of a soft rose-pink at the outer edges shading to a distinctly white centre, and have a delicate beauty. The growth is quite tall, perhaps 5ft., and a little heavier than one would expect from these roses, but otherwise similar. Fragrant.

OLD GARDEN VARIETIES OF THE SCOTCH ROSE

These are double-flowered garden varieties of *R. pimpinellifolia*. I therefore have little right to include them with the Species, but place them here to avoid making too many divisions and thus causing unnecessary complication. They appear to have been largely the result of pure selection from the Species. We grow *R. pimpinellifolia* seedlings in large numbers, mainly for municipal authorities, and I have frequently noticed that there will nearly always be a few individual bushes with at least some sign of blush-pink in their flowers. I assume that this group is the result of selecting individuals of this kind. They were, as the name suggests, developed in Scotland, and indeed they are ideal roses for the more extreme climate of the North. It is difficult to say when Scottish interest in these roses began, but in the early 1800s, Dixon & Brown of Perth were probably the first nurserymen to grow them on any scale. Later the firm of Austin & McAslan of Glasgow listed 208 varieties, but there is no mention in their catalogues of those that we grow today. We may assume that a few of them at least survive under other names.

Although the Scotch Roses flower for a very limited period early in the season, and are not particularly showy, they do have certain virtues, not the least of which is the dense, bushy, compact nature of their growth. These bushes are covered with pretty little flowers in season, and the result is a charming picture. They are also extremely tough, and will grow under poor conditions, particularly on sandy soils. This gives them a special value which it would be difficult to replace with any other garden rose. They nearly all have their own pleasant perfume.

ANDREWSII. Small semi-double, deep pink flowers of rather cupped formation. Dense, bushy growth of about 4ft. in height.

DOUBLE BLUSH. Blush-pink flowers, deepening towards the centre and paler on the reverse side. Height 4ft. A pretty little rose.

DOUBLE WHITE. An excellent shrub and the best known of these roses. It forms a fine, well rounded, dense and bushy plant of about 5ft. In May and early June it is studded with small, double, deeply-cupped flowers with a delicious fragrance.

FALKLAND. Semi-double, delicate pink flowers fading almost to white against a background of greyish-green leaves, provide us with a charming effect. Height 4ft.

GLORY OF EDZELL. This attractive rose is always particularly welcome, as it is one of the first of all to flower. It has single, clear pink flowers that pale towards the centre. A sprightly little shrub of 5ft.

HARISONII ('Harison's Yellow'). There is some doubt as to the origin of this rose, but it was probably raised by George Harison of New York in 1830. It is almost certain that it is a hybrid between a Scotch Rose and *R. foetida.* It forms a rather slender, upright shrub of 5ft., bearing bright sulphur-yellow double flowers which are cupped at first and open to a more flat formation, usually exposing their rather darker stamens. The foliage is of a slightly greyish-green. It provides a most satisfactory exclamation mark of bright colour in a border of Old Roses before most of them are in flower. Fragrant.

MARBLED PINK. Small semi-double, cupped flowers, opening wide with the outer petals turning back. In colour it is blush-pink at first, marbled darker, becoming almost white. It forms an attractive, low, dense but spreading shrub of 3ft. in height. See page 369.

MARY QUEEN OF SCOTS. I do not have this variety at present, but understand it is a charming rose. It has small, double flowers coloured a mixture of purple and lilac-grey, paler on the outside. There is a legend that it was brought from France by Mary Queen of Scots. Height 3ft.

MRS. COLVILLE. A shrub of 2½ft. in height, thought to be a hybrid with *R. pendulina.* The flowers are single, crimson-purple, white at the centre, with yellow stamens. The young wood is red-brown, and it bears elongated hips of darkest red.

SINGLE CHERRY. Small cherry-pink flowers, with a lighter reverse and prominent stamens. Height 3ft.

STANWELL PERPETUAL. The first Old Rose I grew and still a favourite of mine. It was discovered in a garden in Essex, and introduced in 1838 by a nurseryman called Lee, of Hammersmith. It is highly probable that it was the result of a chance cross between *R. piminellifolia* and an Autumn Damask, as it is unique among Scotch Roses in that it is reliably repeat flowering. Its growth is more lax than is usual in these roses, and the foliage a rather greyish-green, but otherwise it is typical, showing little sign of the Damask parent. It is not so free-flowering as the others in this group, but this is made up for by a succession of later blooms. The flowers start as the most perfect little cupped buds of clearest blush-pink. These open to flat, semi-double, rather informal flowers of about 3½ins. across, with quilled petals and a button eye. They have the most delicious fragrance. The height is about 5ft. Like all these roses, it is very tough and hardy. See page 369.

WILLIAMS' DOUBLE YELLOW ('Double Yellow', 'Scotch Yellow', 'Old Double Yellow', 'Scots Rose'). This is similar to 'Harisonii' and probably came from the same parents. It was said to be a seedling from *R. foetida,* raised in 1828 by John Williams who lived near Worcester, and must have been a chance cross with a Scotch Rose. At first sight it is easy to confuse it with 'Harisonii', but closer examination reveals it is much nearer in growth to its Scotch parent. It has pale green carpels, not stamens, in the centre of its small bright yellow double flowers that open to an informal formation. These have a strong fragrance, similar to that of *R. foetida.* In Scotland it is known as 'Prince Charlie's Rose'. Height 4ft.

WILLIAM III. A dwarf bush of no more than 2ft. in height, suckering freely when on its own roots and forming a dense thicket. The flowers are semi-double, purplish-crimson fading to lilac-pink, and are followed by small, round, maroon-coloured hips.

ROSA PRIMULA. This rose is similar to *R. hugonis,* to which it is closely related, having the same finely divided, fern-like foliage and dainty yellow flowers carried along its arching branches. These are of a delicate primrose-yellow, with a light scent, and it is one of the first roses to flower in mid-May. It is also known as the 'Incense Rose' for the fragrance of its foliage — a fragrance which will carry far on the air. It may be expected to grow to 6ft. and as much across. A native of the region spreading from Turkestan to Northern China. First discovered near Samarkand by the American collector F.H. Meyer, 1911.

ROSA × RICHARDII. This interesting rose is also known as *R. sancta,* the 'Holy Rose' or the 'Sacred Rose of Abyssinia'. It was probably a natural hybrid between *R. gallica* and *R. phoenicea.* It forms a sprawling but shapely bush of 3ft. in height and 4ft. across, and bears large pale pink flowers in small clusters. It was introduced into Britain by Paul of Cheshunt in 1902.

Not only is it one of the most beautiful single flowered roses, but it also has a long and intriguing history. Dr. Hurst speculates interestingly on its origins. He suggests that St. Frumentius, who brought Christianity to Abyssinia, may have introduced it to that country in the fourth century, and that it was planted in the precincts of Christian churches and thus preserved throughout the centuries. He goes on to relate how in 1888 the eminent archaeologist, Sir Flinders Petrie, discovered the remains of this rose twined into garlands in tombs in the cemetery of the town of Arsione of Fayoum in Upper Egypt, near to the Labyrinth Pyramid. This would date them to a period between the second and fifth century A.D. He also tells us of Sir Arthur Evans's excavations at Knossos in Crete. Here Evans found a representation of a rose that was part of a wall painting and which Hurst felt bore a striking resemblance to the 'Sacred Rose'. This is probably the earliest picture of a rose ever found. See page 350.

ROSA ROXBURGHII (*R. microphylla;* also popularly known as the 'Burr Rose', the 'Chestnut Rose', the 'Chinquapin Rose'). An unusual rose from China and Japan, it forms a vigorous shrub of about 7ft. in height and the same across, with stiff, angular branches and attractively flaking light brown bark. It has strong hooked thorns in pairs, just below the leaves. The leaves themselves are long, with up to fifteen evenly-arranged leaflets. The flowers are usually solitary, 4ins. across, and of a clear pink fading to white, with plentiful golden stamens, the stalk and calyx being covered with prickles. These are followed by large, round, bristly hips (hence 'Chestnut Rose'). The whole effect is that of an attractively gnarled shrub. In cultivation prior to 1814.

ROSA ROXBURGHII PLENA. This is a double form, probably of Chinese origin, and thought to be of great antiquity. The flowers are very full, giving the appearance of a beautiful Old Rose. They have large, pale pink outer petals, while the numerous shorter centre petals give a deep pink effect. They have a light fragrance. Height 2½ to 3ft. A curious and interesting rose. Introduced to Britain by Dr. Roxburgh, from Canton, 1824.

CANTABRIGIENSIS, *Species Hybrid. One of the best of the* Rosa hugonis *hybrids, with typical dainty flowers and fern-like foliage.* *See page 347.* Calvert

ROSA CANINA ANDERSONII, *Species Hybrid. A good garden shrub which is probably a Dog Rose hybrid. See page 342.* Knight

ROSA PIMPINELLIFOLIA DUNWICH ROSE, *Species Hybrid. Note the attractive mound-like growth. See page 360.* Knight

ROSA SETIPODA, *Species Hybrid. A fine 10ft. shrub, beautiful in flower, leaf and fruit. See page 373.* Calvert

ROSA CANINA HIBERNICA, *Species Hybrid. Probably a hybrid between* Rosa canina *and* R. pimpinellifolia, *with bushy growth and dainty flowers. See page 342.* Knight

ROSA MOYESII, *Species Hybrid. One of the finest Species Roses, with bright red flowers followed by long pitcher-shaped fruit.* *See page 357* Knight

STANWELL PERPETUAL, *a recurrent flowering hybrid between a Scotch Rose and an Autumn Damask. See page 363.* Knight

MARBLED PINK, *a garden form of* Rosa pimpinellifolia, *and a good example of a Scotch Rose, all of which are useful for poor conditions. See page 362.* Knight

ROSA MULLIGANII, *one of the most massive of the Species Climbers, and ideal for growing in a tree.* *See page 378.*
Warren

HIGHDOWNENSIS, *Species Hybrid. A good form of* Rosa moyesii *with cerise flowers and rather fuller growth.* *See page 358.* Knight

ROSA FEDTSCHENKOANA. *Species Hybrid. Attractive grey-green foliage and a natural ability to repeat flower. See page 345.* Calvert

ROSA VILLOSA. *Species Hybrid. Good grey-green foliage and massive hips. See page 374.* Page

ROSA CANINA. *This and the illustration above right show the great variation of colour to be found in this rose.* Page

ROSA CANINA. *Species Hybrid. The Dog Rose of our hedgerows. See page 341.* Page

ROSA FOETIDA PERSIANA. *Species Hybrid. A double form of this Species Rose. Rich yellow colouring. See page 346.* Calvert

GREENMANTLE. *Species Hybrid. A hybrid of* Rosa eglanteria *— the Sweet Brier — with fragrant foliage. See page 344.* Calvert

ROSA RUGOSA. This important species is the parent of the Rugosa Hybrids, and I have dealt with it in the section on those roses in Chapter 8.

ROSA SERICEA (*R. omeiensis*). A vigorous, usually thorny shrub, occurring in a wide area extending over Northern India, the Himalayas, North Burma and Western China, and first collected in 1822. It is unique amongst roses in that its flowers have only four petals, although occasionally it is to be found with the normal five. These flowers are small, white or sometimes yellow, 1½ to 2ins. across, cupped, with the petals only just overlapping; they are held very closely along the branch early in the season in mid-May. The foliage is small and fern like with many leaflets; the hips are small, red and pear shaped. Height 10ft. *R. sericea* does not make a great show in the garden, although the growth and foliage are attractive. It has given rise to a number of forms and hybrids. The following three are worthwhile.

ROSA SERICEA HEATHER MUIR. The most beautiful form with creamy-white, scented flowers which are much larger than the species — about 3ins. across. These are produced with great freedom over a long period throughout the month of June. It will form a very large shrub of 10 by 10ft. or more. The hips are small and orange-red. It was named after the creator of the famous Kiftsgate Garden. Mrs. Muir obtained the original seedling from E.A. Bunyard, and it was eventually distributed by Sunningdale Nurseries in 1957.

ROSA SERICEA PTERACANTHA. This unique rose differs from *R. sericea* in the enormous size of its red thorns. These are triangular and flat, up to ¾in. wide at their base, and are the rose's chief attraction. When young, they are a translucent red-brown so that the sunlight shines through them, giving a brilliant effect. For this reason it is worth placing the rose where the sun can catch it, and cutting it hard back annually to produce new growth and, consequently, young thorns. Alternatively, it is sometimes useful as a barrier to halt both four-legged and two-legged intruders, for no rose has quite such a formidable armoury. The flowers are white, similar to *R. sericea,* with four petals, and not very conspicuous, although they have a certain quaint charm amongst the thorns. 8 by 6ft. Western China, 1890. See page 353.

ROSA SERICEA PTERACANTHA RED WING. A hybrid with *R. hugonis,* which has similar large red thorns, although they are rather smaller than those of its Pteracantha parent. The flowers are creamy-yellow, and it forms a graceful shrub with fine fern-like foliage. Height 8ft.

ROSA SETIPODA. In every way a beautiful shrub: in flower, leaf, fruit and general demeanour. It will grow to about 10ft. in height and the same across. The foliage is very fine, the leaves being about 7ins. long, with nine neatly formed leaflets of a glaucous-green, and with a slight Sweet Brier fragrance. The flowers are quite large for a species, 2½ to 3ins. across, opening flat, the petals turning back slightly at the edges. They are held nicely poised upon thin, bristly purplish stalks, have a light fruit-like fragrance and appear in the latter part of June. The hips are very large, orange-red, flagon-shaped and bristly, with persistent sepals. A native of Central China, brought to Britain by E.H. Wilson in 1895. See page 367.

ROSA STELLATA (*Hesperhodos stellatus*). A native of the South-western U.S.A., from the west of Texas to Arizona, this is a wiry, thicket-like shrub of about 2ft. in height, with grey-green stems, pale sharp prickles and hairy, deeply-toothed leaves of three leaflets, rather similar to those of a gooseberry. The flowers are solitary, 2 to 2½ins. across, soft rose-pink in colour, with deeply-notched petals and yellow anthers, having something of the appearance of a cistus. The hips are round, brownish-red and about ½in. wide. It is very hardy, but likes sun and a well-drained soil.

ROSA STELLATA MIRIFICA ('Sacramento Rose'). Similar to *R. stellata,* but more vigorous, attaining 4 to 6ft. in the wild, usually with leaves of five leaflets. The flowers are slightly larger and it is more free flowering than *R. stellata.* It requires similar conditions. Both are roses of some charm.

ROSA SWEGINZOWII. A very vigorous shrub that is similar to *R. moyesii* in many respects, but larger, growing to 12ft. in height and the same across, with very large thorns and numerous bristles. The flowers are rose-pink, 1½ to 2ins. across, and held in small clusters. These are followed by long, bristly, flagon-shaped, orange-red hips. It is a native of North-west China. Introduced 1906. See page 353.

ROSA VILLOSA. Also known as the 'Apple Rose' for the exceptionally large size of its round hips which make a fine display in autumn. It is a vigorous, well-formed shrub of 7 by 7 ft, with large, downy, grey-green foliage, against which its clear rosy-pink flowers show themselves to good effect. These are about 2½ins. across, with slightly crinkled petals and a light fragrance. A native of Central Europe and Western Asia. See page 372.

ROSA VILLOSA DUPLEX. ('Wolley-Dod'.) This is a semi-double form or hybrid of the rose described above. Although it may be a little shorter in growth, it is otherwise similar. In spite of this, the chromosome count suggests that it is, in fact, a hybrid of a garden rose. The hips are less plentiful and perhaps a little smaller, the flowers rather larger, but we have the same attractive combination of flower and leaf. It is known to have been in existence prior to 1797.

ROSA VIRGINIANA. A dense, suckering shrub, notable for the varying colours of its foliage. This is bronzy when young, becoming green, and finally turning to autumn tints of red and yellow. The stems are tinged with red, and have few thorns. The flowers appear later than many other Species and continue from late June to early August. They are quite small, cerise-pink, paler at the centre, with pointed buds. The hips are small and bright red, persisting throughout the winter. It will grow to 4 or 5ft. in height, and sucker freely on its own roots. A useful rose for municipal planting or for the more natural areas of the garden. Many seedling strains of this rose have become rather mixed and show distinct signs of hybridity. A native of North America.

ROSA VIRGINIANA ALBA. A white-flowered form or hybrid of the rose described above, with green stems and pale green leaves which do not turn to autumn tints. Height 4 to 5ft.

ROSA WARDII CULTA. *R. wardii* is a native of South-east Tibet and is not in cultivation. *R. wardii culta* is a form of this rose collected by Kingdon Ward and distributed in 1924. It is another Species of the *R. moyesii* type, being rather similar in growth and foliage. Its flowers are white, with a mahogany-red central disc surrounded by yellow stamens. In fact, it is sometimes known as the 'White Moyesii'. The growth is arching, the foliage light green, and it will grow to 6ft. in height and 5ft. across. There are very few thorns.

ROSA WEBBIANA. A pretty Species closely related to *R. willmottiae.* It is of dense growth, with slender, reddish-brown, twiggy stems in long, arching sprays, along which are borne pale lilac-pink flowers, each about 2ins. across, with a slight scent. These occur in early June. They are followed by narrow flask-shaped, scarlet-red hips of about ¾in. long, making a particularly dainty display; indeed, few other Species can match it in this respect. The foliage is made up of up to nine small, finely-divided leaflets. It will grow to about 6ft. in height and 6ft. across. A native of the Himalayas, Afghanistan and Turkestan, it grows at from 6,000 to 18,000ft. First cultivated in 1879.

ROSA WILLMOTTIAE. Of all the Species, this is perhaps the most graceful in growth and foliage. It is a prickly shrub of 8ft. in height and rather more across, with arching growth bearing small, finely-divided greyish-green foliage, giving a dainty spray-like ferny effect. The flowers are small but pretty. They do not last for very long, but while they do they provide a pleasing picture. Their colour is lilac-pink with creamy stamens. Later, there are small pear-shaped orange-red hips. A native of Western China, collected by E.H. Wilson in 1904. See page 352.

ROSA WOODSII FENDLERI. *R. woodsii* is a variable shrub native to central and western North America. *R. woodsii fendleri* is the form usually seen in gardens, reputedly found in the southerly areas of this region — sometimes as far south as Mexico — although it is quite hardy. It forms a dense bush of 6 by 5ft, and has graceful growth, greyish-green leaves and small lilac-pink flowers with creamy stamens. These are fragrant and borne singly or in small clusters. In autumn the branches are hung with round, shiny, red hips that persist well into winter. These are perhaps its greatest asset. First cultivated in 1888.

ROSA XANTHINA SPONTANEA CANARY BIRD. One of the most popular and best known of the Species, mainly because of the deep yellow colouring of its flowers. Although it is a good shrub, I am not quite sure it deserves such pre-eminence. It has 2in. flowers, graceful growth, chocolate-brown bark and dainty fern-like, grey-green foliage. The hips are dark maroon, but not very conspicuous. An excellent rose, although not always very robust and it is inclined to suffer from die back unless on its own roots. Height 7ft. See page 353.

CLIMBING SPECIES ROSES

Apart from the shrubby Species, there are a number of good Climbing Species. In the wild these would climb over shrubs and into trees to find the light. The majority of them are of the Synstylae family (see below) and of very strong growth, producing large sprays of small, white flowers.

In addition there are a few Climbing Species of other families. These vary considerably and include some exotic roses of great beauty (see pages 381-382). Unfortunately, many of them are rather tender, but where this is the case they are usually well worth trying on a warm wall.

Nearly all the Climbing Species are best left to their own devices, with little pruning, at least in so far as space allows. They will require very little other attention.

CLIMBING SPECIES OF THE SYNSTYLAE FAMILY

Species of this family are so distinct as to make it helpful to include them in a section of their own. The name refers to the fact that all these roses have the styles of their flowers in one piece, and not separated and held individually as is the case with all other roses. This is the simple way in which botanists identify them. It is by crossing Species from this family with garden varieties that all our Rambler Roses have been developed.

A reader who is not familiar with the Synstylae roses might be excused if he complained that they seem to be all very much the same. They do, however, vary greatly in height, and as we get to know them better we find that they have many subtle differences which are hard to put into a few words. They usually have a strong, sweet fragrance, and flower with exceptional freedom. They include some dramatically tall and rampant roses ideal for growing in trees and over bushes, and indeed for covering any large structure.

ROSA ARVENSIS (the 'Field Rose'). A common rose of the British hedgerows, flowering after the Dog Rose and having rather smaller white flowers. It also grows wild over much of Europe. A climbing or trailing Species it is usually found scrambling over bushes. From a horticultural point of view it is mainly important as the parent of the Ayrshire Roses.

The flowers are borne in small bunches along reddish stems, and are followed by ovoid, red hips. Contrary to what we often read in books, it is fragrant and is indeed the 'Sweet Musk Rose' extolled by Shakespeare and Spenser. This rose will grow to a great width if permitted — perhaps 20 by 10ft. in height. It is worth growing in wild places, and is sometimes used for roadside planting.

ROSA BRUNONII (*R. moschata nepalensis,* the 'Himalayan Musk Rose'). A variable Species and one of the most beautiful of this family. A native of the Himalayan region, extending into China, it grows extremely vigorously, to a height of 30 or 40ft., making it excellent for climbing into larger trees. The foliage is particularly fine, with very large, elegantly poised leaves of seven widely-spaced, long pointed leaflets. These are grey-green and downy on the underside. The flowers are creamy-white, about 1½ins. across, with yellow stamens, and are held in very large clusters in late June and early July. They have a strong fragrance. This Species is not completely hardy and can be caught by severe frosts, but it is entirely worthwhile in most areas. First cultivated in 1822.

ROSA BRUNONII LA MORTOLA. A superior form of *R. brunonii* in almost every way, and should generally be grown in preference. It has larger white flowers of about 2ins. across, which are held in larger clusters. The leaves also are larger, more grey and more downy. In other respects it is as described in the Species above. Height 30 or 40ft. It was named after the famous garden in Italy, close to the French border, and was brought from there to England by E.A. Bunyard. It was introduced in the U.K. in 1954.

ROSA FILIPES. A strong and rampant climber that will grow to 30ft. The flowers are white and borne in large corymbs. They are of a pronounced cup-like formation, and each is held on a long, slender thread-like stem. They have a strong fragrance and are followed by very small oval hips. We do not grow this Species — it has been almost entirely superseded in the garden by *R. filipes* 'Kiftsgate'. A native of West China, first collected by E.H. Wilson in 1908.

ROSA FILIPES BRENDA COLVIN. A seedling from 'Kiftsgate' described below. It has all the strength of that massive rose, and small single flowers in large clusters. The difference lies in the colour: this is a soft blush-pink which quickly turns to white. Unfortunately, the pink is so indistinct as to be almost white in massed effect. There is a delicious fragrance. A chance seedling discovered by Miss Colvin, first distributed by Sunningdale Nurseries in 1970.

ROSA FILIPES KIFTSGATE. This is the form of *R. filipes* usually sold by nurserymen. It has become well known among keen gardeners as a climber for large trees and there is no better rose for this purpose. It is a prodigious grower and an astonishing bloomer. It can easily achieve 40ft. and bears enormous corymbs of bloom, sometimes with hundreds of flowers. Individually these are small, cupped and creamy-white with yellow stamens. They have a strong fragrance. It can at times be a little choosy as to the position in which it is grown, and refuse to live up to its reputation as a massive grower. The late Mrs. Muir of Kiftsgate Court, Gloucestershire, purchased this rose from E.A. Bunyard in 1938. Where he obtained it from we do not know, but it was eventually introduced by Murrell (U.K.) in 1954. Mrs. Muir's original plant is now some 60ft. in width, and over 40ft. high. See page 352.

ROSA FILIPES TREASURE TROVE. See Chapter 10.

ROSA HELENAE. A native of West China, collected by E.H. Wilson in 1907. It is a vigorous Climber that will grow to 18ft. in height. The flowers are small, about 1½ins., creamy-white and held in dense, well-rounded clusters of about 6ins. across. They have a strong fragrance. The hips are small, ovoid, orange-red and hang gracefully from the branch. The foliage is dark green with seven to nine leaflets, and there are strong, hooked thorns. This is a useful tree climber where *R. filipes* or *R. mulliganii* are too big; it may also be grown as a large shrub.

ROSA MOSCHATA (the 'Musk Rose'). Not, in fact, a wild Species, but a rose of ancient garden origin. It may have been brought to England in the time of Elizabeth I and has many romantic associations. Later, it had an important effect on the breeding of garden roses, being one of the original parents of the Noisette Roses. On a sunny sheltered wall it can be very fine, but in a less favourable position it may not be so impressive. The flowers are single (sometimes semi-double), creamy-white, and held in widely branching sprays. It has two important merits: its delicious musk fragrance, and the fact that it does not bloom until August, and then continues until autumn. Height about 10ft.

ROSA MOSCHATA PRINCESSE DE NASSAU. At one time known as *R. moschata* 'Autumnalis', this has semi-double flowers of creamy-buff. They are held in dainty sprays, appearing unusually late in the season (in August), continuing until autumn, and are exceedingly sweetly scented. This rose needs and deserves a sheltered position in full sun to hasten the blooms. We know nothing of its origin, but it has many similarities to a Noisette, which in fact it may be. Height 8ft.

ROSA MULLIGANII. For a long time this rose has been available from nurserymen as *R. longicuspis,* but according to Bean's *Trees and Shrubs,* it should properly be known as *R. mulliganii.* This is going to be rather confusing for a little while. *R. mulliganii* vies with *R. filipes* 'Kiftsgate' for the position as the largest tree-climbing rose. It is usually not quite so strong, but will reach 30ft., and has fine, glossy, almost evergreen foliage, with leaves of seven leaflets, the young shoots being tinted with brown. The flowers are creamy-white, almost 2ins. across, and are held in huge broad trusses of anything up to 150 individual blooms. They have a strong fragrance. In autumn there are small orange-red hips. It flowers late in the season, from the end of June to mid-July. A native of West China, it was collected by F. Kingdon Ward in about 1915. See page 370.

ROSA MULTIFLORA (*R. polyantha*). A vigorous Climber or shrub sometimes used as a root stock in this country, but more often on the Continent. For this reason it is frequently found surviving in gardens, long after the garden rose which was budded on to it has died away. However, this is not to say it is not a useful garden plant, although it is perhaps a little stiff in growth as a Climber, and there are better Species. It has considerable value for large-scale planting in municipal landscapes, as it grows very vigorously, forming a great mass of tall growth. For this purpose it should be grown from seed. It bears tight clusters of small, 1-in. creamy-white flowers with golden stamens in late June and early July. These have a strong fruity fragrance which carries extensively. There are small, oval, red hips in autumn. Its dimensions as a shrub are 7ft. high by 10ft. across; as a Climber it will grow considerably taller, and may reach 20ft. or more in a tree. It was one of the ancestors of the Multiflora Ramblers and the Polyantha Pompon Roses, eventually influencing the Floribundas. It is thus one of the most important ancestors of our Modern Roses. A native of North China, Korea and Japan. Known to have been in Britain before 1869.

ROSA POLYANTHA GRANDIFLORA. This is usually known as *R. gentiliana,* but it is more likely that it is an *R. multiflora* Hybrid, as no one seems to have any knowledge of it in the wild; and more conclusively by the fact that the styles of its flowers are separated, indicating it is not a pure member of the Synstylae family. In late June to mid-July it bears masses of small, single white flowers in rather small clusters. These have orangy-red stamens, a strong fruit-like fragrance, and are followed by light red hips which last well into winter, making a fine display. It flowers freely and has plentiful, glossy foliage, which is tinted with bronze at first. Height 15 to 20ft. It is thought to have been brought from China, and introduced in 1886.

ROSA RUBUS (*R. ernestii*). A vigorous Climbing Rose closely related to *R. helenae.* The flowers are 1½ins. across and are borne in tight clusters of up to forty. These are creamy-white at first with a tint of yellow at the base of the petals and attractive orange stamens at the centre. They have a particularly strong Multiflora fragrance, and appear from late June to early August. The blooms are followed by a good display of small orange-red hips. The leaves are made up of five of more leaflets which are downy beneath and have a purplish colour when young. Height 20ft. A native of Central and Western China. First discovered by Dr. Henry about 1886.

ROSA SEMPERVIRENS. This Species is a native of Southern Europe and North Africa and is best known as the parent of the beautiful Sempervirens Hybrids. It is, in fact, an attractive Species in its own right, with larger flowers than others of this family and of pleasing individual character. These are borne in small clusters on long, graceful, trailing growth. They have a slight fragrance. The foliage consists of five to seven leaflets and is almost evergreen. Not entirely hardy in the British Isles.

ROSA SETIGERA (the 'Prairie Rose'). There is some doubt as to whether this should be regarded as a shrub or a Rambler. It is so large that I think for most garden purposes it is best treated as a Rambler, when it will climb to 15ft. In late July and early August it bears small sprays of 2-in. rose-pink flowers that fade almost to white. These are followed by small, round, red hips. The foliage is of an attractive dull green colour. It is a useful rose for growing in a small tree or over bushes, and has the added attraction of coloured flowers which are unusual in this section. Where space can be found it is also an excellent shrub, sending out long, trailing stems and forming a mound of sprawling growth. It is a native of the Eastern United States, and has been used in the breeding of Rambler Roses, more notably 'American Pillar' and 'Baltimore Belle'.

ROSA SINOWILSONII. This rose has the most magnificent foliage of all the Species, and it is grown mainly for this reason. The leaves are of a dark, glossy green, very large, and may be up to 1ft. in length. They are deeply corrugated, tinted with purple beneath, and have seven leaflets. The flowers are not outstanding, being white, 1½ins. across, and borne in small sprays. Most unfortunately, it is not completely hardy. I am not sure how tall it will grow, as the frost has always cut it short in my garden. I notice *Modern Roses* states 50ft. It was brought from China to Britain in 1904 by E.H. Wilson, who was responsible for bringing so many good Species from that country, so much so that he became known as 'Chinese Wilson'.

ROSA SOULIEANA. A very strong, loose-growing Climber or shrub, with long, arching stems, distinctly greyish leaves, and hooked yellow thorns. The flowers are pale yellow in the bud, opening white, about 1½ins. across, and freely produced in clusters. There is a fruity fragrance. Bunches of small, ovoid orange hips make a good show in autumn. As a Climber it will grow to 12 or 15ft. without difficulty. As a shrub it will create a mound of growth 10ft. high and the same across. It is excellent for wild areas, where it can be grown as a shrub or into trees and over bushes. In the British Isles it may be cut back by cold frosts. Collected in West China by Père Soulié, and sent to France, arriving at Kew in 1899.

ROSA WICHURAIANA. A vigorous, trailing rose, native to Japan, East China, Korea and Taiwan. Best known as the parent of the Wichuraiana Ramblers, it is a useful garden plant in its own right. It will make excellent ground cover where space permits, sending out trailing growth of great length which will keep close to the ground or climb into bushes and trees with the help of its hooked thorns. It does not flower until August, when it has attractive pyramid-shaped clusters of small white flowers shading to yellow at the centre. These have a strong fruit-like fragrance. The foliage is a bright, glossy green and almost evergreen. Later we have small, ovoid, dark red hips. It is also a most attractive Climber, growing to 20ft., its long shoots hanging gracefully from their support.

OTHER CLIMBING SPECIES

ROSA BRACTEATA (the 'Macartney Rose). A most beautiful and exotic rose, but unfortunately not completely hardy in the British Isles. It will, given a warm and sheltered wall, survive most winters, certainly in the warmer parts of the country. The flowers are large, up to 4ins. across, pure white, with a silky texture and a large boss of orange-red stamens. They are fragrant and borne singly on short stalks, with attractive, large, leafy bracts around the buds. The fruit is globular and orange-red. It has fine, smooth, dark green leaves with up to nine leaflets, and is almost evergreen. The growth is bushy, to about 12ft. in height in a suitable position, and it will in warmer climates form a good shrub. Unusually among Species it continues to flower until autumn. It is a native of Eastern China, collected by Sir George Staunton, and brought to this country by Lord Macartney in 1793. In the warmer regions of the Southern U.S.A. it has become naturalized and is regarded as something of a weed in certain areas. It is one of the parents of the beautiful 'Mermaid'.

ROSA GIGANTEA. The most splendid of the wild Species Roses. Sadly, it is too tender to be grown in the British Isles, except in the very warmest areas, but even then it seldom blooms. In its native habitat of South-west China and Upper Burma the flowers are very large, 5 or 6ins. across, and may be pale yellow, cream or white, with large, overlapping petals and a boss of golden stamens. The fragrance is similar to that of Tea Roses. It has huge, 9-in. glossy dark green leaves, and will make massive growth to as much as 50ft., even 80ft. in warm climates. The hips, too, are very large, about 1½ins. across, and globular. Indeed, it is in every way gigantic. Gault and Synge, in their *Dictionary of Roses,* tell us how the giant hips are sold for eating in the bazaars of Manipur State. Discovered by Sir George Watt, 1882, introduced by Sir Henry Collet, 1889.

R. gigantea is of particular interest to us as one of the great influences in the development of Modern Roses, and this has been discussed at some length in Chapters 3 and 4. It was this rose, above all, which was responsible for the transition of Old Roses to what we now call Modern Roses. It is so huge and so different that it was certain to change the whole character of garden roses.

ROSA LAEVIGATA (*R. sinica, R. cherokeensis*). A vigorous Climber or shrub, with dark green leaves which are unusual in that they each have only three coarsely-toothed leaflets. It has 4-in. creamy-white, deliciously fragrant flowers borne singly or in pairs in late June. This is another beautiful but tender Rambling Species. It will flower well in this country, but requires a warm wall if it is to survive. A native of China, it has adapted itself to the wild in south-eastern North America, where it has become known as the 'Cherokee Rose'. Growth 20ft. Introduced 1759.

ROSA LAEVIGATA HYBRIDS

ROSA ANEMONE (*R. anemonoides, R. sinica* 'Anemone'). This is a hybrid of *R. laevigata,* probably with a Tea Rose. It is more delicate in appearance than the former, with sparse growth, less foliage and finer stems. The flowers, however, are very similar to those of *R. laevigata,* and are of supreme beauty, being a clear shell-pink, lightly veined with deeper pink and paler on the reverse side. In spite of its refined appearance it is hardier than *R. laevigata,* but still requires a warm wall. It starts flowering in early June and, although not repeat flowering, continues over an extended period. It will grow to 15ft. in a suitable position. Slight fragrance. Bred by J.C. Schmidt (Germany), 1895.

ROSA LAEVIGATA COOPERI ('Cooper's Burmese Rose'). This is a Species closely allied to *R. laevigata,* and a native of Nepal, North Burma and South-west China. Its flowers are large, about 4ins. across. They are held singly and are of glistening pure white, with a large boss of yellow stamens. It has fine, very glossy foliage, with three (occasionally five) leaflets. Unfortunately it is tender and has failed to flower in my garden, although at Sissinghurst Castle it flowers freely early in the season on a sunny wall. In England it will grow to about 12ft., although in its habitat it is a giant. We have a plant under glass where it flowers freely and would no doubt grow to a great length. It was first brought to this country by Mr. R.E. Cooper, and grown at the then National Rose Society's Trial Ground at Haywards Heath, in 1931. Our stock was brought to us by Mr. and Mrs. Cooper-Willis from Nepal, where they saw valleys of it growing to the tops of tall trees, and sweeping in long, trailing stems almost to the ground. This must be the most wonderful rose spectacle in the world.

ROSA RAMONA. A sport from *R. anemonoides,* discovered by Dietrich and Turner of California in 1913. It is similar in every way, except for the colour of the flowers. This is cerise-crimson with a greyish tint on the reverse. A very beautiful rose. See page 352.

HULTHEMIA

This is a sub-genus that was previously classified by botanists as part of the genus *Rosa.* It is closely related to the rose, as is illustrated by the fact that the two have been successfully hybridized.

HULTHEMIA PERSICA (*Rosa persica, R. berberifolia,* 'Rose of Persia'). This is an interesting shrub that occurs in the semi-desert conditions of Iran, Afghanistan and neighbouring U.S.S.R., where it is a common sight. It forms low, twiggy, spiny growth of about 2½ft. in height, spreading by means of runners. The foliage is silvery-grey. The flowers are small, about 1½ ins. across, of deep golden-yellow with a red-brown blotch in the centre. No rose is of quite such a brilliant yellow. Later, there are small, bristly hips. In its native territory it is extremely hardy and persistent, and I understand it has been known to push its way up through concrete. It is not easy to grow in a northerly climate, but not impossible if given a warm, dry position. First introduced to Europe around 1790. See page 352.

× HULTHEMOSA HARDII (*Rosa* × *hardii*). This is a bigeneric hybrid; reputedly *Hulthemia persica* × *R. clinophylla.* It has larger and finer flowers than *H. persica.* These are bright golden-yellow with a bright red-brown eye at the centre. I have never seen it in flower, but understand it is beautiful. It is a rather straggly plant and somewhat subject to mildew, but will grow to about 6ft. with the protection of a warm wall. Raised at the Jardins du Luxembourg, Paris, 1836.

MODERN HYBRIDS OF HULTHEMIA

As early as 1880, Thomas Rivers, the famous rose specialist of the time, predicted that *Hulthemia persica* would probably be the parent of an entirely new group. He, of course, saw it as a species of *Rosa,* and was not to know that it might not be quite so simple as that. Nonetheless, there are signs that his prediction may well be about to become true. In 1964 Alexander Cocker obtained seed of *Hulthemia persica* from Iran, and gave some of it to Jack Harkness who grew the Species and hybridized it with a number of true roses. Attempting to hybridize between two separate genera is no easy matter, but Jack Harkness succeeded in doing this with a number of roses and states in his book *Roses* that he had successfully hybridized *H. persica* with 'Ballerina', 'Buff Beauty', 'Canary Bird', *R. chinensis* 'Mutabilis', 'Cornelia', 'Fru Dagmar Hastrup', 'Margo Koster', 'Mermaid', 'Perla de Alcanada', 'Phyllis Bide', 'Roseraie de l'Hay' and 'Trier'.

It was the bright central 'eye' of *H. persica* that appealed to him, and no doubt the bright yellow colouring and extremely tough growth, but there is more to his hybrids than this. They form appealing small shrubs of unrose-like appearance. Their growth is bushy and rather sprawling, with flowers of distinct character. I would like to see them bred further, not just as an improvement on the rose, but as something quite different. Here are two varieties Harkness has introduced. Unfortunately they have proved difficult to propagate and stock is not plentiful.

EUPHRATES. Sizeable clusters of single reddish-salmon flowers, each with a prominent scarlet eye at the centre. These are produced freely on an excellent spreading bushy plant of 2ft. in height. The leaflets show considerable variation in shape, which is a feature of the Persica hybrids. *R. persica* × 'Fairy Changeling'. Harkness (U.K.), 1986.

TIGRIS. Attractive semi-double, canary-yellow flowers with red centres. The growth is lax, dense and spreading, with many thorns and light green foliage providing a gooseberry-like effect. It flowers in June and July with occasional blooms appearing later. *R. persica* × 'Trier'. Harkness (U.K.), 1985.

Chapter 12

ROSES IN THE GARDEN SCENE

There are many ways to enjoy roses. They may be grown without thought for their effect in the garden, as a thing of beauty in themselves, for their flowers alone. A collection of roses may be gathered showing all their varying habits and forms. For this purpose they can be planted in rows in the kitchen garden. The gathering of such a collection can be a source of great pleasure and interest.

Many people find exhibiting an exciting, interesting and sociable hobby, though some more highbrow gardeners consider this to be a rather trivial pursuit. I do not agree with them. One of the charms of the rose is the fact that although it is nearly always beautiful, it does not easily achieve its full perfection. Other flowers can be relied on to turn out the perfect bloom every time. Not so the rose. Its flowers are of such complexity and delicacy that they only achieve perfection by degrees; seldom is the ideal achieved. Thus they are good subjects for competition.

Others see the rose as a cut flower for the house, and it is indeed most valuable for this purpose. As I have said, it is particularly suitable for an architectural setting in the garden, and it is only to be expected that it would be equally at home inside the house. There is endless scope for artistry here, particularly in combination with other flowers, and there are few better ways of getting to know roses well, at least in so far as the flower is concerned.

Having said this, most of us will, quite correctly, see the rose as a garden flower. As such it is supreme. In beds, in borders, on walls, over trees and bushes, on arches and pillars, in gardens formal or wild — in whatever type of garden, the rose has its place.

There is a further contribution the rose can make and one it is important not to forget. This is its value for what is known today, somewhat awkwardly, as amenity planting — its use in public places. Here it could make a much larger and more varied contribution than it does.

It is, however, the rose in the garden that we are chiefly concerned with here. As I begin to assess the many possibilities open to us, I have to confess I am somewhat bewildered by their multiplicity. The best I can do is to take them one at a time and cover them as completely as I am able. It is not possible or desirable in a book to give exact instructions on the planting of gardens. All that I can do is to give a few ideas as pointers as to the direction the gardener might take and to outline some of the ways in which roses might be used.

The art of gardening is, thankfully, something that has to be done by the gardener himself. He can learn much from books, by taking advice, and by visiting other people's gardens, but in the final analysis it comes down to what pleases him. As a piece of general advice, I would simply say that he should not be too easily satisfied, nor should he be afraid to take a chance. If he is not happy with a planting or layout he should change it, or even remove a plant altogether. In this way he will gradually get closer to his ideal.

ROSES IN THE BORDER

Of all the places in the garden in which we may grow roses, the border is the most likely. For this roses have many virtues and few weaknesses.

Hybrid Teas and Floribundas are not ideal for mixed borders. Their habit of growth and often harsh colours do not mix well with other plants. In spite of this, if we are careful in our selection, suitable varieties can be found. I have in mind such roses as 'Iceberg', 'Escapade' and 'Dainty Maid', but of course there are others. This does not mean that more typical varieties cannot be satisfactory when grown in a border on their own, particularly if we choose sympathetic colours, and avoid using too many of the strident shades. Other plants may be grown with them, but they should be used only to complement the roses — violas and pinks are good examples. Care must always be taken to ensure that these other plants do not compete too strongly — I have seen violas climbing up rose bushes and smothering them completely.

It is, however, the Shrub Roses that are best suited for the border, particularly the mixed border. Even though they are not, of course, herbaceous, they are very much at home in the herbaceous border. The slightly heavy character of some of their flowers and their rather haphazard habit of growth seem to associate well with herbaceous plants, while the prominent and shrubby nature of the rose can give structure to a border.

The Old Roses are ideal, with their soft colours and fragrant flowers. Many modern Shrub Roses are equally suitable and often have the advantage of repeat flowering, thus greatly extending the season. I should also like to put a word in for the English Roses, which have been bred with this use very much in mind, having the old type of flower while continuing to bloom intermittently.

There are also roses that are particularly suitable for the shrub border. Here it is best to look for those of more natural growth. Certain of the modern shrubs, for example 'Cerise Bouquet', 'Dapple Dawn',

'Frühlingsmorgen', 'Vanity' and the single flowered Rugosas, will look very much in place. Among the Old Roses, it will be necessary to pick those with more simple flowers, like *Rosa alba semi-plena* or the Damask 'Celsiana'. Perhaps best of all are the Species and their near hybrids, almost all of which would be entirely at home with other shrubs.

Most borders today are not exclusively devoted either to herbaceous plants or to shrubs, but are a mixture of both, and here a wide range of Shrub Roses will be found useful. The rose has one very practical advantage in all borders — it flowers when most of the shrubs have finished flowering and before many of the herbaceous flowers have begun. Whether your border be herbaceous or shrub, or a mixture of both, roses fill a very important gap. What is more, they frequently continue to flower all the way up to winter.

I suggest that, in larger borders at least, there are advantages in growing roses in groups of two or more. Three is often ideal. Roses frequently form rather ungainly shrubs and can become bare at the base. If they are planted in close groups they will grow together to form what is, to all intents and purposes, one plant, and will look altogether fuller and more natural in growth. This is particularly important when the shrub happens to be repeat flowering, for repeat flowering is not natural to a rose, and puts an added strain on the plant. In a closely planted group there will be, so to speak, more than one access point to the soil, thus making a better performance possible. I am aware that this idea does add considerably to the cost, but rose trees are not expensive when compared to other items on which we might spend our money, and Shrub and Old Roses in particular do live for a very long time. This, however, is in the nature of a counsel of perfection — individual shrubs are entirely adequate, particularly when well grown. With the larger, more arching shrubs planting in close groups is not necessary at all.

Many people reading this book will be Shrub Rose enthusiasts, or I hope potentially so, and if they cannot have a rose garden will at least wish to have a border of roses. Certainly this is a very good way to house a collection, something that may, if so desired, be added to and subtracted from over the years. Indeed, collecting roses can be a hobby in itself. Two borders would be better still, with each facing the other and a pathway down the middle. This path may be of grass, stone, concrete paving, gravel or brick. A good background is a great advantage, either a hedge, wall or trellis-work. Borders should be of sufficient width — 3 or 4 yds., or even more if space permits. Some shrubs are quite large, and it is nice to have a variety of heights in order to obtain a more interesting effect. Where it is only possible to have a narrow border, it will be necessary to use smaller shrubs and avoid the larger kinds which might eventually take over. A careful combination of perpetual flowering roses with those that flower only in the summer will ensure continuity of bloom. Other plants need not be excluded, but select with care only such as will enhance the beauty of the roses. Borders of two main flowers will create a double interest. Irises are a good example. They flower before the rose, and provide an excellent contrast in the form and colour of their leaves.

There are many Shrub Roses, indeed some of the very finest, that even so have a difficult habit of growth. A prime example of this is 'Constance Spry' which, though excellent as a Climber, forms a large, sprawling shrub. Its growth goes all over the place. This can have its attractions, but is difficult in a confined position. A solution to this problem is to erect a wooden fence, with a single rail, around the shrub, rather in the way that trees are protected from livestock in park land. This will vary according to the size of the shrub, but will usually be comparatively low. The growth can thus be contained within a rectangle or triangle, the more central growth being held up by the outer growth. In this way we may obtain a nice shapely shrub. There is no need to worry about the appearance of the wood, as it will form an added attraction in itself. It may be worth tying some of the growth to the woodwork; in fact, with a little artistry in the tying of the branches, we can add to their beauty. This is a method employed with great success by James Russell at Castle Howard. Many roses benefit from this treatment, even those which at first sight would appear not to require it. A low, light structure around such varieties as 'Charles Austin' and 'Gertrude Jekyll' can encourage them to spread and further enhance their already not unattractive growth. The stretched-out stems tend to shoot more freely, encouraging continuity of bloom. Climbers and Ramblers, more particularly, can be converted into excellent large shrubs with the aid of such support. Some Old Roses are very floppy in growth, and they too will benefit. Ugly, upright, Hybrid Perpetuals, can be trained to take on a degree of elegance.

ROSE GARDENS AND FORMAL AREAS

There are many roses that are suitable for the more natural areas of the garden, but if a choice is possible most of them are really more at home in a formal setting. Roses are briers by nature and distinctly informal in habit of growth, far more so than most shrubs. They may thus be said to be informal plants for a formal setting. Incongruous as this may seem, such a combination is, for me at least, the most beautiful of all. It is only necessary to visit gardens like Hidcote Manor in Gloucestershire, or Sissinghurst Castle in Kent, to see what I mean. When a natural and informal planting can be held within the architectural structure of a formal layout, it is frequently then that the most satisfactory effects can be achieved. This is perhaps more true for roses than any other plant.

In larger gardens it is the areas around the house that are usually the most suitable. Climbing Roses on walls and over walls; Old or English Roses close to paved areas, in formal niches, along paths, and so on. In the average small garden the question does not really arise, as this is by its very nature intimate and around the house.

Every rose lover's ideal would be to have a rose garden; a garden of roses, although not everyone has the opportunity. If such a garden is surrounded by a wall this has many advantages, for walls not only make a good background, but are useful for Climbing Roses, particularly if some of these are inclined to be tender. It will be necessary to take care in the choice of colours to go against them. A hedge would be almost as good. A yew hedge is particularly desirable. This can be grown more quickly than many people think, and is in some ways better than a wall, for its dark green provides a better background than anything I can think of. Another good idea is to enclose your rose garden with trellis or rustic work. This can be covered with Climbing Roses.

The layout of a formal rose garden requires much thought. It may be in a great variety of patterns and much pleasure can be had in drawing up the design. Careful attention to the proportions of both border and pathway, and between one bed and another, is most important, and skill and thought can in fact render the garden a satisfactory piece of architecture. Paths may be in a variety of materials: grass, paving or gravel. Brick or cobblestones form another possibility. A mixture of both, perhaps woven into patterns, can be very pleasing. All these have their own particular attractions. Edging is essential where there is gravel, and here stone or concrete can be used. Edging plants like closely-clipped box will add much to the charm of the garden.

Formal gardens are frequently better for having a focal point, either at the centre, or perhaps towards one end; a point to which all paths may lead. A piece of sculpture would be ideal and add much to the atmosphere, and perhaps give it a human dimension, providing a lift to the whole scene as nothing else can. Alternatively, there may be a centre bed of roses, possibly of some particularly imposing variety, or a weeping standard. Again, there could be some structure clothed with roses; perhaps a pyramid or other form covered with Climbers, or even a temple-like structure or summer house, all of which might also be clad in roses. These latter constructions may, if so desired, be formed of trellis-work.

We might fill our garden with beds of Hybrid Teas and Floribundas, and perhaps surround these with borders of Shrub Roses. Providing the Hybrid Teas and Floribundas do not swamp the shrubs and Climbers with over-brilliant colours, this can be nice and make a very colourful picture. It is usual to recommend beds of one variety only. I am not sure that this is essential; it might be worth planting carefully chosen blends of different shades of one colour in each bed. Alternatively I should like to suggest that the beds be planted with Old Roses, English Roses, and Modern Shrub Roses of appropriate size. It is now possible to have a mixture of recurrent-flowering small shrubs that are entirely suitable. These will provide continuity of bloom, and other old once-flowering varieties may be intermingled with them, or perhaps confined to the surrounding borders. I think this would be the most beautiful of all rose gardens. When we

THE BEAUTIFUL *Victorian Garden at Warwick Castle.* Edwards

A VIEW OF *the rose garden at David Austin Roses, Albrighton, showing Old Roses and Climbers.* Page

ANOTHER VIEW OF *the same garden at David Austin Roses, Albrighton* Page

A FINE EXAMPLE *of 'Léontine Gervais' growing on a pillar, with 'Dentelles de Malines' to the left.* Page

ROSA ALBA MAXIMA. *A tough and very old rose, seen here with the contrasting foliage of a hosta.* Knight

DOUBLE BORDERS *with roses at Sissinghurst Castle, Kent (National Trust). The narrow brick path with wide borders is most satisfactory. Note how the other plants blend in with the roses* Page

AN OVERHEAD VIEW *of the borders at David Austin Roses, Albrighton.* Page

PAUL'S HIMALAYAN MUSK *growing over the stump of an old tree.* Knight
ROSA WICHURAIANA *charmingly laced around a cottage window.* Page
Both scenes in Mr. and Mrs. Christopher Dumbell's garden at Worfield, Shropshire.

speak of rose gardens, it does not mean that we should exclude other plants, as these can provide contrasts and harmonies and be a great asset. They may also be used to fill the gap before the roses bloom.

Finally, although it may be asking for the impossible, my ideal would be as follows: that our naturally informal roses should be enclosed within a formal framework of beds and hedges, or whatever, and that this should further be surrounded by an informal planting of trees. Thus we have the informal, enclosed by the formal, and this again enclosed by the informal. This seems to provide a calm that is unequalled by any other arrangement.

STANDARD ROSES

Standard Roses are not very fashionable at the present time. This may be due to their high cost, for they are expensive to produce. It is perhaps more likely that it is the result of the more natural form of gardening now in vogue, for Standards are essentially for formal areas. As tastes appear to be changing a little in favour of formal gardening, perhaps the Standard is due for a revival. For those whose interest in the rose extends beyond Hybrid Teas and Floribundas, it will probably be because they cannot buy the type of rose they require, or they may not have thought of the possibility of other roses in this form. In fact, there are a number of so-called Shrub and Old Roses that make better Standards than the conventional Hybrid Teas and Floribundas. Shrub Rose specialists usually grow at least a few Standard Roses, but the range is inevitably limited, as it is not economically possible to grow numerous different varieties in small numbers. Probably the best solution is to get a nurseryman to grow your requirements to order. A few will do this.

The opportunities for using Standard Roses are not very plentiful. In a formal rose garden they can be very effective, particularly where the other roses are of low growth. Here they bring height and form to the whole. Unfortunately most Shrub Roses are a little too tall, so that the head of the Standard does not appear sufficiently high above them. Indeed, it is possible that they are best used with other plants of lower growth. It is also pleasing to see them planted, at regular intervals, along both sides of a path. Here they can provide an almost Renaissance-like effect. If we can find a place for these roses, I think we should; few features attract more attention than a really well-grown Standard or Weeping Standard. Well grown is perhaps the key, for they do require careful nurturing.

By no means all roses are suitable for Standards, even if we could buy them. Most good specialists grow a fair selection of the Hybrid Teas and Floribundas, but these often tend to be too upright in growth, so that the flowers can only be seen from the sky. There are important exceptions, such as 'Iceberg', which is perhaps the best variety of all for this purpose. Looking a little further afield, the rose 'Little White Pet' forms a most perfectly symmetrical head of dense growth, and produces its flowers repeatedly. 'Ballerina' has large, shapely heads, and also repeats well. Other than these, the English Roses, as a group, excel all the rest. It just so happens that the growth of many of them is ideally suited to this purpose. If we choose those of spreading or bushy growth, such as 'The Countryman', 'Cymbeline', 'Heritage', 'Lilian Austin', 'The Reeve' and 'Yellow Button', these will fill the bill exactly. 'Graham Thomas' and 'Mary Rose' are perhaps a little too upright, but they form such magnificent heads that they may be worth while, especially in a sunken garden. They seem positively to relish standing on the top of a stem. In their case this should, ideally, not be too tall.

Where the length of the flowering period is no problem, some of the Old Roses can be charming. The finest Standard I ever grew was a 'De Meaux'. It had the most perfectly formal head, evenly studded with small pink flowers, like a piece of embroidery. Such varieties as *R. centifolia,* 'Empress Josephine', 'Marie Louise', *R. gallica officinalis* and 'Rosa Mundi' can be very good.

It is important to prune Standards carefully so that they do not grow to one side and become ungainly. A strong support is essential, for they do tend to become very heavy. Such a support should be either of metal or tanalized wood. Untreated wood will soon rot in fertile soil, and nothing looks worse than a Standard Rose leaning awry.

Weeping Standards make a dramatic effect when suitably placed. They are particularly useful when a focal point is required. It is also possible to visualise them situated at regular intervals in a border, or possibly in a row against a wall. They are, of course, Rambler Roses budded on a standard stem, and it is essential that the varieties chosen have thin, trailing growth, such as we find in many Wichuraiana Hybrids. Stiff Climbers will not weep properly. 'Albéric Barbier', 'Crimson Shower', 'Débutante', 'Félicité et Perpétue' and 'François Juranville' are good examples of roses that can be used for this purpose.

CLIMBING ROSES ON WALLS

What a wealth we find among the Climbing and Rambler Roses, and what a diversity of usage is possible; how much poorer our gardens would be without them! They provide us with more scope than any other kind of rose.

The most usual place for Climbing Roses is on the wall of a house. Climbing Roses can make a beautiful house more beautiful, and turn an ugly house into a thing of beauty. For this purpose it is often better to use Climbers than Ramblers. Some of the Multiflora Ramblers tend to get mildew in such a position; other classes may sometimes be too strong. Having said this, Ramblers can provide the most dainty effects, although this will be only once in a season. For others, such as the Banksian Roses, a wall is both desirable and essential. The most common method of support is to hammer nails into the mortar, and tie to these. A more effective method is to attach either trellis-work or wire mesh to the wall. It is then quite easy to thread the growth through this as it develops. A further idea, and perhaps the best, is to stretch parallel wires along the wall, about 1 or 2ft. apart, and thread the growth behind them. The wires should be attached to vine eyes (loop-ended metal stems, driven into the wall), which will hold the wires at a short distance from the wall of the house. Unfortunately vine eyes are no longer manufactured, but could easily and cheaply be made by a blacksmith. All this might sound rather elaborate, but a little extra work beforehand will save a great deal of trouble in the years to come. It is not only the walls of the house that can be used in this way, but also garden walls in general. Roses may sometimes be grown not only up the wall, but also encouraged to climb over the wall from the other side and tumble down into the garden. In such cases a Rambler Rose of flexible growth will be the most suitable and provide the most natural effect.

There is one problem about which I constantly receive enquiries. This is the question of roses for planting against north or east-facing walls. Hybrid Teas and Shrub Roses usually look a pathetic sight when grown in such a position. In general, roses require the sun. In spite of this, there are Climbers that will do quite well without direct sunlight. 'Zéphirine Drouhin', as I have said in the description of that rose, is one of the very best for this purpose. It actually seems to thrive better on such walls, and does not suffer from mildew as it does in the sun. I have found 'Golden Showers' to be very similar in this respect. Some Rambler Roses seem to do well, 'Albéric Barbier', 'Félicité et Perpétue' and 'May Queen' are examples. Other roses include 'Gloire de Dijon', 'Madame Grégoire Staechelin', 'Madame Plantier', and 'New Dawn', but there are many more. The taller varieties of the Alba Roses, though not usually regarded as Climbers, are particularly good. They are happier than most roses in the shade, and the lack of light will draw up their growth to a greater height. They are among the best for an east-facing wall, where they have to withstand the cold east wind. 'Maigold' is also useful for this position.

A warm sheltered wall is a valuable asset, enabling us to grow some of the more tender Climbers, such as the Banksian Roses, the Climbing Tea Roses, and certain Climbing Species. A south wall is very good, although a west facing wall is often ideal. Here, the thaw after a frosty night will not be too fast, as the sun will reach it later in the day. If the sun strikes the young sappy growth too early in the morning, the thaw will be very rapid, and thus do more damage.

I have suggested the Albas for a north wall, but these can also be useful on other walls, for in fact many shrubs make good Climbers. The division between Climber and shrub is a somewhat arbitrary one. A few examples include 'Alchemist', 'Cerise Bouquet', 'Cornelia', 'Dentelle de Malines', 'Felicia', 'Fritz Nobis', 'Madame Isaac Pereire', 'Pleine de Grâce', *R. chinensis* 'Mutabilis', 'Scintillation', 'Shropshire Lass'. Many others will occur to the reader. Although these may not be tall, some of them have the advantage of being repeat flowering, and they are ideal for lower walls. A rose like 'Constance Spry', which is often regarded as a shrub, is perhaps better on a wall. Among other English Roses 'Abraham Darby', 'Cressida', 'Hero', 'Leander' and 'Lucetta' are equally good as shrubs or repeat-flowering Climbers. This is particularly true of 'Abraham Darby'. Almost any Shrub Rose that is inclined to be tall and loose growing is likely to be suitable where a wall or fence is there to encourage taller growth.

PERGOLAS, ARCHES, PILLARS AND OTHER STRUCTURES

The use of Climbing Roses is not of course confined to existing buildings, but may include a wide variety of structures expressly built for them. The pergola is perhaps the most impressive of these. Careful planning is necessary if it is to be successful. It is best and more appropriate if it conducts people from one part of the garden to another, along a path of genuine, practical use. It may look a little contrived when the path is constructed to take the pergola, although this is permissible if nothing else is available. Various materials can be used. Rustic poles are the cheapest and most usual. These can be entirely satisfactory, but it is best if the uprights are quite thick. The cross bars need not be so heavy. It is essential that all timber should have been treated under pressure against rot, otherwise, within a very few years, the whole structure will have decayed at the base. Uprights of brick or stone, or perhaps some form of reconstructed stone, are more impressive, but also much more expensive. It is essential that they be of fairly substantial proportions if they are to look correct and stand permanently. With these materials the cross members may be of sawn timber. A further method is to construct your pergola from trellis-work. This not only looks attractive, but has the practical advantage that the growth can be woven through the trellis, thus elminating tying.

The selection of roses to be used on a pergola requires careful thought. A lot will depend on the width and distance between the pillars, but even quite short distances will require relatively strong roses. The choice lies between Climbing Roses, which are usually perpetual, and Rambler Roses, which are not. The fact is that they are expected to travel rather a long way. Many roses will do this with ease on a wall, which has a natural tendency to draw them up. It is quite different with a pergola. Much will depend on your soil and the attention that you are willing to give to the rose, particularly in the matter of pruning. If you use Climbers, you will have the advantage of recurrent flowering, but it is necessary to choose strong varieties. It is perhaps best to plant Ramblers. They are, on the whole, more flexible in growth, far taller, more robust, and will provide a more natural, bower-like effect. It is, I think, better to have one magnificent show than to have a less plentiful but more continuous one. With Ramblers, the season of flowering can be extended by growing other climbing plants such as clematis and honeysuckles together with the roses. This can be most pleasing, but take care that they are not so strong as to swamp the roses. A strong plant of *Clematis montana* can take over the whole structure.

Among the many varieties that we might use are 'Albéric Barbier', 'Bobbie James', 'Cécile Brunner' (climbing), 'Claire Jacquier', 'Félicité et Perpétue', 'François Juranville', 'La Perle', 'Lawrence Johnston', 'Léontine Gervais', 'Madame Grégoire Staechelin', 'May Queen', 'Paul's Himalayan Musk', 'Sanders' White', 'Vicomtesse Pierre du Fou' and 'Weetwood'. Almost any Climber or Rambler will be satisfactory, so long as it is tall, vigorous and reasonably flexible in growth. The ideal rose would be one that tends to have blooms that hang slightly on the stem.

Arches provide an attractive picture in gardens of a more formal nature. Climbers and Ramblers are suitable for these. They can be placed along a path at any position, but are particularly satisfactory where it is desired to mark the division between one part of the garden and another. A further idea is a series of fairly closely placed arches, rather like a pergola that has not been linked up. Arches need not be narrow and upright in appearance, but can, where the width allows, be quite broad. Again, an arch may be placed against a doorway in the manner of a porch, and used in this way can provide an attractive and romantic effect. It is necessary that the building should be suited to this treatment: generally it should be of a modest rather than grand nature. Arches are not difficult to construct and can be made of a variety of materials. Many garden centres supply them ready made, but this may be an expensive way of acquiring them. A very simple and quite satisfactory arch can be constructed by the use of 'Weldmesh' grid. This is a heavy form of wire mesh. It is stiff and can be bent into any shape you may desire and will require little further support. The growth can be threaded through the wire, as with trellis-work. Apart from this, all the materials suggested for pergolas are equally suitable for arches: rustic poles, stone, brick, and trellis-work. It is also possible to use iron hoops, such as we find in Victorian and Edwardian gardens. These would have to be bought ready made, or perhaps made to order by a blacksmith.

Almost all Climbers and Ramblers are suitable, providing they are not excessively strong. With arches, the gardener may wish to have recurrent-flowering varieties, although here again it is often the Ramblers which are the most appropriate. Broad arches will, of course, take stronger roses.

There are occasions when a free-standing pillar can contribute to the garden scene: to give height to a border, or to provide a point to which you may wish to attract the eye. Pillars may be of the materials suggested for arches and pergolas. Simple larch poles are often used, though thick sawn timber looks much better — sometimes it is possible to find old timber for this purpose. Brick or stone are imposing. Height may vary according to the position in which the pillars are to be placed, and the size of the rose to be grown. It is possible to visualise a very large pillar of considerable height. This could be clothed with a very tall Rambler. The training of the rose is best done in spiral form, by wrapping the growth around the pillar. This will not only look more attractive, but will also encourage the rose to break all along the stems. Climbing Roses on pillars, when trained vertically, tend to produce flowers only at the top where they cannot be seen well, leaving a bare base.

Choice of varieties requires some care. Ideally we would like to have a rose which flowers from top to bottom and, while being strong enough to reach the top of the pillar, does not grow so rampantly as to get out of hand. A few suggestions are 'Blairi No. 2', 'Crimson Glory' (climbing), 'Crimson Shower', 'Cupid', 'Dream Girl', 'Easlea's Golden Rambler', 'Félicité et Perpétue', 'Gruss an Teplitz', 'Iceberg' (climbing), 'Léontine Gervais', 'Maigold', 'New Dawn', 'Phyllis Bide', 'Zéphirine Drouhin', and most of the Modern Climbers, but there are numerous others.

A variation of the pillar is the tripod. This has the advantage that the growth is on a slight slant, thus encouraging flowers at the base. It is also very useful for very strong Ramblers for which the gardener may otherwise have no place. Tripods can create beautiful effects when smothered with billowy growth and bloom, which will in time obscure the poles. They should be tall if they are not to look insignificant. Rustic poles are usually used for this purpose. Angle iron is another possibility. Tripods are perhaps best suited to Ramblers.

I think I have illustrated how numerous are the uses for Climbing and Rambling Roses, but their scope does not end here. All manner of cubes, pyramids, tunnels, arbours, summer houses, screens, etc., are possible. For such purposes lattice-work is ideal. It is so adaptable and can be cut into all manner of forms. Anyone who has been to Roseraie de l'Hay, near Paris, will know what I mean. There are endless possibilities for the use of the imagination. Such structures can add much to the charm of a rose garden, or indeed to the garden in general. Ramblers are ideal for this purpose. They can often be neatly trained into the form required, covering it with bloom.

GROWING ROSES OVER TREES AND SHRUBS

One of the most beautiful and natural ways of growing Ramblers is to train them into or over trees and large shrubs, or even over hedges. To some people this may seem a little ambitious at first, but in fact this is not so. The wild rose is by nature more often than not a plant of the thicket, making its way through other trees and shrubs. It would, in the wild, have found the sunlight through the upper branches of trees. Our garden Ramblers are not so very far removed from these wild roses.

Many gardens have old fruit trees that contribute little in the way of fruit. These are ideal subjects to carry Ramblers and Climbing Species. The roses can be allowed to climb amongst their branches at will. We shall thus have a second blooming after the first blossom has gone. Varieties should be chosen according to the size of the tree. Too heavy a rose can smother a small tree, and may result in its premature demise.

The recipients need not necessarily be fruit trees. Almost any tree is suitable, providing it is not too strong for the rose. Ramblers can bring light to the darkness of conifers. There are interesting examples of this at the Royal National Rose Society's gardens at St. Albans, where roses can be seen making their way up large conifers. Climbers, Ramblers, and indeed strong lax growing shrubs, growing in a shrubbery or in some more wild area of the garden, can be encouraged to thread their way through shrubs and over hedges. They will often do this of their own accord. Here a mixture of art and chance can come into play. By training a long growth here and there, as we think most suitable, the rose can be encouraged to spread, and a wild and natural effect will be achieved. On other occasions it will be necessary to cut growth away where it is becoming out of hand and perhaps overcoming a valued shrub.

For large trees, there are a small number of very strong Ramblers that can be used. The most famous and one of the best of these is *R. filipes* 'Kiftsgate'. This can achieve heights of 30ft. and more, producing masses of small white flowers in very large sprays. Not far behind this is the species *R. mulliganii,* which is almost equal in vigour and provides massive heads of single white blooms. Other strong varieties include 'Albéric Barbier', 'Bobbie James', 'Paul's Himalayan Musk', *R. brunonii, R. brunonii* 'La Mortola', *R. rubus* and 'Wedding Day'. For smaller trees a great variety of other Ramblers may be chosen according to size.

The most difficult aspect of growing roses into trees is getting them started. The tree will be well established and its roots will have spread thickly throughout the soil around it. The conditions there will be very poor and probably dry. There may also be partial shade, so always plant on the sunny side of the tree to avoid the shade as far as possible. The secret is to dig out a fairly large area of soil and replace it with new soil, at the same time mixing it with very generous quantities of farmyard manure or compost. This should be at a little distance from the tree, where conditions will be more favourable. When the rose is planted, train it along a cane towards the branches. Water and fertilise it well for the first year or two. Soon it will be making its way into the tree, and eventually it will be able to look after itself. Such a rose can be an important feature in a garden, and extra care when it is planted is well worth while.

HEDGES, SCREENS, BARRIERS AND FENCES

Roses, properly chosen, can form beautiful hedges and screens. I say properly chosen, because if the reader's experience is restricted to a hedge of 'Queen Elizabeth' and the like, he may have his doubts. It is a comparatively rare sight to see a really fine example of a rose hedge. This cannot usually be achieved by the use of the majority of Hybrid Teas and Floribundas. There are, however, numerous Shrub Roses that are very suitable for this purpose. No rose can be expected to produce the neat, trimmed appearance of a yew hedge, but that does not matter, as a rose hedge is intended to be something quite different. It will form a long, billowy mass of bloom, at the same time providing an impenetrable barrier.

The first point to decide upon is the height. It may be a tall hedge that is required, surrounding all or part of the garden. It may be something of more modest size, perhaps to provide a division within the garden. Again, it may be quite short and used as an edging for a border. We require roses that are as dense and bushy in growth as possible, such as will have a shapely form when clipped. This should be done each spring to encourage suitable growth.

Planting distance will vary in accordance with the size of the shrub. It will also depend to some extent on how long you wish to wait before it fills into a full hedge, although this will not be very long in any case. Three or four feet is usual for large shrubs, down to 1½ to 2ft. for the smaller kinds. For a very small hedge it may be best to plant as close as 1ft. apart. In each case much depends on the variety. It is usually not necessary to plant a double row; a single row will be adequate.

Suckers can be a problem. When these occur, it is an unpleasant task removing them from beneath a bushy hedge. Fortunately, the roses that will be used are usually strong, and therefore take up more energy from the stock, leaving little for suckering. This problem can be overcome, to some extent, by planting the bushes deeply, placing the union of the stock and the rose 4 or 5ins. beneath the surface of the soil, thus discouraging growth of suckers from the root stock. This may lead to suckering from the scion in varieties like 'Rosa Mundi'.

There is another question that we have to ask ourselves. Do we have a hedge of one variety, or of many? My instinct is strongly in favour of the former. The trouble with mixed hedges is that they can become unbalanced; some varieties will always get the upper hand and grow large at the expense of the rest. Even so, the mixed hedge need not be ruled out. It does furnish us with the opportunity of growing a large number of different roses in a small area, a not unimportant consideration in a small garden. Careful management by pruning may help by discouraging the greedy members, although they usually get their own way in the end. The important thing is to choose varieties of similar strength, in so far as this is possible. A hedge of one rose, on the other hand, can be a

NOZOMI, *a small Ground-cover Rose seen here falling towards a pool at Mr. and Mrs. Christopher Dumbell's garden at Worfield, Shropshire.* Page

ROSA PAULII, *Species Hybrid; 'Officinalis', Gallica Rose; and the Rambler 'Wedding Day', in one of the borders at David Austin Roses, Albrighton.* Price

ANOTHER SCENE *in Mr. and Mrs. Christopher Dumbell's garden, showing* Rosa mutabilis *with delphiniums, the grey-leaved Ruta and other herbaceous plants. The Rambler on the house is 'Alexander Girault'.*
Page

TWO FAMOUS FRENCH *rose gardens, showing roses planted in a formal style. Top, Roseraie de l'Hay, Paris. Above, Roseraie du Parc de Bagatelle, Paris.* Thomas

ROSES AND FOLIAGE *plants growing in a garden at Heslington, Yorkshire.* Thomas

A GRASS PATH *in an Essex garden between established borders of old roses, together with geraniums, alchemilla and other plants* Thomas

OLD ROSES *and contrasting foliage plants at Sissinghurst Castle, Kent (National Trust).* Thomas

CLIMBING ROSES *surrounding the pool at the Royal National Rose Society's 'Gardens of the Rose' at St. Albans.* Thomas

A VASE *of Old Roses attractively arranged by Mrs. Ann Dakin of Brewer's Oak, Shifnal, Shropshire*
Knight

magnificent sight, with all its bloom appearing at one time, and we can expect the growth to be uniform.

The choice of varieties is broad. On the whole, as I have said, Hybrid Teas and Floribundas are not suitable, with one or two exceptions. They are far too stick like and open, although 'Iceberg', for example, can form a very good low-growing hedge. For a large hedge or screen, many of the Species and Species Hybrids are excellent. A hedge of *R. hugonis* is almost certain to be magnificent, being covered with yellow in late May, and with lovely fern-like foliage for the remainder of the summer. Much the same can be said for others of its close relations, and indeed many other species of dense growth. 'Complicata' will provide a glorious show of large, single, Dog Rose-like blooms. It is possible to have a wonderfully fragrant hedge by planting the Sweet Brier, *R. eglanteria,* or perhaps one of the Hybrid Penzance Briers. *R. rugosa* and *R. rugosa* 'Alba' are both good, have a natural ability to repeat flower, and also produce very large hips. *R.* × *micrugosa* is worth considering: the growth is very dense and it has fine foliage; the flowers are beautiful, but not so plentiful as we might wish, particularly when cut as a hedge. 'Cerise Bouquet' will form a magnificent broad hedge of 6ft. with elegant sprays of flowers. 'Nevada' and its sport 'Marguerite Hilling' are two of the finest of the larger kinds and will form dense hedges. At this point it should be mentioned that tall hedges of this kind will need a considerable width in which to develop: if we clip them severely they will simply make new growth without providing bloom. Be careful to fit the rose to the size of hedge required. This will not matter so much in the case of most repeat-flowering roses, as these can more easily be kept within bounds.

Going down a little to something rather smaller, the Hybrid Musks may be used. Such varieties as 'Buff Beauty', 'Cornelia', 'Felicia' and 'Penelope', are probably the best. Among the Modern Shrub Roses there are a number of useful hedging plants. 'Ballerina' has just the bushy growth we require, and provides the ultimate in repeat flowering and reliability.

Old Roses and roses of the old type, carefully chosen, can form a charming picture. Almost all the Albas are suitable, with the possible exception of 'Queen of Denmark'. English Roses, like 'Heritage', 'Mary Rose', 'The Miller' and 'Windrush', provide continuous bloom and form good medium-sized hedges. The two single-flowered varieties, 'Red Coat' and 'Dapple Dawn', are particularly suitable, as these are compact in growth and very continuous in bloom. Short hedges, either as the edge to a border, or as divisions between various parts of the garden, can also be charming. The best known for this purpose is 'Rosa Mundi'. This can be clipped to 2ft. or so, and will make a beautiful little hedge covered with quantities of fresh, striped flowers. A more continuous effect can be achieved with such English Roses as 'Wife of Bath' or 'Bredon'. Getting even closer to the ground, it is well worth considering the more bushy varieties of the Patio Roses. I could, in fact, go on making suggestions, but with careful observation gardeners will find many more suitable roses.

We are sometimes asked for roses that will form a strong barrier against trespassers or unwanted visitors, such as dogs and other livestock, or even people. The most ferocious defender of all is *R. sericea pteracantha,* described in Chapter 11. It has the largest of thorns and they are very numerous; the growth, too, is very dense. Any person or animal getting through a close planting of this rose deserves to succeed, for it is virtually impenetrable. Many of the Rugosas are almost equally impenetrable, as are many of the Species. At a lower level, most of the Scotch Roses (*R. pimpinellifolia*) are useful.

Fences can often be improved by training Climbing Roses along them. In this way we can rid ourselves of what may be a somewhat bare and unattractive object, and at the same time find room for a few more roses. Taller screens can be erected from rustic poles, trellis-work, and so on. Such structures, with roses trained on them, may be used to provide privacy.

GROWTH, FOLIAGE AND FRUIT

It is easy, when choosing roses, to become preoccupied with the flowers alone. There are other considerations as, for example, the sweep and grace of their growth, or perhaps their bushy, twiggy habit. To watch the rose growing prior to flowering can be a pleasure in itself: at first the swelling of the buds, often starting surprisingly early in the year; then the breaking leaf; after this the growing leaves in all their variety and freshness; eventually, the young flower buds of every shape and size, up to the first glimpse of the petals.

All rose foliage is beautiful, but there are certain roses that may well be used primarily, or even exclusively, for their foliage. Perhaps the best known of these is *R. glauca,* which has pretty but rather insignificant flowers, but the most attractive coppery-mauve foliage. The Alba Roses, which provide us with some of the most attractive flowers, also have fine, grey-green leaves; as do the Species *R. fedtschenkoana, R. soulieana, R. villosa* and *R.* 'Dupontii'. *R. hugonis* and its many relations and hybrids have fern-like foliage, so also do *R. willmottiae, R. woodsii fendleri,* and others. *R. macrophylla* and *R. sinowilsonii* have particularly magnificent large foliage. By the careful combination of these with other roses and other plants we can achieve pleasing effects. The foliage of many roses provides attractive autumn tints late in the year. *R. rugosa* and many of its varieties are good examples, as are *R. nitida* and *R. virginiana.*

Other factors, too, should not be forgotten. Thorns and bark have their part to play. I have never had much time for the idea that we should develop thornless roses. This would be comparatively easy, but the rose would lose something of value. Bark may vary in colour from yellow-green to red and brown. It will also vary according to the stage of growth.

Many of the wild and more natural roses have but a short period of bloom, although make up for this with colourful hips. These come in various shapes, colours and sizes. They may be black, as with the *R. hugonis* and *R. pimpinellifolia* types, or they may be orange, but more usually they are red. They can be small, as with the rambling species or the shrubby species *R. willmottiae,* or they may have massive hips like small crab apples, as is the case with *R. villosa, R. rugosa* 'Scabrosa', and *R. macrophylla* 'Master Hugh'. The most elegant are those of flagon-like shape, such as we find in *R. moyesii* and its forms, and again in *R. macrophylla.* This succession of leaf, flower and fruit amounts to a very important contribution to our garden shrubs as a whole.

It is not unheard of for the nurseryman to receive a request for a rose of a certain colour, of Old Rose formation, strongly fragrant, repeat flowering, disease free, that will also bear hips — all on the same plant! Most people will appreciate this is impossible. We can have a combination of most of the virtues, but rarely do we get them all in one species or variety. Double-flowered roses do not usually produce hips. In recurrent-flowering varieties, hips are not particularly desirable, as they take up the plant's energy and prevent further flowering. This is why we dead head our roses. There are exceptions to this rule, as for example in some of the Rugosas: *R. rugosa* is a repeat-flowering rose by nature. It also produces fine hips, and we thus have the situation where we find green hips, red hips, and flowers on one shrub at the same time.

ROSES WITH OTHER PLANTS

Shrub Roses associate happily with a great variety of plants. It is hard to go very far wrong in placing them, but it is, I think, important to avoid mixing them with flowers of too strong a hue, as this may overwhelm their usually softer colours. Most people never really consider such matters and still achieve good results. There is, however, no doubt that a little planning can often lead to very pleasing effects, and certain plants spring immediately to mind. Here, then, is a small selection of plants that in my opinion associate well with roses and which will in some cases extend the season of flowering in a border. The list could, of course, be very much longer, but it may provide a starting point from which the reader will be able to develop his own ideas.

ACHILLEA. Beautifully feathered silver foliage. 18ins. to 2ft. Summer.

ACONITUM PANICULATUM NANUM. Blue flowers. Will blend in with a wide colour spectrum. 3ft. Late summer.

AGAPANTHUS. Round umbels of blue or white upright flowers. A good contrast to roses when planted towards the front of the border. 2½ft. Mid- to late summer.

ALCHEMILLA MOLLIS. An ideal companion for Shrub Roses. Flowers lime green. 18ins. Early summer.

ANEMONE JAPONICA. Pretty flowers with a refined elegance, in whites and pinks. 4ft. Late summer to late autumn.

ANTHEMIS CUPANIANA. Single pure white daisy flowers above dense silver foliage. For the front of a border. 1ft. Spring to summer.

ARTEMISIA ABSINTHIUM LAMBROOK SILVER. Silver-grey finely cut foliage. 3ft.

ASTRANTIA MAJOR. Numerous airy white flowers held above attractive deeply cut foliage. 2ft. Summer/autumn.

CALAMINTHA NEPETOIDES. Flowers mauve-white, giving a pleasing hazy effect. Aromatic foliage. Bees love this plant. 1ft. Summer to autumn.

CAMPANULA. Particularly good varieties for association with roses are *C. lactiflora, latiloba* and *persicifolia,* giving a soft blue or white combination which highlights the pink blooms of roses beautifully.

CENTAUREA HYPOLEUCA JOHN COUTTS. Pink flowers, leaves pale green, white beneath. Seldom without bloom. 2ft. Early summer.

CRAMBE CORDIFOLIA. Attractive coarse foliage. A noble sight when the branching stems give way to gypsophila-like clouds of white scented flowers. 6ft. Use only where scale allows. Early summer.

DELPHINIUMS. Charming effects can be achieved by combining the long blue spikes of delphiniums with pink roses. 4 to 7ft. Summer.

DIANTHUS. Pinks are ideal companions for roses, with their attractive old-fashioned flowers and grey foliage. Their only drawback is their fragrance which is so strong it can overwhelm that of the roses, at least at a distance. Old varieties flower once, modern varieties flower throughout the summer.

DIGITALIS. A few foxgloves rising up between Shrub Roses can provide a pleasing picture. They will probably seed freely, and the subsequent plants should be thinned out so that they do not become too much of a feature.

GERANIUM (Cranesbill). There can be few flowers more suitable as companions for roses. They give little trouble, have beautiful foliage and dainty unobtrusive flowers. Numerous species and varieties are available, most of which are ideal. Here are three: 'Johnson's Blue', with finely cut leaves forming dense cover, beautifully-veined lavender-blue flowers. 1ft., early summer to autumn. *G. renardii,* sage-green rounded leaves, white flowers with a suspicion of violet, 1ft., early to mid-summer. *G. sanguineum* 'Lancastriense', dark green leaves and clean pink flowers, 9ins.

GYPSOPHILA PANICULATA BRISTOL FAIRY. A dainty airy plant, which everybody will know. 3ft. Summer.

HEMEROCALLIS. Like lilies and irises, these plants with their rush-like leaves and lily flowers, provide an excellent contrast to roses. There are innumerable varieties that might be used. 2½ to 3½ft. Summer.

HOSTA. Plants with large, beautifully-sculptured leaves which vary greatly between species and variety, both in form and colour. They make an ideal contrast to the growth of roses. Bell-like flowers on tall elegant stems. For better foliage choose a shady position. 18 to 40ins.

IRIS. Irises are often recommended for association with Shrub Roses. They have the advantage that the majority of them flower before the roses, thus extending the flowering period of a rose border. Spiky grey-green foliage forms a pleasing contrast, although this can become a little shabby towards the end of the season.

LAVENDER. There can be few more satisfactory plants for planting with Old Roses — particularly in a formal setting. In growth, flower and leaf lavenders are ideal and add to the old world effect where Old Roses are grown.

LILIUM. Lilies approach roses in their importance in the history of garden plants and are, in fact, ideal companions for Shrub Roses, their clean-cut elegance contrasting with the softness of the roses. *Lilium martagon, candidum* or *auratum* might be used, among others. It would probably be best to avoid some of the massive brightly-coloured hybrids.

LYCHNIS CORONARIA ALBA. Grey basal leaves, branching grey stems, simple white flowers. 3ft. Summer.

MALVA MOSCHATA ALBA. One of our most beautiful native plants, with finely cut leaves. White flowers often with a suspicion of pink in the evening light. Seeds itself, but not a nuisance. 2 to 2½ft.

NEPETA × FAASSENII. This dwarf catmint requires little description. It starts to flower in June and gives a good display well into the autumn. Use formally as an edging, or informally in a mixed border. 3ft. Summer.

PENSTEMON. Although rather tender, these have lovely colours and a long flowering season. 'Evelyn', rose pink, 18ins. 'Apple Blossom', blush pink. 'Garnet', claret-coloured flowers. 'True Blue', a lovely soft blue.

PEONY. In larger borders peonies may be used. Like the irises, they come before the roses, and later their large foliage forms an ideal foil, often turning to autumn tints later in the year.

RHAZYA ORIENTALIS. A discreet plant with willowy leaves and wiry stems, producing soft blue flowers over a long period. 18ins. Mid- to late summer.

RUTA GRAVEOLENS. A most attractive blue-green dainty leaf. Cut this plant hard back in mid-spring, the leaves are so much more glaucous when young. 2ft. Ideal for the front of a border.

SALVIA. Both herbaceous and sub-shrub types are good companions for roses. The choice is wide, some are tender but many are hardy. *S. argentea,* basal leaves woolly and almost white, branching stems with white flowers, 3ft., summer. *S. nemerosa* 'Superba', a bushy plant with numerous erect spikes of violet flowers and crimson bracts over a long period, 3ft. A dwarfer form, 'Lubeca', 18ins., is ideal for the front of the border, giving a hazy effect. Summer.

STACHYS MACRANTHA. Dark green indented leaves clothe erect stems with mauve flowers. 3ft. Summer.

STACHYS OLYMPICA. This well known silver 'Lambs' Ears' goes well with Old Roses. The variety 'Silver Carpet' is a non-flowering form and makes an ideal edging or ground-cover plant for roses. 18ins. Mid-summer.

THALICTRUM SPECIOSISSIMUM. Very striking. Although often reaching 5ft. in summer, when planted as a single specimen, it will not overwhelm the roses due to the nature of its growth. It might be termed a 'see through' plant. Glaucous blue-green divided leaves and complementary stems. Heads of fluffy lemon-yellow flowers which some gardeners prefer to remove.

VERBASCUM (Mullein). Most species of verbascum associate well with roses, their long spikes shooting up between Shrub Roses.

VIOLA. There are many beautiful violas to choose from; I am particularly fond of the species *V. cornuta* and its forms. All are evergreen, with small green leaves which form a complete ground cover. They flower in early summer and last well into the autumn. 12ins. Planted at the base of a rose, they are capable of hoisting themselves to as much as 3ft. This can be attractive when the rose is tall enough not to be swamped. The type plant is a rich deep violet. The following two varieties are my favourites — 'Lilacina', a cool slaty blue and 'Alba', which is one of the cleanest whites.

ROSES WITH CLIMBING PLANTS

Where we are using Rambling Roses on pergolas, pillars and other structures, it is an excellent idea to combine these with climbers of other genera. The Ramblers bloom mainly in late June and July. This season of flowering can be extended with the help of a careful selection of climbers like clematis and honeysuckles. It is necessary to be careful in selecting such companions, in order to avoid the one overcoming the other, and to provide a succession of bloom.

ROSES FOR WILD AND WOODLAND AREAS

For those who are lucky enough to have wild areas in or close to their gardens, or better still, open woodland, there are many roses that will be entirely suitable. It is to the Species and less-developed roses that we must turn for this purpose. Much of what I said in the section on growing Rambler Roses through trees and shrubs will also apply here. Apart from this, there are many Species and varieties of a shrubby nature that are suitable for such areas. Nothing could look more natural or pleasing. *R.* 'Cantabrigiensis', *R.* 'Headleyensis', *R. hugonis, R.* 'Macrantha', *R. moyesii, R.* 'Paulii', *R.* 'Paulii Rosea'; the Sweet Briers; *R. 'Complicata', R.* 'Dupontii', *R. macrophylla, R. glauca, R. willmottiae, R. woodsii fendleri,* are a few that come to mind. Nor should our own Dog Rose, *R. canina,* be forgotten. Moving a little further away from the Species, such garden varieties as 'Cerise Bouquet', 'Dentelle de Malines', 'Frühlingsgold', 'Lady Curzon', 'Pleine de Grâce', 'Running Maid', 'Scintillation' and 'Shropshire Lass' may appropriately be used. Recurrent-flowering roses are usually not able to compete under such conditions, but exceptions can be made; the Hybrid Musk Rose 'Vanity', the English Rose 'Dapple Dawn', 'Marguerite Hilling', 'Nevada' and 'Red Coat', and some of the more natural of the Rugosas: 'Nyveldt's White', *R. rugosa, R. rugosa* 'Alba', 'Roseraie de l'Hay', and so on, but as always with such lists, there are many more.

Rambler Roses need not necessarily be grown as Climbers. They will, if planted in close groups of, say three of one variety, build up into thick mounds of growth. These are particularly suitable for large, more natural areas of the garden.

All the roses that I have mentioned should be successful under semi-wild conditions. The important thing is to get them off to a good start. Equal care should be taken in the preparation of the soil as for roses in the garden proper. After this the weeds must be controlled in order to get the shrub going. As the roses become more mature this will become less important. One method of controlling weeds is to place black polythene around the roots. This will smother the weeds. Larger groups of roses will defend each other and have a better chance of survival.

I should like to take this opportunity of airing an idea of mine that has become something of an obsession. May I suggest that the Shrub and Climbing Roses, such as I have mentioned above, should be planted in large gardens, in order to get away from the tyranny of the rhododendron. Rhododendrons are, indeed, one of the most valuable of shrubs, but many large gardens seem to consist of them and them alone. Once the short splendour of their flowers is over, there is nothing to follow except the dark of their foliage. It is true that they provide an easy and cheap way of covering extensive areas of ground with minimum upkeep, but if some of the larger Shrub Roses could be added to these, they would contribute variety and continuity after their flowering was over, as well as colourful hips and dainty contrasting foliage. Of course, it would be necessary to ensure that the soil around them was not too acid. I often think that the more highly developed rhododendrons are to the large garden what the Hybrid Teas and Floribundas sometimes are to the small garden — rather too much of a good thing.

GROUND COVER

I have discussed a new group of roses which are known as Ground-cover Roses in Chapter 8, but ground cover is not restricted to these; there are many other roses that might be used for this purpose.

R. wichuraiana is the first that comes to mind. It is a natural creeper that will travel far, clinging to the ground. Not surprisingly, many of its hybrids also have something of this capacity. It is important to select only those of thin, lax, growth. These will, like their parent, make low growth and be covered in bloom in season, requiring little in the way of attention, except to be kept in bounds and the occasional removal of old and dead wood. They are ideal for bare banks and areas where spacious, but otherwise disused, ground needs to be covered. Such roses can be encouraged in this habit of growth by pegging down some of their stems, thus ensuring that they fill the desired area.

If we are willing to interpret ground cover in a rather broader manner, to include roses of taller but still spreading growth, we may plant such procumbent varieties as 'Constance Spry', 'Dentelle de Malines', 'Pleine de Grâce', 'Raubritter', *R.* 'Paulii', *R.* 'Paulii Rosea', 'Running Maid', 'Scintillation', as well as some of the more bushy Ramblers like 'Félicité et Perpétue'. All these are excellent for filling large areas of ground, particularly in public places.

Species like *R. pimpinellifolia* and its varieties are, by their very nature, ground-covering plants, as are *R. nitida* and *R. virginiana.* These are quite low in growth, and sucker naturally, creating a thicket as they grow. They are ideal for difficult conditions and poor soils. For this purpose they must have been grown on their own roots, that is to say from seed, and not on root stocks, otherwise they will not spread as we would wish. Some Gallicas are also ideal for this purpose: 'Officinalis', 'Rosa Mundi' and 'Tuscany' in particular. It will be necessary to grow them from cuttings, to enable them to sucker naturally. Alternatively, bushes may be planted deeply. In this way the garden variety will soon develop its own roots.

Having said this, we must not forget the new group I have placed under the heading Ground-cover Roses. These usually do not cover quite so much ground as many of the roses mentioned above, but some of them are repeat flowering which makes them more suitable for smaller gardens.

COVERING BUILDINGS AND UNSIGHTLY OBJECTS

Many gardens contain unsightly objects, which may be essential in themselves or very difficult to remove. Manholes, oil tanks, and the stumps of old trees, are examples. One solution to this problem is to cover them with Climbing Roses or Shrub Roses of a sprawling nature. The roses chosen will vary according to the size of the object. Often they will include those recommended for ground cover.

Sometimes there are buildings which we would prefer not to see, as for example garages and sheds. Here we may use really large Ramblers, where the space permits, and an offending building can be virtually obliterated and turned into a thing of beauty.

ROSES FOR DIFFICULT CONDITIONS

As rose specialists we receive a continual stream of letters enquiring about roses suitable for planting in positions that are, for one reason or another, difficult. The most frequent of these is shade, either under a tree or on the north side of walls.

I should make it clear that no rose will grow under the heavy shade of trees. There are, however, roses that will grow in partial shade. For this purpose I have already recommended the Alba Roses, and these are probably among the best as a class. Some of the species hybrids such as *R.* 'Andersonii', *R.* 'Complicata', *R.* 'Paulii', *R.* 'Paulii Rosea', and the Sweet Briers are satisfactory. The more robust of the Modern Shrubs, as for example, 'Frühlingsgold', 'Shropshire Lass', 'Ziguenerknabe', should be suitable. The Ayrshire Hybrids will match the Albas for this purpose. They are, of course, Ramblers, but could be allowed to wander at will under such conditions. It is best to avoid repeat-flowering roses, for it is too much to expect them to produce more than one crop in anything but the best position.

Shaded north walls are less of a problem, and these have been discussed earlier in this Chapter under 'Climbing Roses on Walls'.

Those who live close to the sea have particularly difficult problems. Here they frequently have to contend with wind, salt spray and perhaps sandy soil. As with all such problems, it is a matter of degree, depending upon the situation. *R. pimpinellifolia* and *R. rugosa* can be found growing well on sand dunes close to the sea, but most people will require something more than these. It has to be admitted that seaside gardens do not favour roses, but then nor do they favour many other plants. If it were practical to build a tall wall or larch-lap fence around a small area, it would no doubt be possible to have a charming courtyard rose garden with all manner of roses, particularly if some good soil was brought in.

For the average seaside garden, I would recommend Rugosa Hybrids. They are tough and hardy, and most will be recurrent flowering. Others for these conditions are the Scotch Roses; certain of the shorter English Roses such as 'Bredon', 'Pretty Jessica', 'The Miller', 'Wife of Bath'; Ground-cover Roses; Patio Roses. Polyanthas are also tough and reliable. We might add to these certain Modern Shrubs such as 'Ballerina',

'Frühlingsgold', 'Little White Pet', 'Martin Frobisher' and 'The Fairy'. Old Roses should do better than most, since they only have to flower once. Climbing Roses can be a problem, except when they are given a protected wall. Those who wish to grow modern bush roses would be well advised to confine themselves to the stronger Floribundas.

There may be very poor areas in a garden where it is difficult to grow anything. These may be excessively sandy, of rank clay or chalk. Few sites are so poor that they cannot be improved, except, of course, where there is very little soil at all. The secret is to add copious quantities of humus, and mix this thoroughly with the soil. The varieties mentioned for seaside gardens should be suitable. We might add certain taller roses like 'Francis E. Lester', 'Pleine de Grâce' and 'Zigeunerknabe'.

Frequently we are faced with a dry bank that is very poor because the top soil has been removed in the process of landscaping. It is a good idea to use strong growing Ground-cover Roses for these positions. Suitable roses are mentioned in the section on this subject.

Some of us have the good fortune to live in hilly areas, high above sea level. For gardening, this may have disadvantages. Here, at least in the British Isles, the season will be short, and the rainfall heavy. Much the same can be said for the more northerly areas of Scotland. In the more extreme parts it would be best to grow Old Roses, particularly Scotch Roses and Albas. The season may be so short, that a second crop of flowers is not possible. More Modern Shrub Roses can also be satisfactory, but we will probably have to be content with little more than one period of flowering.

ROSES FOR SMALL AND VERY SMALL GARDENS

Most of what is said in this Chapter applies equally to small and large gardens. Nonetheless, there are obvious differences, particularly in the choice of varieties. Most owners of small gardens confine themselves to growing Hybrid Teas and Floribundas, and these are in many ways ideal. I am, however, sure that most people reading this book would like to grow a wider range of roses than just these alone. The trouble is that many may feel this is not possible because Shrub Roses are too large. It is the word 'shrub' that is the problem. It seems to suggest something of large dimensions, but this is not necessarily true. A large proportion of the Shrub Roses are no bigger than the Floribunda 'Queen Elizabeth'. Another complaint is that they flower only once in the summer. This is true of many of them, but there is still a wide selection of Shrub Roses that do repeat flower.

If we look through the Old Roses, that is to say in Chapter 2 — Old Roses I, we find that many varieties are not large. Some of them are not more than 3ft. in height, and most of the remainder can be pruned to keep them in hand.

The majority of Old Roses in Chapter 3 do repeat, and will thrive under close pruning as well as any Hybrid Tea, although they will lose some elegance of growth. With such treatment they will produce finer individual flowers. The Portland Rose and its varieties are excellent small shrubs, with flowers of true Old Rose charm. 'Comte de Chambord', 'Jacques Cartier' and 'Rose de Rescht' are three of the best. The China Roses are nearly all of small growth in our climate, and repeat flower better than any other roses. Their slender growth takes up little space. Among the Bourbons and the Hybrid Perpetuals there are numerous beautiful Old Roses that, with hard pruning, will repeat well: 'Boule de Neige', 'Ferdinand Pichard', 'Madame Pierre Oger', 'Reine des Violettes', 'Reine Victoria', to mention but a few, are all suitable.

Coming to roses of the present day, many of the English Roses were bred with the small garden in mind. They also have suffered by bearing the title Shrub Rose, which of course is what they are. Most rose specialists agree that to list a new rose as a Shrub Rose can be the kiss of death in so far as the popular market is concerned. In fact, most English Roses are ideal for small gardens. They have the advantage of combining Old Rose flowers with reliable repeat-flowering qualities and, without being too large, they usually have shrub-like growth. Most lend themselves to hard pruning and can, if desired, be treated like a Hybrid Tea. So grown they lose some of the attraction of shrubby growth, but take up less space. When pruned in this manner they will flower even more repeatedly.

There are other, more modern Shrub Roses worthy of consideration. 'Cécile Brunner', 'Little White Pet', 'Perle d'Or', 'Snow Carpet' and 'The Fairy' are all exceptionally good small garden roses. So too are the Polyanthas, the Miniatures and more recently, the Patio Roses.

Wherever the garden is small, the rose lover will make maximum use of walls and fences for Climbing Roses — a wall is a potential bed of roses in itself. The walls and fences of a small garden add up to a sizeable area. An arch or arches might also be considered. With careful thought such a garden can become a bower of roses.

It is surprising how many different varieties can be gathered into a restricted area. Moreover, the small garden owner will come to know his roses more intimately and thus reap more pleasure from them individually.

There are many who do not just have small gardens, but very small gardens, of the pocket-handkerchief type — a few square yards. For these it has to be admitted that most of the beauties of the rose are not possible, but there is still quite a lot that can be done. Roses may be grown in pots, troughs, window boxes, as well as small borders. Here it is that the Miniature Roses come into their own. These really need intimate surroundings if they are to be properly appreciated. If they can be planted in a raised position, so much the better. Patio Roses have been bred with just such surroundings in mind. We need not stop here entirely. There are a number of slightly larger roses that may be considered. Among the English Roses, such varieties as 'Bredon', 'Canterbury', 'Dove', 'Fair Bianca', 'Pretty Jessica', 'Prospero', 'Wife of Bath' and 'Wise Portia' will all fit in well. From other classes we might choose 'Cécile Brunner', 'Jenny Wren' and 'Perle d'Or', and one or two Miniature Old Roses: 'De Meaux', 'Burgundy Rose', and so on. Here again we may plant a Climbing Rose wherever it can be fitted in.

Finally, I suggest that, even in small gardens, not every rose should be short; a few taller varieties should be included, and this will help the general structure and provide a more interesting picture.

ROSES IN POTS, TUBS, TROUGHS AND BASKETS

This section leads on naturally from the last, for roses grown in containers of one kind or another lend themselves ideally to small gardens, although not exclusively so. At our nursery we are frequently asked if it is possible to grow roses in this manner. Our answer to this question is 'Yes', but that they require careful attention. It has to be admitted that roses do not like a restricted root run, nor do they like to have their roots baked in a sun-exposed pot. In fact, they are not the easiest of subjects.

It is important to use a properly balanced potting compost. I would recommend that it should be a soil-based, not a peat-based compost. It is equally important that there should be ample drainage. Do not forget that roses grown in pots and other receptacles are entirely dependent on the gardener for their survival. Watering must be regular and thorough — even a short period of drought can lead to rapid deterioration and the death of the plant. Likewise, feeding is vital; soil in containers quickly becomes depleted of sustenance and the regular application of fertilizer is most important. Do not allow the rose to become pot bound. Move the plant from smaller containers into larger ones before this happens. Alternatively, where this is not possible, take the rose out and remove some of the soil and roots, then replant the remaining ball of soil and roots back in the pot, surrounding it with good potting compost.

Courtyards, paved areas, patios and so on in larger gardens may be enhanced by roses grown in this way. City gardens are often small and paved; flat dwellers are usually restricted to balconies.

By growing roses in containers, it is possible to create pretty miniature gardens. Such areas may be regarded as an extension of the house or flat.

Indeed, the plants themselves can be brought indoors for short periods when in full bloom, but only for short periods, otherwise they will soon deteriorate.

Any rose can be grown in a pot if required, given a large enough receptacle, but usually it will be a repeat-flowering rose of not too large a size. Our experience in growing roses in containers for the Chelsea Flower Show has proved that English Roses are particularly suitable for this purpose. They are much more easily grown in pots than Old Roses. Certain compact Modern Shrubs like 'Ballerina', 'Little White Pet' and 'The Fairy' are good. Polyanthas, Patio Roses and Miniature Roses are excellent.

The container in which the roses are to be grown is worthy of careful consideration. Fortunately a large variety of shapely and well-decorated pots, urns, troughs, etc., are now becoming readily available. These, with suitable plants, can greatly enhance the garden. Tubs also are suitable, and have the advantage of often being large and not too expensive. Indeed, it is always advisable to err a little on the large side.

The idea of growing roses in hanging baskets is a recent development made possible by the introduction of suitable roses, and may sound a little unlikely, but can in fact be very successful. Perhaps the best rose for this purpose is 'Nozomi'; with its naturally creeping habit it will hang down from the basket to give a most pleasing effect. For smaller baskets 'Snow Carpet' would be ideal, as would 'The Fairy', certain of the Ground-cover Roses, and the more prostrate of the Patio Roses. For baskets that are at eye-level, Miniature Roses might be tried.

Mr. Paul Edwards has introduced me to a much older idea, popular in Victorian gardens. Roses and other plants were crammed into what were, in effect, large wire mesh baskets. These might be very large, perhaps 6 or 10ft. long, or even more. They would be lined with moss and filled with soil, and then planted. These would be situated in the garden where they would create the effect of a giant basket of flowers.

ROSES FOR MUNICIPAL PLANTING

Here we have an enormous field in itself. The greater part of what I have said throughout this book is equally applicable to parks and public planting in general, for this is, in fact, only gardening on a larger scale.

Hybrid Tea and Floribunda Roses are widely used by most public authorities. Large numbers are planted each year, and there is much to be said for this, as they are so colourful and are seldom without bloom throughout the summer. I would also like to encourage the use of Shrub Roses and Old Roses. They are already used very successfully by a number of authorities, but I am sure that they should be grown much more widely. These roses have a softening effect upon what may often be otherwise rather harsh settings. Their more gentle colours and natural growth seem to be just what is required. They also give the parks' superintendent an opportunity of providing planting that is a little different, without going into all the complications of exotic plants and shrubs. The work of such people is complicated enough at the best of times. A rose is a rose, whether it be 'Super Star' or some rare and unusual old variety; the cultural problems are much the same. Almost everyone loves roses; their appearance in greater variety leads to greater interest from the public.

Choice of variety will vary enormously according to where roses are to be used. In more confined areas the rules are very much the same as for the garden. The roses will, of course, need to be reliable, hardy and, if possible, recurrent flowering, although it would be a shame if too much emphasis were placed on the latter. For larger, less personal locations, rather special roses are required: strong, well-formed shrubs that flower freely even under adverse conditions with minimal attention. They should also be as free from disease as possible. Hybrid Musks, Rugosas, and most Modern Shrubs are ideal. The Old Roses are also useful and grow easily and well, although I would not usually advise varieties from Chapter 3 — Old Roses II. The larger, stronger growing English Roses are entirely suitable. Many of the species are very useful for planting in large drifts.

In the choice of roses for public planting, we come up against a problem of the 'chicken and egg' kind. Authorities often require large numbers of one variety, sometimes very large numbers. The average nurseryman usually grows only a very limited range in such quantities. For this reason the parks' authorities, quite rightly, limit their plans to the roses they know will be available. Again, in his turn, the nurseryman restricts himself to what he knows will be asked for. What is needed is a great deal more liaison between the two. It would be better still if roses could be grown on contract, so that the authority gets exactly what it requires. In spite of this, many interesting and beautiful Shrub Roses are available if a little trouble is taken to look for them.

It may be fruitless to go very deeply into the matter of the selection of varieties, as the parks' superintendent will have his own ideas. I will not attempt to make any suggestions as to suitable Hybrid Teas and Floribundas, but a short list of Shrub Roses may be a help. This could, and should, be extended much further.

MODERN SHRUB ROSES: 'Ballerina', 'Cerise Bouquet', 'Dentelle de Malines', 'Fritz Nobis', 'Frühlingsgold', 'Frühlingsmorgen', 'Golden Wings', 'Little White Pet' 'Marguerite Hilling', 'Marjorie Fair', 'Nevada', 'Pleine de Grâce', 'Raubritter', 'Running Maid', 'Scarlet Fire', 'Scintillation', 'Smarty', 'The Fairy', 'Zigeunerknabe'.

GROUND-COVER ROSES. Most of the roses in this section are ideal.

HYBRID MUSK ROSES. 'Buff Beauty', 'Cornelia', 'Felicia', 'Prosperity', 'Vanity', 'Wilhelm', 'Will Scarlet'.

RUGOSA ROSES. These are particularly suitable, and many are already widely used. I suggest 'Blanc Double de Coubert', 'Fru Dagmar Hastrup', 'Lady Curzon', 'Mrs. Anthony Waterer', 'Nyveldt's White', *R. rugosa,* 'Roseraie de l'Hay', 'Sarah Van Fleet'.

ALBA ROSES. All these are very worthwhile, being amongst the hardiest and most reliable of roses, with pleasing grey-green foliage. *Rosa alba* 'Maxima', *R. alba semi-plena* 'Celestial', 'Madame Plantier', 'Maiden's Blush', 'Queen of Denmark'.

DAMASK ROSES. 'Celsiana', 'Ispahan', 'La Ville de Bruxelles', 'Madame Hardy'.

CENTIFOLIAS. 'Chapeau de Napoléon', 'Fantin-Latour', 'Ipsilante', 'Tour de Malakoff', 'Paul Ricault', *R. centifolia.*

MOSS ROSES. 'Comtesse de Murinais', 'Maréchal Davoust', 'Old Pink Moss', 'Shailer's White Moss', 'William Lobb'.

BOURBON ROSES. These are not very suitable, but the following are exceptions: 'Adam Messerich', 'Bourbon Queen', 'Commandant Beaurepaire', 'Georg Arends', 'Honorine de Brabant', 'Variegata di Bologna'.

SPECIES ROSES. Almost all these are useful. I would particularly recommend the following: *R. californica* 'Plena', *R.* 'Cantabrigiensis', *R.* 'Complicata', *R.* 'Headleyensis', *R.* 'Macrantha', R. macrophylla, *R. moyesii* 'Geranium', *R. moyesii* 'Highdownensis', *R. nitida, R.* 'Paulii', *R.* 'Paulii Rosea', *R. pimpinellifolia* 'Grandiflora', 'Double White', 'Double Yellow', 'Lutea Maxima' and 'Dunwich Rose', *R. eglanteria* and its varieties; *R. glauca, R. sericea pteracantha, R. villosa, R. virginiana, R. willmottiae, R. woodsii fendleri.*

RAMBLING ROSES grown as shrubs would be particularly useful for large-scale planting. It is possible to visualize huge drifts of these, creating a magnificent effect, when closely planted. I am sure if the planting was done to some depth, there would be little trouble from suckers. I am surprised that they have not already been used more widely in this way.

ENGLISH ROSES can be recommended with confidence, particularly the stronger growing kinds, their robust more natural growth, repeat-flowering qualities, soft colours and varying form of flower, making them particularly suitable. I would suggest the following varieties: 'Abraham Darby', 'Belle Story', 'Charles Austin', 'Cymbeline', 'Dapple Dawn', 'Dr. Jackson', 'Gertrude Jekyll', 'Graham Thomas', 'Heritage', 'Leander', 'Lilian Austin', 'Lucetta', 'Mary Rose', 'Red Coat', 'Wenlock' 'William Shakespeare' and 'Windrush'.

Every sizeable town should have a rose garden. Few features will give more pleasure. If this can include as many different types as possible, the interest and pleasure will be so much the greater. Some towns already have extensive collections. Not infrequently, where they include Old Roses, they are presented as 'historic' gardens, something that is by no means essential. Such a garden need not be expensive to maintain, particularly where a high proportion of Shrub Roses is included.

ROSES IN THE HOUSE

One of the great pleasures of roses is to cut and arrange them for the house. Whether this be a single bloom in a narrow-stemmed jar, or a magnificent bowl, roses will bring life to a room as few things can. Thus we shall be able to enjoy them in a more intimate and quite different way, and come to know them better.

As a rose breeder and nurseryman, I frequently cut blooms and bring them indoors in order to study them more closely, but I cannot claim to be any kind of expert or to have any particular theories on flower arrangement. In the main, I would prefer a more simple and apparently casual effect. To obtain this is not so easy as it may seem for roses are not the most obedient of flowers. They have a bad habit of flopping over and looking in quite the wrong direction, and it is hard to get them to stand just as one would wish. It will nearly always be necessary to have something to hold them. Various holders are available on the market. Oasis or crumpled wire netting may also be used. I sometimes place a small jar within a larger bowl to act as support. There is room for considerable ingenuity here. Alternatively, if we go out into the garden and pick a large bunch of roses and simply dump them in an upright bowl, this can often result in beautiful chance effects, with the aid of a little adjustment.

The association of differing varieties gives scope for thought. The bright colours of the Hybrid Teas and Floribundas are a problem. Even the Old Roses, with their more sympathetic colours, do not associate quite so easily when cut. It is helpful to pick a bloom and place it against other roses before making a final decision. It will then soon become clear which will give the most desirable result.

Not only colour, but also form and size of flower should be taken into consideration. Too many large and heavy blooms together in one bowl can sometimes look a little clumsy. If they can be associated with smaller-flowered roses, or sprays, these will have a softening effect that is altogether more pleasing. The sprays also help us to hold the heavier blooms in place.

Roses need not have the bowl to themselves; they mix very well with other flowers. In fact, it is easier to arrange them in this way, and we can often create beautiful pictures. The following are just a few suggestions as to flowers which can be arranged with roses.

Alchemilla mollis with its yellow-green starry flowers and rounded soft green leaves; the large shapely leaves of any of the hostas; gypsophila for its dainty many-flowered sprays of small pale flowers.

Larkspur, particularly the paler blue, can give a pretty cottagey effect and looks especially well with roses of pink shades, as do nigella and cornflower. Copper beech can be very useful, providing a good foil, particularly for red roses. Honeysuckles are lovely in combination with Old Roses. Ferns also might be used, as well as ivies. Among the roses, the dark foliage of *R. glauca* will enhance most shades, particularly the apricots and reds. Other species with light feathery foliage, such as *R. willmottiae,* also have a place. Once again, I have to say 'and so on', for in reality there is no limit to the variety of possibilities.

I will not attempt to suggest the best roses for flower arrangement. To me they are all suitable. It will, however, be found that some last longer than others. It is best to cut roses early in the day, before they receive the heat of the sun. If they can then be plunged up to their necks in water, and taken out later for arrangement, they will subsequently last much longer. The ends of the stems should be cut off while under water. This is because the freshly cut stem will otherwise begin to heal or callus, even in the seconds that elapse between cutting and placing it in the water, and this prevents it from taking up water. Such precautions can greatly extend the life of the flower. A few of the bottom leaves could also be removed.

Chapter 13

ROSE CULTIVATION

Rose growing is not difficult. It is easy to surround it with a mystery that is not warranted. Good results can be achieved with little more than common sense and a minimum of attention. In fact, many who grow roses do so with no more than this. To insist on more would be to bar the majority of people from growing roses in their gardens. In spite of this a little extra skill, care and knowledge will help us to achieve better results. One thing is certain, the more we put into our roses, the more pleasure we shall get out of them.

CHOICE OF SITE

The choice of position for roses depends in part on aesthetic, and in part on practical considerations. There are certain conditions that roses do not like. They do not like shade, not even partial shade, although, as we have already seen, there are some roses that will withstand this better than others. They do not like competition from tree roots, nor do they like the drip from the outer edges of trees. Many Shrub Roses look particularly well when mixed with other plants and shrubs, but it is very necessary to take care that these others are not such as might compete too strongly with the roses. This is particularly important when the roses are first planted; once they have risen above their neighbours it is rather less crucial. The soil should be of reasonable depth and in good condition. It should also be well drained. It is not possible to grow roses in waterlogged soil.

SOIL PREPARATION

Usually the gardener does not have much choice as regards soil type. He has to make the best of what is there. Without doubt most roses are happiest in a heavier soil where they will grow far larger and more strongly than in other soils. With adequate manuring, good results should be easily obtained. If you have an exceptionally heavy clay this may cause some difficulty at first, but it can be overcome by mixing in liberal quantities of humus and by using a planting mixture around the roots of the rose.

Light soils and medium loams are entirely suitable, but the roses will require more generous treatment, particularly if the soil is very light.

The real problems arise in limy or chalky soils. Roses do not like too much lime. They prefer a soil that is either neutral or very slightly acid. I am sometimes a little dismayed when I meet out customers — so many of them seem to have chalk gardens, and I cannot help wondering how our roses are faring. Fortunately this is a problem that can be overcome, but it does require some expenditure and effort. Large quantities of humus should be mixed with the soil, particularly immediately around the rose, although it is better if this does not actually touch the roots. The humus will neutralize the alkalinity and help retain moisture.

Peaty soils are the most difficult of all. Here, the only solution is to import soil and place it in the area around the rose to a depth of 1ft.

Care in the preparation of the soil is very worthwhile. A rose, if it is a Hybrid Tea, will thrive for ten years or more. If it is an Old Rose or a Shrub Rose it may well continue for much longer. We are therefore making a long term investment, and it will really pay dividends if we do the job thoroughly. If the soil can be dug some weeks before the roses arrive, so much the better. Thorough cultivation to a spade's depth, together with the careful mixing of soil and humus, will make a great difference. In addition to this, it is worth breaking up the subsoil with a fork as you dig; this will help drainage and enable the deep tap roots to go well down. If you dig up an old rose bush you will usually find that there are few roots in the first foot of soil; most of the growth is deep down. In spite of this, the humus should only be mixed with the top 12ins. of soil; beneath this it will be unable to work effectively.

The reader will have noticed the emphasis I place on humus. I regard this as crucial in growing good roses. Its use is not really necessary with very strong roses such as the Species, but with repeat-flowering roses it is essential if we are to get the best results, particularly later in the year. The humus may take various forms: well-rotted farmyard manure, compost, one of the various proprietary brands, or peat. The first two are best, but peat is a good alternative. It is not a bad plan to use peat together with the other forms of humus. It is very long lasting and has a good effect on the condition of the soil, mixing in well, but has little nutritional value.

If you are unable to apply humus, at least use a proprietary rose fertilizer. Indeed, a dressing of fertilizer early in the spring after planting will be desirable in any case. Potash is vital for roses, particularly on light soils which tend to be deficient in this. Heavy soils often lack phosphates. Sulphate of potash is a good source of potash, and bone meal an excellent natural source of phosphates.

REPLANTING ROSES IN THE SAME GROUND

There is one point above all I would like every rose grower to heed. When the soil has had roses grown in it for any length of time, say five or six years, it should not be replanted with roses. Such soils will be what is usually known as 'rose sick'. This does not mean the existing roses will not thrive in it indefinitely, but when the ground is replanted with new roses, it is quite probable that they will fail to grow properly. This is true even when extremely healthy and robust roses have been taken out. The exact nature of the problem is not fully understood; it is almost certainly due to microscopic organisms known as eel worm, but poisons from the roots of the previous roses may also be involved.

Fortunately this only concerns the area immediately around the bush or shrub. If it is possible to move even a little way to one side of the previous rose, there should be no problem. Where this is not practical the answer is to remove the soil from the area where the original rose has been, to a width of about 2 to 4ft. across, and 1ft. in depth, according to the size of the rose, and replace this with a mixture of one part humus to three parts good soil from another area of the garden. Where rose beds are involved, it will be necessary to remove all the soil and replace it. This may seem a little extreme, but I think it is worthwhile. Far better, if you can, to move your new roses to a different part of the garden. Another more simple method is to sterilize the soil before planting. It is possible to obtain chemicals especially for this purpose from your garden centre.

For those who do not feel inclined to go to these lengths, the problem can be mitigated by the use of large quantities of humus. The problem of rose sickness is greater in light soils that tend to lack humus and, in my experience, much less in humus-rich soils.

PURCHASING ROSES

There are two ways in which rose trees can be purchased — bare rooted or in containers. There is now a generation of gardeners which tends to know only the latter, or to think there is something rather risky about the former. This is quite wrong; both have their virtues, but on balance I would favour the bare rooted. The best roses tend to be sold thus, while the smaller bushes find their way into pots, into which they fit more conveniently. Not only this, but roses are never really happy in containers, and unless the garden centre has looked after them well, there is a danger they may be poor specimens.

If you require roses that are in any way out of the ordinary, it will be necessary to buy through mail order — unless you are lucky enough to live near to a suitable rose specialist. It is not practical for the average garden centre to carry any more than a very limited range. When buying from a rose specialist it is advisable to order well in advance. The grower has to plan his crop some two and a half years ahead, and it is not always possible to predict what the demand will be. Varieties will inevitably become sold out.

PLANTING

I will deal with the bare-rooted roses first. These may be planted at any time between November and March. If they are not purchased locally, they may arrive either at a time when you are not able to plant them immediately, or when the weather or soil conditions are not suitable. In this case, they should be temporarily heeled into the ground by digging a small trench and covering the roots with soil. They will then be quite safe for many weeks. If the soil is frozen when the roses arrive, they will be all right in their packet for three or four weeks, so long as they are kept in a cool but frost-proof building.

Planting should be at such a depth that the joint at which the rose has been budded on to the root stock is just beneath the surface of the soil. Make a hole of adequate size to take the roots, spread the roots out evenly, and fill in with soil, treading it down gently with the feet, being careful not to get the soil too solid. It is very worthwhile using a special planting mixture for this purpose. This can be made up of half peat and half best garden soil, together with a sprinkling of bone meal. Alternatively, a ready-made mixture may be bought. This will give your rose a much better start and, incidentally, if your mixture is kept dry, make it possible for you to plant when the soil and weather conditions are less than perfect.

If you wish to move established plants, this is entirely possible providing they are not too old and gnarled. Roses often seem to relish this treatment. Before doing this, it is vital to prune the bush very severely, removing all old and dead wood, and cutting it almost to the ground. This will mean that the roots of the plant, which will have inevitably been badly maimed, will not have to maintain too much growth in the early stages.

The planting of container-grown bushes is very much the same as for those with bare roots, except that it is important to avoid breaking up the soil when removing the bush from the pot. It is best to cut away the plastic with a knife, or, if the container is a solid pot, to knock the bush and soil out whole. The advantage of a container rose is that it can be planted at any time of the year. Having said that, it has to be pointed out that such roses, when planted later than June, will by the following year usually be little further ahead than a bare-rooted rose that has been planted the following winter.

If we are planting late in the season, say late March or early April, it is advisable to keep an eye on soil moisture. The ground can easily become dry before the roses have had time to make roots. In such cases give a heavy watering that will go deep. This is doubly important in the case of container roses that are planted out of season. It is easy to think that they are quite safe in their little ball of soil, but this can quickly dry out.

Climbing Roses require special consideration when they are planted against a wall. It will frequently be found that the soil here is very dry, even in a damp period. For this reason there are more failures with Climbing Roses than among any other type. The plant is unable to get a start in life without sufficient moisture and will not grow strongly for two or three years, until the roots have been able to move away from the wall. To alleviate this problem, plant the rose at least 1ft. from the wall, and instead of arranging the roots in the usual circular manner, spread them away from the wall towards the more moist soil. Even then, a regular soaking of water is often necessary for the first year.

PRUNING

My remarks in the first paragraph of this chapter are particularly pertinent here. Pruning is not difficult, and much latitude is possible. It is something of an art and it can be interpreted, in some degree at least, according to the type of shrub or climber that is required. Used in this way, it becomes an interesting and enjoyable task. I have from time to time, while progressing through the various classes of roses, made notes on the subject, but it would perhaps be convenient to summarise it here in a more general way.

OLD ROSES THAT DO NOT REPEAT FLOWER (Chapter 2). It is possible to leave these virtually unpruned, although a fairly substantial thinning of older, less-productive wood will become necessary after a few years. This will make way for new and more vigorous growth. At the same time it may be desirable to shape the shrub according to your own taste. Different people may interpret this in different ways. It may be thought worthwhile to preserve elegantly protruding branches, even if this upsets the symmetry of the whole. If pruned in this way Old Roses may become too large for many gardens, and although they will provide a mass of bloom, they will not produce the finest or largest individual flowers should such be required. A more usual method is to cut back the strong main growth by about one-third of its length, at the same time cutting the side shoots to one-third and removing the old, dead and spent wood completely. In this way you will obtain a more compact, although sometimes less elegant, shrub.

All these roses are best pruned as soon after flowering as possible. This encourages new growth, which will in turn produce the best flowers in the following season.

REPEAT-FLOWERING SHRUB ROSES. In so far as their pruning requirements are concerned, repeat-flowering Shrub Roses usually present quite a different problem to pruning Old Roses that do not repeat flower. Their long season of bloom makes heavier demands upon them, and closer attention is desirable. It is necessary to remove the small, twiggy side shoots and, at the same time, to cut away some of the old growth to encourage the new. Be careful not to remove too many or too much of the stronger branches in the early stages (as these will form the structure of the shrub) or the rose may fail to become a shrub at all. Something of what I have said about the roses that do not repeat flower applies to those that do repeat flower. Try to avoid a too-clipped appearance — there is no virtue in pruning for pruning's sake. We are trying to produce an attractive, shapely shrub.

China Roses require little pruning, other than the removal of some of the old wood. Hybrid Perpetuals often make tall, upright bushes, and with such roses growth may have to be reduced to half its length in order to achieve a presentable shrub. English Roses include a whole variety of different habits of growth, and pruning is dealt with at some length in the introduction to Chapter 6, but broadly speaking it is the same as for other repeat-flowering Shrub Roses.

Pruning should be done during the winter, to enable the shrub to make an early start, thus making possible a second crop of flowers.

HYBRID TEAS AND FLORIBUNDAS. New bushes should be pruned back to within 5ins. of the ground at planting time. Thereafter their stems should be cut to about half their length. Weak, twiggy growth is cut away, as are dead and diseased branches. As the main growth ages, some of it should be cut harder to encourage strong new stems from the base. Pruning is probably best done in March, although it can be done earlier. Early pruning encourages early flowers so long as the young shoots are not damaged by late frosts.

CLIMBING AND RAMBLING ROSES. Climbing Roses, which are in the main repeat flowering, should be pruned during the winter. Pruning them is quite simple. A Climber consists of the main long stems which do the climbing, and short side stems coming from these which produce the flowers. All we have to do is to remove some of the main stems each year where they can be spared. These will be those that are becoming weak and unproductive. Having done this, we cut back the smaller side shoots to about 3ins.

Rambling Roses are even more simple to prune. It is only necessary to remove some of the older growth from the plant to ensure renewal and to avoid it getting out of hand. Where the area for growth is more or less unlimited, as on trees or over large structures, the plant can be given its head for a few years. In this way, a more natural effect will be achieved. In fact, I would go so far as to say that with most Ramblers, the less we interfere with the growth, the better. In the case of the Multiflora Hybrids it is necessary to remove more of the basal wood, as they tend to become choked with growth at this point. There are certain exceptions to these rules. Banksian Roses should be left unpruned as should 'Mermaid' — all it requires is an occasional thinning.

SPECIES ROSES. These are wild and natural roses and require little pruning other than the removal of old and spent wood once the shrub begins to mature. This is best done during the winter. Do not allow the shrub to become too full of dense and dying growth.

STANDARDS. Pruning is the same as that recommended for other roses, according to type. Try to keep the head wide and shapely, not too upright or spiky. Pruning to an outward facing bud will help in this respect. It is desirable to have a neat, almost formal head of growth, or perhaps slightly arching growth. Weeping Standards require an occasional thinning. Try to avoid the removal of long, weeping stems, otherwise the head may become too bushy. Further suggestions for pruning various groups, classes and individual varieties of roses will be found under the appropriate headings.

MULCHING, FEEDING AND WATERING

This is not necessary on the largest and most robust of shrubs, such as the Species Roses. Nor is it entirely essential for once-flowering roses, as for example the Old Roses, although these will be greatly improved by such attention. With repeat-flowering Shrub Roses, English Roses, and the Hybrid Teas and Floribundas, it does become very necessary if we are to have quality and continuity of flowering. It is true that acceptable results can be achieved without such care, but a little extra assistance in this direction yields results out of all proportion to the effort involved. This is particularly true with soils that are less favourable to roses: light sands, chalk, limestone, and so on.

Mulching is the most important. If roses are given a good mulch each year, or even every other year, most other cultural considerations fade into insignificance. Mulching helps to maintain the moisture in the soil through drier periods, and this makes continual flowering possible. It provides plant food, it reduces susceptibility to black spot, and has a smothering effect on weeds. Various materials can be used. Rotted compost is excellent. It is worthwhile gathering your garden and household waste for this purpose, but it should be given ample time to rot down. Perhaps the simplest method is to use bought materials such as peat or forest bark. These are free from weeds and easy to handle. The feeding value will be less, but this can be corrected by the application of fertilizers.

When growth begins in the spring, a dressing of one or other of the various proprietary rose fertilizers should be applied. This should be repeated in June or July as the first flush of flowers is passing in order to encourage the next. A good general fertilizer is suitable, but it should contain a high proportion of potash, particularly on light land. Roses demand large quantities of potash, more than most other plants.

Many people who grow repeat-flowering Shrub Roses are disappointed to find that their plants frequently fail to make a second crop. Even Hybrid Teas and Floribundas sometimes do not flower as continually as we would wish. Obviously we cannot have repeat flowering without growth, and growth is entirely dependent on the availability of moisture. It is of little use applying fertilizer to a rose if there is not the moisture to make it available to the plant. Even in a climate like our own, there is rarely sufficient rain to maintain moisture at the necessary levels throughout the summer. I am certainly not going to suggest that watering is anything like essential in this country, but it can contribute considerably to the performance of our roses. There are excellent automatic watering systems available which will make the task very simple, and they are not expensive. If you do decide to water, give a good soaking. Even one or two such soakings in the course of an average summer will make all the difference. This is particularly important after the first flush of flowers.

SUCKERS AND DEAD HEADING

Most roses are budded on to root stocks and this inevitably means that from time to time there will be suckers, that is to say growth from the stock. Suckers are not difficult to detect, as they arise from somewhere below the point where the rose was budded on to the stock, and their leaves are usually very different from those of the garden variety. With the Alba Roses we can more easily be deceived, as they are closely related to *Rosa canina* from which most of the root stocks we use in this country have been developed. A great deal of trouble will be saved if suckers are removed early on; it is much easier at this stage, and little of the energy of the plant will have been wasted. A knife is the best tool for this purpose — try to cut away a little of the bark together with the sucker, otherwise the sucker will quickly re-emerge from the same point.

The removal of dead flowers is not essential, but the plant retains a much tidier appearance if this is done. Roses are by nature single flowered, but man has made them into double flowered. For this reason the petals tend to stay intact even as the flower dies, and they are often unsightly.

Dead heading is more important in the case of repeat-flowering shrubs and Hybrid Teas and Floribundas, for if these produce hips they will take up the energy and inhibit further flowering. Of course, where hips are to be desired, as with the Species, no dead heading should be done.

DISEASES AND PESTS

Considering how widely the rose is grown it cannot be said that it is particularly subject to diseases and pests. By and large, the rose is able to live with most of them. They become more of a problem when many roses are grown in close proximity. This is, of course, true of nearly all plants. We hear a great deal about elaborate spraying, but this is not always essential, although it is more important with the repeat-flowering roses.

Perhaps the biggest problem is blackspot. Few roses are completely resistant to this disease, and it might be said to be the greatest single drawback of the rose. Anyone who can breed roses that will resist blackspot will be doing a great service. Unfortunately in the breeding of such resistance we can lose many other desirable characteristics.

With modern sprays and equipment, control both of diseases and pests is not too much of a hardship. The important point is to start spraying early in the season. Most problems start in quite a small way but quickly mutliply. If you can halt them at an early stage, treatment will be much easier and more effective.

Here is a list of the main diseases and pests, together with the appropriate chemicals to control them.

DISEASES

BLACKSPOT (*Diplocarpon rosae*). The symptoms of this disease are just as the name suggests — black patches appear on the leaves, with yellow at the edges. These will grow and multiply and may, if left unattended, defoliate the whole plant. Blackspot is worse in the country or in any area where the air is clean, but some varieties are much more susceptible than others.

The most effective spray at present is one which contains bupirimate-triforine. This should be applied as directed both on leaves and stems, at the time when the leaves are emerging. This early spraying is most important. It is then recommended that spraying should continue at ten to fourteen day intervals, but this is a counsel of perfection. With most roses, a further two sprayings at the normal rate in late May, June and July will keep the disease sufficiently in check.

Good cultivation will help in the avoidance of blackspot. Adequate feeding and mulching is important, but avoid the excessive use of nitrogen. Poor drainage and the shade of trees will also encourage this disease.

POWDERY MILDEW (*Sphaerotheca pannosa*). A white powdery mould appears on the leaves and buds. The leaves may turn yellow and purple and eventually wither and drop prematurely. The buds may fail to open. Use a spray containing bupirimate-triforine as soon as the disease appears, and continue as suggested for blackspot. Do not allow mildew to develop too much before spraying.

Here again, good cultivation encourages healthy growth. Mulching, watering and feeding will help to prevent the problem in the first place. Excessive nitrogen provides soft growth which mildew thrives upon. Climbing and Rambler Roses are particularly susceptible.

ROSE RUST (*Phragmidium tuberculatum* and other species). This is one of the worst diseases, but fortunately is not common. Orange swellings appear both on upper and lower leaf surfaces in spring. Later in the season, rust-like patches appear on the underside of the leaf and eventually turn black in August.

Normally you will not have to worry about this problem, but where it does occur it is important to catch it early. Spray in mid- to early May, when the first infection appears. An effective spray is one which contains oxycarboxin. It is vital to spray the underside of the leaf — the upperside is not important.

Rose rust occurs most frequently on hot, dry soils and where the soil is deficient in potash. It occurs more often in a wet season, or where there is a prolonged heavy dew. Certain varieties of rose are much more subject to it than others. Alba Roses and Rugosa Roses, which are normally so trouble-free, may be affected. Most other Shrub Roses are immune.

PESTS

APHIDS. These may be green, orange, reddish or black. Most gardeners will be familiar with them. They feed off young shoots, starting in the spring, and multiply rapidly if not checked. Eventually they will cause distortion of the leaf. Excreted honeydew dropped on the leaves often grows a black fungus known as 'Sooty Mould'.

Control is not difficult, and numerous systemic sprays are available. Spray when the insects first appear. When purchasing, make sure that the chemical is not a hazard to bees or other useful insects.

LEAF-ROLLING SAWFLY. The leaflets become tightly rolled and a greyish-green grub may be found inside. This problem chiefly occurs where roses are in the shade of trees.

It is only possible to spray for prevention before the curling of the leaf occurs. When you have this problem it will be necessary to wait until the following year and spray in May with a spray containing fenitrothion.

Having provided this short list of troubles, it is important to stress that we should not regard rose growing as a continual battle with diseases and insects. Frequently these will not occur. We only need to treat them where they show signs of becoming a real problem. We ourselves do minimal spraying in our nursery garden.

GLOSSARY

ANTHER. The part of the flower which produces pollen; the upper section of the stamen.

ARCHING SHRUB. A shrub in which the long main branches bend down towards the soil, usually in a graceful manner.

BALLED, BALLING. The clinging together of petals due to damp, so that the bloom fails to open.

BARE-ROOT ROSES. Roses bought without soil, not in a container.

BASAL SHOOT. The strong main shoot that arises from the base of the rose.

BICOLOUR. A rose bloom with two distinct shades of colour.

BOSS. The bunch of stamens at the centre of a flower.

BRACT. A modified leaf at the base of a flower stalk.

BREAK. New growth from a branch.

BUDDING. The usual method for the propagation of roses by the grafting of a leaf bud on to the neck of a root stock.

BUD-SHAPED FLOWER. I have coined this term to describe rose blooms that are in the form of a Hybrid Tea, i.e. flowers that are of high-centred bud formation and mainly beautiful in the bud (as opposed to those of Old Rose formation).

BUD UNION. The point on the root stock where the bud of the garden rose was inserted.

BUSH. I use this word to describe closely pruned bedding roses, as for example a Hybrid Tea.

BUSHY SHRUB. A rose of dense, rounded growth.

BUTTON EYE. A button-like fold of petals in the centre of a rose.

CALYX. The green protective cover over the flower bud which opens into five sepals.

CANE. A long rose stem, from the base of the plant, particularly as in a Rambling Rose.

CHROMOSOMES. Chains of linked genes contained in the cells of plants and animals.

CLIMBING SPORT. See Sport; the climbing form of this phenomenon.

CORYMB. A flower cluster that is flat-topped, or nearly so.

CROSS. See Hybrid.

DIE BACK. The progressive dying back of a shoot from the tip.

DIPLOID. A plant with two sets of chromosomes.

FLORE PLENO. Double flower.

FLUSH. A period of blooming.

GENE. A unit of heredity controlling inherited characteristics of a plant.

GENUS. A group of plants having common characteristics, e.g. *Rosa.*

HEELING IN. Temporary planting of roses when conditions are not suitable for permanent planting.

HEIGHT. The heights given for individual varieties are only approximate. Much will depend on soil, site, season and geographic area. The breadth of a rose bush or shrub will usually be slightly less than the height.

HIPS OR HEPS. Seed pods of a rose.

HYBRID. A rose resulting from crossing two different species or varieties.

LEAFLETS. The individual section of a leaf.

MODERN APPEARANCE, ROSE OF. Rose that usually has high-pointed buds and smooth foliage, similar to a Hybrid Tea Rose.

MUTATION. See Sport.

OLD APPEARANCE, ROSE OF. Rose with bloom of cupped or rosette shape, rather than the pointed bud and informal flower of a Modern Rose; the plant usually having rough textured leaves, i.e. Gallica, Centifolia, etc.

ORGANIC FERTILIZER. A fertilizer made from natural materials rather than chemicals.

PERPETUAL FLOWERING. A rose that continues to flower in the same year after the first flush of bloom, though not necessarily continually.

PISTIL. Female organ of a flower consisting of the stigma, style and ovary.

POLLEN PARENT. The male parent of a variety.

POMPON. A small rounded bloom with regular short petals.

QUARTERED. A flower in which the centre petals are folded into four quarters.

QUILLED PETALS. Petals folded in the form of a quill.

RAMBLER-LIKE. I use this term to describe roses bearing large sprays of small blooms similar to those of a small flowered Rambling Rose, particularly a Multiflora Rambler.

RECESSIVE GENE. A gene that is dominated by another, rendering it ineffective.

RECURRENT FLOWERING. See Perpetual Flowering.

REMONTANT. See Perpetual Flowering.

REPEAT FLOWERING. See Perpetual Flowering.

ROOTS, ROSES ON THEIR OWN. Not budded on to a stock; grown from cuttings.

ROOT STOCK (STOCK). The host plant on to which a cultivated variety is budded.

RUGOSE. Leaves with a wrinkled surface.

SCION. A shoot or bud used for grafting on to a root stock.

SEEDLING. A rose grown from seed. In the context of this book, the offspring of a variety.

SEPAL. One of the five green divisions of the calyx.

SHRUB. A rose that is normally pruned lightly and allowed to grow in a more natural form, as opposed to a bush which is pruned close to the ground.

SPECIES. A wild rose.

SPORT. A change in the genetic make up of the plant, as for example when a pink rose suddenly produces a white flower.

SPREADING SHRUB. A shrub on which the branches tend to extend outwards rather than vertically.

STAMEN. The male organ of a flower, consisting of the filament and anther, which produces pollen.

STIGMA. The end of the pistil or female flower organ.

STYLE. The stem of the pistil which joins the stigma to the ovary.

SUCKER. A shoot growing from the root stock instead of from the budded variety.

TETRAPLOID. A plant with four sets of chromosomes.

TRIPLOID. A plant with three sets of chromosomes.

UPRIGHT SHRUB. A rose in which the growth tends to be vertical.

VARIETY. Strictly speaking, a naturally occurring variation of a species. The popular meaning, so far as roses are concerned, is a distinct type of rose.

BIBLIOGRAPHY

American Rose Society's *Annuals,* from 1917.

Bean, W.J., *Trees and Shrubs Hardy in the British Isles,* 8th edn. revised.

Bois, Eric and Trechslin, Anne-Marie, *Roses,* 1962.

Bunyard, A.E., *Old Garden Roses,* Collingridge, 1936.

Dobson, B.R., *Combined Rose List. Hard to Find Roses and Where to Find Them,* Beverly R. Dobson, Irvington, New York 10533, 1985.

Edwards, G., *Wild and Old Garden Roses,* David & Charles, Newton Abbot, 1975; Hafner, New York, 1975.

Ellwanger, H.B., *The Rose,* Dodd-Mead, New York, 1822; 1914.

Fisher, John, *The Companion to Roses.*

Fletcher, H.L.V., *The Rose Anthology,* Newnes, 1963.

Foster-Melliar, Rev. A., *The Book of the Rose,* Macmillan, 1894; 1910.

Gault S.M. and Synge P.M., *The Dictionary of Roses in Colour,* Michael Joseph and Ebury Press, 1970.

Gore, C.F., *The Book of Roses or The Rose Fancier's Manual,* 1838; Heyden, 1978.

Griffiths, Trevor, *The Book of Old Roses,* Michael Joseph, 1984.

Griffiths, Trevor, *The Book of Classic Old Roses,* Michael Joseph, 1986.

Harkness, Jack, *Roses,* Dent, 1978.

Hillier's *Manual of Trees and Shrubs,* 4th edn., 1974.

Hole, S. Reynolds, *A Book about Roses,* William Blackwood, 1896.

Hollis, L., *Roses,* Collingridge, 1969; 2nd edn. with new illustrations, 1974.

Jekyll, G. and Mawley, E., *Roses for English Gardens,* Country Life, 1902; reprinted Woodbridge 1982.

Keays, F.L., *Old Roses,* Macmillan, New York, 1935; facsimile edn. Heyden, Philadelphia and London, 1978.

Kordes, Wilhelm, *Roses,* Studio Vista, 1964.

Krussman, G., *Roses,* English edn., Batsford, 1982.

Lawrance, Mary, *A Collection of Roses from Nature,* 1799.

Le Grice, E.B., *Rose Growing Complete,* Faber & Faber, 1965.

McFarland, J.H., *Modern Roses,* 8th edn., McFarland Co., U.S.A., 1980.

McFarland, J.H., *Roses of the World in Colour,* Cassell, 1936.

Mansfield, T.C., *Roses in Colour and Cultivation,* Collins, 1947.

Nottle, T., *Growing Old Fashioned Roses in Australia and New Zealand,* Kangaroo Press, 1983.

Paul, William, *The Rose Garden,* 10th edn., Simpkin, Marshall, Hamilton, Kent & Co., 1903.

Pemberton, Rev. J.H., *Roses, Their History, Development and Cultivation,* Longmans Green 1908; rev. edn. 1920.

Redouté, P.J., *Les Roses,* 1817-24.
Ridge, A., *For the Love of a Rose,* Faber & Faber, 1965.
Rivers, T., *The Rose Amateur's Guide,* Longmans Green, 1837.
Rose Growers' Association, *Find that Rose.*
Ross, D., *Shrub Roses in Australia,* Deane Ross, 1981.
Royal National Rose Society's *Annuals,* from 1911.
Shepherd, R., *History of the Rose,* Macmillan, New York, 1966.
Steen, N., *The Charm of Old Roses,* Herbert Jenkins, 1966.
Thomas, G.S., *The Old Shrub Roses,* Phoenix House, 1955.
Thomas, G.S., *Shrub Roses of Today,* Phoenix House, 1962.
Thomas, G.S., *Climbing Roses Old and New,* Phoenix House, 1965.
Thompson, Richard, *Old Roses for Modern Gardens,* Van Nostrand, New York, 1959.
Warner, C., *Climbing Roses,* Tiptree Books.
Willmott, Ellen, *The Genus Rosa,* Murray, issued in parts 1910-14.
Young, Norman, *The Complete Rosarian,* Hodder & Stoughton, 1971.

MAIN AGENTS FOR ENGLISH ROSES

The following are main agents for the English Roses described in Chapter 6. These roses are also becoming available through numerous other nurseries and garden centres. (At the time of going to press this list was up-to-date, but changes may occur. For further information write to David Austin Roses at the address below.)

UNITED KINGDOM
David Austin Roses,
Bowling Green Lane,
Albrighton,
Wolverhampton WV7 3HB,
England.

FRANCE
Georges Delbard,
Malicorne,
03600 Commentry,
Paris, France.

GERMANY
Ingwer J. Jensen,
Hermann-Lons-Weg 39,
D-2390 Flensburg,
West Germany.

HOLLAND
Kwekerij 't Hulder (trade only),
5821 EE Vierlingsbeek,
Overloonseweg lla,
Holland.

De Wilde Bussum (retail only),
Kwekerij Pr.,
Irenelaan 14,
P.O. Box 115,
1400 A.C. Bussum,
Holland.

ITALY
Rose Barni,
51100 Pistoia,
Via Autostrada 5,
Italy.

SWITZERLAND
Richard Huber AG,
Baumschulen,
Dottikon,
Postcheck 50-11595,
Switzerland.

AUSTRALIA
The Perfumed Garden Pty. Ltd.,
47 Rendelsham Avenue,
Mt. Eliza, 3930,
Australia.

CANADA
Hortico Inc.,
Robson Road,
R.R.I. Waterdown,
LOR 2HO,
Canada.

NEW ZEALAND
Trevor Griffiths & Sons Ltd.,
No. 3 R.D.,
Timaru,
New Zealand.

SOUTH AFRICA
Ludwigs Roses C.C.,
P.O. Box 28165,
Sunnyside,
Pretoria 0132,
South Africa.

U.S.A.
Wayside Gardens,
Hodges,
South Carolina 29695-0001,
U.S.A.

Most of these nurseries also grow a wide selection of Old and Shrub Roses.

GENERAL INDEX

Bold figure numbers refers to illustrations

INDEX OF ROSES

Bold figure numbers refer to illustrations